Last of the Rhodesians

Chronicles of an African anarchist

The Gokwe Kid
Dick of the Bushveld

Karl Greenberg

Copyright

The Gokwe Kid – Dick of the Bushveld
Published 2012

This book remains the copyright of Karl Greenberg.

All rights reserved. No part of this publication may be reproduced stored in a retrieval system, or transmitted in any form by any means, electronic, mechanical, photocopying, recording or otherwise, without the prior permission of the author.

Copyright©Karl Greenberg, 2012

Contact the Author:

gokwekid@gmail.com
www.lastrhodesian.blogspot.com

Last of the Rhodesians
Chronicles of an African anarchist

The Gokwe Kid
Dick of the Bushveld

PART ONE

Dedication

This is for my sons: Timon and David.

Yes, my lovely boys, it has taken a little longer than planned to answer your ultimate bed time anecdote request –

"Daddy, tell us another story about the time you were in Africa and had to shoot tourists."

CONTENTS

The Gokwe Kid - Dick of the Bushveld

PART ONE

CHAPTER 1:

RETURN OF THE ROGUE RHODIE   2

CHAPTER 2:

RECRUIT COPPER KARL GETS CRUELLY CROPPED   12

CHAPTER 3:

A WHITER SHADE OF PAIN   18

CHAPTER 4:

DRESSED AS A TREE; I COME TO HUNT THEE   35

CHAPTER 5:

BAD BLOOD   51

CHAPTER 6:

PHILOSOPHICAL PONDERINGS: PLEASURE AND PAIN ARE PRE-EMPTED BY PAYDAY AND PERCEPTIONS OF PLEASURE PAID   65

CHAPTER 7:

INFAMY! INFAMY! THE BSAP HAVE IT IN FOR ME   78

CHAPTER 8:

INTO THE GOKWE GULAG GOES GRIEVING GREENBERG   88

CHAPTER 9:

HE WHO WIELDS THE RULER RULES   98

CHAPTER 10:

TEACHING TRIALS AND TRIBULATIONS   105

CHAPTER 11:

THERE IS LIFE IN GOKWE – BUT NOT AS WE KNOW IT   117

CHAPTER 12:

TRIGGS TEACHES TRICKS OF THE TRADE - MEANWHILE WEEPING WILLOW KEEPS A-WEEPIN'   127

CHAPTER 13:

CRY THIEF AND UNLEASH THE PUPPY OF LAW   136

CHAPTER 14:

BLACK PEASANTRY AND WHITE ELEPHANTS   144

CHAPTER 15:

'GOOD GOLLY!' - WHAT A LOAD OF GOBBLEDYGOOK   155

CHAPTER 16:

THE FELLOWSHIP OF THE BINGE   170

CHAPTER 17:

LANDIES, LIONS AND LIES   179

CHAPTER 18:

DRIVING, DATING AND A LOT OF CHUTZPAH   187

The Gokwe Kid - Dick of the Bushveld

PART TWO

CHAPTER 19:

THE GREAT BATTLE OF GOKWE 197

CHAPTER 20:

PEOPLE ARE DYING BUT AT LEAST THE MUPPETS
ARE ON TV 218

CHAPTER 21:

SEX, SUICIDE AND SILLY COWS 223

CHAPTER 22:

LORDS OF THE BINGE: THE FELLOWSHIP CONTINUES 234

CHAPTER 23:

PETRIFIED PEASANTS - LEND ME YOUR EARS FOR I NEED
SOME WHEELS 240

CHAPTER 24:

PLEASURE AND PAIN 254

CHAPTER 25:

DUMDUMS, DEATH, DUMPING AND A CAT CALLED CAT 257

CHAPTER 26:

MERRY CHRISTMAS, I NEED A STIFF DRINK! 267

CHAPTER 27:

PULLED OVER WHILST PULLING ON THE PISS   274

CHAPTER 28:

WHEN THE LION FEEDS, I HIT THE JACKPOT   279

CHAPTER 29:

HOW THE CHAIN OF COMMAND WORKS WHEN THERE IS
RADIO SILENCE   292

CHAPTER 30:
THE RISE AND FALL OF THE GOKWE KID

PART 1 - SUPER SLEUTH STRUTS HIS STUFF   302

CHAPTER 31:

THE RISE AND FALL OF THE GOKWE KID

PART 2 - 'STUPID IS AS STUPID DOES'   313

CHAPTER 32:

THE RISE AND FALL OF THE GOKWE KID

PART 3 - SAVAGING THE SAVAGES   322

CHAPTER 33:

THE RISE AND FALL OF THE GOKWE KID

PART 4 - HASTA LA VISTA, GOKWE   331

CHAPTER 34:

'AND…THE WINNER OF 1978 RHODESIA'S X-FACTOR IS…PO
GREENBERG!' (FAME AT LAST - TRIUMPHANT, THE GOKWE KID
ARISES FROM THE ASHES – ONLY TO GET BORED WITH IT
ALL.)   337

CHAPTER 35:

THE BEASTIE BOYS SAY – (YOU GOTTA) FIGHT FOR YOUR
RIGHT (TO PARTY)   346

CHAPTER 36:

A GOOK IN A KIA, BACKING A WINNER, AND A MAD GERMAN   354

CHAPTER 37:

THE GREATEST RHODESIAN WANKERS OR THE MASSACRE OF
ALLAN WILSON AND THE SHANGANI PATROL REVISITED   363

CHAPTER 38:

THE LEOPARD AND THE DONKEYS PLUS - GOOKS! RUN FOR
YOUR LIVES   369

CHAPTER 39:

THE ROAD TO PERSPICACITY – PART ONE   383

CHAPTER 40:

THE ROAD TO PERSPICACITY – PART TWO   392

ACKNOWLEDGEMENTS   402

'Rhodesians Never Die'

We're all Rhodesians

And we'll fight through thick and thin,

We'll keep our land a free land,

Stop the enemy coming in

We'll keep them north of the Zambezi

Till that river's running dry,

And this mighty land will prosper

For Rhodesians never die.

Clem Tholet and Andy Dillon

CHAPTER 1:

Return of the Rogue Rhodie

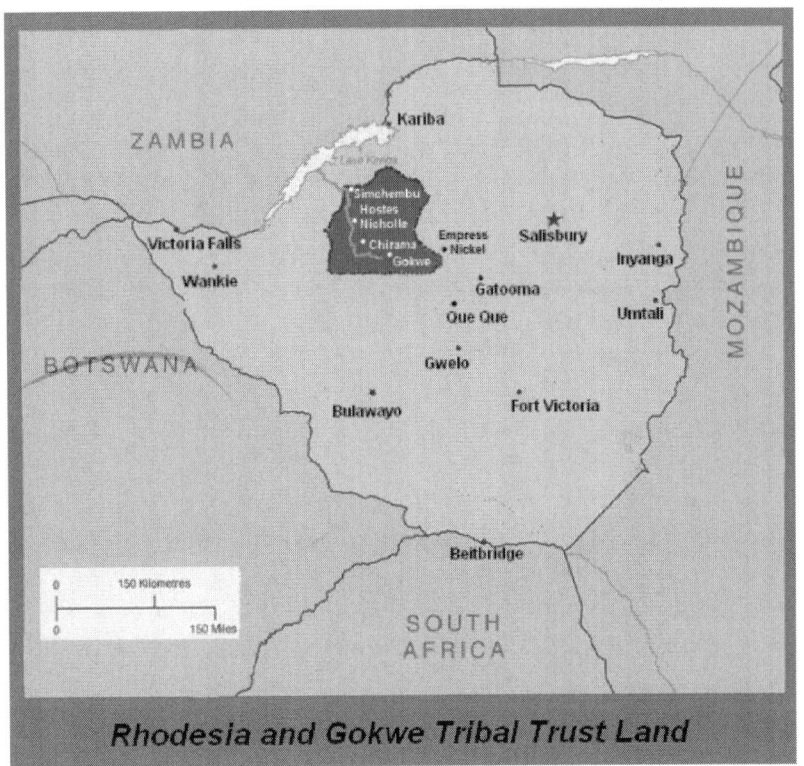

Rhodesia and Gokwe Tribal Trust Land

"Jannie van der Merwe, your Captain speaking, Ek se! We have arrived at dodgy Salisbury International Airport in the illegal Republic of Rhodesia. Those Whenwes returning to fight a hopeless cause – you can stop whining now. Thank you for flying South African Airways."

I staggered from the seat and collected my piles of cabin luggage. A mouse seemed to have died in my mouth overnight after my downing of half a dozen vodka, lime and lemonades freebies to get me to sleep. Forgetting I was now considerably taller in my new platform shoes I moved to the top of the stairs leading to the tarmac and brained myself on the Jumbo's exit door.

"Karl. Yoo-hoo, Karl." Screams of adulation pierced my ears as I tossed the gorgeous locks of softly undulating brown hair from my shoulders and took in the sight of my ululating adorers yelling from the terrace public gallery. Stephanie Brooks, Clare Finlason and Lorraine Trenchard waved enthusiastically. It was a bit confusing at 6.00am on a chilly August day in the southern African spring of 1976. I was expecting my step-mother, Katherine the history teacher, to pick me up. Still, having a few groupies screeching away did wonders to my ego. I was returning in triumph to save Rhodesia.

My landlocked, scrapping little land, barely the size of Texas, was surrounded by hordes of evil, commie black tyrant-controlled basket cases such as Zambia and Mozambique. Rhodesians only had one semi-friendly escape route to the south over what Kipling called, 'the great grey-green, greasy Limpopo River'. And, those rooinek hating Boers couldn't be trusted either!

I observed a few of Africa's 'happiest blecks' unload the luggage as I trundled to the terminal across the world's longest civil runway. At a mile long the thing could have, at a pinch, accommodated the future Space Shuttle. Local Rhodie lore was that when the slopes down south got themselves some new 747s, our lot rang them up and asked how long the runway must be extended to.

"Ag, man, make it a click, hey."

Of course, this caused confusion. Is a click a mile or a kilometre? Rather than ask, hence showing ignorance of the outside world, they just settled on the extended version. I suppose, because of sanctions, the phone line to Seattle was blocked, otherwise they could have just asked some tech bloke at Boeing and saved a few uppity peasants having their maize fields buried under tarmac. Nowadays we have Google and it's the uppity peasants that are getting buried under the tarmac by Mugabe.

I was a tad worried after collecting my luggage. I had to go through customs and didn't fancy declaring anything. I had lied at the check-in (aim for the pretty girl, give No. 1 smile, flutter long eyelashes and get away with 15 per cent excess, while not mentioning you have a mountaineer's rucksack packed with stereo equipment you intend to sneak on board as hand luggage). Of course, all shit broke out on the plane at Heathrow as I wobbled aboard with the thing on my back. The white stewardess (no blacks allowed on this plane), wasn't having any of my snake charming.

"Listen," she hissed into my ear, as I sat smugly down, "I know exactly what stunt you pulled here. I'm getting this put into the hold and have a good mind to report you," she huffed while dragging my rucksack away.

Report me to whom? Who cared? They had threatened me a few years ago when I was visiting my bio-mother in the UK and got caught thieving face creams and eau de cologne from the toilets. Now I had just moved house and the white supremacists were paying for it...hah-hah. No wonder I was the black sheep in my dysfunctional family!

Still, I now had to sneak the black market past the white one into Rhodesia. I put on my dark Ray-Bans to cover guilty eyes. There was no 'Nothing to Declare' fast-track lane - not even for farmers. All arrivals were treated with the same contraband suspicion called 'Customs' and the staff were duly called 'Customers', because if they fancied anything that looked dodgy, they could legally confiscate it. As I entered the 'Customs' small room I glanced at a faded Air Rhodesia poster advertising Flame Lily weekend package getaways to Victoria Falls, and another for Lake Kariba with its incredible dam wall, adorning the plain, white walls. In the 11 years I had lived in Rhodesia up till now, I hadn't previously seen either.

I had a bad feeling I was about to be fingered...

"Anything to declare?" the smartly-attired officer, asked rather inhospitably. He was decked out like a tropical cruise ship captain in pure white with fancy rank flashings on his shoulder epaulettes.

I had to think fast. It didn't help that I looked like David Cassidy from the Parakeet family. My plumage of bright green included a pair of Oxford bags, enough to laminate the landscape luminously, and I had a better suntan, since Rhodesia was just crawling into spring and I had returned from the UK's hottest summer on record. Not only that, his hairstyle cut a clean-cut image, while mine looked liked it needed cutting to get clean.

"Oh, erm, I have a few music tapes, and I am here to join the British South Africa Police." That threw him a bit.

Behind him on the wall was a framed picture of our Great White Bwana, Prime Minister Ian Smith. That was him who told us we had the happiest 'blecks' in Africa. His droopy eye, damaged in a Hawker Hurricane crash while fighting the Eyeties for the motherland in WWII, stared accusingly at my luggage.

"Do you have any books or magazines of a pornographic nature?"

Of course I did. I had stuffed into my luggage one of the hottest books around, Xaviera Hollander's *Happy Hooker*, along with the latest *Playboy* and *Penthouse* magazines, but I wasn't exactly going to tell him that. In this country even Wilbur Smith was called a sexual pervert by our Victorian censors. Nor was I going to inform him that I had half a discothèque's sound system that could reap a nice amount in import duty; a litre of Captain Morgan's 73 per cent proof rum; a super cool digital watch and four tins of Brut 33 deodorant I had purchased at Woolworths on special offer, instead of the rip off $10 down at Barbour's (Rhodesia's version of Harrods, minus the Arabs and most of the stock). All in all, I was carrying a rogue's treasure trove, but as a true Rhodie, I wasn't letting on. *Walls have ears* and *Guard against Gab* was by now well-known government slogans to stop us inadvertently spilling the beans to the enemy.

I showed him a couple of the latest UK pop albums by Mike Oldfield and 10cc.

"How much foreign currency have you brought into the country?"

"Sixty British pounds," I replied. This was not good. Fifty of them had been a goodbye and good riddance present from my bio-mother. The next few weeks were going to be tough, but I was hoping to shift the porn for a few bucks.

And then I was steered through into the awaiting arms of my fans.

Lorraine's old man, Jimmy Trenchard, owned *Le Coq d'Or*, a nightclub in the centre of Salisbury. It held live gigs and was frequented by brain-dead, testosterone-fuelled Rhodesian Light Infantry troopies on 10 days Rest and Recreation (R & R) who kicked other fellow armed forces half to death while competing for any available jiggy-jig. Hence, Jimmy had a bit of coin and his Suzie Quatro look-alike daughter could go to school in her own Mercedes. The other arriving Whenwes went home in dilapidated Rixi Taxi Renault 4's or sun-faded Datsun 120Ys and the occasional pseudo BMW Cheetah (named after the animal, not the fact sanction-starved Rhodesians had been nicely cheated by these crappy kit cars.) There was still no sign of the accident-prone second-hand donkey and wooden scotch carts, but at the rate petrol was being rationed, I guessed it wouldn't be long. Well, at least my darling fans chaperoned me home in style.

Unfortunately, despite my seven month absence and my amazing transformation from a scrawny short back and sides with floppy fringe, into a *Top of the Pops* one-hit-wonder, none of the girls were interested in popping a wondrous hit with me on the back seat. Actually, it soon became apparent I had been used as an excuse for them to get off school for a day. Besides, as they were also just over 18, and wrapping up A-levels for university entrance, they were hardly likely to be caught messing with someone their own age who had barely scraped through O-levels; regardless that I looked like a half Jewish David Cassidy clone.

So, while I did all the talking, the Mercedes cruised through the poorer white suburbs of Hatfield, Queensdale and Cranborne. The standard-sized gardens, two thirds of a football pitch - many littered with huge outcrops of weathered granite boulders - showed off the occupant's income. If it looked shit it meant they couldn't afford a borehole and a full time garden boy. Then the car's retreads crossed the main railway line, (the only one actually), and we entered the city centre. We passed street names of pioneers, explorers, missionaries, and land-thieving imperialists - Moffat, Stanley, Rhodes, Livingstone *et-al* - with old Dutch-style gable houses and shops either side. And then up Second Street, heading north, passing some of the 'skyscrapers'; crossing over Jameson Avenue with Cecil Rhodes' statue stuck in the middle of the road, and so into the suburbs where the proper upper middle-class whites lived – Alexander Park, Avondale and Borrowdale – among the many of this city of a quarter of a million people of all races. I think the indigenous population had its own versions of income graded urban habitats, but they weren't in sight, or in mind - segregated mentally and physically. Land possession: the first of white Rhodesia's bane.

Judging by the peace and harmony of Salisbury it was hard to believe that Rhodesia was at war. The open spaces; intense colours; neatness, cleanliness and pleasant smells of nature; the amazing weather and laid-back populace of black, white and in-between – this was the jewel of Africa. Once taken by its addictive allure it was a place to die for. And that was the problem. Not all the 'blecks' were happy. It seemed that some had progressed from being mere cheeky munts and kaffirs in need of a good snotklap to sort them out, into terrs and gooks that needed slotting. The former derogative terminology was used by boorish Rhodies, the latter, by all of us. The rest of the mad planet considered them Freedom fighters. Hah! From this distance in time, did they get it wrong or what?

It was nice to be home again. The suburb of Mount Pleasant was okay, I guess. Here the iron-rich soil was a deep red, but with no giant boulders common elsewhere the verdant gardens of sub-tropical fauna had nothing adventurous about them. But most did have a swimming pool (except us). Arriving at 14 Sims Road I was rapidly booted out the car as it appeared the wicked wenches had other plans. Julia, the ageless multi-purpose maid, known locally by the uneducated uncouth as a Nanny, was delighted to see me, and I was greeted with happy babbling in her Shona lingo and much clapping of hands. Besides a few swear words, most Shona was gibberish to me. Local indigenous languages were not on our school curriculum, unless you count Afrikaans. I proudly managed to get a mark of 'U' (ungraded), for my O-level exam in that incomprehensible guttural tongue. Actually, I also failed English, but managed to scrape a pass when I did the exam again.

Her English was rather limited but she understood her daily duties: make tea by 6.00am, set dining table for three daily, clear table, wash up, ironing, vacuum, dust, polish the patio, prepare vegetables, baby sit and weed the garden (her favourite chore). All for $13 dollars a month. She wasn't allowed to use the washing machine or the stove – they were considered too technical. And on no accounts was she to touch the pressure cooker or the Kenwood cake mixer - God forbid (nor was I come to think of it!). She was allowed to use the iron, which, as they were made in Rhodesia, fell apart under her heavy hand on a regular basis. The Hoover was built in the 50s and was almost indestructible.

I unpacked Precious (as my beloved mini hi-fi was named) and waited for the rest of the clan to turn up - usually about half past one - after school finished for the day. The family consisted of Michael, my 7-year-old half-brother, 16-year-old step-sister, Bridget, and my petite, strict and correct step-mother. My old man had passed into the beyond in '74 and was pushing up daisies in the Jewish cemetery at Warren Hills. I missed him as much as heaven did. But, the family diagnostics is for another story – suffice to say my school years loosened many bolts in my head, assisted occasionally by clips around the ear hole from father dear, but this tale is about the next traumatic period in my constantly unstable life.

The last seven months had been rather dramatic and traumatic. As soon as school was out for ever, I scavenged more of my rapidly dwindling inheritance and went back to my roots – Salford – a real dump of a place. A city within the city of Manchester in Great Britain – except there wasn't anything great about it. Suffice to say it is a story in itself, but to summarise:

I started my career by stashing blocks of butter into the fridges of Liptons supermarket for £17 a week; progressed to an indoor pool attendant and finally gave up my ghost's roots while on £45 a week (before tax) working in a cotton mill factory as a labouring lackey. I had tried to join the Royal Navy as a trainee officer. I passed the exams but was thrown onto the street when they found out I was from Rhodesia. It seemed that the counter-culture of the 60s, so recently ended, had made the British completely paranoid about white people from Africa. They had sent us there in the first place, the uneducated idiots!

I was homesick and wanted out of this place where people my age in conversation used genitals as adjectives in every other word, punctuated with grammatical variations of the four letter word for sexual intercourse. Idiots, all of them, 99 per cent of whom had never heard of Rhodesia - and those that had thought I was a mass murderer - or at least a plantation slave driver.

I wrote to the British South Africa Police (BSAP), the Rhodesian police force as it was known, hoping for a ticket home. I mean, they actually promoted these kinds of deals. Unfortunately for me I received a threatening letter spelling out I was being considered a deserter unless I returned pronto. To this day, I still can't figure this out. I left as a minor, with British citizenship. So, as a British adult subject I applied for the free ride, but was told that because I had registered at the age of 16 (all white boys had to) I was theirs and was due to start fighting. I still don't get it. Well, that's beside the point. I got step-mom Katherine to spring a one way ticket (to be paid back), after bio-mother said she was happy to see the back of me as long as she wasn't paying - and here I am.

The next day was a high-speed lesson in naivety. I decided to hitchhike to my old school, just in time for the 20-minute 10.00am break, and check out some chinas. Normally, I would have used my bike but sadly it was rather wrecked and besides, wearing my peacock outfit along with the extreme heels I would have probably been wasted on the tarmac at the first corner.

"Yussus man! I thought you were a chick, Ek se!"

That charming comment came from the rather dodgy driver of the Peugeot 404 that picked me up. But things were to get worse as I stumbled on to the rugby field where several hundred kids (whites only), ritually ate sandwiches and mobbed the Dairyboard ice-cream vendor (black only), for the limited plastic bags of Bengal Juice, a beloved chocolate flavoured milk drink.

"Bloody hell, Greenberg, you look like a morph! You turned queer or what?" asked my good friend Tim Bell in greeting. "Hah-hah, you look like you're wearing a friggin' dress, you long-haired fairy."

This comment, accompanied by snickers and giggles from dozens of straw boater-wearing tarts and macho rugger-buggers in their scrotum tight khaki shorts and rain-shrunk, dirty brown porkpie hats, had me rapidly losing confidence in my fashionable superiority. I was waking up to the fact that Rhodesia was still stuck in some weird kind of time bubble and my apparel was sending some bad messages.

I needed a plan B before I was either raped or mugged. I hitched into the city centre and stupidly changed my British dosh at the bank. I didn't know about black markets then. I just presumed that's where the indigenous population bought mealies and oddly shaped tomatoes - while in the meantime our government was practicing it wholesale.

The exchange rate was a farcical 80 pence to the Rhodie dollar. I then invested in a pair of blue suede Bata trainers and, with gritted teeth, a pair of locally-made denim jeans with the dubious name of Spurs. Later, I was furious with myself. I should have kitted up with the much coveted Wrangler or Levi brands instead of the whirling dervish, bloody stupid Oxford bags. Now I was down more than $20 but, besides the long hair, I looked relatively normal. Thus attired, my next visit would be down to BSAP headquarters to sign my life away: *Pro Rege, Pro Lege, Pro Patria** (For King, For Law, For Country.)

*The motto of the BSAP. Rather odd as we had no king, the laws were rather dodgy and the country was internationally recognised as illegal).

rhodie babes - Clare, Stephanie and Lorraine
Pic - Beri Hayter

Memoir mutterings

The Stephanie Brooks mentioned has nothing to do with American mass-murderer Ted Bundy's girlfriend of the same name. I must remember to tell Steph she still owes me a new copy of the Happy Hooker. I lent it to her and after much screaming many months later, a quarter of it was presented back to me in bits with the pages glued together. It seems the sex mad pupils of Mount Pleasant High couldn't get their hands on it fast enough and it was chopped into segments and passed around.

I really should email Lord Sugar of the UK version of The Apprentice fame. It was his firm that sold me that dodgy Amstrad amplifier. It cost £40 in those days and was the cheapest in Dixons at the time. The stupid 5-pin input had been soldered in mono mode (which I eventually fixed), but the output for the tape deck to record never worked. That's what you get from buying from a former barrow boy!

Salisbury International Airport. Crazy, but families visited it as a Sunday outing. For a few cents you would gain entrance to the balcony overlooking the runway and have tea and sandwiches and get all excited when planes arrived or took off.

The statue of Cecil Rhodes was given a wide yellow stripe down its back when Rhodesia passed away. It was removed by the new government shortly after Independence in 1980 and placed in a garden at the back of the National Archives in what is now Harare.

Glossary

China. Nothing to do with the bastards that were equipping and training Mugabe's 'Liberators'. It was and still is a friendly Rhodie referral similar to the British 'mate' or the modern version 'M8'.

Eyeties. Italians. Many of them ended up in Rhodesia as POWs during WWII. At the end of the war they decided it was a far better place than bankrupt bombed Italy, and settled as residents.

Ek se! The phonetic full stop applied to the end of a spoken sentence. Considered trailer trash Afrikaans and means the English etiquette equivalent of 'Oh, I say!'

Mealies. Local lingo for white maize (corn).

Morph. From 'morphing' (to change). Refers to homosexuals, or men too much in touch with their feminine side.

Nanny. African female adult.

Rooinek. Red neck. Derogative term for white Rhodesians (and South Africans) and used by *Rock spiders* and *Slopes* (Afrikaners) in a vain attempt to placate themselves for losing the Boer War.

Slotting. From slot, to shoot/terminate life.

Snotklap. The ability to hit someone with the open hand so hard against the side of the head that the recipient's mucus would spurt from the nostrils. My father was an expert at this. Sadly, I was the only family recipient of this type of education designed to drum some sense into me.

Whenwes. Comes from White Africans abroad tending to start a conversation with 'When we lived in …".

Yussus. Jesus.

CHAPTER 2:

Recruit copper Karl gets cruelly cropped

My obsession with joining the BSAP started when, as a pre-teen, I had read all the Alfred Hitchcock's *The Three Investigators* books and then, as a teenager, all the *Detective Hardy Boys* novels. I was convinced I had a natural talent for hunting down criminals by piecing clues together as I had nearly always concluded who the baddies were before the final chapter. However, nowhere in these American collections did it refer to beating up people with heavy objects to coax them into confessing quickly, and thus save writing so many chapters. I would find out about that trick later.

So, it was with rather naive expectations that I joined the ranks of the 'Blue and Old Gold', in anticipation of achieving the rank of Detective Chief Superintendent before my 21st birthday. When I filled the application form at police headquarters I was told I had just made it in time for the next day's entrance exam. Hey? I hadn't known about that bit. So much for being a great detective. If I failed, it would be conscription in the peasant army for poor little me. God! The mere thought of it gave me a panic attack. The idea of being a Neanderthal troopie 'Brown Job', nearly made me drop one. The army bastards had already sent me a fat envelope with my call-up papers. If I wasn't accepted by the police I would become gook fodder. While I truly did love my country, I had absolutely no intention of dying for it. I was back for the Rhodesian way of life – braais, booze and babes, preferably in the sun, and getting well paid for it. And certainly not for the $77 a month average conscript troopies got for going into the bush, while armed up to their smelly armpits and fighting some very nasty individuals that were officially called terrorists or insurgents or the grander title – Communist Terrorists – or CTs for short. We just called them terrs or gooks. Later I learnt that they were the same as us – freedom fighters! We wanted to be free of them and vice versa. Living on a keyboard of ebony and ivory in perfect harmony is fine, as long as the big keys remain white.

On the application form it showed the wage structure. With my five O-levels, I would start on an income of $222 dollars a month, before deductions, etc. That would have been about £200 British pounds then. That sounded like a fortune when you take into account a bottle of Coke (because of sanctions there was no such things as cans of beverages) was still 5c in the supermarkets, and a pint of beer in the discotheque was 35 cents. Hidden in the small print was a line that said 'if', and it was a big if, I pass all the future exams I might make inspector in seven years. Since I hadn't actually calculated on taking any exams at all, this sort of set back all my ambitions of replacing the present incumbent Commissioner by the ripe old age of 25.

What was apparent when I turned up for the exam - after preparing for it in my usual way, by doing sod all - was that I had unquestionably the most beautiful head of long hair and, along with my gobby manner, it made me as popular as an empty beer crate at a mental institute's annual piss-up. The exam couldn't have been that difficult because most of the 30- odd applicants also passed and, after meeting them briefly during the smoke breaks, I realised that some of them were verging on the imbecilic. So, subject to a medical examination, I was in.

According to the rumours, you had to be pretty brain-dead or a complete spastic if you failed to sneak (bribe) your way past Morris Depot's mad incumbent police doctor, and not get a clean bill of health. When I turned up for my medical, I was a nervous wreck. According to the medical examination form that the senile doc would fill in, three of the criteria could be a problem for me.

Two were psychological. I had to allow him to insert his finger into my anus and feel about for haemorrhoids, and then let him fondle my balls, while I coughed in embarrassment. I wasn't sure what the reason was for this but the thought that my nuts and arse might fail me at such an early stage in my life was extremely traumatic to say the least. Imagine telling your friends you were not accepted into the police force because your piles were bigger than your testicles and your odds of being a homosexual porn-star were up shit creek. (Rhodesian macho humour is rather tedious.) The third problem was physical. I had flat feet, and although they never bothered me, on paper, I didn't qualify.

However, all this fear was unfounded. My blood pressure was checked; I weighed in at 65kg, measured up to 174cm and was asked if I felt "alright". About joining the police? What a daft question. Well, for sure, I wouldn't be here otherwise, would I? Actually, what he meant was if I felt perfect in the body. The mind didn't interest him: that would soon become obvious from the amount of lunatics I would meet as fellow recruits, which included my old china from Allan Wilson High School, Tim Addison, and his new side kick, Jeff Swindells.

That very first night at Morris Depot I was introduced to perhaps one of the wealthiest men in Rhodesia. The police recruit barber, Santos. A tiny man of Portuguese extraction, who had fled neighbouring Mozambique during its bush war, had seemingly been trained by sheep shagging Australian shearers. He would arrive twice a week and set up shop in the evenings inside the recruits' bar, *The Left Right Inn*. In a few buzzing seconds with a massive electric hair clipper he converted my David Cassidy looks into an ugly, round ball, topped with brown sandpaper. For the privilege of having next to no chance of pulling any birds in the foreseeable future, I was forced to hand over a dollar. I was rapidly running out of them.

My intake, Recruit Patrol Officer (PO) Squad 8/76, was designated a squad instructor. He would be responsible for teaching us marching, first aid, self defence and riot control. He also took us for PT and would inspect us before we went off to any other lessons. Unfortunately for me, Inspector Mike Lambourne was the ultimate keen, very mean, killing machine, with a black belt in judo and was a champion weight lifter. He was also one of the biggest men I had ever seen. His regulation cap had been adapted so extremely that its angled hard peak touched the bridge of his nose. It made him look like a nasty Nazi in khaki. With a fist as big as my head and his forearms matching my thighs for size, my half-Jewish anus twitched with fear of this man.

Day One of my new career was used to kit out us fellow recruits. Mighty Mike used his expertise to shout and scream at us into some kind of bunch that might resemble a squadron formation, and had us tripping and stumbling, still wearing our various motley civilian clothes, to the Quartermaster's store. Here we would be issued with all that was necessary for a professional policeman for the next three years. The massive amount was supposed to be packed in a huge, blue, sausage-shaped canvas bag almost as large as myself. There were never-ending trips to the counter to collect stuff: heavy, dark khaki wool trousers and a long jacket for winter. Also jodhpurs, khaki shorts and a short-sleeved safari suit-type jacket for town duties, and grey, open-necked shirts for rural areas. Rubber-soled boots for running around in the bush, leather-soled boots with steel studs for marching noisily on tarmac and normal leather shoes to go with the long khaki, blue-topped socking. There were leather leggings that went from the ankle almost up to the knee that were usually for town duty, and worn, presumably, if you expected to be savaged by dogs. Green canvas leggings were supposed to be for wandering around rural places if you expected to be savaged by snakes. Then came rubber truncheons (presumably for beating senseless any savaging dogs or snakes), hard hats for riots, and soft leather gloves with huge, white, plastic fins, for riding motorbikes - if we would ever get to see one.

After you called out your size and were issued kit, you had to sign for the lot. It all had to be handed back when we left. If something got worn out on the way, that was not a problem, but if it was lost or stolen – you paid for the replacement. Name and number noted on paper for everything. A blue lanyard to wrap around the left shoulder, its clip end holding a shiny stainless steel whistle, would be hidden in the top left shirt pocket. Steel handcuffs, hairy green socks, a stunning leather belt with the magnificently embossed buckle of solid brass with the BSAP emblem of a lion speared by assegais. Then we received our full fighting kit (my protests that I was sure not to need this went unheeded.) Two pairs of heavy cotton shirts, trousers and French Foreign Legion-type caps, all in the deep shades of Rhodesian bush camouflage. One green nylon sleeping bag (known lovingly in the trade as your Fart Sack), aluminium pots and water bottles to put in or on the light green canvas contraption called a web kit. This muddle of straps, flaps and odd shaped pockets resembling a builder's harness for away trips, was designed for maximum efficacy of combat efficiency. It was supposed to carry all that we would need for fighting Charlie Tangos. Not that I was particularly keen on that idea. I had joined the police to serve souls, and not to shoot holes in them.

Along with the uniforms, each recruit was paired up to share a room and a batman (I always wondered if any of them did a bit robbin' on the side), to be our own personal slave. He was there to make our beds, which for some insane reason had to have the sheets and blanket folded in a special way, resembling a giant square hamburger, and placed at the end of the bed. He also had to wash and iron our clothes, and for this privilege, we had to give him each $55 a month out of our hard-earned money. This was exploitation, but I had no chance of getting Julia to move in. This was bad news. I had barely started work and was already in debt to my half-owned slave vassal. As the American confederates are so fond of saying – *If I had known it was going to work out like this; I would have picked my own cotton!*

Memoir mutterings

There still seemed to be some invisible link to the mother country, otherwise what was wrong with the name 'Rhodesia Police'? I suppose it just didn't roll off the tongue with the same amount of ambience as BSAP.

It all started in 1889, when 500 armed volunteers accompanied the pioneer column of Cecil John Rhodes' British South Africa Company crossing the Limpopo and setting up a camp by a kopje some three hundred odd miles to the north. By the time it was realised it wasn't the previously-scouted kopje they were supposed to have reached it was too late and the future capital, Salisbury, was born. The Great White Hunter, Frederick Courtney Selous, had been their guide and as punishment for these major mindless meanderings he was shot in the head by a kraut sniper in German East Africa (but that wasn't until the First World War).

In 1891 the Mashonaland Mounted Police was formed in the north and was soon followed by its southerly counterpart, the Matabeleland Mounted Police, plus the municipal force called the Southern Rhodesia Constabulary. By 1909 the word 'Company' had been dropped and the whole lot, along with the neighbouring Bechuanaland Border Force, became amalgamated as the BSAP. Elements of this force served in the Anglo-Boer war as well as the First World War.

Glossary

Blue and Old Gold. The regimental colours of the British South Africa Police.
Brown Job. Member of the army.
Kopje. Hill.
PT. Physical training.

CHAPTER 3:

A whiter shade of pain

We have all seen Hollywood films with armed forces' recruits jumping up and down, running in circles, swinging like monkeys on ropes to land in mud puddles, marching around like robots etc, etc. Huge, loud horrible men sporting gay moustaches shout obscenities about the mothers of the sweating, straining fuckers, and this bit tends to turn the chicks off in these kinds of movies as bloody boring. Normal, alpha-type males love this stuff. They would be glued to a bottle of beer and shout enthusiastically-
"They are Men of Men," whilst passing wind, belching and scratching at their holes.
The long suffering partner cruelly thinks he should be shouting, "They are Morphs of Morphs!" because of the way they go on about comradely brotherly love and the next thing they all get dressed as cowboys and bugger off to Brokeback Mountain where they can happily bond together…

Everyday would start the same. Someone with a penchant for getting up early, called the 'burglar of sleep' or bugler, would smartly march to the front of the parade square. There, as two fellow immaculately dressed early birds ran up the flags of Rhodesia and the BSAP; he would start parping away on a shiny brass bugle. Not that we would ever get to see this; it was still 5.30 in the morning and we were all fast asleep - till the parping started. I would no doubt awake from an erotic dream about my former maths teacher, or perhaps the geography teacher with the massive mazams (although there was a rumour that the BSAP put the anaphrodisiac 'bluestone' in our tea to stop us pulling our wires), and then it was all a rush to the communal ablution blocks for the traditional triple *S* - Shit, Shower and Shave. Luckily for me, I could control my movements until I could do it in relative peace without being surrounded by guttural grunts and the stench of several dozen expelling bowels. I didn't have to shower in the morning. I did it before I went to sleep and never suffered from sweaty nightmares, unlike some others who would wake up smelling like a baboon's armpit. Thirdly, my hair growth hormone levels were still relatively mediocre, and a quick skim over my face with an electric razor in the evening would suffice. This left me with ample time to have a quick wash and get changed. Then the day would begin. It sort of went like this:

PT first thing in the morning was torture. Before we were subjected to a fast hop, skip and loads of jumping, we needed to be inspected. In fact, before any lessons, all 93 of us (three regular, one National Service and one woman squad), would be inspected simultaneously by our instructors. This occurred on the football-field sized tarmacked hard square, adjacent to the hallowed, grass parade ground and directly in front of the large mess hall that catered for our culinary needs.

Every uniform had its own quirky problems when it came to passing the all-knowing gaze of Inspector Lambourne. While the PT green vest we wore was rarely an issue - keeping the white shorts and tennis shoes (known to us as *tackkies*), perfectly unblemished, was. We soon learnt to keep a small piece of chalk in the pocket, so as to touch up any inadvertent scuff marks we may have incurred on the way from the bedroom to the tarmac. Any creases in the freshly ironed shorts was a definite no-no, so that entailed us all walking like we had carrots stuffed up our arses, as we stiff legged it to the inspection ground.

Inspector Lambourne always pushed us to our limits, and beyond. For the first couple of weeks I would land up vomiting from exertion. This rather painful act had to be done while still running. PT was quite varied. Besides the usual push ups, chin ups, obstacle course, running up and down the spectators stands at the police rugby grounds (a real killer, leaving many a recruit with wobbly knees, heaving his guts up from oxygen starvation), we went on tourist trips. Once a week, we exited the police grounds and ran five clicks through the magnificent National Botanical Gardens as large as a suburb. It didn't see many tourists though. It had a reputation for being the place to have covert sex. One car park area among the exotic plants was a known jiggy-jig sanctuary, while it was rumoured that the tract of virgin savannah-woodland was a breeding ground for illegal fairies. Quite often we would bump into the black recruits from Tomlinson Depot. They were super fit and would cruise by us in perfect ranks - maybe looking for the fairies to beat up.

The fittest in our 23 man squad was Jan, a 28-year-old former member of the South African Police force (SAP). He had played for the SAP rugby team and had been a personal guard outside their Prime Minister's private residence. Jan was about my height, but packed with trained muscle. He could run in those tackies like Jesse Owens, covering 100 metres in 12 seconds flat. I asked him one night, while chilling in the recruits bar, why he had abandoned what looked like a good career to become a policeman in Rhodesia.

"Because I want to kill as many Kaffirs as possible," he replied in his thick Afrikaans accent.

I must admit I was surprised. That had never occurred to me as being a reason to join an establishment that was supposed to protect its people, not to terminate them! By pure coincidence, about a year later, I was to bump into him again. It had been in the police singles' quarters in Salisbury and there he was, kitted in camouflage from head to toe. He had enough pouches stuffed with spare magazines for his rifle to open up his own armoury. Grenades dangled down from the chest webbing straps like bunches of miniature green pineapples. His wish had finally come true. He had joined Support Unit on full-time counter-insurgency tours and was more than delighted to boast his kill count. The only reason he hadn't joined the army was because he knew he would be paid a hell of a lot better as a policeman. A really strange man, but I admit I rather liked him. In every weird respect he was a gentleman, although his uncontrollable hatred towards blacks was beyond my comprehension.

When it came to the final PT exam, although I could not complete eight laps of the earthen, standard running oval in 12 minutes, I still achieved a 93 per cent pass. I had become pretty fit (except for the hair style).

Then of course you did drill. Swinging arms, stomping feet, eyes right and all the bullshit.

At least PT was multi-tasking to some extent. Learning to march - better known as drill - was not. I suppose there are many reasons why every governmental force on the planet insists that their recruits learn drill, but to me, it seemed pointless. It hurt my feet and turned some of our squad permanently into brainless robots. And there was, of course, a uniform for this; blue cotton trousers and open, grey, V-necked short-sleeved shirt.

The most important part of it all was the footwear. A pair of our leather boots had gone to the cobblers and been returned with 12 steel studs hammered into the heel and soles. There was a very simple reason for this. It was to make as much noise as possible while marching. The only time you actually walked in them was on the way to inspection. The chances that you could land up in hospital with broken legs or worse were rather good, because these things were like skating on thimbles, such was their grip on the highly polished corridors. It would only occur to me years later, why Lambourne, as he marched in front of our grouped squad, always seemed to know that some one was out of step - he had heard it! 46 stamping feet of steel, on hard gravel impregnated tarmac, made an incredible din when working in perfect choreographed movements. Lambourne could pick up if two were not beating in step – mine.

I was a bit of a drill spaz, on top of being lazy. When it came to swinging my arms, I just couldn't be arsed with the effort to get them exactly 90 degrees to my body, and what for? They were very happy hanging down my sides as I march. Mighty Mike had a bad habit of stepping to one side, allowing us to pass, and instantly pounce on me. Re-education consisted of being forced to march around holding half a brick in each hand; which was extremely uncomfortable. This caused havoc in the ranks, as I staggered around smashing them inadvertently into my fellow recruits. After each of these painful lessons, my kind and understanding colleagues never failed to give me a few thumps and insults, such as, 'stupid wanker'.

Thankfully, I wasn't the only one who had difficulties mimicking a drunken Buzz Lightyear. There were also a couple of other drill wasters, one of them was 'Woody', the squadron's self-proclaimed highly qualified 'street fighter'. Woody was very popular, for the simple reason that he was a natural born clown, without even knowing it. He had double jointed elbows which he could freakily bend down at such an angle, as to appear they had been snapped. He loved giving us a demonstration of his bizarre prowess while at full march, his arms flapping up and down, like they were his Toy Story namesake. Many a loud snicker would cause our Mighty Mike to stop us marching, and demand an explanation for disarray in the ranks. We never snitched.

Whilst some of our squad thought that polishing their kit and marching around like robots was the best thing since goose stepping Nazis, my mediocre interest in the subject was reflected in my final note…65 per cent. This was not good.

"Man down, man down, call a medic!"

We all know these words from loads of war films. Well, in the police we were all supposed to be trained medics, but I still wouldn't place my life in the hands of some of the members in my squad…

First Aid lessons were also under the tuition of Mike Lambourne. I already had the impression he was more talented in activities that made people require first aid prior to hospitalisation, rather than trying to patch them up. We would all sit in a cramped class room and pay as much attention to absorb the rudiments of sentience preservation as we did at school in religion classes. So much for saving life and soul!

Mighty Mike looked distinctively uncomfortable behind a desk. In fact, he couldn't fit under it and his giant, leather-clad legs would straddle either side of the desk as he tried to get comfortable on the tiny chair. He would then attempt to teach us using a well-thumbed text book. This was as effective as teaching the dead that if they stuck around in a cave long enough, Jesus might come to the rescue.

I didn't care. I was unquestionably the most highly qualified in the class. I had years of Boy Scouts and St Johns Ambulance Brigade experience behind me and I had even bandaged my poor teddy's eye after I had poked into the back of his head at the age of two. While I could artificially resuscitate Lazarus if need be, the others would struggle to open a box of plasters in a vain effort to patch up a shot lung. The only time my fellow First, Second and definitely Third World Aiders perked up with any show of interest was when they found out that the Israelis had discovered that if a shot victim had lost so much blood that his veins had collapsed, you could cut slashes in the drip tube and shove it up his arse! Fancy that! No thanks, I would rather bleed to death.

Having lost ground against my fellow recruits in my vain quest to perhaps actually pass out in the top three of my squad, I was banking on the First Aid exam to recuperate any missing points.

The task of testing our knowledge of the BBC (Breathing, Bleeding and Consciousness), was done by a full time medic from the army. Not only did he appear as if he had just come off the bottle 10 minutes prior to turning up, the bloke looked so wasted I thought he had been hanging off his own beer drip every morning for the last 20 years. Before he started with our so-called examination, he unpacked his First Aid kit and demonstrated on one of us how to administer a drip. After much tapping of veins and squeezing of the victim's upper arm, he plunged the needle into the reluctant volunteer and, after hanging the drip bag up on a small tripod, proceeded to ask various easy questions directed to the entire class. Most of them were met with blank looks and I answered as many as I could. I was growing more and more alarmed at what was happening, but not as alarmed as the poor recruit whose lower arm now had a huge lump the size of a baseball growing under the skin. The bloody drunken fool had missed the vein and half a bag a saline fluid was taking residence in the hapless recruit's forearm. Our super proficient examiner hastily pulled the needle out after this was brought to his attention. I actually expected the stuff to come out like a pressurised water spout, but sadly, much to my anticipated curiosity, it didn't! The recruit was then assured that he wasn't going to spend the rest of his life looking like a one armed, Popeye the Sailor Man and that his new super large muscle would dissipate in a few hours.

Then the idiot, so pickled on drips, morphine or whiskey, announced that he would give us all a blanket pass of 73 per cent! I was furious. This stab in the back would set me back dearly when it came to the overall average pass result. And God help anyone getting shot needing 'real' First Aid. Imagine the scenario –

"What are the chances of the man living, Patrol Officer?"

"About 73 per cent, sir."

"That's fantastic, how do you know this?"

"I got a blanket pass in First Aid."

Obviously, joining the police also meant you were supposed to know a bit about the law you were sworn to uphold. In most democracies, ignorance is not an excuse for breaking a law you didn't know existed. In a white minority-controlled country such as ours, we all broke the law, such as drink driving, and then pretended we were so pissed that we forgot it wasn't allowed. Unfortunately, the annual death toll on the roads was rather high due to this bad habit; although, not as bad as the lightning strike toll.

Lawyers have to go to university for years to understand anything about law, but we recruits were expected to cram the lot in our daily lessons lasting two hours. Take away weekends and the occasional day 'teacher' was sick, I reckon we had maybe 100 hours of the most boring lessons possible. Our teacher was a thin-faced inspector with an enormous caterpillar sitting below his nose like Groucho Marx. The man had the charisma and auditory skill of Rhodesian made *Eveready* batteries – leaking acid and running out of juice within minutes of being installed.

As summer progressed it became harder and harder to concentrate. After an active morning of physical exercise in a progressively hotter sun, followed by a large lunch, I tended to nod off in the class. There were no fans or air conditioning and even with the windows fully open, it did little to stop the lethargy that inevitably crept over us. Sadly this had not gone unobserved and when Groucho sprung a surprise test on us – what does, *Modus Operandi* mean? It meant that I, along with most of the class, had to type it out 100 times as punishment. Presumably we would know what it meant in the future.

In law class we sat behind rows of ancient wooden desks that didn't even have drawers, all stained a dark greasy brown from decades of recruits sweating over them. Addie always sat next to me. We had been mates at Allan Wilson High School but after I went to Mount Pleasant High, the contact stopped. Now by pure coincidence we were back together again. He didn't look like the strongly built swimmer of those days anymore. At the tender age of 18 he was already showing a beer gut and puffed away on strong Madison cigarettes. Smoking was allowed in class as Groucho had one singeing his moustache nearly non-stop. Addie's bad habits were due to the fact he had been a police cadet in the provincial town of Karoi for the previous two years and had been allowed to drink under the age limit. That's what you call having the law on your side. To make himself look older he had a rather poor excuse of a moustache crawling out of his upper lip in a confused manner and still had the annoying habit of hiding my pen.

There wasn't much in the way of decorations in the law classroom, except one object which would constantly be looked at and discussed – a huge map of Rhodesia with coloured pins pushed into it representing every police station in the country. It was a known fact that a recruit would rarely get a station anywhere near home and there was constant banter that the most useless recruits would be sent to 'hot spots' whilst others would be given plums like Kariba or the Victoria Falls tourist resorts.

One afternoon, 7/76 and the women recruit squads were crammed into the law classroom for a special treat. We would be given a lecture by two members of CID. It was my intention to become one of them, but it turned out you needed two years of service before you could even apply for consideration. I had forgotten to detect that fact. Some of the anecdotes they told were stuff of legends. There was the forensic expert with a photographic memory and a data bank installed in his head, who after dusting for prints on a stolen car, handed the investigating officer a note with the name and last known address of the culprit!   Things became really interesting when the topic turned to illicit drugs. Holding up a large, transparent plastic bag full of some odd looking green stuff, one officer announced,

"This is a haul of dagga that we recently confiscated. I want you to pass it around, feel and smell it, to give you an idea what to look for."

Dagga (*Cannibas sativa*), otherwise known as marijuana, was, according to the following quote from *Encyclopaedia Rhodesia*, closely allied to crime: 'When smoked it produces aggressive tendencies and stimulation of the senses. Obvious symptoms are red eyes and a disoriented manner. The person inhaling the stuff becomes exceedingly thirsty and his breath has a sweet smell.' *(What a load of bollocks. Actually it should read – 'When smoked by former BSAP Patrol Officers in their 50s it produces desires to empty the fridge of all beer and chocolate, followed by the senseless stimulation of writing a memoir that keeps at least one person (the author), in spasms of giggles before falling asleep.')*

By the time the bag returned to the officer at the front of the class, two thirds of it had mysteriously disappeared. The CID man's next announcement left us all without any doubts that he wasn't exactly impressed with the quality of us future upholders of the law.

"My colleague and I will now step outside for a cigarette break. When we return, it is expected that the bag will be full again. If it is not, you will all be stripped searched, including the women, and anyone in possession of even a miniscule amount will be sitting in a cell for quite a while."

There were roars of laughter as half of the class room went sheepishly up and emptied their pockets. Some of us had only taken a pinch or two, but a couple of the culprits had been greedy enough to take whole handfuls. I, of course, as a future upholder of the law had taken none; only because I was a coward.

Trips out of the law classroom were rare. One of them was to a mock car crash. Armed with blank Traffic Accident Report Booklets (TARBs) we were supposed to take down details of the incident, note the drivers' names, record any witnesses and draw a sketch of the scene with exact coordinates. The worse entries were then read out in the class by our miffed-off teacher. For example; it was explained that when sketching out a vehicle accident, you do not take measurements from curb side parked automobiles to the crash scene, but rather from the objects that remain immobile for a considerable time - such as sign posts or a handy sized tree, but not the one the car hit.

Another day trip was to a 'Blacks Only' morgue at Harare hospital, recognised as one of the finest in Africa, to watch an autopsy. Presumably there was a legal reason for this. There was plenty of space for all of us to gather around and watch the dissection of an AMA. What hit the senses first was the stench - an all impregnating sickly sweet smell of semi-cooked decaying meat - and a few of us popped outside for a quick spew. This particular deceased had died in an accidental fire in his grass hut. The purpose of the autopsy was to prove this was so.

The body had been taken from the fridge and placed on a large porcelain slab which was designed so that blood would drain away into a gutter installed in the floor below. The black mortuary assistant was a bit of a clown and thought to entertain us. Large tracts of the deceased's outer skin had peeled off into flimsy, crispy black rolls exposing pinkish flesh. His arms, still suffering from *rigor mortis*, sort of stuck up in some weird gesture and the power of this was amply demonstrated by the assistant who pulled one arm down and let it spring up again whilst grinning at us. I think most of us had expected a leg to pop up in response like in some scary film.

Then, taking a scalpel, he slit the skin on the head from ear to ear, and with an awful sucking type sound, pulled half of the man's face down, so his forehead touched the chin. After doing the same to the rear of the head, the skull was cut open with a hacksaw, exposing the brain. This organ was pulled out, and after being weighed, was sliced up like an onion ready to be *sautéed*. The white mortician in the meantime was giving a running commentary as his assistant continued. Having now ascertained that the man had not died from a stroke or tumour, the next bit was the abdomen. The ribcage was crunchily cut apart with what looked like giant hedge trimmers and with brute force pulled apart. Lungs and heart received the same treatment as the brain. It was here that evidence was found of the true cause of death - smoke inhalation. The sliced open oesophagus and lungs were full of black soot. (At that point some of us dashed outside for a quick fag to absorb some soot of their own.) Liver and kidneys were duly chopped up as well. Next, the stomach was cut open and inside it could be observed the last supper swimming in gastric juices. 'Jesus help me' I thought, for at the sight and stench of semi-digested sadza in black sooty sauce was unbearable at that point, and even I was starting to feel a little queasy and went out for a gulp of fresh air.

Now that the insides had been turned into mince meat on the outside, it was time to put them back in. However, the pile of stinking mess was simply popped into the empty stomach cavity and with a few stitches the skin was pulled over the huge mound, making the man look nine months pregnant. To add insult to terminal injury, the face was pulled back and tied back on with such force as to leave the corpse grinning stupidly. For a bit of fun, the assistant then played a little drum-roll on the hollow head with a couple of steel scalpels. What a laugh! (Not.)

After this dissection, another corpse was promptly thrown onto the slab and at that point I suggested to Addie we wander off and see if we can find a shop selling some Cokes. This unfortunately was a bad move, as when we wandered back at a leisurely pace half an hour later, everyone was in the police truck and a seriously hacked-off Groucho was about to start spewing blood - ours!

By the time it came to take the final exam, my knowledge of the law was still basically what my father had beaten into me – hypocrisy. As a result I scored a paltry 67 per cent, barely above the minimum requirement, and my rankings were slipping badly.

Another bit of fun and games we played was in self-defence and riot control.

I am an expert at self-defence. I still have a yellow belt in the ancient discipline of *Legitquick*, which so far stood me in good stead. I never went near any riots, and certainly I had no inclination to control one. (Although, I have often wished to start some.) Still, it was part of the curriculum and it was obvious that our squad's own home grown, mountain gorilla would 'teach' us the tricks of the trade. These took place in my church, the gym hall. Lambourne usually asked for volunteers to demonstrate some strange ways of how a man, the size of King Kong, could subdue a rioting teen (intent on attacking Kong's foot whilst using nothing more than his testicles), would be castrated with a swift kick to the groin hard enough to punt the teen's balls out of his ears.

The whole thing was ludicrous. If Lambourne had been the rioter and attacked the entire squad, our only defence from instant dismemberment was death. But, we had a few laughs. One particular useless recruit, who never failed to spew on PT, was singled out for the 'choke lock'. This would be achieved by crossing the lapels of the poor recruit's judo tunic at the throat and yanking hard enough so that his blood supply was cut off to his head. The wretch was then left twitching spasmodically on the floor until he came around.

Twice we caught Lambourne out. When asked for a volunteer for a demonstration of an 'elbow lock', Woody was more than happy to have a go. As Lambourne exerted pressure against the joint, Woody let out a massive scream, and 'broke' his elbow. The look on Lambourne's face was just too much. He had honestly believed he had snapped Woody's arm! The other occasion was when I was called out. This was the 'grab rioter by lapels, fall back, place foot in rioter's stomach at the same time and toss him over onto his back.' Hah, I wasn't a former gymnast for nothing. The force Lambourne used propelled me up high enough for me to do a neat somersault, land on my feet, and leg-it before he got up…

Since I like to chat, radio instruction should have been a breeze, but for this module, we were supplied with no radios. So saying

"Roger, Roger, Over and Out and my real name is Charlie," into our ballpoint pens soon got rather tedious.

We were taught about Shackle. It was a code we were to use when on patrol looking for CTs and needed to phone home and tell base where we were. I thought I didn't really need this because I wasn't planning on going on any of these gook chasing patrols. After all, I had joined the police, right?

Wrong, but I find this out sooner rather than later. Meanwhile, learning Shackle was a bit like using a logarithm book. No big deal, so our instructor, a tall, pleasant Section Officer, who had a black belt in karate, allowed us to chat about anything of interest. When the teacher asked if any of us had any training in the grand, ancient, and noble art of self defence, Woody let slip he was a 'street fighter' *par excellence*. Not a good one apparently. When he picked a fight with another one of our squad members, a rather odd farmer's kid, he got the shit kicked out of him. However, Woody gained even more respect by taking his humiliating defeat like a gentleman, and differences were patched up...

Everyone passed with 80 per cent and to round up the Morris Depot training there were typing lessons.

What can be said about typing lessons? They were a complete disaster. I did so well, I still type with two fingers, while looking at the key board. A skinny woman, Annie Lovell, about forty plus going on to infinity (judging by the makeup, tight top and short skirt), was our tutor. A huge plastic screen, hanging on the class room front wall, was painted with the keys. It had flashing lights that lit up as plinky-plonky poor porno type music shattered our frazzled nerves. The idea was to 'touch type' by just looking at the flashing letters, but the typewriters were dinosaurs and fingers got jammed between the keys, carriages stuck - but the music and flashing lights played on.

When Groucho forced us to write the definition of *modus operandi* out a 100 times; some recruits were so desperate they paid professional secretaries to do it. I managed 40 lines and didn't give a toss for the consequences.

I passed with 52 per cent. Now I was in big trouble and slipping badly down the rankings but at least my scores were better than the ones I used to get at school. And I still had to be taught to be a killer, so it was time for us big boys to get our toys.

Messing about and learning about small arms would become one of my favourite lessons. Instruction would be taken at the police armoury and taught by Section Officer (SO) Tony Wesson, who had a weird sense of humour and was at the time a bit of a celebrity for doing something no one else had done. Namely; meeting up, shaking hands and chatting with a bunch of serious hard core gooks - and live to tell the tale. This was because a very curious incident had happened that kept us all in a state of confusion for a short time. It was called *The Kissinger Peace Proposals* or, in clear text...we, the white minority, had surrendered!

On the evening of Friday the 24th of September 1976, barely a month after I had joined the police, the Prime Minister Ian Smith announced to a rather shocked nation that his government had accepted the terms put forward by the American Secretary of State, Dr. Henry Kissinger. All of us had huddled around radios to hear it (I actually recorded the entire speech), and while we had little clue what had been going on behind the scenes the gist of it was that there would be the end to white rule within two years and, as a prelude to an interim government being formed, a cessation of terrorism. Then, the idea was, that after two years all the blacks would get the vote, not just the ones that earned at least $1000 dollars a year, which of course meant a black majority-ruled country. During this build up, our illegal sovereignty would be replaced by the old one – the United Kingdom.

All of this was rather confusing as most of us didn't have much of an idea what was going on. We knew there were loads of gooks running around raping, killing, pillaging and generally being really bad-ass out there in the bush and the Rhodesian defence forces were losing men almost daily, but the politics was rather hazy. The press was censored and it would be a long time before I found out who Bob Marley was.

Anyway, after the speech we thought it was a perfect excuse to go on the piss and get totally shit-faced down at the Left Right Inn. Now that we were once again law abiding, decent, civilised subjects of Her Majesty and not land thieving, racist, imperial colonists as we were depicted north of the Zambezi, we sang some old favourites. *God Save the Queen* (pre-Sex Pistols version, although with hindsight theirs would have been more appropriate) and *Rule Britannia*. We even considered staggering to the Botanical Gardens and sing *I'm Just a Sweet Transvestite* with the fairies who, in theory, could now come out the closet as western liberalism finally entered our Victorian time bubble. Our black barman, even after being told he was now British and could get a job pulling pints in London, and could even use the municipal swimming pools and library, was nonplussed by the excitement and shut up shop at the usual time.

The following day, a hastily organised meeting for all recruits was made in the gym hall. During this question and answer session with senior officers, many serious fears were carefully addressed:

"Do we get paid now in British pounds because I need to import a new battery for my digital watch?"

"Do we have to make our own beds?"

"Will the price of beer and fags go up?"

No one could answer, so we simply went back to the daily routine. It all came to naught anyway as it appeared that the nationalist leaders were not informed of the deal. In the first few days of euphoria and confusion, SO Wesson made friendly contact with a group of 'freedom fighters' and chatted about the so called ceasefire. They had then returned back to the bush with a promise to meet again, but they never did after it had become apparent the whole thing was a lemon.

It was here at the armoury we were given a weapon that would become so much a part of our lives. A brand new SA FN FAL 7.62 NATO Battle Rifle. This name is quite a mouthful and would generally be referred to by the initials FN and certainly never use the derogative word – *Gun*! If one of us inadvertently referred to their rifle as that, they would be forced to stand at attention, holding it out in the left hand, and with the forefinger of the right pointing first to the rifle, start chanting the immortal lines -

"This is my rifle." Then the hand would be lowered to the genital area with the finger pointing at your dick,

"And this is my gun." The hand would return to pointing at the weapon, still held aloft,

"This is for shooting." The finger would finally be pointed back to the trousers,

"And this is for fun!"

The slang term for the rifle is gat, although no one seemed to have a clue where that came from. Woody, upon receiving his, promptly engraved into the plastic stock that covered part of the barrel, TTTT. This he explained was his gat's name - Terry The Terr Terminator. A few of the others also decided to give their big boy's toy a name, but none matched Woody's wit.

SO Wesson was an extremely knowledgeable man in the science of ballistics and I was absolutely fascinated with the subject. We were taught to strip and re-assemble many various models of small arms, both ours and 'theirs'. Police forensics were quite sophisticated and SO Wesson explained that after any contact between the Goodies (us) and the Baddies (them), all expended cartridges of the terrs would be salvaged and examined. The firing pin of each weapon left a unique indentation and it was possible to work out which group of terrorists had been responsible for being serious bad ass. It also contributed evidence to help send a captured gook to the gallows.

Most of us enjoyed the lessons and comprehended the mechanical functions of the weapons, except 'Poor old Guy'.

'Poor old Guy' was 19 and a tall praying mantis stick of an apparition. He had come out only six months before with his parents from the United Kingdom. What the hell for, I never really gathered, but rather than go into the army he was trying to become a policeman. He was completely out of his element and, while trying his hardest, he had very little chance of ever being capable of exuding authority. During one lesson, SO Wesson, completely frustrated with Guy's total inability to understand the functions of a 9mm pistol, had pulled the breech block back and told the innocent Guy to insert his long slender forefinger into the exposed chamber. As he did so, Wesson released the breach block, leaving Guy with small tears of pain in his eyes, holding aloft the pistol suspended from his forefinger. The force had made the cold steel cut deep enough to bring blood.

'Poor old Guy' didn't pass-out with us, he was put back a squad. He had no enemies; everyone was his 'new best friend'. We felt quite protective towards our 'Poor old Guy'.

At the armoury there was a small museum, if you could call it that. In a room that led off from the main hall where we were taught, there was a collection of artefacts from the war. All around the wall were posters and grainy black and white photographs of atrocities committed by the terrs. Mostly the victims were black. All of them were unarmed civilians - peasants, caught between the security forces and the 'liberators'. We had little historical background knowledge of the nationalist struggle. It hadn't exactly been on the curriculum at school. As I said, what little we knew was what we had read in the local papers. To us they were just gooks, trained by Russia or China to steal our country. *It was as simple as that!*

Weapons training was an excellent education but sadly there would be no examination to test our new knowledge. Our rifles would stay housed at the armoury until we left Morris Depot. They came out every day for an hour or two for drill, as it was now incorporated into our marches. They wouldn't actually be fired until we all went for COIN (Counter Insurgency) training. There we would be taught how to use these weapons to kill gooks, and dogs and snakes that try to savage your leggings.

Memoir mutterings

Mike Harvey (he pops up in the story a bit later), while editing this part, was rather excited about this chapter and wrote -

'You are portraying an interesting time when schoolboys are evolving into hairy men, being disciplined and shaped with harsh depot training, with individual recruits having mixed ideas of what it is going to be all about and how different every one is!'

The expression 'bugger off' was well used in my time in Rhodesia. I was really shocked when I eventually looked the word up at the age of 33!

I never did understand the film Brokeback Mountain. Why are they called 'cowboys' when all they did was herd stupid sheep rather stupidly!

Glossary

AMA. African Male Adult.
Bluestone. A military urban legend. A chemical additive, usually copper sulphate or bromide, was allegedly applied into drink or food to stunt sexual desires. Many recruits complained but it was actually the rigours of training that left the manly part too exhausted to play with.
CID. Criminal Investigation Department.
Contact. Firefight between opposing armed groups.
Dagga. Cannabis.

Lemon. Waste of time/anti-climax.
Mazams. Female breasts.
Sadza. Cooked mealie meal.
Spaz. Spastic
Spew. Throw up. Vomit.
Support Unit. A Para-Military combat unit, known as *Blackboots*.

CHAPTER 4:

Dressed as a tree; I come to hunt thee

When I joined the BSAP the idea that I would actually get involved fighting in the terrorist war hadn't really entered my head. Salisbury was peaceful enough. The war seemed to be in far flung places. Sure, the news on the radio and what was written in the press told of atrocities and death of friends and foes alike, but it never really occurred to me that as a policeman I would be taking any part. Besides, we were all led to believe that we were easily winning the war or at least containing it. BUT, just in case, we would be sent off to Domboshawa, to learn to become soldiers.

Less than an hours drive east of Salisbury, this was a place of unspoilt beauty of Msasa trees and bush savannah, set in the Chinamora TTL (Tribal Trust Land) of rolling hills with huge gomos of domed granite. It was also famous for beautiful examples of Bushman paintings. The Domboshawa cave had been used for centuries for rain making ceremonies and many of the paintings had been ruined by the soot of countless fires. However, there were still some fabulous relics of hunting frescoes of great interest.

It would be in this idyllic setting that for the next 18 days we would live like happy campers in primitive conditions and at the end of it return as lean, mean killing machines. Well that was the idea. In fact – forget it. If it took the army four months to train the average troopie, there was no way in hell that we would learn the fine art of counter insurgency in the short time allocated. Our job was to stop enough bullets till the pros arrived - assuming that we have a radio and the time to send our dying coordinates in Shackle to anyone bothered tuning in. 'Cannon fodder' springs to mind.

The other major problem was the instructors - a pair of complete and utter wankers. A wanker, according to the *Urban Dictionary* (online), is - *Someone that thinks they're 'cool' but in reality is a total knob jockey.* These two were wankers of the highest order. The one in charge was a middle-aged bespectacled inspector with a beer gut and a face that looked like it had received a blast of birdshot from short range – or rather, elephantshot. The scarring could easily be put down to a severe case of teenage acne which, more than likely, had led him to have an upbringing of constant bullying - so that now, as far as the human race was concerned for him – it was payback time. I will call him Insp. Pockface here.

His side kick was in his middle 20s and had the rank of Lance Section Officer (LSO). This imbecile had a pathetic excuse for a blondish moustache attached to a fat, swollen, sweaty red face. Both he and Pockface had a lot in common – primitiveness, uncouth, sadistic, thick as shit, and having a great taste in the fine art of consuming Castle beer. Crate loads of it! SO Beergut (as I will call him), surpassed even his master when it came to how much hairy stomach flesh protruded between the strained buttons of their sweat stained, grey uniform shirts.

Squads 7 and 8 would be taught together. We were dressed in our crispy fresh, embarrassingly brand new camouflage and had stuffed our combat kits into our sausage bags. So, along with unloaded rifles, we were all loaded onto a couple of open-backed Bedford trucks for the trip to our new homes. There were mountains of strange-looking objects piled into the back and we tried making ourselves comfortable and dry. Not from any rain, but from lads who suddenly needed to urinate off the back only to have the stuff whipped back as fine spray. One of the smokers in the rear of my truck had found an oddly shaped wooden box with a hole at the top and along with some others, used this enthusiastically as an ashtray.

When we arrived at our destination and started unloading everything, Pockface went mental at the sight of the improvised ashtray because it was an active gook landmine. What the hell we were doing with one of those is beyond me, but I did feel a little queasy with the idea that second hand smoking could have really killed me! The 'campsite' had a round tin hut where all the supplies of food and ammunition would be stored. This was called the magazine. Inspector Pockface had us all lined up and divided the 40 of us into five units of six men and two of five men, each unit henceforth known as a stick. Each stick had a leader, randomly selected by being older and perhaps wiser than the majority of us. My stick had Jan as the leader. This was good because if any gooks did pop up, I could rely on him to sort it out while I ran away. Among my compatriots were Addie and a stocky-built kid from Bulawayo, who had become a great friend, Jeff Swindells. Unfortunately, we also had 'Poor old Guy'!

Our leaders were then told to find a spot among the boulders and bush scrub for his stick to make a camp, leave all kit still packed, and report back with rifles in 20 minutes. When we returned, Beergut had mysteriously disappeared and Pockface had arranged for us a little moving-in party. Pointing to a gomo, about 1½ clicks away, he announced,

"Each stick is to take two cartons of ratpacks from the magazine and carry them up to the top of the gomo and back. The last stick to return will be rewarded by having to do it again."

Grinning with that sneer I would grow to loathe in a very short time, he went on, "In case any of you idle fuckers think you can pull a fast one, SO Beergut is already at the top to keep an eye on you. Now – GO!"

Bloody hell, he's kidding or what? A carton of ratpacks is huge. They came in a cardboard box. They were about the size and weight of the kind of builders' bricks popular with rioters in the name of democracy and calling for freedom. I reckoned there must have been 96 of them in the cubed carton held together with two nylon straps. What you were looking at was a standard sized washing machine with the weight of a full load of wet clothes. This is heavy and sadly - I had no brother to carry this load up a hill and back. As well as transporting this cumbersome weight through the bush for the only reason of going there and back, just to see how far it was, we had to carry our empty rifles as well! Empty. How stupid was this? We could be robbed by looters on the way and had no ammunition to shoot them and we would then starve to death!

It quickly became apparent that two men would be needed either side of a box, each holding one bottom edge in cupped hands and then forced to run with their bodies twisted at an angle. The three 'free' men would carry all the rifles. We would change places every few minutes, but with 'Poor old Guy', barely able to carry his own weight, he was left to stumble behind holding rifles. Jan, being unquestionably the strongest of us all, stayed longer on the box than the others. It was absolute agony and often the box would slip from palms soaking wet with sweat and plunge to the ground. The pace was gruelling and the bush was filled with the roars of the stick leaders egging their men on.

By the time we staggered back into camp, my head felt it would explode from the pounding blood. The rainy season hadn't started yet but there had been a couple of piddling gooey streams we had splashed through in the ravines between the huge outcrops of boulders, filling our boots and chaffing our feet raw. My forearms were in burning agony and my hands could barely uncurl. Out of the seven sticks we had managed a respectable 3rd place. It was getting late by that time and the sun was setting rapidly. As I drank greedily from my plastic water bottle, filled with piss-warm water, now tasting like the nectar of the Gods, I watched the sticks battle it out. I then observed one of the most incredible feats of strength and determination, ever.

Squad 7 of 76 had only 17 men. As they had been at Morris Depot a full month ahead of us, the powers that be had decided that this lot would play with the 'gee -gees' (Equitation Instruction). My squad had promptly all piled into the recruits' bar to drown themselves silly with happiness on hearing the good news. The most feared things in Morris Depot were in the stables. They were full of the most cantankerous, evil minded poison on four legs. Every three to four months these horses received new victims and gave them a really hard time. Many a morning roll call of that first month would expose the depleted ranks of 7/76, lined up a few paces away from us. Some of them tried to stand with glazed eyes of pain in the sick-call ranks. The semi-dead, still dressed in full PT gear, their exposed flesh swathed with bandages from vicious bites from sadistic nags, hung pathetically against each other. Another member of their motley crew had actually been hospitalised with concussion; after having a perfectly shaped horse shoe imprinted into his forehead whilst attempting to inspect a rear hoof for trapped stones.

One of the recruits in 7/76, Dave Meaden-Kendrick, was nicknamed after the initials in his surname, 'M-K'. He was a year older than me and almost as huge as Lambourne. M-K's size just oozed power and when his four legged piece of Devil's offspring had nipped him on his tender flesh under the left tricep in the first week, it would be its last nasty stunt. M-K's revenge was pure poetic justice. M- K smashed his huge, bunched right paw, straight into the side of the nag's head, stunning it instantly, so that it fell to the floor in a pile of spasmodically kicking legs. As he told us all later,

"When the fucker woke up, it decided to be a very good dog."

Brave man. I would have shot the thing and then beat it with my riding whip. Nothing more satisfying than flogging a dead horse.

Now I and the others watched with absolute astonishment as M-K walked into the camp, alone, carrying one of the cartons! He had put those huge hands inside the nylon bindings and held them like you would rucksack shoulder straps, balancing the carton, a third more than my own body weight, on his broad shoulders and back. The veins in his neck bulged from the effort, and his well tanned face streamed sweat as he dropped the box down with a mighty thump and… wordlessly trotted back into the bush…to fetch the other one!

Other exhausted sticks staggered in, their members collapsing on the ground, some vomiting from the fatigue. And then, silhouetted against the dying sun, bathed in a red hue, the great hulk of M-K appeared again, his body bent over almost double, holding the incredible weight on his back, as even his herculean strength started to fail him. Blood dripped from where the thin nylon straps had cut into the flesh of his palms. Those of us, still twitching on the ground with oxygen starvation, thought this was the retro-reincarnation of the crucifixion of the messiah; using a packed washing machine instead of a heavy wooden cross, as whispers of …

"God… you see that?" and,

"Holy, Jesus Christ all mighty!"

Some lifted their eyes to heaven in adoration whilst others, hallucinating badly now, thought they could see Pockface and Beergut, dressed as Rhodesian centurions, whipping him, while slugging greedily from bottles of chilled Castle beer.

And my response to this amazing apparition - it's a shame I couldn't swap him for 'Poor old Guy'. Behind M-K followed the remnants of his stick, their faces displaying the embarrassment and anguish of their humiliation, but thanks to the super-human effort of their leader, they would not be last.

Pockface and Beergut (who had wandered in behind the last stick), appeared well pleased with their introductory course in sadism.

"All of you take a ratpack each and make your graze. Except you lot," Pockface said, now pointing at the poor bastards who had come in last, "who will now take the cartons and do it again. SO Beergut will not be coming with you, but I will be watching with binoculars, so make sure you all do some vigorous waving from the top of the gomo, otherwise I will send you back again."

I was just glad it wasn't our stick doing it again. I grabbed a box of ratpacks along with a rather buggered miniature Camping Gaz cooker and after the rest of the cartons had been manhandled into the magazine, we went off to make dinner.

With light fading fast, it was time to look what was on the menu...

Now ratpacks or ratz for short, are not like the fab meals we had been served on the airplanes of those days long gone by; for nothing is so far away as yesterday... Breakfast consisted of cute little cocktail sausages and delightfully crispy bacon slices, nestled gently against a steaming, mushroom omelette. A fresh bread roll with curls of cold butter - bobbing delightfully among ice cubes - served alongside the glass of divine orange juice. I don't remember what was for lunch, but dinner...ah, orgasmitron! Fillet steak (done just right) in pepper sauce, with freshly steamed bright green beans and itzy-bitzy shiny, juicy carrots, and half a dozen croquettes with the soft potato mash encased in bright golden yellow breadcrumbs and eaten with perfectly polished stainless steel cutlery, and you could swill this down with as much fine wine or beer as you wanted and then dab your delicate lips with a fresh white linen napkin, before lighting up a smoke from the light offered by the stunning stewardess, who smiled so seductively as she cleared your tray, then made sure your pillow was puffed up right and helped you open the plastic bag with your own souvenir blanket...and that was in the peasant class!

No, sadly, ratzs are nothing like this. No Harry Potter in this story.

I had seen these boxes before. When I was 15 and had been visiting best-friend Stephanie Brooks, her brother Mike (who was doing his call-up with the army), would bring a couple of half empty ratpacks home with him during his R and R. We had experimented with them in the kitchen and usually fed the dog with the results.

I just love children sized shoe boxes with little neatly packed mysteries in them. Sure enough there were lots of surprises. A quick look at the rest of my sticks ratzs revealed that we had three different types of 'One Box, One Man, One Day'. Stamped on the side of each light brown cardboard box was a letter. C, G or H. The idea of this was to give everyone a change of diet everyday. Digging through the contents, it soon became clear that the initials actually stood for: Crap, Gore and Hideous. As the packs were designed to be used by survivors of a nuclear holocaust, the things were almost indestructible and, in theory, would stay fresh till the end of the world. Plus, they were certified as edible, whether you liked it or not.

Basically, all *ratpack* types would have the same stuff in them. The different types were due to the contents of the supplied tinned food and the kind of starch. A quick visual examination could be described so:

Common to all ratpacks –

1. A (my) palm sized, very sticky transparent plastic bag, filled with orange or green sugar. This was supposed to be 'cool drink'. For some strange reason this bag always seemed to have burst and made the rest of the contents adhere to each other like super-glue. Once you had the stuff in a cup and applied water, you were treated with a vile taste resembling nothing like oranges or lime, and a mass of wet, semi-dissolved sugar swirling around at the bottom.

2. Another transparent bag, about half the size of the sticky one, which looked alarmingly like it contained four teaspoons of dried semen. In fact, it was supposed to be milk powder that you combined with the next two bags.

3. A small bag of cigarette tar, the same size as the semen bag, which appeared as having been scraped out of the lungs of a chain smoker. This was the coffee! When boiling water is added you spent some time twirling a defoliated twig in it (no teaspoons), and then you shook in some sugar and milk powder. The milk powder flatly refused to dissolve, and immediately gathered in small lumps on the surface and no amount of twirling could get them to do their proper job of integrating with its dark brother. (See! – black and whites don't mix well!) When it came to drinking the stuff, the lumps would stick to your teeth and when you bit into them, you were rewarded with the sensation of chewing on a sweaty sock.

4. A bag of off-white sugar the same size as the 'cool drink'.

5. A packet of four bullet-proof, light brown oblongs that fitted

neatly into your top breast pocket around the heart area. These were biscuits or hardtack as they are correctly known, and are made from wheat flour, salt and water and then baked extremely hard. The things could last for years and were almost indestructible. It was claimed they could stop a bullet, so that's why we kept them in our shirt pocket. They were close to inedible and attempting to eat them without being softened in the 'coffee', you had a good chance of breaking all your teeth.

6. A bag, same size as the sticky stuff, resembling salted small white pebbles. Well, they were as hard as pebbles, but not quite as hard as the biscuits. These were peanuts. Not the nice Willards roasted type that you bought in the supermarket, these were the rejects. These were the nuts that fell on the floor whilst they were being pulled out of their shells. They were left to lie there for weeks till they became rock hard. Now they were so devoid of moisture, that whilst attempting to chew them, they set like concrete as soon as it had collected every drop of saliva in your mouth. You then used the twiddle stick from the coffee to pry the soapy tasting muck from the roof of your mouth where it had decided to take up permanent residence.

7. An aluminium, unmarked toothpaste tube, but filled with some stinking green/yellow pus. Inside was an incredibly greasy load of semi-rancid margarine. This tube obeyed Murphy's Law every time it was squeezed. Instead of coming out the narrow hole exposed after removing the screw top, it instantly unravelled its rear end and fired its rotten guts all over your combat trousers. Since you couldn't eat the biscuits, you now used them to scrape the greasy gunk from your crotch, leaving a lovely large stain. Since the stuff ponged so bad, you wouldn't dream of cooking with it, so it got promptly chucked. Even the ants gave the stinking glob a wide berth.

8. Some huge yellow salty pills. These were to be taken every day to combat salt loss due to excessive sweating. They tasted vile.

9. A box of *Lion* matches. Besides for making *foja* (fire) they could be used as tooth picks and ear cleaners. My mate Addie used them as weapons. He had this very annoying habit that after he lit up a fag, he would place the used stick in the crook of his folded first finger and then use his thumb to flick it into your face.

Starch Options

1. A bagged handful of off-white, rock hard, wedding confetti. This was rice. Not the kind Uncle Ben would eat. The stuff took ages to cook, drank water like a fish and because there was no sieve available - it tended to turn into mush. If you added the sugar and the milk-powder it became the world's worst rice pudding.

or

2. A bagged handful of yellowish hard tubes resembling a gutted cheap ballpoint pen, now chopped into finger tip sized bits. Officially it was called *macaroni*, but any resemblance to its Italian origins was lost in translation. When mixed with milk-powder and sugar, it just beat the rice pudding in the competition of the worst things you can put into your mouth without gagging.

The Tin Options

Each tin was approximately 200grams (7 ounces) and had no paper labels. Upon opening them, the strange contents could be one of the following –

1. A blue boiled egg, some badly cloned Heinz type beans, and a dwarf's circumcised penis, otherwise known as a cocktail sausage. This was the ultimate in bad eggs, so to speak, because the egg, which took up 80% of the tin, stank like a stink bomb and looked the same colour of a freshly hung corpse's bloated face. It sat ponging away in some orangey coloured sauce that had a few brave beans wallowing in it whilst the baby sized dick hid under it.

We were actually warned about these tins. We were not to open them if the tin ends looked suspiciously like they were being pushed out from the inside. This unique feature in tinned food was due to the fact that the egg had finally come of age, and the frenzied bacteria that were happily eating it had farted so much, that the bulging ends would erupt imminently. There were rumours that the Selous Scouts, a unique fighting unit, would use them as grenades against the gooks.

or

2. Frankenfarters. These deathly pale objects were called this because they resembled Frankenstein's fingers - after the nails had been neatly guillotined off and the bones pulled out. They smelt like they had been breeding in a swamp and once ingested they tended to produce abdominal gas that a gook could smell from a click away.

or

3. More tiny penises, drowning in a thick orange swamp full of dodgy beans. This was really the same as the tin with the egg, but without it. This moved the food from inedible to barely edible.

4. An occasional and rare imported tin of pilchards in tomato sauce and on the most wanted list. They tasted so lekker they would be traded for promised blind-dates with fellow recruits' virgin sisters. Judging by some of the ugly buggers we had with us, you would have to be blind to date any of their sisters... or mothers for that matter.

Now certain members of our trainee buddies in arms were wise to the fact that ratpacks are used only in desperation. Jan, our leader was way ahead on that scale. His sausage bag really was full of swag. Out came real tins of just about any produce available in the shops and he soon had himself a regular feast prepared. Why hadn't I thought of going shopping before we went on COIN? That was because I flatly refused to use my pay to feed my-self. I would rather starve... and so I did.

Another clever device Jan had brought with him was called a *tin opener*. An amazing device that could open tins! I hadn't thought of bringing one of these either. His was a SAP issue, a tiny folding hook type metal thingy, that hung around his neck on a shoestring. A little larger than a thumb, it was a flat piece of hardened steel with a folding flat blade. With leverage, the punctured tins contents would slowly be exposed. We now had to queue to open our food. Meanwhile, 'Poor old Guy', in frenzied desperation, had thrown his tin numerous times at one of the huge granite rocks that dotted around our 'camp site' until it burst its guts all over the show and then scraped the stuff into his aluminium 'cooking' pot…

So, after an excellent evening meal under the magnificence of the southern hemispheres' stars, we all gathered around a lovely roaring fire, popped open Castle beers and locally made firewater, and sang comradely songs such as *Rhodesian never die* and *This land is your land, this land is whiteman's…',* and regaled each other with stirring tales of the time the Rhodesian rugby team beat the All Blacks 10-8 in 1949. And then, full of fighting spirits we would retire to our bivouacs and fart-sacks. (So-called because of the gas produced in the sleeping bag from one's intestines struggling to digest the ratz)… Sadly, only the sentence in brackets is true.

The bivouac was supposed to protect you from the elements. This piece of high tech protection was also called a poncho because in the middle of the green parachute silk type rag, there was a huge hole in it through which you stuck your head and this thing was to stop the rain pouring over the rest of you whilst on bush patrol. When it came to sleeping time, you tied the hole up and with lots of string, the corners of your batman cape was then stretched and attached to four trees that had miraculously grown in exactly the required configuration for your new sleeping quarters. Of course we had no string, but Jan had.

So that meant the rest of us just sort of used it as a groundsheet-cum beggar's blanket and hoped to hell it wouldn't rain. You then spent the night tossing and turning, moaning in agony as every tiny rock and tree root pushed up through the thin nylon of the sleeping bag, into the soft and bony parts of your body.

We had to sleep fully clothed, minus our boots. This was a good idea as the nights at this altitude tended to be rather chilly. There was a secondary purpose to this also – instant action stations in the event of a surprise attack. Someone would scream out 'Red Alert' and we would clamber out of our fart-sacks, slip into combat boots and be firing at the enemy in seconds.

Actually, what really happened was the first thing I would be fighting was my sleeping bag and poncho that had somehow had me trussed up like a spider's victim. After somehow unravelling myself, I fell over as my unbuttoned trousers were gathered about my knees, all the time trying to disentangle my shirt from the poncho that was reluctantly refusing to let go. Meanwhile, in complete darkness of course, it is presumed the enemy are almost on top of you. Don't panic! Now having managed to disengage with the poncho/bivouac/spider's web, I do up my trousers, find the boots and turning them upside down, noiselessly beat the shit out of them on the ground before placing them on my feet. This was to set free any scorpions, baboon spiders or snakes that might have taken to your putrid, sweaty damp footwear as the perfect home to move into. Next thing I notice is that I can't find my rifle and my socks must have come off in the fart-sack. Otherwise I was ready!

Next day, as we lined up staggering from lack of sleep and feeling rather scruffy, we were promptly cheered up when recruit Scummy from 7/78, the ultimate piece of dog-shit, tried to resign. Now, Scummy is of course not his real name. I know his real name, but as I don't have anything nice to say about this 'person', I will for legal reasons refer to him as Scummy.

Scummy was an enigma and a dodgy one at that. He was the perfect non-Rhodie. He had quite a reputation that was as ugly as his face. Scummy was a lot older and pushing 30, and while claiming to be a hot shot civil engineer from the UK, he hadn't comprehended the mechanical functions of a toothbrush as he had a thick line of scum covering his protruding front teeth. He liked to show-off, to anyone who was vaguely interested, some of his photos portraying himself in the UK. There was one of Scummy next to his expensive sports car, Scummy standing in front of his propeller driven private plane, Scummy at some hot-shot nightclub supping champagne with babes, etc. When asked why he had quit what appeared to be a successful career with all the trappings of the jet set, he had replied that life had become boring and thus, on a whim, had joined the BSAP. Very strange indeed! And... the bull-shit about babes was also very suspect because we all thought he was a morph. Morphs were about as popular in Rhodesia as the Jehovah Witnesses and Collins Encyclopaedia salesmen. As for morphs, they had to be discreet otherwise they got a bashing while the latter peddled their books for free, which were promptly binned, and the other unread lot filled every white middle-class bookcases which had the salesman laughing all the way to the bank.

Scummy had already spent some time in 'the box' for disobeying a direct order. He had flatly refused to get on his horse. He never gave a reason but it boiled down to pure cowardice - he was frightened of the thing. I could understand that, I didn't like the biting, kicking things either, but I would still have gotten on the bloody minded animal. Now, the box really wasn't that bad. It formed part of the guard house, situated at the main entrance to Morris Depot and comprised two lock-up cells complete with high grilled-windows. Whenever a white police officer was punished for some misdemeanour within the police force's own code of conduct, he could be locked up for a period of up to two weeks. The condemned would be let out during the day and would be watched over by a depot recruit. I did this very boring task once – guarding – not as a naughty boy. The 'prisoner' sat on the grass verges that were all around the place and pulled weeds out. This was very mundane, so most of the time was spent chatting with the equally bored prisoner. At five o'clock the convict would be returned to his cell and be given food from the canteen. About the only bad thing about the box was the fact you would be given a short recruit-style haircut, but in theory the convictions, depending on how serious they were, could affect your promotion chances.

Now, the BSAP couldn't actually incarcerate the tosser *ad-infinitum* for refusing to ride a horse, so a sort of deal was made. He would get up with the others, get dressed as if to go riding and then spend 90 minutes standing alone on the parade ground till the lesson was finished...

So now, back in the bush and us lot still feeling a little blurry in the head from a miserable nights sleep, we were all standing in our sticks in front of Pockface, whose face, now a bright scarlet laced with white acne scars, was about to explode. Scummy, with all his kit packed in his blue sausage bag, was moaning away about how poorly he had slept, and how he had now definitely decided that a career in the BSAP wasn't quite up his street or backdoor. And dictated to Pockface his request – "So, if you don't mind, I would like a lift back into town, or failing that - call me a taxi."

None of us laughed. After all, we were all fine Rhodie gentlemen, being brought up to respect a condemned man's final request before being hung or shot, regardless how ludicrous the wish was - which in Scummy's case had pushed the boundaries of incredulity.

Inspector Pockface was a right snarky bastard, but even he excelled in wit now.

"Certainly. Sadly we need the vehicles today, but let's see what I can do." Pretending to hold a radio microphone, he went on, "Hello, is that Rixi Taxis 60 666? Good. Please could you send a cab to the secret BSAP counter insurgency camp just on the left of the big cave in Domboshawa. (Short pause) I see, you are not insured against landmines. Thanks anyway."

Unfortunately for Scummy he hadn't found out that at this point - trying to leave the BSAP after you have signed up, was nigh on impossible. Unless you died of course – very quickly – if caught morphing.

Inspector Pockface had no qualms pointing this out to Scummy in front of us as we listened with bated breath.

"For your information, and every other recruit, there is a three month notice to be worked, if the resignation is accepted, which in this case was highly unlikely as – 'I don't like playing soldier and the cuisine and bedding isn't quite up to the normal standards of the Meikles Hotel to which I am accustomed,' - is not on the list of accepted reasons to terminate your contract. Now, you have one choice - shut the fuck-up and do what you're told. If you walk out this camp, I will have you arrested immediately for being AWOL (absent without leave), and personally make sure you fulfil your three year contract cleaning out the shithouses in Chikurubi prison."

Fair enough, I thought, but I was a little bothered with this strange talk of conditions of service. What happened if I simply couldn't be arsed anymore at being a policeman? People did tire of their chosen careers you know. Would I go to jail for that? I definitely hadn't read the small print of my contract. In fact, I think the only part I had read and noted was how much I was going to be paid. The rest hadn't interested me much – till now. Still, I would worry about that at a later date. An incarnadined Scummy now had to use that fine engineering mind of his to reach a very quick solution and so, surrounded by us lot revelling in some fine *shadenfreude*, completely humiliated, he picked up his bag and shuffled back awkwardly to his stick.

So with that morning's pick-me-up, we were told we would now learn how to shoot our gats and how to terminate terrs.

Glossary

Gomo. A treeless kopje.
Graze. Meal.
Lekker. Very nice.

CHAPTER 5:

Bad Blood

I would end this particular day at the rifle range in a filthy mood and with blisters on my right palm (unacceptable resignation grounds) – all thanks to Pockface.

But before I delve into that, I will explain about the 'dog tag' and how it is supposed to save your life. Made of rot-proof, compressed greenish fibre, they were the size of a General Service Medal. The dog tag would be impressed by hand using a metal punch and hammer. On one side it would have BSAP, your force number, and surname. On the reverse it said BL GR (blood group) and underneath was the magic letters needed to fill you up after catching a bad leak - such as being shot or driving drunk into a tree.

We would receive these just prior to going on COIN and to get them we needed to be drained of a milk bottle sized of the sticky red stuff. I wasn't much taken on this idea. As far as I understood, this blood group malarkey could be done with a pinprick to the thumb and therefore no need to have my vital juices sucked out into plastic bags and then given away for free to some riff-raff that had drunkenly cut his throat whilst shaving. Oddly, when the entire squad were delivered to the local hospital, Lambourne announced that this was entirely voluntary but suggested that refusal could lead to dire side effects. He didn't mention what the dire side effects would be after the 'donation'- such as fainting away in a swoon every time we tried to masturbate for the next few nights. Still, in exchange we would get a free cup of Tanganda tea and a Lobels digestive biscuit. Some of the squad had given blood before and that entitled them to a Castle beer! I still hadn't much taste for beer yet - still being a bit of a vodka, lime and lemonade and a Crunchy bar boy - but I tried to con the nurses that I could handle missing a bucket full, purely with the idea of selling my Castle for 25c.

When we finally collected our tags, I was very impressed with my results. I was unique! My blood was so rare - I had visions of making millions with the stuff. I could retire on a pint a month. My euphoria was shattered shortly afterwards when, whilst boastfully gabbling to anyone who would listen, a 'qualified' source informed me that whilst having a 'one-in-ten-thousand' blood group was pretty cool, it would likely kill me. Huh! Now I might have misheard this because it appeared that since infancy my hearing was seriously impeded by the sound of my own voice in constant overdrive, but I gathered that I could only be pumped back to life with replacement of the exact haemoglobin of the same group. Bloody hell - mathematically thinking, I might land up getting some black blood and turn into a goffel. Even worse, it might come from a homo-goblin like Scummy and I'd become a morph!

Jeff was so pleased with his results he tattooed himself, using Rhodesian made Indian ink, B+ on the inside of his left ankle. I thought that was a very clever idea. I am sure most medics automatically knew that having failed to find the neck worn dog tag on a headless body, would find the information they need after a thorough strip search. I was still having anxiety attacks about my ipseity and thought of having my life saving request for my rare blood tattooed in large letters on my forehead. I practiced a sketch with a Neo-magic felt-tip pen, while looking in the mirror, but decided it looked silly when it came out in reverse.

Back on the rifle range, and with this terrible fear of being punctured and left to die because the blood bank's exclusive luxury department cupboards were bare, (sanctions?), I lay down in a row with my stick, received a handful of cartridges and was told by Pockface that we would shoot in sessions of rounds of 6 - 8 – 5 – 4 or was it 8 -10 – 3 – 6 or: I didn't have a clue because my hearing was again impaired. Rather than receive the wrath of Pockface by politely requesting he talk coherently and perhaps a little nearer so I could comprehend what the hell the moron was going on about, I just kept on firing till everyone stopped – this would lead to grave consequences.

Holding and firing an FN is poetry in deadly action. I loved it as it was the swankiest piece of kit that belonged to me and hadn't cost a cent. We're talking about big money here - plenty of it. Faraday and Sons, the retailers of angling equipment and tackle for hunting gooks on Manica Road in Salisbury, sold them to the public for more than $1000. Work it out - I had no expensive wife/girlfriend, car or home, just a posh Hi-Fi, and now, now assigned under my name - was a beautiful piece of machinery. It would be years later when I owned a second hand Rolex that I could get my rocks off again on man's mechanical creative ingenuity. Forget that the FN is designed to kill - a Rolex is designed to get the owner mugged. What's the difference? Someone always dies.

The first and second session involved us shooting at a Figure 11 target featuring a screaming, bayonet-wielding German soldier (very odd, why not screaming gooks?). Then flags were waved, there was a lot of shouting, we wandered down the 50 metre-long range to see our results, and then Pockface (using a metal twiddle stick), adjusted each rifle site according to the 'grouping' of the bullet holes that had penetrated the target. All very well and good - until it came to shooting for points and the chance of getting the coveted marksman's badge. Surprisingly, Pockface had done an excellent job on my sights and I was shooting bang-on – until I ran out of ammunition. That meant it was impossible to get a high enough score. I had used up too many rounds in the first two sessions. Jeff got his badge…the lucky bastard.

    Our stick would do its turn of patching up the targets for the next group of recruits. This meant cowering in a trench as shots were fired over us. Okay, this sounds stupid, but I did put my head up a bit above the parapet to take a peek at what it looked like being in the firing line. It is very scary shit man! It works like this: Assuming that neither Scummy nor 'Poor old Guy', were next in line to shoot, the odds of collecting one in the head were narrow. This conclusion, in my dumb mind, was because the targets were mounted on wooden poles and you would have to be shooting seriously low to slot me - unless it was deliberate. But, thank God, murder was still illegal in Rhodesia, even if it was a lucky shot (or as some used to say - 'It isn't the bullet with your name on it you need worry about, but the one addressed 'To whom it may concern'). What I experienced was rather disturbing. You look down the barrel of a gun, albeit quite far away, and then you see a puff of smoke. This means, in theory - that was basically the last thing you saw or experienced before your brains were scattered as fertiliser on the earthen man-made ridge behind you. If the bullet missed, then other senses kicked in - such as sound and smell. There would be a sharp snap, like a whip cracking, and then a 'whoomp' as a piece of pointed, brass coated lead ploughed into the piled soil behind you.

At this point in time the actual 'pop' of the fired rifle could be heard, and depending on the wind direction, there was that smell of burnt cordite and me defecating into my incompetent combat trousers with fear of being a terminated AB Rhesus Negative. Many scientists thought that the aroma of burnt cordite was an aphrodisiac, as scores of ex-combatants, being paid five bucks a lie, claimed they would get a root at the whiff of it. Actually, they are wrong. In my honest personal opinion, the smell made my brown ring twitch almost uncontrollably, allowing a small and nasty smelling odour of canned blue egg to sneak out. My little stiffie that was, according to Darwinian principle of instinctively mortal preservation, could be only used in procreation, was now apparently responding with the inane desire to have a small white flag of surrender attached to it – presumably by using some left over sheet of bog roll.

SO Beergut had spotted my antics and, using a bit of mnemonics, such as screaming his tar-filled lungs out with swear words, persuaded me to keep my head low. Actually, he and Pockface would do a lot of this kind of shouting as panic-struck recruits waved armed rifles around in confusion of arming and loading a machine far above the intellectual capacity that their heads contained. Still, no one had been hurt yet. Just as the whole shebang was being wrapped up; we had a visitor. Another inspector turned up for a little rifle practise and a posing Pockface demonstrated his immense knowledge of weaponry by shooting off several magazines on fully automatic. This is rather a pointless exercise unless you have a habit of trying to shoot a flock of wild geese as they take flight. The FN can be set to automatic, but it requires shifting the safety catch 270 degrees (the safety on the AK 47 was a touch of genius. Automatic mode was set between 'off' and single shot. The idea being that the average peasant using the weapon would in panic ram the catch all the way down, thus preventing the user wasting loads of ammo.) There is a reason for this as Pockface demonstrated. As the rounds chased each other down the barrel at the rate of three at a time, the barrel would, from the force, ride up and to the right. This is extremely difficult to control.

As we all waited in the trucks to take us back to camp, Pockface finally finished playing Audie Murphy, and came over.

"You", he said, pointing to me, "take my rifle," and handed it up high enough for me to grab the protective stock. As my clutching hand went out, with a malicious grin he dropped it lower, and I instead grasped the almost glowing, white hot barrel, dropping the weapon immediately.

"You insane mother fucker," I screamed. My doe-like hazel-brown eyes glittered murderous steel, and leaping from the truck, roaring like a deranged elephant in musk, I bellowed

"I will cut out your beer sodden liver with a rusty bayonet, you utter twat, and force feed it to you," as my fellow recruits roared their support.

A nice thought, but actually all the recruits were laughing their stupid heads off and Pockface said

"Dropping a rifle, and an officer's at that, is a punishable offence. Get down, pick it up and give me 40 push-ups."

The only push-up I could think of was sticking said bayonet 40 times up his brown eye, but sadly I had no bayonet and so with blistered hand, I meekly complied. My revenge will come later, when this book is published. Knowing my luck he has already passed on to the great brewery in the sky.

The next couple of weeks became a haze of running around, shooting loads of blanks at each other in a vain attempt to grasp the rudiments of patrolling in the bush, and being able to cope with three basic scenarios

The first was where we were having a nice little walkabout and our 'Point' spotted a bunch of gooks. These walks never took place in single file, which was rather a pain as the bush isn't like a rugby field, more likes rocks and plants and trees that get in the way. So instead we had different formations similar to a five-a-side football team. One formation was supposed to be shaped like an inverted 'V', (called an 'arrow'), and another was sort of like the markings of a dice depending how many were in a stick. Point simply meant the poor bastard at the front. Point would then point out the close proximity of gooks by hollering out

"Gooks! Run for your lives," whilst legging it asap past the bloke called 'up the rear'. 'Up the rear' meant 'You bring up the rear position.' It is the opposite of point and tended to be my favourite spot due to my bad blood. (And Scummy's - for literal reasons.)

COIN - me and Addie
Pic - Gokwe Kid

Presuming that Point wasn't me, he would then send silent signals with his hands, much like sign language used by the deaf. Ours seemed more like used by the dumb as most of them were incomprehensible. Generally, we were then were to make a plan of taking cover and sting 'em when they came within hearing shot, but I never could figure that out because once you're shot in the head, you tended to hear nothing.

The second scenario was when we were having a nice walkabout. All of a sudden you hear the sounds of very angry hornets buzzing around your head. This is a good sign because it means you are not dead yet. Someone would then holler out –

"Gooks! Run for your lives," whilst legging-it asap past the bloke called 'up the rear'.

Presuming that 'point' isn't me, he was now no longer required to send finger semaphore as it wasn't really relevant with all the banging of rifles being fired, the screaming as we crashed into each other and the trees that always seemed to be in the way, and all of this in a cloud of spent cordite. Now, according to our training, we would go from the defensive to the offensive using the strategy known as 'Attack is the best form of defence'. The idea behind this clever plan was that as we couldn't run away faster than fired bullets, we might as well meet them head on (great idea since we had no helmets). This would presumably spook the gooks who would then be overcome by our superior fighting skills and surrender. They would then agree to go back to being well behaved garden-boys and cooks and barmen, and forget the whole liberation nonsense of getting farms and brand new 4x4 twin cab Mitsubishis for free. Usually we just hung the cheeky bastards – legally of course. We were gentlemen, not the *KU KLUX KLAN*.

And the third and last scenario was the ambush. This is quite good fun as you spend a lot of time doing nothing. You and your stick would dig out holes for foxes (rather daft as we had none in Rhodesia), hide in them and simply wait until some gooks, taking a nice walkabout, would wander past. When they entered the so-called 'Killing Ground', someone would shout "Gooks! Run for your lives," while legging-it past the bloke called 'up the rear', who was asleep by now.

Actually, the ambush stuff was rather boring, but Addie and I had an idea to liven things up a bit. We worked out that by ramming a used blank cartridge into the flashguard at the end of the barrel of the FN, when firing a blank it propelled the spent cartridge a fair distance at some speed. Things went a bit pear-shaped when I connected with one member of a stick (playing at being gooks), on the head, making a neat cut in his forehead. Ah! Nice one! First blood! This was exciting; I was getting a taste for all this. Of course Pockface made a fuss and asked who did it - but I wasn't going to snitch. You never snitch on your best mate, even if it was me.

Our bush war fighting capabilities experience was then enhanced by being taught how to use nasty exploding metal pineapples called grenades. What cute little things they were! Remarkably, they resembled the ones used in World War II films. That was because that was exactly what they are. A Mills Mark II with a use-by-date printed on the box – 'Third World War' – which wasn't exactly very convincing and rather hard to pin down. Still, we were allowed to play with them a bit until it was time to actually use one.

A rather simple device, it had a split safety-pin that held back a handle or striker lever, that when released, set into action a chain reaction which very rarely worked. These antiques were better off being sold as souvenirs on *EBay*. You could make these very dodgy things 'safe' by unscrewing a large base plug at the bottom and removing the detonation device. This was done whilst we all practiced. Each of us in turn would squat with Pockface or Beergut in a larger foxhole designed for lions and then standing up shout the words "Pin." At this time your left hand ring finger had removed the ring holding the splint of the grenade, now curled up in your right hand, and was waved triumphantly in the air. Then you would shout "Grenade," and throw it. It's bit like shouting "Fore" in golf.

The grenade was then supposed to be propelled by brute force into the hordes of oncoming gooks, depicted by a circle of more large wood mounted posters of German soldiers. This was all very tame. Then we were allowed to play with them charged and ready to 'Rock and Roll!' Sadly, there weren't enough to hand around. Sanctions, yet again, had damaged Rhodesia's ability to acquire deathly museum pieces. I wasn't bothered not to be able to have a go as I didn't really fancy having half my body torn apart when the ancient thing went off prematurely.

We all took cover a short distance behind the bunker where the 'chosen few' would now take turns lobbing one. We would watch the antics sitting up till the scream of "Grenade!", and then had to lie down and wait for the 'kaa-thump' as it went off, followed immediately by a buzzing sound as the end-plug went zipping over our heads. Fifteen grenades would be thrown by the lucky volunteered and it was then that Beergut's true purpose in life would become apparent. While none of them exploded in anyone's hands, thus ensuring the future's first mobile phone 'hands free' operators - 50 per cent didn't explode at all!

So what do you do now? It appears you do not wander over with an old supermarket paper bag, pop it in and toss it into the rubbish tip. Nor it would appear that taking pot-shots at it was allowed, which was a shame as I would have fancied that. Nope – Beergut was sent out to make it safe after we waited five minutes. Hah-hah, what a job man! I would rather pluck stings from angry scorpions than crawl out weeping and moaning about my horrible lot, while dragging several feet of cordite-filled detonation cable.

Instead of simply training a monkey to think that there were some nuts inside and getting it to unscrew the plug and remove the dodgy detonator, the BSAP had trained a larger one to wrap cord around it, and then crawl moaning all the way back to the lion sized fox hole. This was done with no blast protection at all, not even a helmet, just a pair of sunglasses to keep out the glare. Then Pockface would assist by pushing the plunger on the hand-wound electric powered detonator, just like in the movies. Whoom! The thing would explode.

This was fine entertainment indeed, but the best bit was left till last when Richard Berton, a rather skinny bloke in our squad, took his place. Beergut was by now a gibbering gibbon gagging for beer from all the exercise he had done. So, Richard does the business, pulls the pin, screams "PIN", followed by "GRENADE", and throws with all his might.

Now, it is well known in the military forces the world over, that for reasons unknown, live grenades tend to be thrown a lot further than dummy ones, and Richard's was no exception as it went an enormous way – vertically. Straight up into the air, like a plumbline in reverse. All eyes followed it up till it reached its zenith and then, almost in slow motion, plummeted to earth to land perfectly between the pair of them. For the first time in his miserable career, Beergut must have hoped this one would be a dummy too, plus he had the advantage where he wouldn't have to crawl anywhere to terminate it. Instead, he did a brave thing, and threw his mighty belly onto the evil pineapple in a vain hope to save Richard's life.

Like hell he did! He screamed "Oh Shit!" grabbed Richard by the scruff of his neck, dived over the earthen lip to safety as the grenade went off. That was sadly the end of the day's entertainment and we went 'home' to our camps to make dinner, giggling like schoolgirls who had just seen their headmaster run over by a car. Richard of course, was in some kind of shock.

That night Beergut got his revenge…

Another inconvenience of COIN was guard duty. The magazine with all the supplies and ammunition needed to be protected from any terrs that might find it easy pickings. So we all had to take turns parking our arses near it 24/7. During the day, this was a godsend of laziness but, night was different. Each stick took guard duty rotationally. The plan was simple. One member of the stick would sit by the magazine for two hours in the dark, fearfully fondling with his genitals, as weird sounds emanated from the surrounding bush. At the end of each shift, he would wake the next contestant for a round of 'pass the timepiece' for the watch. My superlative chronograph was very practical for this job. It was the very latest in the cheapest digital watches on the UK market.

COIN - magazine guard duty - but i am smarter because i wear BATA
Pic - Gokwe Kid

While others would have to use a match to see the time pass so slowly, mine flashed it in neon red. It had the hour, minute, second and even the date. All this at the touch of a button. Amazing. There were a couple of drawbacks. It was useless in daylight. The Rhodesian sun was rather bright, which meant telling the time was rather difficult because before you could tell anyone, you first had to read it. Made of rather poorly constructed stainless steel, it had a dark red plastic square face. To actually find out what hour of the day it was, it meant pushing the button, then quickly encircle the watch with the right hand then raise both arms up to an eyeball and peer into the manmade cave you had created. This had to be done rather quickly, otherwise the 'save power' mode kicked in and left you looking at two blank faces. The first being the watch while the other was the person who asked you the time in the first place. This entire time-telling took some time and meant I had to stop whatever I was doing, and drop everything, except my rifle of course - this was clamped between my legs.

The other problem that now occurred on night watch was that the cheap shite watch ate batteries like they were made in China on purpose. That second shift of keeping one's eyes peeled for gooks finished it off, as all of us checked the LED readout every couple of minutes. I even confess that in absolute boredom I kept the button pressed in to watch the seconds count down. Anyway, late that evening, Beergut turned up, pissed out of his head. Our stick wasn't doing watch. Not that it made any difference.

Beergut and Pockface lived the life of Riley compared to us poor recruits. They had a huge tent with all the trappings, including camp beds, gas lights and a huge paraffin-powered fridge stocked with beer. I had in comparison a digital watch and a warm bottle of Coca-Cola I was hoarding for a special occasion. They ate fresh food. I ate cardboard boxes as they tasted better than the contents. Now, it was known among us, that in theory, either Beergut or Pockface would have to be in their canvas hotel every night in case all hell broke out. This could either be a riotous mutiny against our conditions or if the gooks decided we were easy meat, which we were, and one or the other of them would then control the sticky situation in either scenario by shouting loads of swearwords.

That night, Pockface needed his usual lashings of the golden nectar down at the nearest country club and, because Beergut was still traumatised from his experience of playing as a dispensable bomb disposal expert, he had been allowed a crate or two to settle his ragged nerves. When he returned alone, around about eleven, guess what he found guarding the magazine? A hungry jackal sniffing at the door. Beergut bellowed and raged until some dopey head wandered up, buttoning his fly, explaining it wasn't his fault because the bloke before him hadn't woken him up.

By now we were all awake as Beergut screamed for us to get to the magazine immediately. Dishevelled and bleary eyed we gathered in the lights of Beergut's Landrover and were told we could all take a hike. Not as in bugger off, but as in run into the bush where there was a huge puddle of red mud and wallow in it for a while like warthogs having a bath. This was deemed punishment and after half an hour of deep cleansing mud therapy, we were allowed to return to our hovels and fill our fartsacks with clods of wet clingy earth. Now that should have been that.

First thing in the morning, we sullenly lined up in front of the pair of twats. Then Pockface announced a weapon inspection. I had to admire his tactics as we couldn't be hung for the same crime twice. Well it was bloody obvious that after the little escapade the night before, it was hardly likely that we had spent half an hour stripping our weapons and cleaning them from the contents of a stinking bush mud sump. Yup, our rifles had been dragged through the filth as well. There was one big golden rule that could never be broken. Unless our FN was in the armoury, or in a locked gun cabinet, it never, ever left your side – ever! It became an appendage.

After a drama queen type inspection we were informed that a nice little 10 clicks jog was just what we needed to cheer us up and to remind us to keep our weapons nice and clean. Pockface was smart enough to allow us to hastily retrieve our water bottles so as to counter any future manslaughter charges. And so off we went, and went, and went.

This time it wasn't a bush run - it was on the road. First a dirt one, then onto the main Salisbury to Inyanga highway. All this time, while Beergut drove, Pockface stood in the back of the open Bedford truck urging us on with profanities. Stragglers were supported by stronger members, who in turn swore profanities. We no longer ran in sticks or even a neat group, but as punch-drunk marathon trainees. It didn't help that cars zoomed by, Rhodies waving enthusiastically and blowing kisses at all us 'brave young men'. With Addie carrying Jeff's and my rifle, we dragged Richard along. At least we didn't have to look after 'Poor old Guy', because he was in hospital. Lucky 'Poor old Guy'? Actually, he had nearly died.

It had happened a few days earlier when he said he couldn't get out of bed and thought he had the flu. Me, as No 1 First Aider, concluded that the symptoms of clammy skin and pale complexion, along with a headache, seemed close enough, although he wasn't coughing, sneezing or wheezing. He wasn't doing anything, just dying. Pockface had excused him but whenever we returned to camp he complained of being cold and shivered away under his bivouac even under the blazing sun, neither eating nor drinking. By the morning of the third day, with his speech now incoherent, I re-thought my diagnosis and proudly announced that 'Poor old Guy' was at death's door due to chronic dehydration. So off he went to be attached to a drip for a while. He never returned for the rest of COIN - the lucky bastard.

At some point, Pockface realised we had had enough and stopped the truck. He told us the way home by using a shortcut. Following a farmer's fence we were allowed to walk back. How kind. But the biggest surprise was when we got back to camp. There in front of the magazine were four crates of beer.

"It's my birthday, so each of you may help yourselves to a couple."

What a slimy git! He might have bought off the others, but not me. Besides, the beers were warm, and as I didn't like the stuff at that point, I thought of spiriting mine away to sell later. That idea was soon brought to naught.

"Drink on the spot and each bottle must be upturned onto your head," announced Pockface.

"Return the empties and bugger off ... that's it for today."

'Piss-ant' was what I thought of him and went back to my bivouac out my bracket from the gassy stuff, but at least it made the ratpack more palatable.

Hasta la vista, baby. I am now a trained terrorist terminator. Well, not quite. After all the shooting and shouting and running, I thought the odds of me surviving a contact with a bunch of gooks depended on how well they had been trained. I could only hope that theirs was as bad as mine. It seems that with the massive manpower shortage, we were being seriously fast-tracked. Amongst some of the strange lessons were:

1. How to jump out of a helicopter and form a protective perimeter. Then form a protective perimeter and jump into the helicopter. All this using deaf and dumb language as we couldn't hear a thing due to the mighty roar of the engines and the fierce winds caused by the rotor's downdraft. This exercise was rather exciting as we had no helicopter and the 'seats' were upturned beer crates.

2. Watch Pockface explode a Chinese made gook landmine cum ashtray. I haven't a clue what that was all about, but it did make a big bang.

3. Watch Pockface fire off half a dozen mortars into a gomo. I haven't a clue what that was all about either, but it also made a big bang.

There were no final exam results for COIN. Just the fact you survived it meant a pass. It was with a very happy heart that I returned to Morris Depot.

Memoir mutterings

It turns out that all the panic attacks about my bad blood were bullshit. I could have anyone's as long as it had a minus sign and only AB people could have mine! So the bloody stuff is worthless! Just my sodding luck.

Glossary

Goffel. A person of mixed colour, usually black and white. Not to be confused with a zebra. A zebra, incidentally, was explained to daft Germans on safari in Zimbabwe, as a *streifenhausen-klippin-kloppen.*
Root. An erection.
Stiffie. See **root**.

CHAPTER 6:

Philosophical ponderings: Pleasure and pain are pre-empted by payday and perceptions of pleasure paid

Human nature takes great pleasure in people's pain. The Germans have a word for it – *schadenfreude*. Our degree of civilisation is indicated by our use of schadenfreude. If one administers pain for pleasure, or enjoys someone's pain second hand, this is bad. However, on the other hand, someone who takes pleasure in the simple discomfort of a person, especially if it is their own fault, this is good. A perfect example is when Scummy tried to leave the police. Did we laugh or what? But, what happens when it always seems to be me on the end of other people's schadenfreude? It's just not fair....

My paydays at the end of each month nearly gave me a heart attack. Honest 'Coppers'? My arse they were. The thieving swines had stolen hundreds, if not thousands of copper cents from my well deserved pay. Okay, I knew I had to pay tax. All whites paid tax. It came with our skin colour. Tax wasn't that high, about 10 per cent of my $222, but there were more subtractions. Pension contribution? What was that all about? Since I couldn't make Commissioner before I was 25, I couldn't be arsed waiting another 40-odd years to get my money back - besides, I had only signed up for three.

Worse was to come. Don't forget, I am already forking out thousands of cents for a batman who sits on his arse all day talking to fellow batmen as he cleans my boots (I paid for the polish and cleaning cloths). The BSAP had charged me for food and accommodation! I thought it was free, just like the medical cover. At least the bastards didn't charge me for the hundreds of uniforms they made me get cleaned at my expense, or the bullets I had shot off on COIN. Or - for that bloody matter - the bloody FN rifle. Next thing I know I'm being charged for the toilet paper! I hadn't seen anything about this in the small print I hadn't bothered to read. AND, here is the real pain, I had actually had to pay to sleep 18 days under a leaking poncho while eating food fit only for peasant war refugees. I must have been insane.

Okay, the recruit's mess hall served up rather good grub, but had I known I was paying for this, I would have rather bought a can of baked beans and warmed them up under the tap instead of consuming the absurd amounts served three times a day. Oh, and, as for Morris Depot's bedrooms, they were fine. Spotless actually, since I am paying a batman to keep it so…spotless.

That meant we were not allowed to have anything visible of a private nature. Such as: a picture of your mum or have your teddy sleeping on the pillow, or a stereo speaker cable leading from one cupboard (where one speaker and the stereo were hiding) over the door frame and into another cupboard (where the other speaker was hiding). The stereo, my beautiful Precious, my pride, my pleasure, which I had bought and brought all the way from the UK, was my ultimate Precious. Getting a night's marching punishment (known as being 'On Charge') for; and I quote from the bits of paper us sinners were given –

'… and to wit, an inspection of Recruit Dunn and Greenberg's quarters showed them to be in a state of utter dishevel with unauthorised wires criss-crossing the room. Signed, Inspector Lambourn.'

The punishment didn't fit the crime. Alan Dunn, my room mate, howled his head off, moaning and weeping that it was my entire fault. Well, he wasn't that bothered when he listened to his *America* tapes on the coolest stereo in Rhodesia, was he? Tough-titty. At least I got a bit of schadenfreude knowing he would have to share my pain. I will explain the pain in a moment after I have accumulated a few more… and they sort of went like this… well, the way I read them between the lines, as you do:

'…and to wit - Recruits Greenberg and Addison did, unauthorised, wander off during an autopsy to seek pleasure in a bottle of Coca-Cola, and thus making me look like a right twat as we waited for them. I hereby sentence them both to three nights marching to be taken when they have their pass-out party. Signed - Inspector Groucho.'

Addie wasn't having that, nor was I. Three nights - whatever - but not during the passing out party. It was a pleasure we had all contributed to financially with no rebate for non-attendance. Addie, using his police cadet experience, appealed to the highest ranking man in Morris Depot, its commandant, Assistant Commissioner Stuart, who upheld our appeal. We still had to do our punishment, but not when we had the party. Guess who had also been invited and didn't bother? I certainly got a bit of schadenfreude then.

Then of course there was the recurrent 'On Charge', because some uniform bits were 'not' allowed to be done by the batman unless you paid the cheeky bugger extra:

'...and to wit – Recruit Greenberg attended drill inspection in a uniform fit only for a beggar on the corner of Union Avenue and First Street. His rank flash's daft little brass backing plate hadn't seen any Brasso for at least a week, and his green Cobra floor polish polished webbing belt had not been touched with said polish since he arrived. I hereby award the said recruit with night marching for one, two, three and four nights as I see fit during the four months I can torture him. Signed, Inspector Lambourn.'

I accumulated a few, and they were a pain. To wit:

'...and the recruit will line up on the parade ground in full drill uniform at exactly 7.00pm. He and his fellow sinners will march as a squad to the main entrance almost a five minute march away. There, they will queue up and write their names in a book. Then they will march back. They are then free to do whatever they please till 7.30pm when they will line up on the parade ground in full drill uniform and march once again to said gate and write ones name in the sodding book again and march back and then they are free to do what ever they please till they must line up on the parade ground at exactly 8.00 pm and blah, blah, blah *ad infinitum*, and this stupid bullshit will go on till 10.00pm and their feet burst into blisters and their arm and leg muscles cramp in terrible pain, hah, hah, hah. Signed – The Bastards of the BSAP.'

Still, we pretty well all got one of these. If you didn't it meant you were unquestionably an arse licking dickhead and would be promoted to Commissioner for your 25th birthday, or of exceptional police officer material and a real pain in the arse for being such a clever-clever. Sadly our squad had a couple of those clever-clevers that had far better exam results than poor little me.

Back to pay day: The first pay day was in cash, what little was left of it after the police stole half of it and Woody came for his share - the Shylock. (Actually, he helped half of us out, interest free.) Most of our squad owed money to Woody. I had turned up at Morris Depot with $10 - with a month to go. I hadn't been that concerned; what with all the free meals and accommodation I thought I had. Ten bucks should easily carry me through 30 days. It didn't. There was always something you needed - like booze.

Booze - the Achilles heel of Rhodesian males and many a female. How we loved it. I misquote Shakespeare here: 'Rhodesians! Drink until you're silly, then wake up and drink yourself silly again - for the pissed will inherit a swollen liver.'

Many would try it and many failed, but The Left Right Inn was a good starting point. This place was an oasis in Morris Depot and no one but recruits were allowed in. The drinking games that went on in there were of legendry proportions with many recruits waking up in hospital attached to a drip due to alcohol poisoning. Great fun! I didn't get wasted every night, but I did pick up a tolerance for vodka, lime and lemonade - what with me still having a sweet tooth. In one session I had great schadenfreude when Jeff lost our little 'How many pure shots of Rhodesian made rocket fuel called vodka, could you drink till you passed out or threw up?' The answer is seven. Then Jeff's eyes went backwards into his head, making him look a bit like he had placed half a ping-pong ball in each socket, shuddered uncontrollably, and threw up in a raging torrent straight at the barman, who luckily ducked in time. But the best piss-up ever was during the VIPs and the highest ranking police officer's Christmas party. Volunteers were asked to serve the dignitaries' drinks. I volunteered because I knew I could get a few sneaky freebies in and maybe borrow a bottle or two of vodka when no one was looking...

There was a mixture of both black and white waiters, dressed in similar fashion of blue tights with a gold flash down the side, and a white, short sleeved shirt. Along with the white gloves, we looked like the Black and White Minstrel Morph Show (less the brilliant white lips). Things went just fine as we served behind long tables set in the magnificent gardens of the Morris Depot Assistant Commissioner Stuart's residence. With awe we served people like Prime Minister Ian Smith and other members of his cabinet, the commanders of the army, air force etc, etc. These were A-list Rhodesian celebrities. The only ones we had really. As far as the 'artistic' celebrities such as TV presenters were concerned - most of them were morphs and stuck around in each other's back yard scenery.

By around 9.00pm, the celebs and their wives started to get a bit rowdy, and several were moaning a lot about the quality of service. What was becoming apparent was that the staff was having a far better party than the celebs. Luckily, the big cats had buggered off early (it seemed they had a serious war to run the next day), so the rest, as far as we were now concerned, were just hooligans spoiling for a fight. Man, did we drink. I witnessed one recruit pour an entire bottle of gin all over a celeb's wife's hand as she stood there being topped up. Another waiter fell into a hedge while opening a bottle of beer.

Oh the pleasure of this all. I was slugging away at the vodka, last man standing, before linking up with Richard, arm in arm, each with a bottle of gut rot and tootled home after (I think) - being dismissed. Oh the pleasure. Oh the pain.

I was rudely awoken the next mourning. I was mourning that morning because I was dying, very badly. Nothing like crying over your own departed, pickled soul. Jeff, and Addie - who had also been there, but the bastard had good tolerance after being a cadet for two years - had a right hard time putting me into my PT uniform. I recall, as they dragged me to the parade ground, that I had to stand in the sick ranks. God help me...I was sick all right. I hadn't felt this ill since the cheese and wine thrash at the 8th Mount Pleasant Boy Scout group's annual general meeting where I had been a waiter too. That's another story.

I stood (sort of), to attention as Lambourn inspected the ranks. Sickies were in the last row. I vaguely recall that Richard, who was a tad under the weather as well, whispering to me to keep still and stop swaying around in ever increasing circles. Before Lambourn could even arrive, I - still in attention position, arms smartly stiff beside my sides, hands clenched, with thumbs pointing down to the floor - bent stiffly over and vomited a bucket load of evil smelling fluid on the parade ground. Well, Lambourn hadn't drilled into us the correct way to vomit, so I should have got some Brownie points for the effort. I then fell over.

I was dead. Forget the fact I had urinated on the Royal Grass a few hours earlier and not been caught. I was done for. I would be marching 'On Charge' for the rest of my career, and then, an amazing thing happened...my guardian angel arrived for the first time.

"Was Greenberg by any chance part of the serving staff last night?"

It was Lambourn. I gathered there were several confirmations of this fact - as if I cared. I didn't want my mummy or teddy at this stage; I just wanted bed and a bucket next to it.

"Greenberg, you drunken piece of shit, get to bed."

Praise the Lord, I was saved. In my rocket fuelled hallucinations, the penny dropped. I wasn't here to have my spirit broken, they were just trying to tame it and control it. I awoke inspired from my vision for about 30 seconds and forgot it. But I also concluded Inspector Lambourn wasn't a bastard who screamed in my dreams "As You Were!" every time I thought of women. No, he was an officer and a gentleman. And he was fair, for nothing was ever said of the matter. He had my respect.

We could also go down to the very posh Police Club overlooking the rugby grounds. There we could chill while watching 'Shape' try to shape with anything wearing a skirt. This boringly bland former member of the SAP (like Jan), talked so much garbage he was a human tranquiliser. There was a lovely snooker table that was free to use and Addie and I would have a few games. But that was about it – except for listening to my beloved Precious with all the self-made tapes of BBC TV's *Top of the Pops* - recorded a few months earlier when the world was saner. We were not allowed out of Depot during the week and had to be tucked up in our beds by 10.00pm.

Weekends we could let our hair down a little (Hah-hah…what hair!) On Saturday mornings we would be given a light inspection in civilian clothes. After checking if we needed another visit by the Portuguese hairdresser, Santos, we were free! Free to do what?

We had to wear a jacket and tie and sign out and had to sign back in before midnight otherwise - while we wouldn't turn into a pumpkin – we'd be on a charge and banned from going out the next weekend. I occasionally hitchhiked to see step-mum, or loafed around town with Addie and Jeff. Saturday night was spent at discothèques such as Barneys and Feathers. Two clubs that were used by the nutters in the Rhodesian Light Infantry (RLI), Le Coq d'Or and Club Tomorrow, could only be visited in full squad strength - as some really nasty fights often broke out. As I said right at the beginning - these troopies or Brown Jobs, were mostly regulars. In other words, they were brain dead. Regular piss-heads more like it. Fuelled on booze, they would spend their 10 days R and R releasing waves of intoxicated adrenalin and testosterone on any one suspected of being a clever-clever, or worse – a morph!

I had a run-in with too much adrenalin while at Morris Depot. One morning I awoke covered from head to foot in strange little red bumps that were rather irritating. Calling in sick, which wasn't a problem as the entire squad refused to come within 50 goose-stepping paces of me, while making signs of the cross, I was allowed to visit the Depot doctor. This was the same lunatic that let me join the BSAP asylum in the first place. After making me strip, I was diagnosed as having something rather odd, and recommended to be injected with 5ml of pure adrenalin over a period of one hour. The nurse who administered the stuff felt rather sorry for me. Not as sorry as I was feeling as I lay on the bed sweating buckets, my heart going berserk and my skin feeling as though it had just been skinned and cured for Satan's latest red cloak.

I was released into the blazing sunshine feeling spaced out my mind and with a sick note exempting me from physical activities, such as drill, for 24 hours. It didn't exempt me from standing in full uniform in the blazing sun while everyone marched up and down. Strangely, Doctor Frankenstein's adrenalin had kicked me into touch, and the next day I staggered into his office, looking a lot like the monster he had created. This mad man then wrote out another prescription for the adrenalin. I was doomed!

I was saved by an understanding nurse who had been sent to murder me.

"Listen, I believe you have prickly heat. I will switch the adrenalin for some antihistamine. If you agree, just nod, but never tell any one."

I nodded. Two hours later I was wolfing down a fine lunch of steak and chips, and was tip-top again.

As for my love life (the greatest of pleasures), I had none, which was perhaps just as well since according to rumours, our tea was laced with bromide (copper sulphate) to stop us jerking ourselves blind each night. But, prior to joining, the 10 days with my long shoulder length hair, giving me stunning David Cassidy looks, along with my digital watch, had me pulling birds like there was no tomorrow. Sadly there was.

In that short time, I pulled a gorgeous 15-year-old red head who offered me her body but I refused because I didn't fancy joining the police with a pending illicit sex with a minor charge over my head; and dumped her after five days as I was running out of time, and her intellectual capacity was rather limited. I managed to get-off with both my next-door neighbours. One, Susan Grundy, denies this to this day…but I remember! I had the X-factor - 'til I joined the BSAP - leaving my ex-babes now asking the 'Y' we bothered with him factor.

Towards the middle of December I applied to visit my former high school for its end of year prize giving assembly. Lambourn had it approved and I was instructed to wear the safari type suit of tunic and shorts. Leg wear was to be brown shoes and long khaki socks. The reason I was going was because I was a special guest of honour; a rare thing indeed. For years the headmaster, Geoff Lambert, had only invited me to bend over a stool and be beaten for various offences such as idleness. But at last year's ceremony, I had surprisingly been awarded the Impala Shield, given to the pupil who, while being neither a prefect nor monitor, had contributed the most to the school. Well, it wasn't for fund raising that's for sure, as I never contributed a cent.

It turned out that my dedication to the gymnastics club was the reason. Although my rather embarrassed step-sister Bridget had collected it on my behalf (I was in the UK by then), I was returning the compliment by donating to the school a trophy I had purchased whilst abroad. It was to be given to any member of the gym team, of any gender, deemed to have contributed the most to the sport. And not just anyone like Keith Bell who spent all his time playing rugby and only turned up for the occasional appearance in the club - and got away with it because he was a brilliantly natural-born gymnast.

By the time I walked to the entrance of Morris Depot I bitterly regretted disobeying Lambourn's orders of foot wear. Because I'm a posing waster, I had opted for the impressive brown boots topped with shiny anti-savaging dog leggings. Until then I hadn't worn them and by the time I staggered in immense pain to Second Street to hitch a lift (no chance of me paying for a taxi), I swore never to wear them again. They cut into ankles, shins and back of knees, and made the tortured victim walk like the Tin Man from the Wizard of Oz with a dipstick shoved up his sebaceous gland. (No wonder Lambourn could only goose-step.)

Arriving at Mount Pleasant School just in time, I mingled with old school mates - who had cleverly decided to get more education - at the back of the packed hall. None of the idiots told me that I had a seat in the front row and when Lambert announced the winner for the trophy, Wayne Panton, he expressed disappointment that I had been unable to attend. I would at this point normally have jumped up and down to get the attention I deserved - but I could hardly walk from the pain in my legs. Oh well.

Then, finally, the big day arrived. We would officially become coppers and, in my case, again copperless.

It rained in the mid-afternoon of December 22, 1976 –but not the typical rainy season thunderstorm that might have crashed and flashed from black skies for an hour or two. They might have cancelled otherwise as it wouldn't go down well if a recruit got a *blitzen* straight down his FN. This was more some incessant piddling drizzle I normally associated with Manchester in the UK - *aka* Mud Island. The rain was rapidly soaking the parade grass as three recruit squads of regular Patrol Officers, one squad of Women Patrol Officers and one squad of National Service Patrol Officers – some 93 white Rhodesian law enforcers –were having their pass-out parade before the reviewing eyes of Rhodesian Deputy Prime Minister, David Smith.

So there I was aged 18½, standing at ease just before Christmas Day, 1976, being anointed with tepid rain among the neat ranks of my squad, straining to hear the Commissioner and other dignitaries address the audience. All I could hear was 'plop, plop, plop'. That was the sound of accumulated raindrops dropping from my No 1 police cap onto my No 1 uniform.

I watched in fascination as the rain soaked across the back of the heavy khaki/olive-green uniform of the ex-recruit in front of me. To my amazement, he started to steam. In fact, we all did. Although it was raining, we were all getting cooked in the heavy outfits. There was also a funny smell, like camels drowning in urine. This added to the very essence of the history of the moment - for our amazing force once patrolled on camels. Maybe the jackets we now wore were made from their carcasses, or horses and donkeys or elephants – for if it moved – a Rhodesian policeman could ride it.

In a few more waffling lines, and more marching around the

hallowed grass, (the one I pissed on just recently) - that was now a swamp, I would be a real policeman called a PO, that meant Patrol Officer, the lowest rank held by a white policeman who conveniently outranked any black one - regardless of age or experience.

Waffle, waffle, was still being babbled through the rain. Something about having cordial relations between police and public.

"This is a very important characteristic of an efficient police force and one which I am sure you will do your utmost to develop," the Deputy PM intoned.

Yeah, whatever. I am bloody soaking man, get on with it.

"Blah blah, going through hard times, blah blah, and the community need hold no fears as to your intentions and capabilities."

The black police band finally started up some half drowned din, which according to the blurb handed out to the spectators, was 'Rhodesians Bold' and 'Kum-a-Kye' (a poor choice, as now we were no longer boys but Men of Men. It was raining them, hallelujah!) That would be our cue to wade off for one last round of soggy goose-stepping.

Mighty Mike Lambourn strode forward with a ceremonial sword which looked like a stainless steel tooth-pick in his huge hand.

"Squad, Attention. Forward ... March!"

The time we had spent learning to march was put into action as we squelchingly followed Rhodesia's living example of the *Colossus of Rhodes* (the Greek one, not to be confused with that English land-thief Cecil), around the huge grassy parade ground. The water sprayed like the Victoria Falls in reverse from Lambourn's boots stamping on the sodden turf. If there had been any sun peeping through the overcast skies that afternoon to blot out, this man could do it. Now here we were marching in unison in fancy jodpurs that looked like trousers with elephant ears. To keep these 'ears' stiff my batman had ironed shavings of Sunlight soap inside until they were stiff as cardboard. Unfortunately, the ears were starting to foam suds from my leg movements and the constant supply of fetid moisture.

Lambourn had taken great care to hide me among my squad. As the crappiest marcher of our 22 able bodied men, I was carefully flanked by bigger squad mates. The idea was that the spectators, among them my step-mum and step-sister, would not get to see much of me as I spasmodically pranced like a warped wood-soaked Pinocchio on the Royal grass. I actually doubted if they could see any details of the five squadrons of drowning rats on display.

Then, it was all over, and there should have been a line up with my squadron for its passing-out photo. It seems the magnesium couldn't fire the flash with all the rain or something. Oh well! No squad photo-shots for remembrance. Not as if any of us would have in any way been visible through the steam still coming off freshly-badged shoulders. It is a crying shame really. Most of them I would never see again and we had certainly all been changed by the experience. It would have been worth sticking it up on Facebook, looking at those fresh-poes faces again and recalling some of the more colourful characters that had made up the recruit squad 8/76.

So that was that - job done. I was a policeman now, ready to bring justice to the streets of Rhodesia - but I wasn't sure which street. A couple of weeks previously we had been asked to write down three options, in priority, of where we would prefer to be posted. This had caused furious debate with the 'experts' claiming that usually you got your second option. Mine went like this –

1. Stay on at Morris Depot and become a drill officer. This was a clever trick as I had zero chance of that since my marching skills were more spazticus than Spartacus. Oddly, John Arnott and M-K did become drill officers. I wasn't surprised, especially by John, who had actually paid his batman to go on holiday for four months as he insisted on doing all the polishing and shining bullshit himself. The only reason he didn't iron his own shirts was because he had to be in bed by 10pm.

2. Salisbury Central Charge Office. This would be fine as it meant babes and booze in civilisation. Addie, the jammy bastard, did get this position.

3. The Mashonaland Province, of which Salisbury was its capital so, in theory, I wasn't that far from booze and babes.

My clever ploy worked wonders and after the pass-out ceremony I received a slip with the words, Midlands Province, and a rail ticket for the night train leaving that same day - so much for a few days off over Christmas. Five others were also given the same marching orders, including Jeff.

I kissed Katherine and Bridget goodbye, shook mighty Mike's huge paw, and went crying to my room to pack my Precious very carefully using the tons of uniform I was to drag around with me.

Morris Depot - Passout parade - Squad 8/76
Pic - BSAP Outpost

Memoir mutterings

Email from Tim 'Addie' Addison –

At the Officer's Christmas Party - while serving two Castle Lagers to an Ass. Com., I pushed them over the table towards him but used a bit too much strength and they both slid off and landed on his feet, upright and one on each. By that stage the brass were also pissed so didn't seem to mind.

Excerpts from Deputy Prime Minister David Smith's speech taken from the BSAP magazine *The Outpost*, January, 1977, page 27.

Of the central characters mentioned no longer in this memoir - 9737 PO Steven 'Woody' Wood was killed in action at the end of '78.

9734 Insp Richard Bertin. Died in a traffic accident 1982.

9733 PO Alan Donn. By purchase. (Bought his way out of his contract.) March '79

9727 SO Jacobus Johan 'Jan' Brummer. Pension and other benefits. July 1980.

7790 Chief Inspector Mike Lambourn. Pension and other benefits. December 1982.

Glossary

Fresh-poes. New recruit.

Get-off. Heavy petting, limited usually to a lot of deep throated snogging and a lucky feel of a breast or two.

Shape(ed). Terminology referring to the act of ***Getting off.***

CHAPTER 7:

Infamy! Infamy! The BSAP have it in for me

That evening, Salisbury central railway station was packed. We had second class tickets. The cabins were almost the same as first class but held six. With all the crap we were carrying there was little space to make ourselves comfortable. Rhodesia Railways was state owned and its stations and rolling stock were kept in immaculate condition. There was no racial segregation, just a financial one. Third and fourth class didn't have dark green leather seats that converted into beds, but you got what you paid for. I was amazed that I hadn't been forced to pay for my ticket, otherwise I would have tied myself to the roof of fourth class.

The brown painted coaches disguised the red dust they accumulated and were pulled by a magnificent 15th class Garratt steam engine. These superb examples of British engineering had been brought back into service as sanctions made fuel scarce. The Rhodesian government had simply exchanged their diesel engines with the South Africans for FNs and ammunition. With Wankie

Colliery being one of the biggest coal mines in the world, we weren't exactly short of the stuff. Besides, the jet black engines riddled with brightly polished brass pipes were a real attraction.

The night train to Bulawayo, the second largest city of a quarter million, in the country's south-west, would take all night. We would be kicked out sort of in the middle, at the capital of the Midlands – Gwelo. Although a mere two and half hour drive away, the train would take six hours to get there. This was because, with a lot of hissing steam, crashing and banging, the train insisted on stopping at every piss-pot town and village en-route. Sleep was impossible.

As we stood on the platform of the pitch black Gwelo train station, I wondered where the reception committee was. There must have been a small problem with communication, for surely they knew I was on the way? Dragging all our belongings outside, we all stood there with thumbs up bums and minds in neutral.

"Do you think we should phone the police," voiced someone after about 15 minutes.

This seemed a good idea, and we all agreed.

"Anybody know the number?"

"999," said I.

"Don't be an idiot Greenberg, this isn't exactly an emergency."

Yes it was. I could get mugged any minute and have my Precious stolen. I couldn't even fight off any looters as my FN had no ammunition.

There was a public pay phone and after looking up the number in the chained directory by the light activated by a push button dynamo, a minor riot broke out over who would cough up the five cents to make the call. I flatly refused because as usual I was flat broke again. Eventually we were picked up by the Charge Office night shift and dumped, bags and all, on the carpet of the single men's mess.

At 8.00am we were duly presented to the Assistant Commissioner and commanding officer of the BSAP Midlands Province, Pat McCulloch. There was a brief "Good morning, did you sleep well?" (Is he kidding or what?) And then we six raw policeman in rumpled uniforms and bottle brush haircuts were given some options.

"I will divide you in pairs between Gwelo, Que Que and Gatooma. I will ask for your overall squad placing. The highest will have first option and then so on down to the last."

This was interesting. It hadn't occurred to me that we might be sent to other towns under his jurisdiction. Things were getting better. I knew I was third in line. The top two chose Gwelo and Gatooma respectively. I could understand Gwelo, they had babes, but Gatooma? The place was so backwards they didn't even have a set of traffic lights. For all I knew they might not have any electricity. I was third in line and had to think quickly. I took Que Que as it was exactly midway between Salisbury and Bulawayo, had electricity to power my Precious and just a two hour hitch hike from Salisbury. The place was even rumoured to have babes.

Jeff took Gwelo. It made sense as that was nearer to his home in Bulawayo. The last two clowns were then split between Que Que and Gatooma. With that decided, half an hour later saw four of us stuffed with our kit into a long wheel base Landrover zipping back towards Salisbury on a wide, well maintained tar road. It all seemed a hell of a waste of rationed petrol. Why hadn't they distributed us properly in the first place, instead of playing bloody musical chairs with me and my Precious?

Now feeling totally knackered with all the nonsense, an hour later I was turfed out at Que Que police station with another recruit from 7/76, David Odendaal, who I knew nothing about, besides the end position he had qualified within his squad — namely, the very end of it.

Into Que Que charge office Odendaal and I went, dragging all our junk with us. There I met my first super black man - Patrol Officer Bukka. A couple of weeks before I had seen some of these black gentlemen dressed in civilian clothing eating together in a separate, glass walled room of the large mess at Morris Depot. They were there because of the Government's change of command system. For the first time, blacks would, could, make the leap to the lowest white rank of Patrol Officer. The first group had all been the highest ranking blacks (Sub-Inspector with one silver bar on the shoulder epaulets), with at least 15 years of immaculate service behind them.

Patrol Officer Bukka must have been in his mid-40s and cut an impressive figure.

"Good morning and how may I help you?"

For a second I thought I was back in the U.K., listening to Trevor McDonald reading out the news on the TV. This man's English put mine to shame, never mind Odendaal who was almost totally incoherent with Rhodie slang and swear words constituting the majority of his vocabulary. While Odendaal puffed on a fag, I explained our predicament.

"I see." Looking down at a large, leather clad open diary, he went on "I am afraid the Officer in Charge of Que Que district has a full schedule for today, but I have pencilled you to be in his presence at 8.00am tomorrow. I will arrange for transport to the single officers mess where I hope you will find accommodation for the night."

In a blink of his eye he had a driver there instantly and off we went.

We were dumped in a couple of empty rooms at Que Que singles mess. We could do what we liked till tomorrow. Well at least I had a bed, and the view out the window of a nicely kept garden was rather pleasing. This all looked rather nice. Assuming I would be stopping here (although I already thought of requesting a better room, perhaps with a balcony, but in the meantime this would do), I had my Precious out in 20 minutes and was soon belting out six-month-old British Top 20 hits.

The delightful sounds soon attracted an audience of jealous fellow off-duty patrol officers. Such sophistication was beyond their *Made in Rhodesia* Supersonic Hi-Fi comprehension. The Dixons own-brand tape deck was a huge affair in brushed satin aluminium finish and two bright blue flashing input/output meters. There was even a button marked 'Chrome'. That was so cool! It meant it played chrome tapes extra special. It didn't have Dolby, unfortunately, as that would have been an extra £40.00. The amplifier was incredibly, British made, an Amstrad. With a slim body and brushed black face, it was really cute and packed a mean punch through my Japanese made Sony Midi Hi-Fi speakers. Nice indeed.

Meanwhile, due to the immense popularity my Precious had created for me, I was invited, along with brain dead Odendaal, to a few drinks down at the local watering hole – The Three Miles Motel. It was so called because it was three miles from the centre of Que Que. Very original. Sounded like fun, so I unpacked the glad rags and got ready.

Eight that evening saw us as a group in the lounge of the place. Slumped in low slung chairs, large coffee table before us, drinks were starting to flow. I ordered vodka, lime and lemonade. That raised a few eyebrows. Did I care? Odendaal fitted into this group like a missing cog – the perfect Rhodie - fag in mouth and the Neanderthal genes forcing the right hand to curl instinctively around a bottle of Castle beer.

There was a serious shortage of babes. In fact, there was just one - a local doctor's daughter. That seemed to qualify her to be considered a possible catch. Still, she had a right pair of mummeries on her and as she got drunker, she progressively attached herself to my witty banter. This was of course far superior to the animal-like grunting of the piss-heads gathering in harmony, like vultures over some easy dead meat. The leader of this group was a certain Nigel Triggs - who would turn out to be my nemesis. All I knew of him was that he was a senior patrol officer in some shit hole called Gokwe.

I will describe this individual in detail soon, but suffice to say I neither paid attention to his gibberish, and his poorly dressed, bleating sheep, as I was busy by that time examining the dear doctor's daughter's tonsils with my tongue. Until, Triggs, a Madison in the corner of his mouth, the smoke making his eyes squint, leaned over into my space -

"Either you or Odendaal will be coming with me to Gokwe tomorrow. Do you know why?"

I didn't have a clue, neither did I care.

"This", pointing to some complete waster slouched in a chair with a Castle beer glued to his hand, "is Joe."

Joe grins stupidly. Triggs goes on.

"Joe was in Gokwe. Joe went mad, went bush, so they had to bring him here. And, this," pointing to another baboon, "is Wheeler, a complete fucking waster."

The Wheeler bloke sort of waves a Castle at me.

"He crawled on his hands and knees begging the O.C. (Officer Commanding Que Que district), to let him back into civilisation. That means we are short of some fresh blood."

Such a charming man. I concluded he was a lunatic and a psychopath.

Meanwhile, the Doc's daughter was getting frisky so reluctantly I called a cab and wished my enjoyable company a pleasant evening talking shite. And with that I said goodnight.

"You are doomed, doomed," the mad man screeched after me.

I had a hard on that was desperate for a bit of luck, even if it cost half a day's wage in taxi fare.

Back in my new room, things were going sweet. My Precious played bosom groping type vibes and I was busily exchanging quantities of vodka tasting saliva when suddenly - Triggs, Wheeler and the spiralling side kick Joe, burst into the room.

"New police boys must be initiated," announced a scary looking blood- shot eyed Triggs.

I inwardly sighed. This was sure to be rather pathetic and I was dragged out to the garden and hosed down. At least the water was rather warm. When I returned my potential hop, skip and jump had hopped, I had no jump, and I wasn't exactly skipping with happiness.

Bang on time next morning, we acknowledged PO Bukka and followed him. A knock on the door and the pair of us faced a toad. A poisonous one at that! Chief Superintendent Scheisskopf, Officer Commanding the district of Que Que looked like a complete tosser.

"Blah, blah, blah," the silly old toad croaked. "I have two positions available in my jurisdiction. One is with Que Que Rural section and the other is in Gokwe. You there," pointing at a very seriously hung over Odendaal, who stunk like a skunk who had spent the night at the brewery, "what is your name and where did you come in your squad?"

Laugh? - I nearly shat. I smelt like roses after my late night shower. Half-legless Odendaal didn't have one to stand on. Was I bothered? Gokwe for him - hah hah. He will be fine there, what with his new best pal Triggs by his side to share smokes and beers and intellectual conversation associated with the chattering of vervet monkeys.

"PO David Odendaal, 17th out of 17, intake 7 of '76 , Sir !," he announced sickly. I was almost laughing out loud as he squirmed in his badly creased summer uniform.

"PO Karl Greenberg, 10th out of 22, intake 8 of 76, Sir!"

Goodbye thick-shit Odendaal, you are off to have some fun with your new family in the middle of bloody nowhere. It's a hard knock life.

"Well then, Odendaal, I will post you to Gok..., hang on, don't you play golf? I am sure I have seen your name in the newspaper somewhere...?"

"Yes SAH!" A stale beer smelling, blood shot eyed, smiling broadly now Odendaal replied,

"I was third in the recent Dunlop Junior Cup. I am also short listed to play for Rhodesia. I was with the '75 Junior team that toured South Africa, and I am so clever with a stick and a white ball I do not need to think at all."

"Excellent old chap, our police golf team is in desperate need for more talent. I presume you would play for them, wouldn't you?"

A terrible rushing sound filled my head and I nearly fainted. This can't be happening; I am being superseded by a drunkard who hits little white balls called 'damn-it' with a stick.

"Of 'course' I 'wood', sir," was Odendaal's very genuine reply. The bastard was almost wriggling with pleasure.

I was in the wrong club big time!

"Greenberg. You will leave with PO Triggs for Gokwe. David, sweet David, welcome to Que Que Rural," this obnoxious, unfair, corrupt bastard of a Chief Superintendent guiltlessly announced.

Oh its David, sweet David, now is it? I felt ill, *Gokwe*, and now the lunatic Triggs on top of that! Desperation makes me speak out,

"Sir! Could I spend Christmas at home first, after all this is the 24th?"

"Don't be stupid Greenberg, you're going with P.O. Triggs at one this afternoon. Dismissed!"

I crawled out the Que Que Charge Office weeping uncontrollably. My back spurted fountains of blood from the multiple stab wounds made by knives embossed with the BSAP logo. *Et tu, Brute?* I had to make it to a phone box. God help me, give me strength to call home and say my final farewell. I needed some rope and a tall tree.

"Double eight, five three oh four," came the soothing tones of step-mum.

"Hi mum, it's me."

"Oh, how nice of you to phone, Karl. How are you? Where are you now?"

"I'm in Que Que," (sob, sob, wail).

"I see, and will you be staying there then? You don't sound very well, have you picked up a cold?"

Cold? Yes I was cold. Most walking corpses are cold. I never met a hot Zombie.

"No, I am not well, (wail) the bastards are sending me to GOKWE, fucking Gokwe."

"Please don't swear. Well, I have never heard of Gokwe… but I am sure you will like it after you settle down."

Like it? Did Aleksandr Solzhenitsyn like his gulag? The only difference between Siberia and Gokwe was the weather! She didn't understand and I only had five more cents.

"They are sending me there with a mad man because I don't play golf!" I screamed, as the pips warning me of imminent termination from the sane world started its countdown.

"Well, I am not sure I understand, but I am sure there will be other sports you can do, and…"

Beep-beep-beep.

I staggered like a drunk back to the mess. The walk helped to clear my mind. I bounced off the Jacaranda trees that lined the roads past immaculately kept gardens with dogs barking their heads off at me. I wanted to beat Odendaal to death with a seven iron. For decades to come, that leering face would haunt me, as when my death sentence had been pronounced by Toady, I had clutched at my heart and nearly vomited from the shock. I wasn't a complete loser because otherwise I might have defecated on the spot. With hindsight I wish I had…onto Chief Superintendent Scheisskopf's desk.

Odendaal's face, that stupid grin, I thought I would never see it again except hopefully amongst the funeral announcement section in the Rhodesia Herald. But that was not to be; for three decades later I was invited to a little bash at a Rhodie friend's house in the UK. My host was Roy Bushell, and he had turned his garage into the most amazing Rhodie pub. I will not go into detail of the incredible collections and artefacts he had. Suffice to say, I walked in, can in hand, and suddenly clutched at my heart and nearly vomited from the shock. I wasn't a complete loser because otherwise I might have defecated on the spot.

The grinning baboon's face was staring at me again. Not once, nor twice, but what seemed to be hundreds of pictures of that same leering grin. Roy asked if I was alright as I stared in complete disbelief.

"That's David Odendaal," I croaked whilst waving a finger at the painful apparition.

"Yes, it is - a fine chap, do you know him?"

Oh, I knew him alright. I have slept with the bastard stuck in my head for what seems forever. If I had ever had the misfortune of seeing his name on a leader board I would have thrown the TV out the window.

"And that is me there when I was captain of Rhodesia, and there is Nicky Price. I am sure you know about him," continued Roy. "There is me and David in Rhodesia juniors and me and David with the rest of the squad who toured South Africa and…"

Okay. I am sorry David that I called you a baboon and used other derogative terminology, but you had upset me. I forgive you now. Perhaps one day we will meet on a golf course and I can show you how well I can swing a club; such as a knobkerrie.

Memoir mutterings

Of the central characters mentioned no longer in this memoir: -
9701 PO David Odendaal. Own request (he didn't sign up again after three year contract expired) August 1979.

The chapter title is an adaption from a line spoken by Kenneth Williams as Julius Caesar in *Carry on Cleo* (1964)

White balls called 'damn-it' – This expression is from a sketch *Yeno lo golf* by the late Rhodesian comedian, News presenter, Wrex Tarr. It can be found on *YouTube*.

Glossary

Knobkerrie. A homemade baseball bat with a bell end.

CHAPTER 8:

Into the Gokwe gulag goes grieving Greenberg

the end of the world is nigh
i am doomed, doomed...

Pic - no idea - got it from the internet

Gokwe – how the hell did I get into this mess? It seemed like only days ago when we filled in our little slips of paper with our posting options. Gokwe was the furthest on my mind; in fact, it's the furthest place on the goddamn map! There had been a large physical map of Rhodesia in the law school room, with little coloured pins denoting police stations. I recalled how we had taunted each other while pointing to that one pin... all alone in the middle of nowhere.

Imagine that the borders of Rhodesia were perfectly round. Dissect the circle with the four points of the compass and fill in clockwise the first three quadrants with things like wine, women and song. From the remaining segment, start to take a line from the centre, that would be about North West, and keep going till the line is exactly midway between the centre and the circumference. Place a pin here and call it Gokwe village, perched on the edge of the Mafungabusi Plateau. Fill the whole last quadrant with bush, no women, no discos and plenty bad men with guns called gooks.

I packed my Precious and dragged all my stuff out to the forecourt. Triggs turned up at the singles mess after lunch. Some other bloke, the same height and build as myself, attired in rural uniform, was also waiting for him with a load of luggage and looking even more miserable than me - if that was at all possible. Triggs told us to throw our shit into the back of the semi-full open-backed Landrover.

"You Greenberg can climb on top of it all, as I'm not driving all that way with three in the cab, and Brockbank here," smiling like a hyena that had just been served fillet steak, at the other poor bastard, "is senior to you."

I watched the suburbs of Que Que rapidly disappear, and then as Triggs drove the Landy onto the wide graded dirt road, we entered the bush.

Bush, bush, bush and more bush, on all sides. It is not as if I didn't know about the bush. I had been camping with the Boy Scouts in the stuff. But then I had always returned to a big house, big garden and a swimming pool after a few days away. I was never that keen on actually working full time in the stuff. Only peasants like Triggs lived in the bush.

This memoir is about me. Me, me, me, not the friggin bush! You want to know what the bush is like? – Google it. I will help you. Type this: bush Rhodesia acacia trees long yellow grass lions gooks dangerous Christmas Eve 1976 end of the world as we know it.

Press *enter* and see my name come up as No1 loser! (Try it. It works!)

The trip seemed to take for ever and I was soon coated in a fine layer of red dust. We overtook a couple of crab crawling rural commuter buses, their roofs packed almost as high as the bus itself, with everything imaginable. Their overloaded and twisted chassis made them career down the rutted road at almost an impossible angle. The front wheels somewhere in the middle of the road, and the rear dragging its arse almost into the culvert.

If I wasn't feeling so sorry for myself, I might have enjoyed this. Triggs handled the skittering Landy easily, swerving neatly around the inevitable peasant owned mombe that wandered across the road. I would have loved to have had some mellow tunes to listen to, but the idea of my Precious becoming Rhodesia's first mp3 player by getting imbedded into my head from the force of a Chinese made gook landmine, kept me rather anxious. While the cab occupied by Triggs and Brockbank was protected with thumb width, blast-proof steel and a roll bar, the back was open to the sky. It would be to the sky I would be going to if we ran over one.

After what must have been about an hour, we rolled into Gokwe village. I could hardly gather my thoughts together before we had come to an abrupt halt outside the entrance to Gokwe police station. With no time to look about and absorb the place, I stiffly climbed down and followed Triggs and the other new boy into the station. Triggs acknowledged greetings from half a dozen black policemen and then knocked on a door bearing the sign OiC (Officer in Charge.)

Chief Inspector Mike Harvey had a nice face, if a little hawkish, and was of average build - maybe late 30s - and sported the standard Donny Osmond fringe of brown hair. He looked tired and drawn - like he desperately needed a holiday – just like me.

"Hello Nigel, everything go okay?"

"Yes sir. I have brought two other Patrol Officers back with me."

"Ah yes, I knew about PO Brockbank being transferred here but I am confused. Who are you?"

'The Boss', as I would soon always know him by, then let his piercing eyes wander over to my crumpled form,

He was confused? What about me? I had been zig-zagged around half of Rhodesia (presumably on full pay), hosed down in a garden by a trio of BSAP's finest drunks, lost a potential jiggy-jig, stabbed in the back by a golf loving toad and forced to sit on an open-top coffin for an hour while eating dust. And I thought I was about to have an imminent heart attack.

"Hello, my name is Karl Greenberg, and there is some confusion because I shouldn't be here at all but I was kidnapped on the way to the airport in the hope of getting the hell out of this mad house."

Of course I didn't really say that. I could hardly think coherently after what I had just gone through in the last 48 hours.

"PO Greenberg, sir, I have been transferred here."

The Boss sighed.

"Nigel, I am sorry to have to do this, but I need you to return to Sengwa base camp immediately with supplies. Take Greenberg with you. Draw him ratpacks for two weeks," and, looking again at me, "Welcome to Gokwe, Greenberg. Sorry we have no room free for you at the moment, so you will be going with PO Triggs here."

Turning once more to Triggs, he continued,

"Nigel, as you pass my house on the way out, please stop as my wife has something for you. Oh, and PO Greenberg, it can get very lonely out here. Please refrain from fraternising with the African females."

Hah, hah, hah - I am in a friggin mental ward now! I've been here exactly two minutes, mumbled half a dozen words and am now being accused of being a potential future nanny knocker!

"Okay sir, I will take Greenberg quickly to the shops, instead of ratpacks. I'll show him to PO Nico Meyer's room. He can leave his stuff there till we get back."

This was all too much for me. Triggs, the mad man, wants me to pay for my own food! I can live happily on ratzs, so long as they are free. As we went out, leaving Brockbank still in his office, The Boss called out

"Have a Merry Christmas and a Happy New Year," sounding distinctly non-festive in my ears as I followed Triggs over to a row of bedrooms.

Pointing to a door, he told me to dump my shit in there and prepare a bag for two weeks in the bush. The room was a troll's pit. It was filthy and had remains of various dead animals everywhere. Skins, skulls, tails and African spears scattered around. And the smell! My delicate stomach almost heaved. Gawd, this was getting worse; trolls were joining the police force along with alcoholic homicidal maniacs, nanny knockers and cerebrally taxed golfers. I miserably kissed my Precious goodbye and met Triggs 20 minutes later sitting impatiently in a fully packed Landy.

"Where are your spare magazines?" he demanded, as I climbed into the passenger side and stuffed my rifle down the side of the door.

I didn't have any. I wasn't one of those that had plundered the ammo shed when we were on our counter insurgency course.

"Do you actually have any rounds in that gat?"

I shook my head in the negative.

"Eish man. There is a box of ammo in the cubby hold. Load up and don't fuck up."

Triggs stopped the Landy at the boss's house, a mere 100 paces away on the dirt road out of the cul-de-sac that Gokwe police station was in. A woman came out and presented Triggs with an aluminium foil wrapped lump.

"Merry Christmas, Nigel, I made a roast chicken for tomorrow." She looked curiously at me.

"New PO, Mrs Harvey, and thanks for the chicken, Merry Christmas."

She smiled kindly at me.

"Hello, I'm Heather Harvey. I am sure we will get to know each other soon."

I had to say something, but...

"Hello, please take me away from this psychopath and be my Mommy for a while till I'm feeling better," wasn't quite appropriate.

I politely introduced myself, hoping she didn't notice the tears of self pity making my hazel eyes all moist. I just thanked her and slumped into my seat.

On the way to the store I spoke to Triggs for the first time since he helped me have a shower. I wanted to know how come I was spending my own money instead of getting free ratpacks? The love of my wallet superseded even my fear and misery for a while.

"Listen, you get $2.50 for every day you're out in the bush, tax free, in cash, but you don't need to spend that much for food."

I shot ram rod straight immediately, my cowardly spine suddenly transformed. I was getting paid extra to go camping! What a great choice of career I had made, for in a stroke, this just had to be the best job in the world! Before we had even pulled up in front of the huge African style supermarket, 'Kambasha', emblazoned in wonky huge letters on the front, I was feeling much better.

When it came to money, my maths worked well, 14 days at $2.50 a day was $35 tax free! Bloody right I didn't need to spend that much on food. I would rather starve! Plus we had a free chicken. I had almost forgotten the shower incident and showed a bit more enthusiasm for the adventure ahead. We quickly bought some tinned food, rice and potatoes, and we were off into the dusk. It was late now and when the sun went, it went down fast as Triggs headed the Landy onto two well worn tracks deep into the darkening bush.

I was physically exhausted and still in shock, but this was getting quite interesting and Triggs had just done me a big favour. His funny look when I bought a crate of Coke to his three of Castle beer should have been warning enough that he wasn't about to become my best long lost china. I was gabbing away as Triggs sank his first beer, after having flicked the top off on the dashboard in one practised swift motion, while skilfully steering the Landy through the darkening skies along the rutted roads. His noncommittal grunts to my chattering and my exhaustion finally overtook me, and I started to nod off; my head banging constantly against the window as the Landy jumped and skittered through the bush. There was nothing to see and Triggs needed all his attention to keep the machine on the road; ramming the yellow gear knob down that engaged the four-wheel drive at the loose sandy parts, and then almost stopping so as to use the low-range to climb through huge puddles of slippery mud, glistening in the dancing headlights. The screaming engine was constantly pouring heat into the cab. Unable to sleep, I took over opening beer bottles and lighting fags for Triggs between crashing my head on the door frame and trying not to smash my teeth while taking a swig of well shaken, warm Coke.

And then we were there, wherever there was. There was a rush of activity. Several dark shapes surrounded the Landy, emptying it. Its headlights dully lit up a small, grey cement brick building with a tin roof. Following Triggs inside, he pointed at a camp stretcher bed.

"That's yours," he said while wiring up a 12 volt car battery to the overhead bulb that was our lighting. I threw my stuff down and placed my sleeping bag onto the cot.

I went out and looked at the stars. The shadowy figure of the night guard flitted by, greeting me quietly and courteously. That amazing heaven, a few clouds covering the mass of stars, so clear and bright and the sounds of the night bush all around. It was Christmas Eve; I was a million miles away from home and feeling very alone. I went to 'bed'.

Oh well, I suppose taking a correct hard look at my situation (after drying my eyes), I had been sent through police academy, deemed fit for service and dumped somewhere and it was now a case of "Right me lad, time for you to start earning your wages. So, stop the mourning, because in the morning - it is time to go to work"

"Merry Christmas, Nigel."
"Merry Christmas," he grunted back.

I awoke refreshed and bored already, but I had to be careful now. First I had to check out what kind of mood he was in, but at least I had Christmas on my side. I wasn't religious, but the Jewish blood coursing through my veins meant I would take advantage of any pagan ritual; so long as it made life easier for me. I got up and put on a pair of boxer shorts and my bright orange Squad 8 of '76 T- shirt.

"What's on the agenda for today?" I politely enquired.
"Nothing. It's Christmas. Do what you like.'"

Really? Let's see. It's seven in the morning and if I drove non-stop for 10 hours, I could be home for a late turkey. Two problems though. I didn't know where I was and I can't drive. Beam me up Scotty!

My Christmas euphoria left me running around looking for the tree with my presents hiding underneath. Triggs, far more sensible, pulled his arms out of his sleeping bag and opened a beer from the crate next to his cot. Taking a huge swallow, he leaned his head against an arm and stared at the ceiling. Great! This is going to be a very, very merry Christmas – and I found no presents.

With little difficulty I sussed out how to get the kettle on the small gas hotplates working and started to make myself a Rhodie style cappuccino. I looked around my new home. It resembled a damp rotting prison cell with a bog-hole and shower *ensuite*. Rather larger than your average kia, it had obviously been designed by a five year old aspiring architect using Lego bricks. Actually, they did the job. This was a lot better than a poncho with its hole tied closed with a bit of string.

We had two rooms. The smaller of them was the 'bedroom'. The larger of the two had a sink on spindly legs to make up the 'kitchen' area. Two ancient wooden desks with school type chairs constituted the 'office'. A small cluttered bookcase held rolls of tatty worn maps and piles of A4 paper, next to dark blue copy carbon sheets. A small folding camp table with canvas chairs was used for 'dining'. A dark green, TR 28 single side band radio that could be charged from the Landrover's battery sat in a corner. This would be our contact to Gokwe police station. And that was that. There weren't any pictures on the mildew stained walls, not even one of Prime Minister Ian Smith.

As Triggs popped the top off another chibuli I thought it was time to check outside. In the camp there were a few black police officers, some prisoners, complainants and witnesses of various ages and sexes. I greeted all and introduced myself and wished them all a Merry Christmas. I was a little concerned that I might be inundated with the whiteman's bane – "My Krisimas Box, please Baas." It is historically unknown when this irreligious habit first addicted the indigenous population of Rhodesia, but I have my suspicions David Livingstone had something to do with it. Just days before every Christmas the demands would start at around six in the morning with the arrival of the milk-boy, followed in perfectly trained synchronisation by the newspaper boy, the bread boy, the vegetable girl and the ice-cream boy. This was then capped by the same request from the family maid and garden boy – all this expense before you had left the front gate. Then it would be the turn of the petrol boy attendant (all six of them), the supermarket boy, who packed and carried the groceries to the car, and just about anyone else that vaguely knew you. Depending on the presentational piety of the hopeful recipient and Christian philanthropist apathy of the Baas or Madam, fortunes could change hands. I took to wearing a Star of David to counter this problem. Thank goodness, the black police and other government employees must have realised I was just a poor white PO, but a couple of cheeky prisoners gave us all a laugh by asking me for a 'Freedom Box'.

In less than 20 minutes I had sussed out the layout. There was a dirt track leading out. The ramshackle shed-like buildings actually belonged to Internal Affairs. Our police presence had necessitated a couple of six-man green canvas tents to be put up. Otherwise, it was just bush as far as the eye could see.

I went inside and read a book. Triggs raped the chicken at lunchtime with hardly a word to me, and I got tossed a few cold bones. He passed out at 6 pm. I read for a bit longer. Never mind, at least the next day was another public holiday. I suppose I could spend Boxing Day playing pocket billiards – at least I was getting paid for it (plus bonus).

Memoir mutterings

Email from Mike Harvey.
"Please refrain however of making any contact with the African female." are quoted, it makes me sit-up and takes me back when I left Depot and remounts to Salisbury Central and its Chief Inspector who addressed the newcomers "Remember laddies, I will have none of my troops fraternising with these native and coloured ladies of the night!" No doubt those early words of wisdom had stuck, well and truly in the old grey matter.

Rhodie style cappuccino - Take two teaspoons of coffee/chicory powder, two of milk powder (bought stuff, not the insoluble junk from ratpacks) and two of coarse white sugar. Add a tiny bit of cold water in the cup and mix it all well till a smooth paste. Then add the hot water. The results are brilliant, no lumps and a creamy head to boot. The youth of today would never be able to do this – they just buy the pre-mixed lot from the shops.

Glossary

Chibuli. Beer.
China. Bosom buddy, maybe not. Polite terminology for a Rhodie to greet and dismiss a Rhodie whether they like them or not.
Eish. A phonetic or written exclamation mark at the start of a sentence.
Kia. A basic brick construction built at the bottom of middle-class whites' gardens to house domestic servants.

not having a merry christmas
Pic - Gokwe Kid

CHAPTER 9:

He who wields the ruler rules

A toe was pushed into my side, and I awoke to the dull glow of the 12 volt light.

"Get up, we are going on a raid," Triggs nonchalantly informed me.

I pushed the button on my digital watch and it glowed 5.00am. I pushed the date knob to check that it was really the day after Boxing Day, and that I had strangely slept through it. I wasn't expecting to do anything on a public holiday, unless I was getting time and a half, which, now judging from experience - was highly unlikely.

Triggs was outside and shouting in mixed Shona and English at the others. I quickly slipped into the rural uniform of open V neck, cotton grey shirt, khaki shorts, long socks and Bata leather boots. Those cool ones with three straps, known as desert boots. They had cost me a fortune, but the police field boots looked pathetic and only our black staff wore those. These weren't regular uniform but out here it was tolerated.

I was soon freezing my bollocks off in the cool dawn and was very appreciative of the heat that soon emitted through the floor and front panel of the cab from the sturdy four cylinder engine. I was slightly apprehensive about all this but as I was still waking up, I wasn't all that switched on. As dawn broke Triggs pulled the Landy up.

"From here we walk," he announced, as he flung his FN rifle over his shoulder.

The three accompanying black policeman silently jumped off the back, all armed.

"How far are we walking?" I chirped apprehensively.

"About four clicks, lets go," and he was off at a furious pace with no sign yet that a Christmas cheer of a crate of Castle had in any way affected him.

How come we were walking so far? Is there no track? I hate walking, and especially walking through the bush. Half jogging across sodden hand ploughed fields from the local inhabitant's subsistence farming, I thought that dirtying my boots was not my idea of things to do while on a public holiday.

"How come we are walking so far Nigel? Can't we drive there?" I whined pathetically.

"Don't be fucking stupid," he snarled at me between ever shortening breaths, "if the suspect hears the Landy, he'll do a runner before we can get to him."

Ah-hah! Karly boy was learning really quickly. One: once I get a driver's license, I'm going to lose a lot of suspects - even if they have very bad hearing, and Two: Triggs was suffering from a bad babelaas of maningi proportions. (In other words, he had a bad head... Ag-shame).

One slog later - a quick raid on a kraal, a wooden door kicked easily off its wire hinges - a short scuffle inside and we were back on the way to the Landy with a miserable looking manacled suspect in tow. I was amazed! Was that cool or what? Triggs and the others were in and out of that man's rondavel like robots. Once the headman of the place had pointed out the hut, it was all over. One suspected thief in custody. Back home we go, what's next?

For the next few days I listened, observed and learned; by watching a 'real Rhodie' do his job - Senior Patrol Officer Triggs. Although born in Gwelo, he had spent much of his youth in the bush on fishing and hunting trips. With a natural ear for languages he had picked up Shona very well, aided by his BSAP father who also knew the lingo. At the age of 24, he had been in the BSAP for five years, and Gokwe was Triggs' fourth posting after failing to get attached to the Support Unit at the beginning of '76. He was quite a tad taller than me at 1.83metres (6 feet) and had a slim wiry frame of 75kgs. Sporting a classic Justin Bieber cut (most males had one, unless you were bald or suffered from the frizzies) of light brown hair, and although clean shaven, he grew some really cool (if forbidden), extra-long sideburns. Triggs certainly cut a very professional figure. That was because that was exactly what he was. He was a policeman under contract and had a job to do.

I was to be his reluctant apprentice and learn some rather unorthodox methods of crime control. A pair of coldish grey/blue eyes observed everything with almost forensic ability as suspect after suspect was interrogated. I would sit to one side in silence as Triggs went about his craft. Watching him in action was like being a rabbit caught in the headlights of a car; leaving me confused and rather frightened at the man's style. It didn't seem much related to whatever we had been taught at Morris Depot. I suddenly realised that as far as this bit of police work was concerned, I had been taught nothing at all! The next few days went something like this:

Triggs would sit behind the larger of the two desks, usually leaning back on the chair's back legs with his desert boot-clad feet resting on the desktop. In his right hand was a large and rather heavy, lacquered copper 18" long ruler, which would constantly be pounded into his left palm at various speeds and strength - depending on the way things were going.

A constable would bring in turn the suspects and sit next to them in front of Triggs. It was the constable's job to translate. Mostly the suspects were male, dressed in ragged, scruffy and often smelly mixes of T-Shirts and long trousers. Many were barefoot with calloused soles of thick skin. The poor sods looked rather miserable, with hands manacled together and shoulders humped over as they answered the many authoritative questions of the constable. The majority arrested were being charged with petty crimes of theft.

Triggs took no notes, just listened casually as the accused would protest his innocence and when the bleating and pleading grew longer and louder; so would the pace of the ruler increase. The question and answer session would be occasionally interrupted by the constable using his knowledge of his race to express his honest opinion from his African point of view.

"PO Triggs, Sah. I am telling you, this man is lying. Aah, I am tired of this rubbish he is talking."

And then, Triggs had enough. With the speed of a striking puff-adder, the ruler came down onto the desk with a mighty smash. Simultaneously, shooting to his feet and leaning over the desk like a striking cobra, he pushed his face right into the hapless man's space. He would start shouting in a mixture of Shona and English. Most of this I couldn't catch as I only knew perhaps two dozen words of the lingo, and most of them were derogative - me a real townie boy. However, the insinuation was rather self-explanatory that he, Senior Patrol Officer Triggs had taken a lot of time and energy typing out sworn statements from two witnesses that swore on their grandmother's grave they saw YOU do it. This means, YOU go to jail. Now, as I can't be arsed to type out a load of lies, just admit to it and there won't be any trouble. This was followed by a few loud intensive smacks of the ruler either on the desk, making everything jump (including me and the suspect), or directed, if the accused was a bit stubborn, a smart whack to the back of his shoulders. This would raise puffs of dust accompanied by some rather drama queen wailing from the about to be condemned criminal without his non-existent human rights.

Besides, in some respects they were lucky. They may even get to see the sights of Salisbury while doing something worthwhile, like trimming the councils' gardens or breeding budgerigars in Chikurubi prison to sell to daft people like my late father. All this and more - like free food, accommodation, new mates and clean clothing. What more could a naughty thief want! They would come out reformed and live happily ever after or join the gooks if they had been mistreated. This was highly unlikely as not even the Rhodesians water-boarded people for stealing two chickens.

I will grant Triggs this, I didn't particularly like his method - but I was certainly impressed with the results. After each and every suspect agreed to their respective guilt, Triggs would start typing up a charge sheet document which would then be placed in a slim vanilla cover. This numbered and dated docket also contained copies of witness statements and the occasional 'Warned and Cautioned' statement. This was supposed to be a precursor before being charged, but Triggs liked to save time and energy by skipping that bit.

And as for typing! What a laugh. The ancient tiny portable machine, nestled in a splitting cardboard case with peeling, fake black leather, could barely cope with the four A4 blank papers of beige/white recycled paper and three well used carbon papers jammed in its carriage roll. To get the antique to actually print through this massive load, Triggs had to strike the keys with such violence it made the suspect shit himself with fear. Triggs kept things short and simple.

"You are now charged with…." such and such etc, Triggs would drone on in a bored tone with the accused, now convinced of his own guilt, answering

"Yes Sir I did it and I am sorry."

This would be shortened to, "I did it." (No mitigating circumstances acceptable. Far too much effort and the judge won't believe him being sorry anyway.)

"Sign your name here."

"I cannot write."

"No problem, make your mark here." Triggs would reply. This comprised of a guided hand making an 'X' on the four copies with the typed statement under the X, 'His Mark' and that was that - job done.

This was fascinating stuff to watch but I had a feeling my own personality tended to be on the side of the underdog and that I wouldn't be running off to Kingstons stationary and bookstore in the near future to get a copper ruler.

It now poured almost every day flatdogs and shumbas big time, for the rainy season was in full swing, and meant we didn't go on raids. Triggs would try to take statements from the camp's live-in complainants, but that became a joke as you could hardly hear a thing over the deluge of rain, which in an ear blasting crescendo pelted against the corrugated iron roof. I tried to talk to him in the evenings when he called shop, and opened his first Castle, but he wasn't quite the chatty type.

I did find a couple of things we had in common though. We didn't like the same music and we didn't read the same books. I also came to the rapid conclusion that he was sick to death of my gabbing gob. But I discovered one of his weaknesses though. He liked to play poker for money! Got ya! One serious error - we used credit on paper and matches as five cent chips. That whiled the nights away, but I had a bad feeling about getting my winnings.

One morning a constable told Triggs that they had no more fresh nyama. That much in Shona I knew. Triggs told him to go out and shoot something. Bad idea I thought, we might be in the bush, but this area was quite heavily populated and I hadn't exactly seen herds of free range nyama wandering about. I thought maybe Triggs was mad enough to be a cannibal. That afternoon we were presented with a shot duiker antelope, a rather small scrawny thing.

Triggs told them to take the lot but bring the fillets. When they arrived he opened a bottle of red wine and left the bloody meat to marinate. I liked doing a bit of cooking ever since I had won first place in a Boy Scout cooking competition; so I watched his culinary preparation skill with interest - there wasn't any.

Around about knocking-off time Triggs put the wine-soaked, coagulated mess on the gas stove and let it fry away for the time it took the rice to cook. Rhodesian rice was nice, but it wasn't exactly Uncle Bens. In fact, if you didn't keep out a wary eye, you landed up crunching on a tiny piece of granite that had gotten through the filtering system. If you bit onto one, you felt your head would explode and would be lucky not to be spitting out fillings and tooth chips. The wine was Rhodesian and was sold commercially for paint stripping if a blow torch failed to do the trick. So there we were that evening, sitting at the little table, fried duiker fillets in red wine sauce and rice. It was friggin vile. So was the rest of the wine. Triggs was clever enough not to drink the filth and stuck to warm chibulis. The meat was as tough as Triggs and just as wiry. I was still very wary of Rhodie wine, recalling my first adventure with the stuff at the Boy Scout's annual general meeting that had caused a riot, but, that as I mentioned previously, is another abominable story.

Memoir mutterings

Email from Nigel Triggs -

I was a hard arsed little shit in those days but having been in the bush a lot before joining the cops and having been close to the black population, I thought I understood their ways...and what was needed to make them talk! Maybe in your eyes I was a cruel bugger but hey, the cops was a tough job....no use spending 20 hours talking nicely when I could get them to chirp after 10 minutes!

Glossary

Ag-shame. A combination of **Ag**, a multi purpose word, usually at the start of a sentence, pronounced like the German 'ach', also a stand-alone expletive, and ***shame,*** an expression used by women on seeing a cuddly animal or crying ***piccanin*** or a wry comment upon hearing about a ***china's babelaass***.

Babelaas. Pronounced 'Bub-ba-lars'. Hangover of ***maningi*** proportions.

Flatdog. Crocodile.

Maningi. Abundance, plenty.

Nyama. Red meat.

Piccanin. Usually a small child, regardless of race. Also anything that is small.

Shumba. Lion, the animal, and also a type of beer.

me at Sengwa base camp

CHAPTER 10:

Teaching trials and tribulations

Before the year was out, a packed Landy driven by a white man turned up. Triggs was being relieved.

I carefully perused the PO getting out the vehicle. A few black policemen were with him. Shift change, except I was staying. I stood well back in fear of perhaps another dangerous loon taking an instant dislike to me as Triggs blabbed a bit with this slightly plump individual with golden wavy hair, a boxer's nose below a serious dark pair of Terminator style sunglasses. Then Triggs was gone. Bye-bye you nutter - so what we got in store next? A cocky swagger as we meet and greet but Patrol Officer Alan Golden was in order. Firstly, he was a Salisbury dude schooled north of the railway divide, mainly at Churchill High School (that was almost as good as Mount Pleasant High), and secondly, he had a brain tuned into themes other than beer and cold shoulders. Thirdly, he played poker too and coughed up his loss.

My new teacher, who had been a PO for 10 months by now, continued my lessons in a rather different style. Now it would be learning about the locals and exploring the area. Alan took me to meet the local chief. Chief Jiri was a man who commanded high respect within his community. He was top of the chain of local indigenous self-government with several dozen headmen under his jurisdiction. In turn, a headman would have several kraal heads, which were authorised to allocate land to the adult males with families living together in a close knit system of kraals. Effectively the chief was the overseer of several thousand people.

Chief Jiri's kraal consisted of many mud and thatch rondavels and a mortar and brick school. The oblong building consisted of plastered half-walls, the rest open to the elements rather than having windows, and it had a low sweeping thatch roof over the structure. The place was spotless. A large blackboard attached to the back wall was the most prominent feature. There were also small, single school desks and stools for about 30 primary school children.

As we arrived, Alan told me that this was simply a courtesy call. Ah, so we weren't likely to be kicking any doors in. When we arrived the chief greeted us from his place seated under a huge acacia tree providing shade over the cleared earthen plaza where he held 'court'. Several headmen sat respectfully in a semi-circle before him. In his 50s with a grey beard, the chief was attired in a mixture of European clothing and home-cured animal skins of uncertain origin.

We greeted all and sundry starting with the chief, politely in English, and in turn were acknowledged with return greetings and smiles of welcome in Shona. The chief called one of his wives to bring us tiny hand-carved Batonka wooden stools, and the gathered entourage made space for us. Alan asked after the chief's health and whether there were any problems. As they conversed, another of the chief's wives appeared with a gourd made out of a dried pumpkin shell that was filled with some evil smelling concoction. Alan accepted the offering, took a long draught, and passed it on to me.

The chief and those whom he had been holding council with, all watched me in anticipative delight. I looked into the gourd and was suddenly reminded of the contents of the stomach of the autopsy I had witnessed. My stomach churned almost as much as what was churning in the gourd. The liquid smelt sour, and was a creamy light brown in colour with tiny bits of crushed red millet floating around. The whole lot sort of fizzed a bit, but not like when you pour Coke into a glass. More like when it has been sitting in a warm glass for an hour. I reluctantly took a couple of swigs of this bitter stuff. Ugh, I knew I would never get a taste for this beer. The assembled tribesmen all laughed merrily at my expression when I put the gourd down to be passed onto the next in line.

"I see our new PO is not like PO Saunders. Where is he? He would drink for hours with us when he came visiting," the chief chortled.

This was very interesting input. So drinking plenty of this stuff was part of the way of going bush! Then a snack arrived fresh from the constant fire, tended a few paces away by yet another of the chief's wives. (At this point I started to think that I would rather be a future chief than a commissioner. All these wives would be very handy indeed!) We were presented with a pile of strange small black things heaped into a pyramid on a well chipped, sky blue enamel tin plate. I looked at Alan blankly.

"There're roasted flying ants," and taking a handful he popped them into his mouth. "Not bad actually," he mumbled between crunching.

I gave them a quick sniff, and finding them smelling quite appetizing, I gave it a go. I was well surprised. They tasted just like heavily salted popcorn you bought at the movies, but only the bits at the bottom of the bag. Remembering my manners, I refrained from polishing the lot off. I did have to shut out my mind's eye of the mental image of the creepy crawler's previous lifecycle as a winged termite attempting to procreate. After every short heavy rain that ended an hour before sunset, the steaming warm earth would disgorge millions of these things that fell in our food and crawled about the place after leaving tons of wings all over our main room's concrete floor.

"PO Golden," said the chief, "we have some problems. The store has no supplies and with no buses running, things are hard and I need fuel for my Landrover."

Alan assured Chief Jiri he would radio Internal Affairs in Gokwe village and tell them to send some petrol down. The chief had taken care of a few small crimes, but there was one thief that he would hand over to us. All this was done through a patient constable who even translated the jokes and banter that delightedly went backwards and forwards. Then came the thorny question of any terrorist activity in the area disturbing the chief's subjects. No, all was quiet here. This was excellent news. We bid farewell and moved on.

I was full of questions. What happened to Joe Saunders here? How come the chief had a Landy better than ours? Why has the local store no supplies?

We drove to the Sengwa River Bridge. This was freaky, because if you simply followed the dirt road straight on, you would fall off the river bank and down a five story high drop onto the remains of a collapsed bridge. Dark brown water was rushing madly past huge broken columns of concrete and twisted reinforcing steel poking out at crazy angles through the torrent. There was another bridge a couple of hundred paces downstream, but the new dirt track leading to it wasn't so well spread out from traffic. Alan wanted to look how the new construction was coping with the Sengwa River now well in flow. Alan explained that the first bridge had collapsed during a flood a couple of years back, and that the new bridge had been built just that winter when the river wasn't much more than a trickle.

We looked a bit apprehensively at the new design structure. Instead of columns, this was a massive solid red brick affair with huge galvanised metal tunnels for the raging brown water to channel through. But the swirling angry mass was starting to back up. Trees, pulled from their precarious holds on the sandy banks by the flooding river on its journey down from the Mafungabusi plateau firstly westward, then turning north, passing through the Chirisa Game Reserve before entering Lake Kariba, had become tangled knots blocking the entrances through the bridge. Now the backed-up water was starting to lick the top, shoving up dirty brown foam bubbles full of bits of bush grass being smashed to smithereens against the stuck trees. No one was making even the slightest attempt to unlock these plugged holes.

The local inhabitants didn't waste time crossing. Instead of nattering to fellow travellers, they dashed across in fear of their lives whilst pushing overloaded bicycles or whipped their donkeys pulling the homemade wooden Scotch carts. Alan said that as far as he knew, the civil engineers couldn't sink decent foundations into the sand bed of the Sengwa, resulting in the collapse of the last attempt. Looking at this latest effort and the mass of water pushing against it, I had the distinct impression that this version wouldn't hold out much longer either. Hence the hectic speed of the crossing. I just hoped we were not driving over it when it did give way.

We stopped at the local store and went in. Sure enough stocks were low. During the rainy season, any trucks and commercial buses were forbidden to drive on the sidaga roads. They would simply become impassable, a churned up quagmire of clay and slush with deep ruts. What little did come through was on small bakkies, but they couldn't keep up with the demand.

On New Year's Eve we played poker. I told Alan about my terrible fear for my Precious. I told him it was in a room where a troll lived. He laughed.

"Why, who or what is the thing that occupies that room?" I asked.

"He is a mentally retarded Afrikaner by the name of Nico Meyer. He likes to sneak off at night, using a police Landrover, and with his issue rifle shoot anything that moves with the aid of spotlights."

Holy shit, I was going to share a bedroom with a natural born killer!

I pictured the ultimate stereotype of a rock-spider: sloped forehead, no neck, beady tiny dark eyes, powerful hairy arms, knuckles scraping the dirt as he shuffled about grunting and shouting in obscene Afrikaans at any black person whilst shooting at anything with horns or riding a bicycle.

"He would sell the meat to the locals and keep some skins and horns and stuff as souvenirs," Alan continued. Looking at my alarmed face, "Don't worry, he got caught and as far as I have heard, he will not be coming back after his little spell in Morris Depot police cell."

Alan set my fear-induced racing heart at rest as he informed me that the mad thing was being transferred to Que Que, from where they could keep a proper eye on him.

So here was another way to leave Gokwe! (Later I met this troll thing and I must confess he fitted my image perfectly, except his arms were not quite that long.)

"What about Joe Saunders? What happened to him?"

"Oh, he had been too long in Gokwe and started to disappear for large lengths of time amongst the local inhabitants. They had him transferred out before he went totally native."

Somehow I didn't fancy this option either. We stayed up to see the New Year through. At exactly midnight, we called in the night guard and had our photo taken by him. Alan brandishes his privately owned .38 revolver and I have the guard's single round shotgun cradled in my arm as we clown about. I actually look quite happy!

Along with the thief that Chief Jiri had handed over, there were witnesses. Alan thought that it was time I tried out my skills at taking a statement from them. My effort was to test and try both Alan and the translating constable's patience, but of course genius can be very frustrating – especially mine.

After managing to stuff the wad of paper and carbon into the dilapidated typewriter, I was ready and listened intently. Every few sentences I would start to hack at the keys. Three hours later, Alan, who had left me alone on this exercise returned, and looked amazed at the huge pile of typed copies. Picking up page one, he read out it out aloud -

"The witness awoke to the crowing of his cockerels greeting another morning approximately between 5.00 and 6.00am because the rising sun was covered by angry dark clouds that threatened rain at any moment. After making passionate love to wife number four and before his wife number three called that breakfast was ready, the witness went outside to pass water and had to give the noisy barking dog a swift kick which sent it howling off into the bush. The witness returned to his abode and waited for his breakfast. Unfortunately the sadza had been over cooked and was rather..."

"Excuse me PO Golden, Sah. The witness and I are a bit tired. Could we take a break please," interrupted the constable.

"Yes, Yes, of course," said Alan as he looked up.

"When should I return with the witness?"

"Tomorrow, tomorrow. I need to talk to PO Greenberg."

I smiled to myself. This was pure brilliance I had written. I still might make Chief Inspector in two years. I thought of leaning back and putting my feet on the desk as Alan continued to read out loud. I could tell by his body language he was impressed.

"...unfortunately the sadza had been over cooked and was rather..." He stopped and brought the paper to me.

"Your spelling is atrocious, what the hell is this word?" He pointed at 'artroshus'.

"Atrocious." I said. It seemed bloody obvious to me. Alan grunted and continued.

"...the sadza had been overcooked and was rather atrocious and the witness gave his wife number three a slap which sent her off wailing into the bush. The witness then stormed out into the coming storm and went down to see if his wifes...wives? God help me... had been lazy and not planted enough mealies as with the good rains he hoped that there would be enough food..." Alan was sweating a bit now. I grinned and leaned back.

"Are you fucking insane? I thought you said you had 'O'level English - not 'O'level Gibberish."

I didn't recall writing that bit, so obviously he was quoting out of context. I leaned forward again and started to sulk. He went on a bit like my late father reading my school report. I hoped he wouldn't hit me. It's not my fault I am also an undiagnosed dyslexia sufferer.

"The judge doesn't want to read this shite. Keep this tripe till you write your memoirs. He wants facts, facts, facts!"

Picking up the huge pile I had so beautifully compiled, he thrust them in my face.

"Please, before either of us have a heart attack; where in this novel is the part where the witness saw the accused steal the fucking bicycle?"

"I was getting to that bit just as you arrived." I was upset now. Alan was shouting at me. I thought he was my friend.

Alan sighed.

"Listen, just cut to the facts. Do you know what a précis is?"

Of course I did.

"Yes, but I wasn't very good at them at school."

"Why not?"

"Well, I tended to take the piece I was supposed to précis, and, I tended to make the précis longer than the original bit I was supposed to précis; because I thought it was missing bits."

Alan sat down. He looked rather tired. I was still sulking that he didn't like my adjectives.

"Didn't Nigel teach you anything?"

"Oh yes, he did. He could get people to chirp real quickly by using a giant ruler. Is this the way?"

Alan looked confused for a moment.

"You don't hit the witness; he is on your side." He stood up and tried to gather his thoughts.

"What is a poem?"

I didn't like poetry but had the answer.

"You take a book and in a few words tell the whole story."

Alan turned triumphantly to me.

"Exactly! Become a poet. It's as simple as that."

I mulled over this for a few seconds while stuffing the tired old typewriter with another load, I wrote

Witness Statement from AMA Lovemore Sibanda

I awoke and left my abode
For urine I needed to dispose
I saw the accused at length
A bicycle he steels with strength.

Signed: Lovemore Sibanda – his mark.

Alan looked at this.
"Now you're getting the idea, but you spelt 'steals' wrong."

I think that Alan rather liked being my teacher. School outings were great fun and very educational. Not only that, the scenery was stunning. The natives seemed cheerful enough and waved enthusiastically as we tootled along. Being paid to play tourist was certainly up there among my favourite ways to earn money by doing the littlest as possible. Ah, this was the life. On the downside, we didn't have a tape deck in the Landy. Bit of a bummer. I just had to imagine the chords of the *Out of Africa* main theme, 'I had a farm in Africa, till the gooks stole it', soaring to the heavens as we zipped through the game reserve, past herds of elephants, kudus and the occasional lions. All I needed now was a wicked wench and a chilled glass of vodka, lime and lemonade, served to me by a waiter wearing white gloves over black hands; to make my life fulfilled.

On one of these safaris, weather permitting, I met National Parks head ranger, Tony, and his wife. This slightly built character was in charge of the 40,000 hectare combination of Chirisa Game Reserve (which was in Gokwe TTL) and Chizarira National Park, on its western border. This was a place of undisturbed beauty of miombo and mopane trees, scattered between bush scrub. Tony had been there almost three years and loved his job with a passion. He had to: this place was about as remote as it could get. At the park headquarters, Hostes Nicholle Wildlife Research Station, which sat on a hill surrounded by yellow and orange mopane trees and where the Sengwa River ran under cliffs of lemon-brown limonite, I was to meet some remarkable people. To get to the complex we had crossed the Sengwa River gorge. The concrete bridge was tiny; barely the length of the Landrover, but below, the river had cut a deep and wide chasm into the soft surrounding rock, creating almost a tunnel with a narrow slit open to the sky.

There was a tiny clique of white people, with a few foreign scientists working on several projects in well-equipped laboratories. The place had been built by the government under the direction of the then Interior Minister (after which the place was named), in the early '70s and was one of the finest research centres in Africa. From one of the scientists I was to learn that one group had come all the way from America to study the place due to an unknown species of bats that lived there. They were using ultrasonic bat detectors and light tags while examining the type of insect prey along with the bats' habitat use. I was seriously impressed, but the best bit was when I met a genial young scientist by the name of Rowan Martin.

In a large laboratory, riddled with bleeping machines with little TV faces showing strange zig-zag lines, Rowan showed me his handmade fibreglass collars with imbedded transmitters that could be attached around an elephant's neck. They used very little battery power, could last 12 months and be picked up by his masts as far as 15 kilometres. On huge maps on the wall, the enthusiastic man showed me where he had his rotational masts scattered all over the area and by triangulating the signal he and his staff had been plotting the route and distance travelled by the herds through the park. He was very excited with the results and I tried to keep up. He explained that by using his masts, Park Rangers on foot, monitoring every three hours, 24/7, and spotters in light aircraft, he had discovered a new, unknown level of the elephant as a 'clan' beyond just within a 'normal' family that could see and hear each other. In fact, there was something going on that didn't make sense.

What I didn't know at the time, nor he, was that this research laid the cornerstone for one of the most amazing discoveries of the animal kingdom – namely, that elephants can communicate over vast areas using infrasonic sound. They use a decibel range so low that we humans cannot hear it.

All this was incredibly interesting stuff, and I was dragged away, reluctantly, by Alan. On the way back to the Landy, I spotted a couple of young whites among the scattered sheds, but they would have nothing to do with us. Alan explained they were Americans on some sort of aid project and insisted on working for the same rate of pay as the blacks. We police were considered bad guys by these Yanks, and I considered them idiots for working for a buck a day.

On the way back to base we came across a troop of vervet monkeys. Alan, besides having his own pistol, also carried his FN and a .303 rifle with which he shot a monkey straight out of a tree, blasting its head to pieces and handing the brainless corpse to the black staff. It was well received as they were desperate for some fresh nyama. Luckily, Alan didn't ask for the fillets or a monkey gland steak. I think I would have been sick.

And then, with most of the crime back-log sorted out or put on hold, and with fuel running low, we were called back to Gokwe village. At last I would be reunited with my beloved Precious.

me and Alan - New Year 1977
Pic - Alan Golden

Memoir mutterings

Of the central characters mentioned no longer in this memoir: –
9139 PO Jonathan 'Jo' Saunders. Retired, Pension and other benefits. November 1981

Email from Alan Golden –
Shot a Kudu outside the park driving down from Chirama once and went through to Hostes Nichole and grilled two fillets to the delight of the Americans and the horror of Parks. Thought I was going to get lucky but only got to cop a feel!

Email from Mike Harvey -
There was Chief Jire and Chief Sai (I think!) south of Chirama (police base) and one other in the Kana area, whose name I can't recall, something like Nkoka; all Ndebele. The people here were generally ZAPU supporters. To the west were Chief Huchu and one other, again whose name I can't remember and both shifty Shonas. These people had been resettled in this wild wilderness with a lack of water requiring a long line of many boreholes to keep the populace happy. Ha! Ha! This was a particularly bad politically, with much cause to complain about, anti-government and very pro-ZANU. All this was situated below the plateau on the way west to Chirisa Game Reserve.

Glossary

Bakkie. Two door cab and open back vehicle.
Batonka. Also known as Tonga or BaTonga, are a subsistence farming tribe split by the Zambezi and Lake Kariba.
Mealies. Maize.
Out of Africa. Theme from the film. I am using a bit of futuristic musical ambience that is set in the not so far distant past. With the advent of music being introduced to eBooks, I thought I should get a jump start. What else could I use – Matt Munroe singing the theme song from the film *Born Free*? Hardly, since most of the populous didn't think so.
Rock-spider. A South African of Boer descent. Not to be mixed with the Australian terminology of the same name which refers to child molesters and the lowest rank in the prison cell inmate's hierarchy.
Sidaga. Seriously sticky shitty red mud. Landrovers were known to love the stuff and would wallow happily in it for hours.
Sadza. Boiled mealie meal made from maize.
Wikipedia. Great place to look up all the acronyms below.
ZANU. ZIMBABWE AFRICAN NATIONAL UNION. Gang of misinformed, murderous gooks led by Archangel Robert Gabriel Mugabe from shifty Shona land thieves origin. They 'rightfully' took the land from the *Rozvi* and *Torwa* tribal states.
ZAPU. Zimbabwe African Peoples Union. Same as ZANU but led by Joshua Nkomo of shifty *Ndebele* (ex-Zulu descent land thieves of the above Shona), origin.

Alan gets us stuck in the mud again
Pic - Gokwe Kid

CHAPTER 11:

There is life in Gokwe – but not as we know it

The first thing I noticed that stood out and caught my attention as we walked into the Charge Office was a great pair of tits. They were attached to a small petite blonde woman of about thirtyish in a very tight grey Police Reserve uniform with a rather short skirt showing some nice leg. Long fingernails painted bright red, along with matching lipstick spread over a pair of succulent and very saucy full lips. What a sight for sore eyes. I had started to believe I would never see a white woman again. She greeted Alan with a smile. She looked at me questioningly. I gave her my number one grin questionably and introduced myself.

"Hi, I'm Karl Greenberg." The little bundle of fun grinned back and stuck her hand out,

"Gail Rowley, pleased to meet you. I'm a part time receptionist here."

Before my hopeful fantasies started to go ape-shit, I was introduced to her husband. Section Officer Mike Rowley. Oh well, back to reality with a bump.

Next, while Alan knocks on a door but gets no reply, I'm busy saying "Hi!" to the black policemen managing the charge office entrance. I observed that Triggs was doing his thing in his own office as we went on to the boss who worked in the last room in the row of offices before the corridor turned right, along the 'L' shape of the building towards the armoury and store room.

The boss welcomed us back and I was given the rest of the day off to settle into my new habitat. We went back down the corridor, open on one side to the elements and lined with breeze-blocks, past the charge desk and radio room and into the largest office with at least five huge wooden desks. Two individuals were typing away furiously at more ancient typewriters, but at least these were normal sized ones like I had used at Morris Depot.

First up was Nick Robinson, a National Service Patrol Officer, easy to spot because of the green shirt. He was a tall lad the same age as myself, with a sharpish nose and sandy coloured hair. We exchanged a handshake and a '*Howzit*' and then finally PO Peter

Brockbank, the miserable looking bloke who had been in the front cab on that fateful afternoon driving up to Gokwe. He looked up at me with clear blue eyes, blinking nonstop.

"I'm your new roommate. You will like it here," Brockbank mumbled miserably. I presumed he was referring to the troll's pit – judging by the slight hint of sarcasm.

Still following Alan we went down a small path past a tiny swimming pool to the white policemen's single quarters. There was a living room, dining room and kitchen incorporated in a corrugated iron roofed building. I was introduced to our cook, Wilson, a tall happy middle-aged African. He greeted me cheerfully. I took an instant liking to the man. Then a few paces further, the row of identical attached bedrooms - Alan's, the troll's and lastly Nick's. Alan pointed out the separate tiny house another 50 paces away with its own carport, housing Triggs, who being the Senior PO, had privileges. I was then left alone.

I cautiously opened the troll's room. I was gob smacked. The only difference from the last time I had been here was that the bed in a corner had real human possessions on it next to a couple of half unpacked suitcases. This Brockbank person had been in this tip for three weeks and done absolutely sod all! And the SMELL! I nearly heaved. It was time to get organised. I went over to Wilson and asked if he could rustle up a few cardboard cartons. No problemo. The boxes duly turned up with Wilson along with a young lad whom the cook announced was to be my new batman. Thomas was maybe 17 going on 15. Bloody hell, that was quick! No need to put an advert in the Rhodesia Herald under employment available -

Wanted, a batman. Must be honest. Is to do all that he is told for his white policeman bwana in Gokwe. (Yes, you heard right, Gokwe.) You will be badly paid but not mishandled as the boss is a nice man.

Nope – none of that nonsense. As soon as my strange white face had appeared in the very black badlands, the peasants were queuing up for a job! After some haggling over how much, we settled on a sum of 15 bucks a month. The smiling young teenager thanked me. So did I, then gave him the bag of filthy stinking clothes from my trip and grinned.

"Washed and ironed by tomorrow please."

"Ok, Sah," and he was off with much enthusiasm.

It wasn't long before he was soon back with Wilson in tow and I had to cough up a couple of dollars to buy things like washing powder.

    I couldn't tolerate the state of the room. This was disgusting. I didn't think human beings could live like this. The boss had earlier confirmed that the troll would not be returning. It was almost impossible to describe the shit I found. Letters from lawyers and final demands scattered in drawers along with an assortment of dirty rancid clothes: bits of animals and stuff created from materials I couldn't work out their origins. Into the boxes went all of it. An hour later, and feeling rather clever, the lot, including the stinking curtains, were out. I gave a shout to Wilson and the cartons were soon placed into storage, although the fire under the Rhodie-boiler would have been the better option. The curtains joined the pile of my filthy kit to be washed after I had Thomas furiously clean the windows, and sweep and mop the concrete floor. In the meantime Wilson had organised a second clothes cupboard and handed me fresh bedding. I had no idea where they had come from and, better still, I wasn't ever charged for. With two beds and two cupboards, the room was beginning to get a little cramped, but I still managed to fit in a small desk, which Wilson miraculously found for me from nowhere, on which my Precious would take pride of place.

    By the time the others knocked off at 4.30pm, I had my screaming baby singing the sweet sounds of the British Top Ten. The other POs all marched in to hear the latest Bellamy Brothers hit *Let Your Love Flow* and commented that they could see in the room now. Ah, the envy. Hah! I had their attention now. After Nick and Alan returned to their respective rooms, I asked new roommate, Peter, why he had let the room stay as it was rather than sort it out. He whimpered pathetically about his girlfriend and how her dad would get him out of Gokwe soon – and some other crazy bullshit. I very quickly came to the conclusion that he was harmless and very, very useless.

    I pestered everyone with my chatter at dinner and listened to some of Peter's drivel when we returned to our room. What a loser! Madly in puppy love with some young chick in Que Que, the owner of the Fair-Mile Motel's 17 going on 18 year old daughter. According to him, he was only here because the Chief Superintendent and this girl's father were friends. Daddy had complained about his *amour* and here he was. Crazy as it sounded it could be true. After I got shafted with a golf club, anything was possible from that bastard of an officer.

I pointed out to weeping willow Peter the illogic of his argument for not cleaning up the room. If big bad Daddy had arranged for his exile, how come he thought the same person would eventually rescue him? The answer that his 'honey' had promised to persuade Daddy to let him back seemed a rather contemptibly inadequate excuse for lying on his bed in the middle of a stinking tip, and moaning his ill-fortune all night.

At seven in the morning, and after a wash and quick buzz with the electric razor, I joined the others in the dining room for a huge breakfast of bacon, eggs and sausages along with horrible coffee. (I would to have to show Wilson how to make my cappuccino.) Then, in my nice clean and very smart uniform of a rural policeman, off I went with the others to work. Past the pool, glistening invitingly, and into the Charge Office. Everyone split to their desks. I had no idea what I was supposed to do. I wandered over to the boss's office and knocked.

"Come."

I walked in and we were alone for the first time. I wondered if I was going to be questioned about any nocturnal bush desires with dark ladies that might have surfaced.

"Sir, good morning, what do I do now?"

"Aah, Greenberg, good morning, settled in then?"

I murmured that I was.

"Good, then I would like you to work with PO Triggs – so better to get the rope and hang of things around here."

Hah-hah, either I had a hearing problem or the boss had a speech impediment. To me it sounded like,

'Work with Triggs and better get a rope and hang yourself.'

"One other thing," he added, "I need $90 from you."

I think I am going penga. What now? Am I being fined for being sent to Gokwe or has he found out I don't drink beer and this is the punishment?

Watching my face with those observant eyes I would get to know so well,

"It's for single Patrol Officer's food and Wilson's wages for December," he explained.

Hang on a moment there. The only food I ate in December, which I hadn't paid for, was a few cold chicken bones from his wife's Christmas present. Now I'm to pay $90 for this? This would make it the most expensive chicken in Rhodesia, if not the entire planet. As for Wilson, I only met the man yesterday and I have to pay him for never meeting him in December? This was all doing my head in.

"Unfortunately the mess books don't add up and the only way to clear the debt is to make all POs pay $90 to clear the debit," the boss kindly explained.

Mess? Mess! It bloody was a mess all right! When it came to my wallet I wanted to know which Einstein was responsible for this stock market crash. Let me guess.

"PO Triggs has done an outstanding job running the books under such difficult circumstances blah, blah, and sadly I am not in the position to simply print money to cover the over expenditure."

I wasn't listening; blood was pounding in my head. I thought I would pass away. This would leave me almost completely skint! Along with other costs, I was still paying back my step-mom $50 a month for my air fare back here. I was close to asking to have myself certified! I mean, I had borrowed money to get a job and now must give my hard earned taxed cash away to strangers who had over spent! They all been having bunga-bunga parties and expect me now to bung them my dosh to cover it? Hah-hah...*ego insanio*!

"...and, if you get Nigel to show you how to fill out your application for bush allowance, I will authorise the payment immediately."

How nice. Give a buck with one hand and take two with the other. I considered kicking up a right old storm. The boss couldn't exactly order me to cough up 10 days pay for nothing, but I was smart enough to realise that this would not start our future relationship on a friendly professional footing.

Well pissed-off I marched into Trigg's office and considered briefly to shoot him on the spot. At least I wouldn't have to pay for the bullet. He was surprised at my tone. With my eyes flashing danger, and my finger itching on the FN's trigger, I leaned over his desk, and between gritted teeth,

"Listen Nigel, I'm being forced to pay out 90 fucking bucks due to your book keeping. I've also been told to be your shadow until I orientate myself. Please show me how to fill in the forms so I can claim my bush allowance money so I can give it all to you and the rest of what is left of my wages."

By the time Wilson arrived at 10 with either coffee or tea for everyone, I had cooled down but became immediately suspicious I was getting knocked here too. Maybe it was $5 a cup here? How else could the bookkeeping be so bad huh?

Triggs had me running little errands that gave me time to meet more people and get the layout of the police station. There was Tess Erasmus, the wife of one of the Tsetse control men. She also had a part time job as a secretary and radio message operator. A nice woman with long hair in a ponytail, largish arse but very amicable to my sunny boy approach.

I found out that the unoccupied office belonged to a certain man of mystery - Inspector Andy Gray. It turns out he was second in charge, ex-Support Unit and looked after the patrolling aspect of the station. When SB (Special Branch) and CID (Criminal Investigation Department,) operated in the area he would also liaise with them. In other words, they were gook hunters. It was his and the boss's part time secretary who frightened the shit out of me. This woman, who didn't fall for my snake charming, was Mrs Trish Anderson whose husband Andy, was tied up with the Tsetse Department cattle section. The grey haired lady in her 50s had a handshake and voice that was enough to toss me back to Alan Wilson Technical High School and my Afrikaans teacher Mrs Smuts who had beaten me every day for two years (hence my tendencies to have panic attacks).

Still, all-in-all, besides being robbed in broad daylight by the police, it had been a nice day and after work ended and not before we had more of the $5 a cup of tea from Wilson at 3.00pm, I went for a swim in the cute, warm swimming pool after paying the attendant $15 dollars to hire a deck chair for my towel, $3 for the chlorine, $20 for the life guard, etc, etc…(not really).

Driving around with Triggs or Peter, I started to get the layout of Gokwe village into my head. From the walls in the large office, covered in 50,000:1 topographic maps, I also became familiar with names and places scattered around the immense size of Gokwe TTL. A few months from now, the Rhodesia Sunday Mail sent journalist, Spencer Ratcliff, to Gokwe. This resulted in a two page spread being published. I remembered the article and three decades later, Mike Harvey wrote out the whole thing for me. I will use segments of it here and the rest as the story unfolds...

LIFE CAN BE VERY TOUGH IN GOKWE 'THE DARK INTERIOR OF RHODESIA' IT'S A DOG'S LIFE FOR SOME.

Gokwe police camp is one of the BSAP's most remote district stations. The police were privileged, in that the camp is the only place in Gokwe with a generator.

Gokwe village, set in a triangle between Que Que and Gatooma in the east, and Bumi Hills in the west, has a population of 500 Africans – and when the children are home from school - 48 Europeans. Chief Inspector Harvey's responsibilities did embrace three Tribal Trust Lands, 300,000 Africans living in 1400 kraals, and an area of about 15,000 square kilometres (5,800 square miles) which form an estimated one twenty fifth of Rhodesia. It is a tough area policed by tough men. Others - because it is their job - tolerate it. And at the end of a hard month's work virtually everyone "itches" to get out for a while.

Gokwe, 140km (87ml)) on a dirt road from Que Que, - the nearest accessible centre – and 150km (93ml) from Gatooma, sees a continually changing society. People stay there for just a few years at most, and it takes a special type of bush-loving policeman to take the life in his stride. Gokwe has no shops, no doctor, no dentist and precious little in the way of entertainment. If a Gokwian wants fresh vegetables or fresh meat, he or she must have it brought in from Que Que on the daily bus. Alas, the veggies and meat are not so fresh when they arrive. Hardships there maybe but, as many Gokwians will tell you, there are several compensations.

Elephant, buffalo and other game roam through much of the outlying districts. Keen anglers can nearly always be assured of good catches, and the view from the top of Gokwe's Mafungabusi Plateau - more than 1300m (4,300ft) above sea-level, is breathtaking. If you want to get away from it, there can hardly be a more suitable spot in Rhodesia.

One person who has been getting away from it longer than most in Gokwe is Mrs Trish Anderson. She has lived there with her husband for more than four years.

"I love it here. I don't feel cut off. I always try and avoid getting into town. I hate shopping, I hate traffic, I hate noise and I hate people. Out here it is so beautiful, especially when you just sit down and listen to the bird calls."

Mrs. Anderson is also a member of the Gokwe Police

Women's Field Reserve, and she says her husband Andy - who is in charge of the district's cattle dipping - as "The Moo Man, Everyone calls him that around here," she said.

The calls of the birds are familiar sounds to the Gokwe's Police establishment. The village's first police post was set up in 1914. In those days it was home for two white and four black men whose job was to preserve law and order among the indigenous Batonka and Shankwe Tribes. Now, with what Harvey describes as a 'continued low profile terrorist presence' in his district, the police strength is far greater.

Throughout the 15,000 square kilometres (5,800 square miles) - which embraces the Kana, Gokwe and Sebungwe Tribal Trust Lands plus the beautiful Chirisa safari area and the rich Copper Queen Purchase Area - there are now four police base camps. Chirama, Nembudzia at the base of the Sedaga north of Gokwe, Chireya by a Roman Catholic mission station, Madziwadzido all along the Ume river and Simchembu camp on the Mapungola hills.

Setting up those base camps was a big enough headache, but getting to them during the rainy season can prove impossible. When the rains come, much of the Gokwe district is turned into a quagmire of black clay called 'sidaga'.

"In a few weeks when the rains get worse, we know that one of our Police posts is going to be completely cut-off for a few days," said Chief Inspector Harvey. He also knows he'll be getting frequent calls for help from his men who have - once again - got a vehicle stuck in the sidaga.

The three TTLs have seen a rapid population increase in the past 20 years. The area - because of its availability of land - has proved one of Rhodesia's most popular African resettlement districts. It's Purchase Area has also proved one of the country's most fruitful.

Last year, African farmers there produced cotton valued at about $5 million.

Away from the 'dark interior' and back at the Gokwe Police Camp, Chief Inspector Harvey - who has lived there for two years - outlined his feelings about life in the bush.

"There are disadvantages but one does get used to it," he said. "Having electricity is a luxury, but one does start to feel a bit caged in after a while. There are some tremendous scenic areas around here and some superb fishing, but one is not as free as one used to be because of the security situation. To live here you have got to enjoy the bush, but the hardships – particularly during the rainy season with the sidaga - can prove interesting. You've got to have a sense of humour."

Apart from the Police camp, Gokwe is also a base for small outposts of veterinary, tsetse fly control, Internal Affairs, health, agricultural, prison and CMED officials. Education for the children of all European officials living at Gokwe is one of the village's biggest problems.

Eight village children are at present away at boarding school, and children below the age of seven either have to miss nursery school altogether, or battle with correspondence courses.

"My five-year-old daughter Sally is missing out on nursery education," said Chief Inspector Mike Harvey's wife, Heather. "Before our son Graeme went to boarding school we tried the correspondence course, but we found it difficult."

Something else that Mrs Harvey finds difficult is shopping.

"It is hard without a European shop here, but there is always someone going into Que Que, and everyone rings round to see if people want anything," she said. "I get into town once a month for my shopping but now I try to grow my own vegetables in my garden."

Not having a doctor or dentist can also be a problem, but the African clinic nearby is always helpful.

"People here are a healthy lot, and it's probably just as well they are." Mrs Harvey believes the secret of successful living in the bush is 'adaptability.'

"You've got to be able to get along with everyone. Some people who come here just don't settle because they are not adaptable," she said.

As one of the few 'privileged' Gokwe housewives to have electricity in her home, Mrs Harvey says she cannot complain. However, there are just two things she really misses.

"I'd rather have my son here than at boarding school, and I never get a chance to have my hair done properly in a salon," she added.

Memoir mutterings

The reporter took many photographs. Sadly, the quality of the scans makes them unusable.
Of the central characters mentioned no longer in this memoir -

9339 PO Jacobus 'Nico,' *aka* 'The Troll', Nicolaas Meyer. Own Request (End of Contract). Jan 1978

Email from Mike Harvey
My wife was not one to feel she lost out not having her hair done and was quite embarrassed over this alleged quote

Glossary

Penga. Insane.

CHAPTER 12:

Triggs teaches tricks of the trade - meanwhile weeping willow keeps a-weepin'

The next few weeks saw me learning the art of law as practised by SPO Triggs - methodical, efficient and almost violence free. This was definitely a really exciting time and I rapidly absorbed the way things worked. The Charge Office was manned only by black constables under the control of a senior sergeant. A constant flow of the local populace would wander in to report any matter referred to the police by their respective local chiefs or headmen.

If this constituted a petty crime, usually small time theft or a drunken punch up, bestiality (which always caused howls of derision and laughter from the black staff), and payment of fines, this would be handled by them. If needs-be, a crime docket would be opened and passed on to SO Mike Rowley for direction. He in turn would either forward it on to the boss or pass it back with instructions for more investigation. I concluded that Chief Inspector Harvey's job must have been rather boring as it just seems to consist of going through tons of paper work and he never seemed to leave his office except to use the toilet.

If the crime involved murder, rape, suicide, major theft or terrorism this would immediately be referred to a white patrol officer. The severity of the crime dictated the choice of investigating patrol officer by experience or availability. Triggs, as the most senior amongst us PO's, handled the big ones and I would receive the most amazing education in hands-on policing.

On one occasion we were sent out to an accidental drowning. Taking a constable as translator, we drove along well-worn bush tracks. The villager who had made the report clutched desperately to the thick roll bars encircling the cab as he gave directions to Triggs through the open window. After about half an hour we arrived and parked a short distance from a circle of huts that made up a small kraal. In the open clearing in the centre there had gathered a large circle of men and women, nearly all sitting on the ground in silence.

Most of the older women wore some form of traditional head dress and all the females sat in that unique African way of legs straight out and unbent, a position they could hold for hours.

In the centre of this circle of inquisitively watching humanity, Triggs and I were led by the headman to two small naked bodies lying on a blanket. Two little boys, brothers, aged maybe four and six - with water still trickling out their mouths and noses - looking almost as if sleeping peacefully in a foetal position. Due to the near proximity to Gokwe police station, this tragedy was only a couple of hours old. I bit my lip, and struggled with tears. I had seen death already, I had buried my father at the age of 16 and, of course, had been to the autopsy of the burnt man whilst at Morris Depot. I wondered if this undignified cutting up would apply to these poor little babies.

Triggs listened intently to the headman's explanation and waited for the constable to softly translate and confirm what he himself understood. It would seem that while most of the villagers were in the fields tending their crops, the two children had slipped away. With the alarm raised by their absence, the kraal inhabitants had found them both at the bottom of the shallow open well the villagers used to draw their water from, a short distance away from the kraal.

We went over to the well to investigate. Nigel's eyes moved rapidly around as he circled the well. He looked carefully at the muddle of footprints and then at the surrounding bush. I realised that he was looking for any signs on the ground that would perhaps suggest a struggle or foul play. There was none. Back at the Landrover he raised the police station (call sign 608), on the radio. We were not that far away and as long as there were no hills between us and the police station, the reception wasn't bad. He asked to speak to Chief Inspector Harvey. When he finished he leaned back against the vehicle's side, placing his rifle across the spare tyre on the bonnet, and lit a cigarette.

"What happens now?" I enquired quietly, not wishing to disturb the silence that filled the senses. It almost seemed that the very sounds of the bush had gone quiet in deference to the terrible tragedy that lay on the blanket.

"We wait. The boss will now telephone the District Commissioner for permission to allow the parents to bury the deceased."

"How come the DC?"

Nigel, never one to impart information unless pressurized, went on,

"Protocol is that the boss must relay this information and the request for permission to bury the deceased to the local magistrate. As we have no resident local magistrate here in Gokwe, the next one being in Que Que, it is a lot easier to pass the request down to the next in line – the DC. The DC is the most powerful person in Gokwe TTL. Only he can then authorise the burial at the recommendation of the police." He paused as I absorbed this.

"Not only that, but in this heat, the picanins need to buried as soon as possible."

An ice-cold statement of fact.

A short time later the radio crackled into life.

"Mobile 1, Mobile 1, this 6 Zero 8 over."

"Mobile 1 here, go ahead 6 Zero 8, over," Triggs replied into the small hand held sender.

"Permission granted for the burial, over."

"Copied, 6 Zero 8, over and out." He hung the hand set back on its clip on the dashboard, grabbed his rifle with non-regulation web sling, and slipped it over his right shoulder and made his way back to the patient crowd of waiting people. Through the constable he told the village headman that the funeral could go ahead. The headman immediately informed the throng and suddenly the most frightening crescendo began as dozens of women started to ululate in ever louder shrieks while throwing themselves around in the dust. We quickly returned to the vehicle and were on the way back to Gokwe village: the incident raising goose pimples on my arm in the stifling heat. I was deeply troubled, but had difficulty putting the strange thoughts into some kind of coherent sense. Nigel was totally silent. He didn't seem bothered by what we had just witnessed.

"Nigel," I began hesitatingly, "why did they all just... sort of hang around all still and silent? No one was crying?" I struggled with my thoughts, the whole tragic scenario, it all seemed so...foreign!

Triggs was no natural born teacher. A shame really, as the man had knowledge you wouldn't find in the best universities. Maybe the problem was also the amazing cultural gulf between us! He knew the names of the local trees – I knew the name of every artist on *Lyons Maid Hits of the Week*. He could manoeuvre a Landy through the worst *sidaga* – I could dismantle a twisted cassette tape and edit out the screwed up bits.

"Eish, you ask a lot hey!" Triggs squinted against the smoke of an ever-present fag hanging from his lips as he concentrated on the road and my question.

"The natives treat death differently to us, hey. And," his left hand waved sort of poetically around before returning to the shuddering steering wheel, "It's, well, look, you will check out a lot of deaths in the future. Just remember to keep absolutely neutral and show respect."

Just after lunch one day, in my second week with Triggs, he was finally getting me to understand the difference between a Property Crime Report Form (PCRF) and a Crime Docket (CD). Usually the former was simply a fast-track initial report where the investigator would record the facts but there was usually no suspect. For example: the accused said he woke up and his bicycle was gone. Anyone see the thief? No. Any suspects? No. However, anything more exciting meant opening a docket with all the masses of paper work of witness statements etc. Once the accused was apprehended the whole shabam would go up the ladder of command and the baddie taken to Gwelo for prosecution or, if a minor offence, get put down, fined, or whatever, by our visiting magistrate. The PCRF and dockets where all the avenues of investigation had been exhausted were also required to be passed on to Mike Rowley who would forward them through to the Officer in Charge, the boss, Mike Harvey. He in turn might return it for more investigation or pass it on to the District Headquarters in Que Que to have the case closed by the officer commanding (*aka* 'The Toad'. I am surprised he had the time - what with all the golf he was playing!).

This heavy cerebral session was interrupted by a seriously heavy wailing commotion outside Triggs's door.

"Ah, PO Triggs, there is a woman here who says her daughter has been raped."

A rape! I hadn't done one of those yet. A hysterical teenage girl was now dragged by an extremely irritated middle-aged woman into Nigel's office. According to the victim, who between wailing sobs confirmed her age as being 15, had arrived back at her village kraal from fetching water, and upon being questioned by her mother why it had taken so long, had claimed she had been raped by her uncle. Their headman had insisted that they report the incident immediately and they had spent half the day walking the seven clicks to the police station.

Taking the constable and the headman, Triggs and I were soon at the scene of the crime where the headman identified the culprit who was busy constructing a hut for himself. The man appeared utterly confused by his arrest and whilst manacled insisted that he was innocent, and in fact, the young 'victim' was actually his girlfriend. To back up his claim, he showed us several well hidden 'love nests' in the bush that the couple had used for their little secret trysts. Triggs was quiet as we drove back, but I thought I recognised he was going into that special zone in his head when he thought someone was taking the piss.

At the police station the suspect was left sitting still manacled on a bench in front of the Charge Office desk, and re-entering his office where the two females still sat, Triggs dropped the blinds cutting out any view to the outside world. As he sat down he picked up the solid copper ruler from his desk. I clocked the 'cut the crap' look in his ice-cold grey eyes and knew what was coming - sort off, but when it came even I jumped in shock.

"You're lying you bitch," he roared and smashed the ruler down flat on the desk in front of the startled pair. Neither understood what he had said, but the tone and action was well obvious he wasn't exactly on the girl's side in this plot. Then faster than a light weight boxer - one, two, three smacks to the head of the girl, always careful to use the flat broad blade. The girl started screeching plenty of *'amaiwe amaiwe'* and crying a serious river, while the mother sat in shocked silence.

Triggs looked at the constable who had accompanied us. "Tell her what her uncle told us and what we saw, and tell the bitch if she lies anymore she gets more of this," and at that he reared up like a angry cobra, shot rapidly around the desk and struck the girl across the back of her shoulders with a loud whack.

The constable told the mother who, to my astonishment, screamed at her daughter and slapped her with real force around the head. The girl tried desperately to dodge the flurry of blows while kicking up a right hullabaloo. I stood, frozen, when suddenly the constable, wiping his sweat-covered brow with a handkerchief, burst into a huge grin.

"Ah PO Triggs, you are right, Sah. She admits to having sex many times with the uncle but made up the lie to hide this fact when her mother caught her coming home late."

"Tell them to get out and bring in the suspect," Triggs ordered the constable. The reprieved man was brought inside.

"Constable, tell this man that he is very lucky and will not be charged with rape. However, he will be charged with having sex with a minor."

Which was a bit of bummer, as the stupid shagger had only been out of prison two weeks after serving a five year sentence for murdering his wife in a drunken, jealous rage. I was starting to get an inkling of the black populace's obsession with sex - along with drink. Although, when you think about it, there wasn't much else to do in the form of entertainment out here.

Evenings after dinner were spent reading and listening to my cool vibes. I kept a constant supply of Schweppes tonic water 'nips' under the bed. Loaded with quinine, plus the obligatory tablet once a week, made sure I stayed malaria free. Years before on a disastrous family holiday to Malawi, Bridget had caught an almost lethal dose of this dangerous disease and I didn't fancy having a bout of that.

Weeping willow Peter usually turned up about 9pm after using a police Landy to drive the couple of clicks to Kambasha's store and running up another day's pay on the phone bill from pouring out accusations of the possible infidelity of his love. He had been banned from using the police phone because of excessive non-duty use. Then I was forced to listen to his wretched love life for half an hour. It seems Plan A of his great escape was failing miserably. Through his heart-wrenching retelling of the same drivel at 10 bucks a night, I got the impression the silly cow was either too scared to ask daddy to pull his weight and rescue lover boy, or she was having a grand time without him and the calls were doing her head in. I reckoned it would all stop once he ran out of money. As the newspaper article pointed out -It's a hard life in Gokwe. At least I had persuaded him to actually hang up all his clothes as a stop-gap measure.

The entire white population of Gokwe village (said to mean beehive), were members of the 'sports club' which meant weekend binge sessions. Sports wise there was a tennis court that was used enthusiastically by the boss and Mr. Roy Wyatt, the District Commissioner. It was in far better condition than the so called squash court. This strange building had been designed by a drunk and built using no spirit levels. The bricks had been plastered with cement and the whole 'Pisa' like construction was in a poor state. Balls would sometimes disappear through holes in the walls or ricochet off at interesting angles from the numerous edges of broken render and zip off out the roof (that being the sky) with an interesting buzzing sound to land in the thick bush outside and lie rotting for years.

The sports club was only open at the weekends from at 7pm on Friday night. On Saturday and Sunday it opened at 11am. Closing time was officially 11pm but more usually it was when the last person collapsed. For us POs there was a slight catch. It was called weekend duty Patrol Officer. While we white policeman didn't work over the weekend, the office was constantly manned and anything out of the extraordinary had to be reported to the PO who stayed behind on standby duty. However, if one of us wasn't in the mood to get completely bullala'd he could stand in for one that did.

The actual sports club's building was nothing more than a large shed of brick under corrugated tin divided into a 'bar' area and 'lounge' area, and the toilets. The place would be powered by its own generator that members would contribute a small fee (the police would pay a cheaper block fee from their own funded Police Recreational Club funds), for the diesel and for the couple of black staff who maintained the place. The club didn't need any bar staff as it made little difference which side of the bar we sat. The bar room also had two dart boards which were used every Friday for a competition to win a chicken (plucked and ready to cook). Over the next few months I would participate in this Rhodie-style recreation whenever possible and meet some of the characters who would populate it, but before that I was sent away…

Memoir mutterings

Email from Mike Harvey -
Note: In PCRF the P stands for property related incidents such as theft and the more serious housebreaking cases where there was no suspect. In the case of all other crime where there was a strong suspect or an accused person, a crime docket

would be opened. Various statements and reports, such as medical, forensic evidence, plans, photographs, fingerprint evidence, fingerprints of the accused with his previous convictions, the accused's warned and cautioned statements and possible charge sheets, for serious offences, all of which together, contain sufficient facts necessary to put the accused away.

The accused person should not be detained without sufficient evidence connecting him with the crime, and the police by law could not detain him for more than 48 hours, before which the accused would be required to be arraigned before the magistrates. In a place like Gokwe where there wasn't a resident magistrate, this was not possible, so authority would be arranged via radio message with the facts of the case to Que Que District Headquarters who would make application on our behalf before the resident magistrate. He may or may not grant a Warrant for Further Detention until the next court date in Gokwe. With the State of Emergency things were very different in terms of the Emergency Regulations where the police could almost detain without trial for 30 days!

My comment to the above –

Hah-hah, what an understatement. Actually, things could get extremely confusing. Occasionally The Toad from Que Que would come up for a visit. Not a very friendly one – more like when schools get pounced on by government inspectors. The Boss would have us all running around like decapitated hukus, making sure everything ran smoothly. This meant we crosschecked the prisoners log with the actual people in the holding cells.

On one occasion we had one young African male too many. No one had any idea what he was doing there. Even more embarrassing was that he had been interred for about two months! Eventually it seems Alan Golden had picked him up on some crime-related incident and in a rush had totally forgotten to enter his name. Then Alan went off on bush patrol and upon returning had no recollection of why he had picked the bloke up in the first place. When asked why he hadn't started to moan about his incarceration, the young lad explained he had been quite happy getting free food and lodging, doing nothing all day but loll in the sun in the cell's forecourt chatting with the other inmates and guards.

To make amends Alan gave him a job as his latest batman. The last one had done a runner. This unique transformation from potential criminal to trusted policeman's batman lasted about a week when Wilson, the cook, caught the bugger thieving from the kitchen supplies. So back to the cells went the batman for his robbin.

Mike Harvey continues -

As a bicycle is identifiable because all cycles should have a registration number stamped on the main frame just below the saddle, the complainant would be asked for make, colour, size, type and registered number of his bicycle. If he didn't know the number, the stolen property would be regarded as unidentifiable, but if he had these details these facts would be Gazetted and published and would be circulated round the country and the case kept open. When there was no suspect and the value of the goods were under R$200 - the docket would be closed "Undetected" No docket, no suspect, no identifiable property and value under $200.

Note: I think it is important that you get the procedural facts as correct as possible so that what you are portraying is more authentic, otherwise you could be accused of not knowing your subject and your account being a load of hogwash and a farce by those who are in the know, which would be a great pity. What I have recorded above is what I can recall but again I may be off beat as well, so the more ex-police you talk to will establish something more to the truth of what we did.

My comment to the above –
Okay boss, will do.

Glossary

Bullala'd. Absolutely wasted on alcohol, a fraction short of being in a permanent coma.
Huku. A chicken.
Amaiwe. Pronounced the same as the Frank Sinatra song, but with an 'A' on the front. An exclamation of fear or surprise meaning 'My mother' in Shona. The Italians say 'Mama Mia'!

CHAPTER 13:

Cry thief and unleash the puppy of law

first patrol - calling home

With Triggs thinking I was suitably house trained, I was given my own desk in the large office along with Alan, Nick and weeping willow Peter. I even had my own typewriter! Then a mere five weeks after leaving Morris Depot, the boss deemed I had garnered enough experience to be sent out alone into the wilds on my first general patrol.

The Gokwe Tribal Trust Lands were divided up into segments including tribal areas, forests, parks, hunting areas etc. The station operated a system whereby petty enquiries and non-urgent crimes were reported and then classified to its geographical locality (*vis-à-vis* distance and time from Gokwe village), and would be placed in that particular area's in-tray in the PO's communal office. There we quickly learnt to hide them until such time as the pile reached the ceiling and could no longer be just put 'temporarily' to the side. The boss would then assess whether the pile warranted some attention and, if so, delegate someone to go and sort out them out. Why he picked me instead of the so called more experienced weeping willow Peter, I had no idea, but he called me in. The boss's office had two complete walls covered with the best detailed maps you could get, all joined together. The Gokwe area, being so large, needed that much space to display in its entirety.

"PO Greenberg, I want you to go into Area 2 on a general patrol and clear up the backlog of reported crimes and enquiries," as he pointed out the intended area to that part of the map south west of Gokwe village and bordering the province of Matabeleland. This place was below the plateau and in an area I would describe as middle bushveld.

"Familiarise yourself with all these reports. I realise you have no driving licence, which quite frankly I think is quite absurd, sending a man out here without one."

That was for sure - none of this would have happened if I had learnt to drive a golf ball. With so few drivers at the station, I was a pain in the arse, having to constantly beg others to drop their own work to chauffeur me around on enquiries.

"I have informed Sergeant Madanire to accompany you along with two GC constables."

Qué? Blank look from me, and I stick an index finger up a nostril (a really bad habit I had picked up from the locals who practised this every time I asked them, "Did you or did you not do it").

"GC - Ground Coverage - work in civilian clothes, picking-up low grade intelligence from the populace; Greenberg." I nodded my head enthusiastically and stopped picking at my brains. The boss continued, "You will be operating from here," putting a finger below a spot called Gwelutshena, well south of some small place called Kana. "It's an all-black police administrated station situated outside our area and jurisdiction, but they know you will be staying for a while. Organise extra jerry cans of fuel and anything else you may need. Any questions?"

"How long will I be away Sir?"

"I would expect at least two weeks, you leave tomorrow, see

me before you go." And that was that.

I spent the rest of the day preparing myself and my group of merry men for the great adventure and challenge ahead. I read through the reported crimes and enquiries and chatted with Sgt. Madanire and the two GC constables about them. I also went up to Kambasha's store and bought provisions for myself. My young batman, Thomas, was also informed to pack food and clothes for the trip.

The date I left on my first enquiry patrol was the January 29, 1977, at exactly 9.40am. I know this because in my excitement, I decided to note everything down in my swanky, leather-covered, police notebook (which I later thieved, along with two others). That morning I saw the boss as instructed.

"Have you everything prepared, PO Greenberg?" he asked, after the formal greetings.

"Yes I have sir!" I replied.

"There has been a report of a lone terrorist wearing a balaclava accompanied by a women in a maxi dress heading into the Kana river area where you will be operating. Unfortunately, we have no further details, so keep your eyes open and be alert. Have you taken extra petrol and a TR28?"

"I still need to draw the fuel after our discussion and I have drawn a Single Side Band (SSB) radio as instructed, Sir."

With that end to the formalities, I was dismissed and joined my crew.

The open back Landrover was packed almost to the hilt; the additional jerry cans had been filled with fuel and already placed into the back of the vehicle along with all the rest of the kit for the patrol. The ground coverage details, Constables Ngoniye and Kapusia, dressed in civilian clothing, along with their bicycles and my batman, were crammed in the back as best as possible. My driver, Sgt. Madanire, didn't drive like Nigel or Alan but drove as he had been taught, handling the Landrover as if it was a fragile teapot. In his late 30s, he had been a policeman all his working life. He cut a very fine figure. Immaculately turned out, he was, like most of our uniformed black policemen, wearing the shiny anti-savaging dog leather leggings. They all seemed to prefer them rather than shoes and long socks. I think they wore them as a sort of status symbol thing.

As we zipped off I thought I had better bring the sergeant up to speed.

"Sergeant, it is your duty to keep an eye on me as I haven't got much of a clue what I am doing, so I would appreciate any advice."

The man looked at me curiously, and replied in immaculate English, "I will do that, Sah." Then he smiled a big broad grin, "I am sure you will do fine, PO Greenberg."

I smiled back big time too, instantly liking the man and glad he was on my side. He must have seen dozens of young white pups come and go in his time.

Now, according to my notebook, I notice that I am half dyslexic! Trying to write this chapter I really struggled to read my own hand writing as it slants from left to straight to right, with badly spelt words spaced, on average, three to a line! I am definitely missing a tickie to make up a bright sixpence! Most of the pages are full of 'incidents' where nothing really concrete gets done. We dashed around here and there, chasing up old crimes, interviewing witnesses, handling petty thefts etc. Then there was the constant flow of information coming over the radio about gook activity in the area. A couple of cattle dips destroyed, a black commuter bus held up (possibly pseudo gooks), and an incredible amount of time spent with the Landy stuck in mud.

In the evenings back at the police camp, I would type up all the necessary paper work. I slept in one of the offices in a sleeping bag on a stretcher while my black companions were housed amongst the resident staff without a murmur. The two ground coverage personnel sometimes spent the night out gathering intelligence, but this was a bit of a lemon. The pair of them were operating in a predominantly Matabele area, presenting them - as members of the Shona tribe - with an almost impossible task. Should their sleeping arrangements, in whatever kraal they would spend the night in, be reported to the gooks, they didn't stand a chance. The pair had one .38 service revolver between them. An even stupider move was the fact that I had forgotten to draw extra ammunition. The sergeant and I had exactly one full magazine each!

There is one incident worth recalling. It was a request from a police station in Rimuka, asking for the apprehension of a suspect, an African Male Adult (AMA) by the name of Munyonde, for housebreaking (HB). A radio message had been sent to Gokwe about three months earlier, along with a docket number and the name and address of the baddie. This system worked throughout Rhodesia. It was relatively simple. After we got directions from the local headman the sergeant wanted to pull up a fair distance from the suspect's kraal. I looked at all the mud lying around and thinking of my poor batman who would have to clean my shoes, I ordered Madanire to drive all the way.

Well, much to his and the ground constables bemusement, I might as well have turned on our blue flashing light and siren (which we didn't have), stood on the Landy roof, waving the blue and gold police flag, firing shots into the air, and roaring through a giant megaphone -

"Thief, here is the BSAP, and I am here to arrest thee!"

The entry I wrote says -

01.52pm: Of to Kana headwaters to pick up accuseds involved in H.B. and theft.

2.30: A/M Munyonde absconded earlier when he saw our Landrover. There was no property belong to him at the kraal.

As we roared up, I saw the suspect legging it into the bush. Oh well! The two constables, upon seeing my embarrassment, told me not to worry, and to wait a few days. They were sure he would be back and

"PO Greenberg, it is better that we go in alone this time."

I heartily agreed, and two days later - the following triumphant entry.

10.27: Met GC details who have been successful in catching Munyodi for Rimuka.

Now, after days of driving around the bush we finally have an arrest. My first one with me (sort of) in charge. I was really pleased. My wonderfully loyal sergeant (well pleased that I am well pleased), took a photo of my brave Ground Coverage constables, the manacled baddie and me in the back of the Landy with my tiny *Kodak 100 Instamatic*. I have this huge grin on my face and one hand on the suspects shoulder in a classic 'you're copped mate' pose. Ah, the empire strikes back! (Cover Photo.)

For some strange reason I handwrote the Warned and Caution statement there and then in my little book. It took me hours! On the inside back cover is an example of this. However, intriguingly it had been changed and a small typed written piece of paper covered the original text. It is attached with a very rusty staple so it is possible to see what had been changed. The line,

'I need not say anything unless I wish to do so and whatever I do say may be given in evidence…'

Had been changed by a recent law to,

'While I have been informed that I am not obliged to say anything in answer to these allegations any failure at this stage to mention any facts relevant to my defence to them may result in court drawing inferences against me. Whatever I say will be put into writing and may be given in evidence.'

'Inferances' (sic) being a rather clever word for me, has 'conclusions' in tiny handwriting above it. This is what he had to say about his arrest -

I do not admit breaking the house but I know the people involved. There names are A/M/A Modomeni July and Modomeni Malani. I saw them with the property. They gave me one jacket and one trouser in order to sell it. I sold this property for R$8 then returned the money to the accused and they gave me R$3. That is all.

I certify that the above statement was made freely and voluntary by A/M Munyonde Muchisero. It was read to him and he signed it.

Signed…X (his mark)

It all seems a huge cost in manpower and equipment for what looks like nothing big deal, but, hey, a crime is a crime! Luckily for all of us, on the way back to base camp we bumped into the District Commissioner on the road, who was also out and about on business. As he was on his way back to Gokwe village it was a perfect opportunity to get rid of miserable looking Munyonde. I certainly didn't fancy popping him on top of the overloaded Landy when it was time to go home.

A couple of days later, with fuel getting low and with most enquiries sort of sorted, we set off home. Besides the fact that for most of the way we were doing some serious slip-sliding away in the sodding mud yet again, the Landy was starting to pick up some complaints. Actually, the problem lay in the fuel pump. It had totally packed in. I hit upon the ingenious plan that if pressure could be brought into the fuel tank, we could force petrol into the small glass filter, and from there it would feed by gravity into the engine. To this end, I got my Thomas to cup his hands around the fuel intake and by breathing in through his nose; keep blowing into the tank till the air pressure did its job.

This worked three times, getting us an amazing five clicks further till the poor bugger nearly passed out from hyper ventilating and chronic petrol fume syndrome, and that was that (I hope he didn't get addicted to the stuff). We were well up a muddy creek and some eighty clicks from Gokwe village. I managed to raise them on the SSB and they informed me that Nick Robertson would be dispatched to rescue us. As the sun started going down I radioed Gokwe again, only to be told that Nick's Landrover was also stuck in the mud and, HE couldn't be rescued till the morning due to lack of vehicles, never mind US! Our predicament was not good. Perhaps by slightly misquoting the genius of Victorian novelist, Edward Bulwer-Lytton, I can truly give a half-cocked vision of the pickle jar we were in -

'It was a dark and stormy night; the rain fell in torrents — except at occasional intervals, when it was checked by a violent gust of wind which swept up through the bush (for it is in Gokwe Tribal Trust Land that our scene lies), rattling along the nearby kraal hut's sodden thatch, and fiercely agitating the scanty clothed constables and spaced out batman in the back of the well shafted Landrover.'

At that point I allowed the three at the back to go to the nearby kraal to spend the night. Sergeant Madanire and I would stay in the Landrover. Not really a very clever idea when I look back now (sitting ducks). After an extremely uncomfortable night the rest of the gang returned at first light and at 10.30am the next day; we were finally rescued.

So, after 11 days of running around - I had one arrest, a petrol sniffing batman and a well buggered Landy. Not actually a very successful patrol, but at the debriefing with the boss he seemed quite pleased.

"PO Greenberg, while it is unfortunate that you were not able to arrest more accused, it is more important that WE, the police of Gokwe, maintain a presence and that we show the people that we are here to work for them and take time and effort to maintain law and order."

I hadn't thought of that. Sounded impressive enough. If he really is as pleased as he said he was, I might as well strike while the poker was still hot.

"Could I have some days off Sir?"

Time off was at the boss's discretion. If you were not duty

weekend PO, your Saturday and Sunday were your own. Unless you had transport that meant one thing - Sports Club. That's it! I had everything in my favour. Four weeks in the bush, three in the office and only one weekend off.

"Have you all the follow-up enquires typed out?"

I confirmed I had. Now I was grateful for those hours pounding away in the evenings on the ancient typewriters.

The boss smiled after making an entry into the book,

"You can have five days off Greenberg, and if you type out your bush allowance, I will sign it immediately for clearance - have a nice break."

Woo-hoo – city lights here I come.

Memoir mutterings

Email from Mike Harvey -

The police post came under Nkai, much like Nebudzia came under Gokwe, and covered the main TTL of that district. The Kana and Shangani Rivers were infiltration routes used by ZIPRA to get into the heart of the country, so it was important, from a security point of view, to have an established police presence in the area with its ground coverage. In those days Gwelutshena, its name may derived from the Gwelo River which ran through that area, was termed a "growth-point", much like Gokwe village.

Glossary

Tickie. Finger nail sized nickel coin worth two and a half cents or threepence in the old money.

ZIPRA. Zimbabwe People's Revolutionary Army. Gooks loyal to Joshua Nkomo.

CHAPTER 14:

Black peasantry and White elephants

I had to move fast. It was almost two in the afternoon. I made a few local phone calls to my contacts within the village to find out if anyone was going to Que Que, but at this hour there was no chance of that. I could have cadged a ride the next morning, but that meant losing a day. So that meant only one other way - using Kambasha's commuter bus service. Another phone call confirmed that one was 'scheduled' to leave at 4.00pm. That gave me a bit of breathing space to get organised. I typed out my allowance claim which was an extra $27.50 - very nice thank you - I desperately needed it. I took a quick bath and packed a small holdall with a few essential items. Thomas was told that after washing all my uniforms from our trip, he could take time off as well. Generously I told him I wouldn't deduct any pay for the days he spent loafing around waiting for my return.

    I dressed in 'civvies' of T-shirt and shorts and went back to the office and had weeping willow Peter drive me up to what might have been considered Gokwe High Street. This small 'growth-point' was about five clicks down the main drag to Que Que. Here one could find tinkers, tailors and gook spies, but no Bata, Woolworths, Spar or anything resembling modern capitalism. The few micro managed retail shops weren't exactly the kind of place whitey would go window shopping - since most of them had no windows. The centre of this chaos was the Kambasha business conglomerate. As the Tribal Trust Lands were effectively blacks only, a smart man who spent his money investing in a beerhall rather than just drinking in it, could make himself seriously rich.

Kambasha himself was a portly man of medium height and was undoubtedly the main man of influence. Not only did he have a small off licence but also owned the huge department store, a slaughter house and butchery. Plus - a hotel (which wasn't exactly rated in the Rhodesian Automobile Association's guide to the best places to stay - unless - you were absolutely deranged, as no white person would ever consider Gokwe Village as a tourist destination), a commuter bus service, a trucking fleet and a second hand car dealership of old 1950's wrecks. In other words this bloke was seriously loaded.

All this entrepreneurship was crammed onto a couple of football field sized land scoured free of vegetation not only by the buildings, but by the thousands of feet of shoppers, commuters, chickens, goats, donkeys, ancient jalopies and ox-drawn carts. It was like some kind of giant, crazy circus show. Young men, drinking beer, hung around playing on the dirt ground (weather permitting) a version of draughts or variations of the ancient game of mancala. Others would excitedly play kicker, the mini table football game at five cents a pop. Women sat around gossiping while rearranging small piles of fresh fruit and vegetables piled on a hessian sack before them. Others formed groups dedicated to the crocheting of intricate needle work with creative designs made of tiny, brightly coloured glass beads. Under the outlaying trees, impromptu hairdressing salons were open with young African women, their sleeping picannins wrapped in a shawl and strapped to their backs worked happily away, as they worked at braiding each other's curly black hair into strange, tightly knit lines. At the same time they kept up a constant chatter, while eyeing and giggling over the posing opposite sex.

Accompanying this unrestricted Fairtrade fare, there was the unbelievable racket of what seemed hundreds of chirping natives, in ever-increasing volume, attempting to overcome the sounds from dozens of radios blaring out the government sanctioned station for the natives. To my white ear it sounded like one constant song in the local lingo played repetitively, accompanied by a guitar with only two tightly stretched treble strings. The din would only be broken up with the chattering of some rather excitable presenter and the adverts for Lever Brothers Lifebuoy soap that makes everything whiter. Sadly, much of the milling humanity preferred to spend their money on other commodities, and as a result they hummed to high heavens. But that wasn't the only strange stench hanging sickly sweet in the humid air. What also pervaded my nostrils was the putrefaction of rotting mangos, tomatoes, onions, bananas, gem squash and other locally grown produce. These well exceeded the 'sell by date' and the discarded produce lay scattered and squashed - to lie fly-covered between blankets of sugar cane skins with their chewed pith; spat on the ground from hundreds of sweet-toothed mouths. Those that preferred savoury snacks gnawed at semi-burnt mealies (corn-on-the-cobs), served by proprietors tending smoky fires created in any suitable dry spot. The nibbled cob cores also ended up on the ground.

As I watched yet another perfectly formed set of teeth expertly strip the hardcore mantel of the cane before biting deep into the soft white inner fibre to chew and suck out the juices contained within, I realised that this was an incredible opportunity to capture on camera the real life of the black Rhodesian. I whipped out my *Nikon* digital SLR with 15 million pixel capacity and 28mm-210mm zoom lenses and shot off, at seven frames a second, over two gigabytes of extraordinary snaps. For good measure I did some video clips and loaded them up onto *YouTube*, knowing they would go viral in seconds. Yeah, like hell I did - to me the place of ponging peasant pandemonium wasn't even worth the 20c developing cost of a picture taken by my Kodak Instamatic. This sort of rural high street is reproduced throughout Africa to this day - so why would I take any notice of it?

After absorbing these exciting (not) sights and sounds for just under a second, I went into the 'hotel', and on to old man Kimbasha's office after meeting, and greeting his number one son, a delightful and very smart individual of my own age -

"Ah, hello PO Greenberg, how are you?" Kimbasha senior

said as he stood up from behind his desk and stuck out his right hand.

"Hi Mr Kambasha," I replied, switching the FN to my left hand so as to accept the proffered greeting, "I am fine and would it be okay to get a lift on the bus to Que Que?" ('Lift', as in, non paying passenger.)

"I am always happy to help the BSAP, in fact, I was wondering if PO Brockbank might want to move into the hotel, since he spends most nights here on my phone," he laughed delightfully. "I will tell the driver you will be accompanying him. In these times of trouble, it is perhaps good he will have an armed escort," he added with a mischievous grin.

I just had to like this bloke. Besides a razor sharp wit, he was for us poor PO's, our life line. He would give us goods on credit, cash cheques, let certain weeping willows sit on his phone for hours, and transport our food from Que Que for nothing. It was well known between us that, should we abuse our privileges (such as a cheque going bouncy-bouncy), old man Kimbasha had a direct hotline straight to Chief Inspector Harvey whom, as you could well imagine, would not be amused.

We went outside, dodging the dirty puddles (at least it hadn't rained for a few hours), and Kimbasha prattled in Shona to a particular bus driver that was having a rather engrossing argument with another compatriot.

"Well, PO Greenberg, it is all arranged. I wish you a pleasant trip."

With that, he left, but I wasn't overly happy with the whole situation because the two drivers were coming close to blows while being cheered by the passengers from each side. It was like watching a football world cup final but not knowing anything about the game, nor the language the screaming fans were screeching in (not helped by a baker's dozen of awake picannins – wailing their heads off to the backdrop of panicked caged chickens squawking their swan songs - 'I don't want to be part of tonight's *sadza* and relish!'). Enough is enough…

It was time to take charge of the peasants. We were already running late, and while two middle aged men fighting each other using short lengths of hose pipe and dragging jerry cans backwards and forwards might have been great posting on *YouTube* for a laugh, I didn't have time for this shit. As the highest person of authority in the immediate vicinity (very easy to do - you just need a white skin and a loaded FN), I demanded what the hell was going on. I did not need to be a right luvvie and fire some shots in the air. Firstly, as usual, I only had 20 rounds. Secondly, what goes up has a tendency to come down. Thirdly, and most importantly, the boss would have killed me for pulling a daft stunt like that.

Now, having got their attention by my mere presence, I was given the following explanation.

"Sah, this driver, he is taking MY diesel, and I am telling him we not get to Que Que if he take any more and he say…"

I couldn't be arsed with this bollocks and thought of copper rulers and Nigel Triggs because I wanted to get home! So, casually waving the end of the barrel of the FN around - as you do when you get a tad annoyed - I spoke with mature authority -

"I will say this only once." This quote came from my school days immediately preceding a beating by the headmaster – and the word 'bend'. It worked then and it worked now, "All aboard - we are leaving for Que Que, NOW!"

And with that the hoards piled on with everything but the kitchen sink - which had to go on the roof rack along with enough household junk to start a bush *EBAY* site.

"Tell me driver," I asked as I jumped into the seat directly behind him, "I presume this trip is non-stop and we are not expecting to pick up any one on the way?"

"Yes Sah, that is correct."

This was good news because I would have had no hesitation sticking my rifle end into his ear hole should any one try to flag us down. I think he got the point of this short conversation. Of course, there was one unscheduled stop…

As the 56 seater, seating 156, commuter bus crab crawled sideways at a heck of a pace down the dirt drag, I kept my eyes following the road ahead as the side windows were too filthy to see through. I would have loved to have had something to play music to drown out the babble from the passengers. A perfumed handkerchief held to my nose, such as the one Michael Jackson used on his visit to Africa, could have come in handy, but that might have upset the locals. Anyway, you soon put up with the rancid smell of unwashed sweaty bodies, mixed with diesel exhaust fumes – either that or spend the entire journey throwing up in sympathy with the dozens of wailing, vomiting and shitting picannins. TIA – This Is Africa.

At this point I wasn't overly concerned that gooks might decide to hold up the bus. If it had been that dangerous, surely the boss, or some of the others would have mentioned this fact. So, I tried to chill, sipping on a warm bottle of Coca Cola while keeping a sleepy eye open for danger. No one sat next to me. My holdall and rifle took up too much space, but the locals all seemed friendly enough to my presence, which wasn't really surprising because without my earlier interference we wouldn't have been going anywhere, which was exactly where we landed up – nowhere!

About an hour into the journey and some 20 clicks from Que Que, with some rather dramatic shuddering, the bus started to fart loudly and went into the death throes of coughing its guts up. Then, before the engine cut out completely, the driver managed to pull over in a massive cloud of black smoke and the thing promptly expired with a final, stinking belch.

I shot from the bus faster than the driver and got the hell away from the thing. This was seriously bad news. Now I was frightened. There was maybe an hour of daylight left. As I watched the irate passengers storm out and either lambast the driver or gather in groups (men) to urinate behind the bus, or disappear (women) into the surrounding bush to relieve themselves, I wracked my brains for a plan B.

'Be Prepared' – the Boy Scouts' motto – sprang to mind. After all, I had been a member until I left in disgrace and I was prepared – I was prepared to car-jack the next vehicle. What else could I do? The bloody bus had more attractions than Disneyland for any joyriding gooks in the near vicinity. Especially since the looting, rape and pillaging in this African theme park came with free entry to anyone with an AK 47.

I decided to put some distance between me and the 'fun fair' and started jogging down the road, spinning around constantly to look for any approaching vehicles. I tried to stay cool. Being so close to Que Que, there just had to be some local traffic and sure enough after what was maybe only 10 minutes, but seemed a hella of a lot longer, I spotted a small, white Mazda bakkie approaching. I stood in the middle of the road, rifle in the left hand pointing forwards and held up my right in the classic police 'stop' traffic arm gesture. I might not be in uniform, but this was definitely police business - this particular case I was now involved in had my very life depending on a successful solution. I just hoped the driver knew his highway code when it came to handling a white highwayman.

"A lift or your life!" I didn't yell at the black middle-aged driver and passenger.

"Are you perhaps going to Que Que?" I did ask the petrified man after he had recovered from nearly running me down.

I gathered he was, so I sprang into the back and without much further ado I was driven to the main tar road to Salisbury. I thanked my rescuer profusely - he had just saved my bacon, but I was too tight to even give him the price of a cup of tea. My next plan was that if I couldn't get a lift by 8pm, I could always doss down at the police singles mess and try again in the morning. Hitching in Rhodesia was easy, especially if you are carrying a weapon, and sure enough, within half an hour I was on the way and the kind driver actually dropped me off outside home just in time before my step-mom had her goodnight cuppa. She was delighted to see me. So much so that once I told her I had a few days off, she excitedly said

"Oh, this is such good timing! Tomorrow is Friday and we can go to Inyanga as soon as I get back from school."

Inyanga! That was not the plan at all. I wanted to check up on some mates and maybe go to a disco or something, not go out back into the bush. The problem was that my step-mom was burdened with a white elephant up in the Eastern Highlands of Rhodesia, nearly three hours drive away. There at the bottom of a long winding dirt road called appropriately, Valley Road, just before the tiny village of Juliasdale (where the famous hotel the Claremont was situated), was a small cottage. This three-bedroomed structure, set in two unfenced hectares, with its own stream, was supposed to have been my father's retirement home. He had invested two years of time and some considerable money in the place. I had hated going there with a passion as there was nothing, nothing to do at all, except go for walks, which Katherine did with enthusiasm. Oh, the scenery of massive granite domes and fir trees and cool climate was very nice – but only for fuddy-duddy tree huggers once they reach the ancient age of 40-odd, and therefore have no interest in the opposite sex or nightclubs.

Bridget, upon hearing the wonderful news the following day, flatly refused to go and promptly made arrangements to spend the weekend with Sharon, her pal next door. Michael, at the age of eight didn't have the choice. Due to the fact Katherine had only managed to scrape enough petrol coupons to get us there and back, there was no point in taking my fly fishing tackle. Which was a bit of a shame because about a half an hour's drive from Juliasdale was the very picturesque Rhodes National Park - that kind empire builder Cecil John had donated to us whiteys so we could get a bit of trout fishing in.

I had actually gone camping and fishing there for a few days just before joining the police with my china Andrew Edmondson (the cheating bastard used spinners). The trip had been rather unsettling. We had struggled to get lifts and we had been the only campers. Not only that I had forgotten that August is still very much winter up there and we had nearly frozen to death. But the biggest problem was our proximity to Mozambique - maybe only a thirty minute crow's flight away. There, Mugabe's gooks had set up their own camps with the sole aim of taking over the trout hatchery. If they happened to come across any tea, coffee and fruit estates on the way, they tended to deal with the owners and workers in a rather uncivilised fashion. However, at this stage of the war, they hadn't got the rich taste for oven baked trout, but were well occupied in murdering missionaries and farmers and mutilating and callously dispatching black peasant workers as 'sell-outs', along with any off-duty security personnel they came across. For good measure their landmines took out many buses and they had great fun slaughtering and maiming livestock. And, just so they could keep up their numbers, rural schoolchildren would be made to 'volunteer' to the nationalistic cause and were marched over the mountains to the camps to be given a proper education.

Now, both Katherine and I knew a little of this, but there hadn't been that much news of the future Zimbabwe nation's liberators progressing as far as where we were going. However, she desperately needed to go up and pay the live-in 'caretaker' his salary and see if the place hadn't been ransacked and been burnt to the ground. Step-mom would have loved to sell the damn place, for as much as she adored the still peaceful retreat; it cost money she didn't really have left over from her pittance of a female teacher's salary. How she coped was a mystery. She most probably cleared less per month than I did - and I was always skint.

So we went up there in her Rhodesian assembled Renault 4, with me waving my FN out the window as a deterrent against any ambushing gooks. Valley Road had a few tributaries leading into cul-de-sacs with several dozen retirement cottages and holiday homes set in stunning scenery. What was immediately apparent was the lack of parked cars. That meant a lot of people were a tad put off enjoying Inyanga's peace and quiet. Luckily, the gooks must have thought the area of little importance because if they had landmined the road, the three of us would have caught our last ride. My old man had done a pretty neat job on the place. He had installed a second-hand diesel pump down at the river which put an end to the caretaker's task of transporting a large tin of water up the long steep recline, before climbing a ladder and pouring the contents into a bowser-sized zinc tank for us to have running water. There was no electricity but we had wall-mounted gas lights, and a wood fire under a Rhodie boiler kept us supplied with plenty of hot water.

On the other side of the river, and up an equally steep hillside, resided our caretaker, Kahlif, and his family. Kahlif was of royal blood, being one of the sons of a local chief. Unfortunately, his abode wasn't exactly princely - more like a permanently damp hovel comprising of two rotting mud huts (it rains a lot in the Eastern Highlands). An open fire of hissing fresh pine logs poured out acrid smoke 24/7. A few scraggly half-drowned maize plants grew in the garden. How he survived on $15 a month with two wives and half a dozen kids was a mystery I didn't feel I needed to puzzle over. I was seething to be spending three days and nights twiddling my thumbs. I might as well have had the five days off in the Gokwe Sports Club!

Extremely annoyed with my unselfish Good Samaritan tour of duty, I had exactly a day in Salisbury before having to head back to base. I made a quick dash into town and popped into Radio City on First Street. I had decided I needed a mini-Precious for away trips and knew exactly which portable radio it would be. Supersonic had just brought out a new model and it was a babe. In military style, it was a pleasing shade of camo green. Best of all, it was powerful enough to pick up Radio Springbok from South Africa and Comrade Robert Mugabe ranting on Radio Maputo from his HQ (far from the any danger), about getting free Mercedes Benzs and farms. The salesman was more than willing to sell me one, provided I could show him my radio licence. Sorry, come again, what's one of those. It seems I couldn't listen to Bob (not Marley) or Springbok for free. So feeling rather annoyed, I trundled up to the post office and got the damn thing for 2.00 bucks. More money spent on nothing.

I spent a couple hours on Monday evening seeing my old school china, Tim Bell, but that was just about it. What a great time off. Next day I had to get back. Getting to Que Que was easy. I had barely time to listen to my new vibes (now powered by excruciatingly expensive Rhodesian made Eveready batteries), before I was picked up and dropped outside the police station. Sadly, there was no official vehicle heading to Gokwe. That left me with two choices – Kimbasha buses again – or take a chance at hitching and hope some whitey was going that way. I opted for the latter and got lucky after a couple of hours of sitting around, when I got a lift with an Internal Affairs bloke. As for me cadging a lift on the bus again in the near future was concerned – forget it!

I had been back barely a couple of days when the boss informed me that I was to go on a Police Anti-Terrorist Unit (PATU) initiation course.

Oh Shit!

Memoir mutterings

The problem was that we were victims of our own propaganda. Ever since the collapse of white rule in Mozambique in 1974 and the rise of Mugabe who, after being kicked out of Zambia by Kaunda, had been allowed by new president Samora Machel to use his country as a base for his gooks (led by Josiah Tongogara), not only was Rhodesia doomed, but the poor bastards up in the Eastern Highlands were going to get it big time. Property prices fell so low you could pick up a farm for the price of a jar of lucky beans – which is exactly what Alexander Fuller's parents did. At the time I was in Inyanga, Fuller (then seven years old), was living on some kip of a farm in a part called Burma Valley. Her old man was in the Police Reserve. She relates this life of poverty in the best seller *Don't Let's Go to the Dogs Tonight*. Coincidently, another best-selling author, Peter Godwin (*Mukiwa* and others), who came from Chimanimani in the Eastern Highlands, lived the life of upper-middle class white. At the time I describe he was a year older than myself and also in the police, albeit as a National Service member.

Glossary

Cheti. A receipt for nothing.
Luvvie. Not Rhodie slang. It means 'drama queen'

CHAPTER 15:

'Good Golly!' - what a load of gobbledygook

Oh no! I hated getting dressed up as a tree and crawling like a leopard over sharp stones with mad nutters shooting rounds off next to my ear. Besides, I didn't want to join PATU. They were well known to be used just as expendable target practice for trigger happy Marxist-Leninists gooks. No chance of wriggling out of this one and with my new mini-Precious packed; I was packed off to Selukwe. This small town was smack bang in the middle of Rhodesia. The only thing I knew about it was that Great White Bwana Smithy had a farm there. This area must have been about as interesting as Central Australia since it also had a huge granite boulder sticking up somewhere a few clicks down the road, but that was about it. (Ayer's Rock is 463km from Alice Springs, but in Rhodesia/Australia land size comparison – it is just a few clicks.)

At Selukwe PATU Head Quarters I mingled with a rather motley crew comprising of a handful of police regulars my age, a load of black police regulars of various vintages and some old toppies police reservists on call-up, all aged over 35. I spotted my Morris Depot china, Jeff, which cheered me up immediately and we agreed to team up and suffer together. We then met our host and practitioner of the fine arts of terrorist termination.

Section Officer 'Mad' Mike Moore, or just Mad Mike, as he was commonly known, was the opposite in every way to Pockface and Beergut. He was at least a hand's breadth shorter than me and his physique resembled those pictures in biology books of men with no skin - just tightly woven muscle. With a short back and sides, a classic Donny Osmond fringe and a Freddie Mercury moustache, he was attired in an immaculate set of perfectly ironed, but well faded camo. A true professional, he even had a fancy leather watch cover to stop it glinting in the sun. He didn't smoke, didn't drink and was as fit and dedicated to his craft as Bruce Lee - and just as dangerous.

Later, when I got to know him a bit better, he told me that he had served with the British First Battalion of the Parachute Regiment during the 'Troubles' in Northern Ireland and had admitted he was 'there' during the Bloody Sunday shooting in 1972. He told me he only quit after the IRA, which had him at number two on their 'to be taken out' list, had set off a car bomb outside a cinema as he and his wife came out from a show. They missed but Mad Mike moved to Rhodesia where it was safer. Yeah, so safe that he was now training us in anti-gook warfare. How much of this man's story is true, or for that matter if it was his real name, I cannot say.

We were then taken deep into the bush where Mad Mike had established his torture centre amongst giant granite gomos and trees and waterfalls and streams and bush and just about everything to make life as uncomfortable as possible. Everything my happy nature lover step-mom would rush to visit. Not me though. We were divided into sticks of five. I made sure that Jeff and I were together by gobbing some bullshit about long lost brothers-in-arms, and had three black regular policemen allocated to us. They were all in their early 30s and looked even sorrier about our lot than we were. The next five days were living hell.

He introduced us to his two assistants. I took one look at them and hollered –

"Gooks! Run for your lives." Mad Mike kicked me up the rear and told me to fall in line.

The two scraggily bearded black men were dressed in weird mixtures of khaki jackets and strange camouflage trousers. They stood casually behind Mad Mike. One carried an AK 47 and the other, slightly shorter than his companion's average height, carried a RPD light machine gun. They grinned wickedly at us. I farted fearfully. They were seriously scary. It was rumoured they were 'turned' gooks. It would soon become apparent that if they had crossed and crossed again or just crossed for the first time, we (Rhodesia) would be well shafted. What Mad Mike had taught these highly intelligent men had made them the fittest, hardest and fearless gooks Mugabe could possibly desire. And they were on my side.

Water was our drink, ratpacks our fare and cordite our alarm clock – when wrapped around a tree and detonated at 5am. Jeff and I were still pretty fit from our Depot days, plus Jeff kept trim by having jiggy-jig exercises in Gwelo. I, of course, was fighting fit from pushing Landrovers out of the mud in Gokwe. But what we were put through was rough on the older men, especially the reservists, who were just called-up civilians.

We were introduced to our log. At twice the length of a camper cot (that we neither had, nor were allowed to bring), this head-width, heavy pruned length of gum tree was painted bright orange. This was just in case it might get accidentally lost. Gum tree was a clever choice as the wood is hard to incinerate even for an ex-arsonist such as myself. Five loops of thick, heavy sisal had been attached at intervals along it. This log was to go everywhere with us. One hand in the loop, the other carried your rifle. Run here, run there and run up a waterfall.

Everything was always a race. Even up a waterfall. Its 30-degree soaked granite slope was almost impossible to get a foothold on, especially while hooked to a log and four others. People fell and some were cut up quite dramatically by sharp rocks. Some of the old boys were suffering hard.

Mad Mike pushed and pushed us:

"Who we fighting for?"

"Rhodesia," we mumbled through our pain. This wasn't good enough.

"Who we fighting for?" he would now scream.

"Rhodesia!" we would oblige in a roar in the hope that he would shut up.

"Did I hear someone say Zimbabwe?"

Cynically I thought - no, not yet, but it might be happening soon. This log-dragging bullshit was an attempt to make us work in harmony. It did until our strength started to go. The matched running rhythm started to disintegrate and the log jerked about. When that happened Jeff and I simply handed our rifles to our co-loggers and, sticking the bastard thing on our shoulders, legged it past the other flaking sticks. The only occasions we didn't drag the damn thing around was when we crawling like leopard, rolling around like dogs, yelling like Apaches and climbing the obstacle course.

Me being the quickest, the fastest, the cleverest etc, meant privileges. For example, I was allowed to listen at very low level to my mini-Precious after lights out for an hour. They went out the same time the sun fell out the sky.

On the last day Mad Mike addressed us.

"It's time to see how much you have learnt. There are two tests. These will see if you qualify to be a member of PATU."

This sounded bad, especially since our pseudo-gooks had even bigger grins on their faces.

"You will race as individuals through the obstacle course. I will make notes on your performance. Secondly, this afternoon, four sticks will take up position for a night ambush. The fifth stick will become part of a terrorist group. Their objective is to surprise the ambushers, take members captive and interrogate them. The PATU role is to spot them first and make effective contact (using blanks, I hoped). We will begin in 10 minutes."

I didn't like the sound of any of this – but it got worse.

"I forgot to mention. During your progression through the obstacle course, you will be subjected to live ammunition and other nasty surprises."

As we lined up for the start of the obstacle race, my mind raced. I knew that the first off the woven rope climbing wall - the first obstacle - would have it made. Everyone after that could only manoeuvre in single file and there was almost no way to overtake.

I hit the top of the wall about the same time as about five other relatively fit buggers and then did what no one had thought of - I jumped - not only down but outwards, while somersaulting perfectly to the ground, then expanding the forward motion with a roll. I was up and running fast. Being a former gymnast sometimes comes in handy. Next came the trench, filled with mud and covered by a tarpaulin. Moving so fast, I was out before the orange smoke grenade Mad Mike lobbed in side kicked off. Then it was leopard-crawling under the barbed wire with Mad Mike's pet gooks going mental with real machine guns firing real rounds. I heard screams from behind me– no time to look back – up the rope like a monkey and swing like an orang-utan to another tree, a bit more hop, skip and jump and home free to watch the debacle unfolding.

Men with hair exuding orange smoke, half blinded, staggered from the mud tunnel, eardrums damaged, as all sorts of crackers and fireworks were tossed around them by Mad Mike and the loony fake gooks. By the time it came for monkey do, the rope was slippery with mud from mine and another couple of quick lads' hands, so it was now push the monkey up the tree, to promptly fall off the spanned sisal. I hadn't laughed so much in a long time. We were given the rest of the day off to prepare for more fun and games. At 5.00pm, they started.

Mad Mike decided that my stick would help his gooks. They instantly took command. Us 'gooks' stayed in camp and counted to 10,000 to give time for the Rhodesian forces to hide. Mad Mike's tame killers would take their new black comrades with them hunting whiteys, while useless palefaces Jeff and I could hang around protecting the torture chamber (a small thatched hut next to the campsite), which they would use to interrogate captured security forces. I thought this plan was sound. They also told me that playing my mini-Precious was a no-no. I didn't argue.

After several boring hours, just before I nearly dozed off, two shadows arrived with a trussed up Rhodie. Frantic muffled scuffles awoke me from my sleepy eye.

"White bastard, what is your name? What is your rank. Where are the others?"

"Fuck you, fuck off you fucking bastards," came the fighting spirit reply.

Fiery stuff indeed and obviously a well-educated individual had been captured. Jeff and I grinned evilly at each other in the quarter moon light; it was nice to be on the devil's side. Shame I didn't have a mini mp3 dictaphone to record this; it was better than being blind and listening to the Muppet show. My imagination was going wild in the near pitch blackness.

Only in the morning would I find out that the poor bastard had been tied up like a star fish to the mud-covered poles of the hut.

"I piss on you and smear my shit in your face, you not tell me name, rank number, where you from, how many more of you?"

There followed a sound similar to urinating in a tin, a gasp and the answer,

"Fuck off, fuck you bastards."

I was well impressed. Being a terrible agliophobic (Fear of pain), I would have spilled the beans faster than they could be heated up as soon as the gooks turned up. I knew if the situation had been reversed, and I had been the captive, I would have started chirping instantly. I would start from when I was dropped on my head by a nurse minutes after I was born. Then about my father who shouted and hit me because he thought I was handicapped from being constantly being shouted at and hit on the head. And I would tell them how Mrs Smuts had beaten me every day at school because I was too stupid to learn Afrikaans and finally that I had been done over for $90 because Triggs had stuffed up the mess books. At the end the gooks would be crying, release me and slip me $10 and wish me well. You think I lie...wait and see.

Obviously bored with this failure, the ghosts slinked off and returned a short time later with a much bigger and noisier parcel. The scuffles were louder now and the answer to the well-rehearsed questions went off at a tangent.

"You fucking kaffirs, touch me again and I will fucking kill you when I am out of here. No stinking munt touches me." All this shouting was in a strong Afrikaans accent.

Oh dear! Someone was definitely not getting into the spirit of things.

Then came the piss and faeces bit, which later turned out to be just warm water and cold sadza pushed into the face, and the new victim went totally ape-shit. Screaming out Mad Mike's name, he swore revenge, and would lay a charge against him and his fucking munts for assault etc.

Next thing a whistle signalled an end to the proceedings and gas lights dispelled the darkness. I told Jeff to wait a bit until others turned up. I didn't want Mad Mike to know we had been eavesdropping. At the appropriate time we sauntered over and fell in with the others. Behind him, with expressionless faces, stood his gooks. Mad Mike told a couple of others to go into the hut and release the 'prisoners'.

One of them, a skinny kid, scuttled over to the rest of us. The other, a brute with a thick neck, approached Moore.

"You want my lads, you come through me first," Moore said.

Instantly the idiot broke down into whining babbling. Mad Mike brushed aside the red-faced fool and ordered him to pack up his stuff. He was being sent back to town, there and then: a big fat 'fail' to be noted on his report.

After that little bit of fun, back at PATU Headquarters in Selukwe next day, Jeff and I were given a B+, while the older tossers got A+. This was unfair, but it was time to split up. As I shook hands and said goodbye to Jeff, Mad Mike called us over.

"Listen, Greenberg, Swindells. You were the best but I have to keep the older ones feeling good. Okay?"

We got it.

Then back to Gokwe, with a nice little leopard paw print PATU badge to sew on my camo shirt: I was now licensed to be shot at. I had hardly started to recover from visiting Mad Mike's theme park when the boss called me in to his office.

"Greenberg, I regret to inform you that I have to allocate three members to go on a PATU bush patrol."

The word 'regret' registered that he wasn't talking to me because it was weeping willow Peter's turn to go happy camping for a while.

"With staff stretched so thin, I will be sending you and two constables to Que Que where you will be integrated into a stick and sent on patrol for a month. Please be ready fully kitted up by 2pm. Any questions?"

Any fucking questions!? Like how come he's sending me into the friggin bush again?

Maybe I had one of those personalities people preferred seeing the shit shot out of it. It just wasn't fair!

I was reminded of a Jewish joke. A bloke is sent to heaven by the Jews to ask god a question. He gets to meet the ultimate Big Bwana and says, "My name is Karl Greenberg and I have been sent by the Jewish people downstairs to ask you - is it true that we are the chosen people?"

"Yes, it is true, God booms. "You are the chosen people."

Karl mulls this for a moment. "Well, could you possibly do us all a big favour and choose someone else for a sodding change!"

So, once again feeling well shafted by the gods I don't believe in, I addressed the boss.

"Sir, I have a question. Is there any chance of having a tad more ammunition for my FN than just one 20- round magazine?"

He handed me the key to the station armoury.

"See what you can find, there's not much in there."

I wandered off and soon returned with two well hammered magazines, an ancient Mills grenade, a Walther PPK James-Bond type pistol, and an extra magazine for it. I could keep the FN magazines and grenade. I moaned a bit about my lack of ammunition and the boss told me to draw an extra sixty rounds in their cartons. What a great way to fight a war – there would be me, taking a nice walk when suddenly, "Gooks! Run for your lives," while firing and changing magazines - once, twice - before hollering, "Cease fire, gooks. I need to get the boxes of ammo out my rucksack and sit down and fill up my magazines. I won't be long, have a smoke and then we can continue with this little fire-fight."

Feeling well miffed, I was soon bouncing my way in a Landy back to Que Que. I spent the night at the police single's mess and next morning met up with another 50 of us. I was teamed with two fellow black Gokwians, a young white PO of such boring personality I forgot he existed immediately, and my stick leader – Section Officer Longskroll.

Longskroll was in his late 20s, tall as a skyscraper and thinner than a matchstick. His first words were, "Have any of you had combat action?"

Well, I thought about that one. I had seen some action with the doctor's daughter and then Triggs and co. had hosed me down, but as for being shot at or shoot at real gooks, the answer was definitely a no. We all shook our heads.

"Well, listen up, I have, and I will make it very clear from the start. You will obey all my commands and, with luck, we will come out of this trip alive."

What a plonker! It was alright for him. He was so thin it would take a real lucky shot to hit him. I reckoned the wind from a passing round would be enough to remove his head from the scrawny neck.

Longskroll looked at my bright red rucksack with horror.

"You are not going on patrol wearing that. It would be like waving a red rag at a bull. Where is your combat webbing kit?"

What a bore the man was - on top of being a right drama queen. Anyone would think we could die out there the way he was fussing. The reason I had the rucksack was that I flatly refused to use the webbing kit we were supplied with. It was a load of shite. It was more complicated than accessing a girl's body-shirt and bra strap one handed, and just as uncomfortable. When the webbing was stocked up with sleeping bag, food pouches, water bottles, ammo pouches - the occupant looked like some tramp carrying his possessions in half a dozen Spar carrier bags attached with bits of string all over his body. They chaffed like hell when walking and the swinging weight would make you run like a drunken sailor being chased by a pimp. I had planned for this moment of confrontation, and using my poncho, promptly made the rucksack disappear and turn into a large green mound. Just like Frodo's invisible cloak. That shut him up.

As PO Non-descript was senior to me in terms of the fact he had passed through Morris Depot two months prior to myself, he was allocated as second in command by Longskroll. That suited me fine - the less responsibility for me - the better. After Longskroll and the other stick leaders received the latest Shackle codes, they were told the designated areas for patrol. We got…Gokwe!

What a laugh. What a way to run a war. So, an hour later we are bouncing back to the police station and into the boss's office. He was also rather confused and after a moment's thought said

"I'll send you to Chirama base camp. From there, scout around the area and talk to the locals. Try to make this more of a meet and greet, hearts and minds-type patrol. There are gooks about but we don't know exactly where."

magic cloak, me and a grenade

Pic - Gokwe Kid

Chirama. An apt name - a mixture of charm and panorama. This would be the start of almost a year's love affair with the place for me. It had been a base camp for years. Used by Internal Affairs, Tsetse Control and the police, it had one of the best views in the world. Although about two hours drive from Gokwe village, it was still on the Mafungabusi Plateau, at an altitude of almost 1600 metres. Perched at the end of a sandy dirt road cul-de-sac, Chirama camp sat on the last jutting spit of flattened earth, before it plunged to the huge expanse of almost level bushveld, far below. The first thing you noticed was the octagonal tin-walled and roofed, and glass-windowed radio shack. A few paces further was a brick and mortar kitchen (whites only) with a huge, black cast iron wood stove. Nearby, built from the same materials, was a Rhodie 220 litre drum boiler, supplying skin-removing, scalding water for the (whites only) shower. Scattered around on the dry sandy soil were large green tents for the various resident field reserve and security personnel. Bang in the middle of the clearing stood a tiny hut, not much bigger than its own front door. This was the long-drop toilet used by all races. A couple of old toppies, reservists, were sort of running the place, having been called up from normal life in the city.

The plan was very simple. We would be taken several clicks into the surrounding area to check a given area for signs of possible gook presence, do a walk about, sleep in the bush for three nights and return for one night at Chirama, and repeat this *ad nauseum* until the month was up. Tedious, but that was what it was all about.

The first few days into the patrol Longskroll showed the stick the correct use of silent hand signals. I invariably placed myself at the rear leaving PO Non-descript as point because if he got slotted, no-one would miss him. At night we took turns to do sentry watch and I will delve into this nonsense later on. It didn't take long before Longskroll clocked that I had put something sneaky into my rucksack – mini-Precious. As I could connect it up with a tiny earphone bud, I believed he wouldn't exactly ban it, so I chilled to the beat while the rest lay in their fart-sacks all night bored out their minds.

During the day we would arrive at kraals where Longskroll would chat to the headman with a constable translating. He would take extensive notes about locals' moans and groans, knowing that no-one would probably ever pay attention to them. I didn't mind this as it was far better lolling under a tree than walking about in the heat. After a few days of this, even Longskroll got bored and started to cheat the regulations. We came across a school building, closed for the end of term holidays, and we set up camp. Longskroll radioed a fake position of the stick in Shackle and, as it was the weekend, was more than happy to sit and listen to Forces Requests on mini-Precious – so long as the volume was down low. He also took time-out to sit us at the desks and using the blackboard explains to us the physics behind the aerodynamics needed to fly an aircraft. He had just qualified for his pilot's licence, so was rather enthusiastic about the subject. This was the first time I would be paid to go to school.

And night watch was also cancelled. Much better if we spread our beds around a little using the theory that if the gooks did find one of us snoring away, the screaming as he was butchered would wake us up - and we'd leg it quick.

One of the members of this highly-trained stick of wasters was a young African constable, Sammy. He had impressed me a short time earlier when he, Nick Robinson and I were travelling in a Landrover. We passed a troop of baboons by the side of the road.

Nick, who was driving, said

"Hey, Sammy, look. Isn't that your family?"

Sammy, in the middle, just smiled politely. I didn't. I thought it was a cheap shot and the little I knew of Nick, he must have been bored, as he was certainly better at humour than this. A short while later, a huge baboon sat in the middle of the road forcing Nick to slow down. Sammy then chirped up -

"Oh look PO Robinson. Have you told your sister yet that you have joined the BSAP? I am sure she will be delighted with the news."

Laugh? I nearly shat. Nick wasn't impressed and didn't say another word. I instantly took a likening to Sammy. I would take any opportunity we had to chat together and we struck up a great friendship. About three years older than me, he was very good looking and highly intelligent, and matched my own satirical sense of humour with 'one-liner' quips of his own. I had no problem letting him use my first name in private. Officially this was taboo.

The only thing of interest on the patrol was an incident involving the shooting of an Internal Affairs District Assistant (DA). We were picked up by Landrover and deposited at a base camp separated by a high mesh fence from an adjoining small bush store. A couple of days before our arrival, the Intaf man had been notified of a suspicious individual at the store. Calling through the fence, the suspect had wandered over, drew a Tokerev pistol, and started shooting. The DA, while attempting to run for cover, had been shot in the buttocks. The store owner got a message to Gokwe police and our stick was directed to conduct a follow-up. We found the man dead in his bedroom, curled up on his bed. The death had occurred a couple of days before and the smell of putrefaction was horrible. The only sign of foul play was a small patch of blood on his trousers. Later I would learn that the autopsy on the body confirmed that a Tokerev pistol was used and it was of interest that the bullet had entered the buttock, deflected off the pelvis and penetrated the stomach cavity causing severe internal injuries. It would have been a long and agonizing death – poor sod.

The body was taken back to Gokwe village and we hung around the camp waiting for a tracker. When he finally arrived and was taken to the scene of the attack (the other side of the fence), the spoor was already four days old and any signs to follow-up long gone, due to the hundreds of footprints of the store's customers. Still, the tracker thought he had found signs of someone's hasty exit into the surrounding bush. Longskroll got himself all excited and started using hand signals as if the gook was hiding around the next tree. We duly set off in formation. What a load of nonsense this was, and sure enough, less than 1000 paces later, the tracker lost the spoor. This was excellent news. With no chance of getting picked up for a couple of days we just lounged about. The only excitement was when we found and killed a rather large black mamba that had wandered into the 'kitchen'.

black mamba - Sammy (middle) and me
Pic - Gokwe Kid

And then it was all over. The best news was that on top of my bush allowance, I would receive an extra $1.25 PATU bonus per day. That, multiplied by twenty eight days made a cool mouth-watering, tax free $91. While the army did six weeks in and 10 days off, we had four weeks in and six days off. Once we got to Gokwe and were debriefed (Longskroll doing all the lying), I made sure the transport back to Que Que for him and PO Non-descript stayed put till I had thrown some civvies together.

When I arrived home, I did a curious thing. I invited Katherine out for dinner. No, I wasn't that desperate to chase my own step-mom, *ag sis man*, and I gathered that she was attractive according to the rather crude comments my china Tim had occasionally insinuated; no, it just seemed a good idea. A sort of a thank you for those times she had tried to shelter me from the worse parts of my father's temper, and her untiring attempts to help me with my school work. I hadn't been an easy step-son, this she acknowledged as these meals became almost a tradition each time I came home for a few days off. I was no longer the prodigal son, now I was the prodigal man.

So on that first dinner date we finally started to get to know each other and I almost felt over warming affection for this stern academic until…the bloody woman, taking advantage of my good mood after absorbing half dozen vodka, lime and lemonades, conned me into going to friggin' Inyanga again! I should have shot her and saved myself a lot of pain.

Memoir mutterings

Email from Mike Harvey:

The sticks were briefed (remember SMEAC – situation, mission, execution, administration, communication!) using a map to identify area of responsibility, briefed on known gook activity and history, the local population, their likely response to the security personnel, other troops in the area, the types of checks and what to look for.

This suggested "happy-go-lucky" attitude was obviously your thinking at the time, but reflecting on it now would you have taken your sentry duty more seriously? Obviously sounding like the proverbial old fart, and looking back 30 years – you have raised my hackles. This was a pet hate of mine - I had personal experience of the senseless loss of life through rank stupidity and irresponsibility. The requirement to be alert was fundamental in all security work no matter how trivial it appeared to be as there was always a possible threat – remember it was at this time that a PATU stick in the Binga area had been attacked at night and several Patrol Officer's, one a son of an ex-member whom I knew, were shot in their pits because they decided not to post a guard! I just wonder how you would have felt now, when reflecting back, if one or all of the stick had been taken out or seriously injured. I KNOW WE DO STUPID THINGS AT TIMES AND FORTUNATELY, IN YOUR CASE, GOT AWAY WITH IT. Do you really want show what a dork you were! Remember there were many police, SA police and Army who senselessly lost their lives through failure to use common sense and follow set parameters. Now that I have rebuked you - in retrospect - we can carry on with your narrative – enough said Harvey! BANG!

Fair enough boss, but you did send me out with only three magazines. And, I wasn't in charge of the stick…

Forces Requests. Presented by the late Sally Donaldson every Sunday afternoon, this was a two hour special on the Rhodesian Broadcasting Corporation (RBC). Members of a family, wives and girlfriends would write in and send fond greetings to their loved ones in the bush. She would read them out in two minutes of sexy, breathless words, followed by a shortened latest pop hit. While we Rhodies were too macho to acknowledge this girlie thing, we were secretly pleased if we got our names called out. When you did you would groan out loud, accusing the senders of being soft. It also became a tradition for the 'victim' to buy a round of drinks. The program was not racially segregated, but 95 per cent of the requests came from whites.

CHAPTER 16:

The Fellowship of the Binge

Ian — Alan — Leon
Beer, Smokes and Rifles - Men of Men
Pic - Alan Golden

I would now be staying for a while at the Gokwe police station. It made a nice change to have a bath every night or a swim. However, my financial woes were still plaguing me despite the extra influx of bush bonus. Plans to make some extra coin were going very pear shaped. Upon my return I had a parcel from the UK containing four plastic cased digital watches sent by my mother. My stainless steel one had given up the ghost, so one was for me and the others I planned to sell for $50 a pop.

Alan bought one and coughed up prompt. Nigel bought one and after fruitless enquiries as to when I would see the readies, I went to the boss, resulting in Nigel chucking the thing on my desk and saying nasty things about my parentage. Then Alan's watch broke so I flogged him the second-hand one for $25. All well and good until a letter from my mother arrived along with a bounced cheque signed by...Scummy. Remember him from Chapter 4?

Yeah, as much as I had disliked the bummer I had, a couple of days prior to leaving Morris Depot, asked if he had funds in the UK, and would he change money for me? I pretended that it was to purchase specialist camping equipment. The wanker gave me some long talk about it being strictly illegal but I handed over $100 in exchange for a cheque made out from a Middle Eastern bank for £50. My mother had purchased and sent the watches without waiting for the cheque to clear. As I was occasionally sending and receiving the station's radio messages, it wasn't a problem to send one to BSAP HQ requesting the present whereabouts of PO Scummy. A couple of days later I found out that the thief had been transferred to the Pioneers, which was basically an outfit that built camps etc for the police. I sent a letter to the stinking robbing morph requesting the return of my money and stupidly sent the bounced cheque as proof. Never to hear from the swine and that was that. Both my mother and I were out of pocket, she more so.

But there was another dark cloud about to piss down on my financial parade. I was called into the boss's office.

"PO Greenberg, I regret to inform you… (now what? I was getting sick to death of these speeches of impending doom) …that unfortunately there has been another complete and utter balls up by that friggin' useless Triggs regarding the accounts for the single men's meals etc, which I know you have hardly had a bite of since you have been eating tins of soup for weeks in the bush. As a result, you are required to donate another $90 to the idiot's book keeping fund. This is regrettable (regrettable alright - it wasn't his bloody money!). If I was you I would shoot him on the spot and throw his carcass to the crocodiles…"

I went mental! Absolutely mental, and headed straight into Triggs's office with murderous intent. I had even opened a crime docket with me as the main suspect. First thing I did was grab the ruler (just in case). I had passed O-level Maths. How difficult was the task he had to do? You don't need fancy Excel spread sheets. The back of a fag packet was enough. Food was bought. Food was eaten. Those that ate - paid. Each PO was entered for the time they were present and had eaten a meal. Add said meals together and divide by said POs. Simples! Oh, plus Wilson's wage.

"Nigel. Show me the books. I am taking over."

"Be my guest," he replied without the hint of an argument or sarcasm.

Vegetables and starches were not a problem as we got them locally but when I checked the cost of the meat I thought this was way too high. It was being sent in from a butcher in Que Que. Ridiculous. We had a butcher at Kambasha's store. It was time to negotiate with old man Kambasha for some really good bargains. I got weeping willow Peter to drive me up and after some haggling, ordered half a cow at $7 akg. Job done. The slaughtered beast was duly presented to Wilson who then had a serious problem working out which end of the beast he had. In fact, what was served up over several meals was just one giant old cow's arsehole. The thing must have died from old age and kept fermented in diesel for a year.

I also forgot we needed things like bacon and sausages. But we did have eggs. I hadn't bothered ordering any chicken as I hoped one of us would perhaps win one down at the sports club. I suggested to the others I purchase a goat. Or what about some donkey instead of roast pork? Duiker fillets in red wine? Perhaps vervet monkey steaks? Wilson could marinate it in gland sauce. If there was supposed to be such great fishing around here, go out and catch your dinner. They should welcome a change of diet.

Sadly, my fellow POs were not very appreciative of my attempts to save them a fortune while appreciating meals of great African-style vintage, and I was threatened with a lynching. I had to swallow my pride and grovelling like Smeagel Gollum before Nigel and stroking his knee –

"Dear Nigel, dearest best friend Nigel, I am so sorry, please take over again." Which he did, with just a hint of a raised eyebrow, and managed to get the whole dog's dinner finally under control.

Now that I was now in some form of 'normal' routine, weekends off meant I was stuck in Gokwe. Nigel had some bird he occasionally went to see down in Gatooma and he would zip off in his car on Friday night and return for Monday morning. When he didn't go - it meant trouble…

The Rhodesia Sunday Mail article, continued…

> He added:
>
> "This is part of old Rhodesia. It is a very close community and its spirit is very good." Chief Inspector Harvey said he had been forced to arrest a Gokwian once or twice, and he

explained:

"This is a very changing society. Sometimes you get a really tough element passing through. You get hard talking, hard working and hard drinking men here sometimes, and the village changes from the quiet place it is now to a real Wild West show with guns being fired off and punch-ups. At the moment, the people here are a nice quiet lot, but the place is erratic."

The drinking started on Friday night down at the sports club. Our PO numbers had increased by the arrival of two new members, whilst Nick Robinson had left for better pastures. One was named Leon DeBeer and with a surname like that I presumed he was of Afrikaans heritage, except for the fact he was extremely well perma-tanned and with a head of very black hair. His other strange habit, besides the love of Castle beer and smoking Madisons, was swearing. I think he suffered from a form of Tourette's Syndrome as it seemed he couldn't string a sentence together without using the f and c word joined together as an adjective to describe his fellow compatriots. He did however have one advantage; he could play a mean game of darts and as a result for the next few weeks we had roast chicken nearly every Saturday. The other newbie was the skinny kid from the PATU course by the name of Ian McKinnon. He was the hard nut the fake gooks failed to break. He didn't look older than 16 but had already perfected the Rhodie hand curl around the beer bottle and fag hanging out the mouth. Neither of these individuals, who shared Nick's old room, were worth associating with as they seemed to lack any form of cerebral capacity.

Down at the club you would meet up with the rest of the white Gokwians. The Postmaster and his wife were friendly enough but he had tried to get me to pay 'import duty' on the digital watches. The corrupt bastard had opened my mail! I simply said no. I suppose he could have confiscated them but he reckoned I might start making a fuss, like crying a lot about my poor financial woes. One bloke, Chris Walker, worked for the Internal Affairs. He could have walked straight out of Wilbur Smith's *When the Lion Feeds*. The man could have been a Fredrick Courtney Selous double. He would sit quietly at the end of the bar chewing a match. He didn't talk much. He once related how he had gone into a kraal and had been savaged by a kaffir dog. Now that is a surprise because an incident like this was rare.

The kaffir dog, KD for short, is a rather unique animal. The correct term for this canine is *Afrcanis*. Whites considered them as cowardly, half starved, tick-infested mongrel curs that only black people kept. A regular KD was of medium-size, with ribs usually visible, a long snout and a yellowish-brownish short hair coats. Whilst we whites thought of them as total uselessness, they are in fact a unique species in their own right because it has been the environment that has moulded them. They are born survivors and what we thought was cowardice is, in fact, their wariness of anything unfamiliar. The stature of the half-starved look was normal. There must have been thousands of them in Gokwe. Every kraal would have several - always yapping at us whites. The blacks loved them for their intelligence (that we whites didn't notice), loyalty and hunting ability.

So it was indeed odd that one should sink its teeth into Chris's boot. Amazingly, after Chris put his FN barrel against its head and pulled the trigger, the teeth were still in his boot whilst the rest of its skull disappeared. Chris also held the record for the yard of ale. This three foot long, trumpet-shaped glass receptacle held 2½ pints of beer. Chris sank it in 14 seconds flat and brought it back up again in two. How wicked is that!

Another weird couple were some Germans. They were in their late 50s and hardly had a grasp of the English language. I think he worked for the Water Department. Weeping willow Peter and I once went night rabbit hunting with him. It was one of the funniest things I had experienced. Günter would give us his .22 rifle to use. He would drive his Landrover up and down the grassy landing strip at Gokwe village screaming

"I zee nufink!," as I sat in the spare tyre attached to the bonnet taking pot shots at rabbits as they tried to dodge Peter's searchlight that he was using from the open back.

Günter would be swerving around and I hung on for dear life laughing hysterically whilst firing one handed. Not a bad night's haul with four rabbits that Günter's domestic servants eagerly had for dinner. It didn't occur to me that we whites could eat them.

Another lad was a manic depressive called Piet. He worked at the government's Central Mechanical Engineering Department

(CMED). A nice bloke who moaned constantly about his lot, which I thought was rather odd as he was a South African, and had no reason at all to be here. He could simply jack it in and go back home.

There was a Supersonic stereo in the bar with a collection of LPs. Sadly, most of the warped things had been used to scrape up vomit and the only record that was playable was the Beatles hits. Even that was badly scratched but a twenty five cent piece resting on the top of the needle's head kept it grinding out the same tunes repeatedly.

So people came and people went - depending on their jobs and circumstances. Some were nice, some were downright thieving, lying swines - like one couple who will remain nameless. As usual, I was skint and the Postmaster, knowing of my desire to make any kind of deal, sold me 60 Rands worth of South African post office vouchers. They had to be redeemed in cash in South Africa within three months. Some nice Gokweians were going on holiday at the time. I gave them the vouchers and they agreed to steal them, spend them, and then tell me a cock and bull story about how their car was broken into and sadly my vouchers were stolen. Except they neglected to tell me the thief had the car key as he owned the vehicle.

But the biggest problem with the weekend sessions was when Triggs was around. Even worse was if Alan decided to go on the lash with him. Then there was aggro.

Weeping willow Peter and I would be awoken at some crazy hour and Alco-popped Al and Psychopath Nigel would throw a screaming 'Wankbank' as they called the poor bastard, into the pool, closely followed by his bed and clothes cupboard. If I was threatened I simply beat them to the pool and happily swam about until they got bored. As long as my Precious didn't get chucked in, I wasn't bothered. Some times they went too far. On one weekend while I was away, they took Wankbank for a bog wash (head held in toilet bowl and flushed) polished his nuts with boot polish and then tossed him with bed and clothes into the pool and went to bed. Dressed only with a sodden blanket, weeping willow Peter went and awoke the boss. You can imagine how impressed he was.

From what I gathered from Peter, the boss awoke the drunken pair and held a court session in our lounge. When asked why they had done it, Triggs answer, "Cos he's a wanker," wasn't quite the excuse the boss was looking for. He then gave an order. "This sort of activity will cease and desist immediately. This will not happen again."

Triggs must have been off his skull because his next statement was a big mistake, "Like fuck it won't!"

That clever reply cost him 10 days leave. Alan got away with two weekends cancelled. They didn't bully Peter again but they weren't exactly going to make him their new best friend. Still, he was welcome to play poker with us. Anyone who thought three red cards and two black ones made a flush was welcome to hand over their money.

Only once did it really get dangerous and much to my amusement and Peter's, we would watch as Triggs came home and decided that his new drinking buddies Leon and Ian had been downright discourteous by not having gone with him one Saturday night to drink themselves to rampant violent hooliganism. Triggs always announced his arrival by zooming up at high speed with his car. He then tried their door. It was locked in anticipation. Not to be outdone, he found a large wooden stave and fired it through the window, spattering shattered glass all over Leon. This naturally awoke him and his screams of rage, along with Triggs's drunken taunts, shattered the peace. Weeping willow Peter and I tumbled out of bed to watch the show. Nigel, now obviously fuelled with his own violent reputation and 'Dutch courage' stupidly came up to the broken window to hurl more obscene references to women's genitals and their apparent relationship to Leon's state of mind. The retaliation came rather swiftly and I was well impressed with the style of weapon used. Flicking his cigarette lighter on, he sprayed a tin of pressurised fly killer over the flickering flame, creating instantly a roaring massive sheet of fire, which should have incinerated Triggs's head to a nicely deserved crisp if his KD instincts hadn't made him jerk back instinctively. This was unquestionably extreme hardcore entertainment with free front seats!

With Triggs in retreat and out of range from the impromptu flame thrower and Leon's hand getting rather hot, he dropped the tin of insect killer, charged out the room and threw his twelve inch bush knife, just missing and imbedding into the ground near Triggs's wide spread planted feet. Triggs, shrieking like a Banshee, snatched it up and hurled it back underhand, slicing through Leon's left calf. Ian was now also outside and grabbed the knife. I also came over and called a halt. The cut wasn't bad but it seemed to have enough effect to get Nigel to calm down and go to bed.

Memoir mutterings

Earlier I said I would not reveal Scummy's real name but I have changed my mind because, while scrolling the BSAP Nominal Roll, I came across an interesting name:

9705 PO Donald 'Scummy' John Bruce, DESERTED, July 1978. Well, well, who would have thought he would have sneaked out the backdoor. Doing a runner was relatively easy. Rhodesia wasn't a giant prison – unless its inmates were poor and only had a Rhodesian passport. Scummy would have simply crossed over into South Africa or even taken a flight out of Salisbury to the UK while on a day off.

Email from NigelTriggs –

That is serious wild west stuff.....can't remember much of it but I do remember together with Nick Robinson throwing one of the oke's beds on the roof after returning from a Friday night piss-up at the club. Boredom and frustration and only ONE thing to do...drink away the days till we got out the place.

Wankbank, eish, his chick was the girl from the hotel for a while, man they were such a ball of fire together… sat there staring into space holding hands and when they did communicate it was a full on wraught. (Arguing.) Man, I wonder what happened to him...obviously a decent fella compared to the hooligans in uniform!

I do remember the extra money for the mess bills - that was thrown at me out the blue - and we used to have to phone the orders through to Que Que and they were delivered on the bus, full of dust. I just asked the lads what they like to eat and I got all sorts of orders, so needless to say I just ordered , ox tails and other exotics. Maiwe, when the month end bills arrived I was in the dwang - way over spent - but the problem was that I was out in the bush for a week and someone else ordered the weekly order and went moggy. I was as popular as a pig in a mosque and you are right, $90 was a bloody fortune - so I copped that one badly - and got a rocket from the bossman....

And, as for the watches:

Shite, the watches were that expensive. Yep, I recall you wanting to break my neck about the bloody things. Next I see you I will give you your $50....plus interest, and buy you a new watch in return. I was a bit of an asshole! Apologies after 30 years!

Tee-hee, I will be coming to collect one day...

Glossary

Readies. Money

CHAPTER 17:

Landies, Lions and Lies

the Gokwe Kid and weeping willow

Pic - Gokwe Kid

When another weekend arrived in April, and being stuck with not much to do, duty PO weeping willow Peter asked me if I fancied a little day trip. One of our base camps was in desperate need of supplies and two constables also had to be taken there.

Simchembu or Whisky-Whisky, as it was sometimes called, was an old RioTinto prospecting camp on the Mapungola hills overlooking the Sengwa River and basin - real Batonka tribe country. Gokwe village and the camp were almost equal altitude - with nothing in between - so it made UHF communications rather good. It was the nothing in between that made weeping willow Peter's statement that we would be there and back that day seem rather dubious. A look at the map made it a 370km return trip down a rutted and potholed dirt 'road', through a tsetse fly zone, a stretch of the Chirisa game reserve and then an area like an insurgent's tourist resort. Supposedly, I would be back in time for a vodka, lime and lemonade at the local Gokwe *Alcoholics 'R' Us* Sports Club before night fall.

Feeling rather bored, and not having much common sense, I agreed to come along for a laugh. Although he was on duty, Peter wasn't required to wear uniform and as I was officially off, I was happy in a T-Shirt and shorts. So I went along. We would take one of the open backed Landies with the two constables in the back. Of course, should we run over a landmine we may have stood stand a chance in the cab, due to its reinforced steel plates, but anyone in the rear would become flying biltong.

There was a constant transport problem. Most of our Landies had number plates starting with 13. Landy 1313 was used for local rounds only. This was due to the fact that it had only two forward gears - first and fourth. This meant the driver shot off at an alarming rate and when his ear tuned into the fact that the engine was about to explode, fourth was engaged. By that time you had to reach the bit of down hill road below the police station before the jolting kangaroo jerking of the near-stalling engine made you motion sick. As this machine was the only resident Landy, I would be occasionally taken for a ride as an assistant gear stick. That was because it had another problem - reverse only worked if someone held it in place with some degree of force with both hands. The boss, of course, sent 1313 to CMED for repairs by the forlorn, overworked Piet, but the application for parts were refused and we were told to apply again when the thing was down to a single gear. I suppose turning up at investigations in reverse would make a heck of a figure of true Rhodie entrepreneurial skill.

There was one special Landy. 873 had a white top and was functioning okay - till weeping willow Peter got hold of it. So, on a clear blue sky day, with temperatures rapidly rising, we left around 10am and were soon zipping along, cicadas chirping away, friendly, smiling natives waving enthusiastically at us as we weaved erratically in the soft dust. Peter was playing happily with the yellow knob of the best 4 x 4 by far we had. I was sipping superheated Coca-Cola (still only 5 cents a bottle), and feet up on the dashboard to avoid the engine's radiant heat. Rifles were well jammed between door and seat, and ready in seconds should we come under fire. There was no need for any supplies as we planned on having a nice lunch at

Simchembu before returning to Gokwe in time for dinner. We went past the cul-de-sac to Chirama camp and progressed in low range to navigate the extremely steep rocky track down the escarpment until we hit the long flat straight where the Landy could really fly. All seemed going to plan and I was enjoying the scenery.

We must have been about 10 clicks into Chirisa game reserve when trouble started. I got a feeling that weeping willow Peter might have been blind from his constant crying and was too vain to wear glasses. For the next thing I know, we are in a deep ditch and I nearly choked on a Coke bottle. The poor saps in the back managed to stay in as we ploughed to a stuttering halt. And now? Weeping willow Peter went into one of those wailing whinging apologies that had made him so popular as a rugby ball. It seems he had been keeping his eye so well on the heat gauge, that he hadn't noticed we were about to go into Titanic mode. Plus, we were overheating.

Was I scared?   Not at all. The place where we pranged was as safe as Fort Knox. Nature had supplied the best anti-insurgent weapons in the world. They are called shumbas, and just love a tasty bit of human. As an extra deterrent, the place was populated with the fastest winged injector of 'Sleepy Bye Bye' disease - also known as human African *trypanosomiasis*. The Africa bit about the name had no racial prejudices or preferences. The disease is a killer and also the bite of a tsetse fly is really sore. What five minutes before had been, "Gee, check out that pride of shumbas under the tree, man, and those poor bastards in the back are getting well bitten," was now, "we are well and truly fucked!"

Of course, I didn't know if they really were man-eating lions but I knew they smelt fear-induced stirring bowels for miles, and homed in on it like – well – lions. The two constables correctly and freely volunteered to walk back to the nearest village to solicit assistance. That idea sounded good to me. I had no desire to walk in 32-degree blazing sunshine while playing hide and seek with some overgrown hungry pussy cats. Besides, neither of us POs could speak the local lingo!

But how we suffered. To keep those evil tsetse flies off our blood we sat in the cab with closed windows till the Cokes exploded. Just as we reached the stage to qualify for the health warning 'Spending more than 5 hours in a sauna is bad for your health', help arrived. A span of six mombes appeared. That the owner had been persuaded to bring them into the park and a tsetse fly area was indeed testament to their willingness to help the law. They had wooden handmade yokes and ropes woven from bark. In a few moments the Landy was back on the road. I am not sure if Peter gave them any money for that. I didn't. It was my day off and not my fault we are now five hours behind schedule.

Do you remember that song,
      'Things…can only get better'?
      Try, 'Things… can only get worse'. They did.
      Half blind, weeping willow Peter sets off again and after a short while informs me that 'she' was on heat. For once he wasn't referring *ad nauseum* to his girl friend in Que Que. Nope, 873 was on heat, and we were still some 80 clicks from Simchembu. Although out of the park, we were now in the badlands where gooks liked to hang out. The Landy had to be stopped to cool down and we needed to report in. The UHF radio was useless here, so I had set up the TR28. These heavy things bounced serious radio waves off the stratosphere. I know they were real 'heavy waves' because it was standard Rhodie radio initiation torture to get the new recruit to hold the antenna while sending. This resulted in 2nd degree burns, a short burst of pain-induced urine by the recipient, and the hilarity from the initiator of this form of torture. The antenna tended to be useless, so it was stretch-out-the-wire-aerial time.
      After reaching 608 (Gokwe) to pass on that we would be late, there was a short debate as how to get the aerial down after I had tied stones to the ends and expertly threw them over very high trees. The wire was strong. The trees were strong. The lions, not knowing any park boundaries and thus still abounded around, were even stronger and we had no wire cutters. In fact, we had nothing really. No Coke, no food, no water and in a couple of hours - no sunlight. Taking cue from the great Frederick Courtney Selous, eyesight loaded with adrenalin (as maybe I was the only one with even the slightest notion of our predicament), I slotted the stones with two shots. I nearly blinded a constable with shattered splinters, but at least we were on the move.
      By now I'm singing, 'Things… can only get worser' and they did.
      873 was in a bad way. We couldn't dare open the radiator cap and what for? We had no water, never mind the machine. Light was

fading fast and as we reached the now dry Sengwa River, we came across an abandoned Bedford supply truck stuck on the only bridge, blocking the way up the escarpment. I am supposed to be at *Alcoholics 'R' Us* and supposedly having a really good time by now.

What happens next is a true account of the rape and pillage of a four cylinder Leyland Landrover engine named 873. It was the start of the dry season and the temperature gauge is in the serious red zone. The constables in the back are threatening mutiny. I want to shoot weeping willow, throw his corpse to the lions and I knew I would be acquitted in a military tribunal. This is the really badlands, people die here, especially white ones. Copper-coated lead instant air conditioning projectiles spring to mind. Custer's Last Stand? Alan Wilson and the Shangani Patrol? Can I think of any more examples of idiots getting their free ticket to the after life?

With everyone weeping for their lives by now, Peter shoved the screaming dying Landy into low gear drive, put her into first, and tore its guts out, first through the river bed, then all the way up that escarpment. With dust encircling the dying African sun, the last bit of steam pouring out the bonnet, and smoke pouring out the exhaust, gooks as far away as Lusaka in Zambia could have heard the din as we limped in to base camp.

The occupants were really backward. They didn't understand that I was just a hitchhiker and stuffing up 873 wasn't my idea. It was also not my fault the Bedford truck broke down. It seems some over zealous driver thought riding the clutch down hill till it hit the bridge was good for its plates. Wrong. They seized. As far as I was concerned I had nothing to do whatsoever with the whole calamity.

"That means we are sending a stick of five men to protect it."

This announcement came from Inspector Gray. *The* Inspector Gray. The man of mystery – we meet at last. A bachelor and maybe late 30s, he was a strong-looking man with a pipe hanging out his mouth from which he constantly puffed away.

Well, at least I wasn't then volunteered to play baby sitter to a Bedford truck but it meant due to lack of available 'eyes' I had to do guard duty for two hours between 2am and 4am. Dammit! This is supposed to be my weekend off. This was definitely the last time I was going out for a little 'pleasure' drive in the bush and not getting paid for it. I couldn't even claim bush allowance.

My pitiful bleating and attempts to persuade Inspector Gray to make that fool Brockbank do my shift as well because it was his entire fault, made no impression of course, but dinner was a treat. A very rare treat actually, considering it was categorized as Royal Game - the stunningly beautiful sable antelope. The saviours of the realm and protectors of the law were short of a fresh joint, and a sable had accidently walked across the rifle scopes when it accidently went off. Very nice. The huge piece of roasted meat was extremely dark coloured and strong tasting (of guilt?). Still, I should be grateful for small mercies. A rather alarmed voice had just reported over the radio that a pride of lions had decided to take up camp under the Bedford for the night and five men in the cab were extremely claustrophobic. Hah hah hah! It's a hard knock life. They should have looked at the bright side. The lions were protecting them from the gooks.

It was quite a large camp. Well set out. A good old Rhodie drum boiler supplied hot water, so a shower was much appreciated. Sandbags encircled the place and at 2am I was sagged over them. By 3am I was having serious hallucinations and kept seeing aliens with glowing red eyes from the direction of the pitch-black bush. It was scary. Every sense was at screaming point. The slightest sound seemed magnified and anything that remotely made a snapping sound became gooks slinking up on us.

Sunday broke. It was another hot and lovely day and seemed a perfect time to do a Mazoe Patrol stunt and fight our way back to HQ. Only difference - the 1896 pioneers had horses, 33 armed men and a wagon protected with sheets of metal against the cheeky blacks that had started a rebellion over some stolen land. We had a cracked cylinder head and just the two of us to negotiate through another rebellion of cheeky blacks STILL moaning about some stolen land. Except this time they were better armed.

Using as many spare containers available we had taken enough water to get us to the base of the Chirama plateau before 873 gave up. By feeding her tortured radiator constantly before she blew her top, it worked. At the base of the last obstacle was a borehole and a water tower with a huge hose. Then, weeping willow did a strange thing. Leaving the engine running, lifting the bonnet, he whacked the radiator cap off with a lump of wood and proceeded to give the steaming dying beast a bath.

The hose end was designed to feed water trailers, not radiators. Anyway, loads of steam later, we stagger back home.

We get debriefed by the Boss. I still protest it was my

weekend off but there's a problem with responsibility for killing 873. I get asked a simple question.

"Did PO Brockbank leave the engine running at Chirama when he refilled the radiator?"

My mechanical abilities were undoing a girl's bra one handed whilst snogging. What kind of question was this? I lied, thinking I save Peter's ass.

"No."

In the ensuing yowling from weeping willow Peter, I realised I hadn't been the perfect witness and tried to change my story. But - the damage was done.

Memoir mutterings

The trashing of Landrovers was a rather bad habit. The record was most probably set by PO John Wheeler, the character I described as crawling into the Toad's office on all fours begging to be let out of Gokwe, but it appears this was just a wind-up story.
Nigel Triggs sets the record straight re: John Wheeler's driving ability.

Email from Nigel.
Wheeler was on his 6th Landy that he either crashed or broke and was relegated to stay at Chirama where his driving skills would not be tested or anyone else at risk. A PATU stick had been deployed along the water tanks line heading north from the base down in the valley...the leader was a Rusty Hustler (not a fan of Alan Golden - he wanted to fork him up all the time...like a bull to a red rag), anyway the stick had been deployed down the escarpment in a Landy by Wheeler, and he returned to base and they patrolled. After some days they wanted to come back so they radioed Wheeler and asked him to pick them up by water tank No.?

So Wheeler, as bored as anything, heads off down the escarpment at one heeluva rate...as he was known to do all the time. So now SO Hustler and the stick decide, let's walk towards where Wheeler is coming from, so they can get picked up quicker. On the walk to the next nearest water tank they decide that they are going to give Wheeler a fright of his life (as there was the usual good spirit amongst the lads). If you remember the road along the tanks is half decent, dead straight and one could build up a head of steam. Wheeler is expecting the chaps further up the road and has head is still down and sending it. The PATU team is now about 3km closer to camp and they hear the Landy humming it down the beaten track. All the whites hide in the bush and they allocate one of the blacks in camo to make Wheeler crap himself. So, as Wheeler is travelling on his own towards them, not expecting to see them until another 3km, the black PATU fella jumps out in the road in front of Wheeler and points his gun at him. Wheeler thinks he is really in the shit now and swerves off the road into the bush on the side to try and evade the "gook"...smacks into a tree with the front bumper which now bends the bumper in a curve and the rear of the Landy is now also wedged into a tree at the back and he is stuck firmly between the two trees....Landy No 7 for Wheeler!

They took ages to get the Landy out from between the trees....after the laughter subsided....and some manoeuvring. Wheeler was in big shit for his exploits and that was his last Landy at Gokwe and Andy Gray issued him with a bicycle to patrol on.

Glossary

Biltong. Raw meat (normally beef), usually cut with the grain, heavily salted and loaded with top secret spices and hung up to dry. Similar, but far superior to the Yank's beef jerky.
Prang(ed). Crash involving any wheeled vehicle.

CHAPTER 18:

Driving, dating and a lot of chutzpah

A couple of weeks after my brush with the shumbas, I was again called into the boss's office. I hoped this wasn't going to be another 'deep regret' speech leading to more money being handed over to Nigel, or the ultimate pain, dressing up like a tree and playing hide and seek with the gooks.

"PO Greenberg, I requested that you be fast-tracked to Driving School as it is becoming a considerable inconvenience having to provide you with a chauffeur when you go on investigations."

I waited for the inevitable big downer.

"Of course, this will be considered an unpaid holiday and you will be required to pay $500 for the lessons and a further $50 to take the test."

Which, thankfully, wasn't the case, but I was always suspicious when it came to magical freebies from the BSAP.

"As such, you will pack and report for lessons on Monday. I expect you will be gone for three weeks. You will be staying at the Cranborne singles mess. Dismissed."

My grin beamed brighter than the morning sun. Oh the pleasure. City lights here I come and this time I couldn't be roped into going to Inyanga. Sadly, I couldn't claim bush allowance, but hey, I was still getting paid to get a driving license.

The boss sorted me out with transport to Que Que and, with a large kitbag stuffed with uniforms (and mini-Precious), I hitched to Salisbury and managed to get home by Saturday. The following day I mulled over how I was going to get to my destination. Cranborne was the other side of Salisbury and at least 15 clicks from Mount Pleasant, and Katherine didn't have the extra fuel, so I was a bit buggered. I had no intention of wasting money on a taxi and didn't fancy dragging loads of kit through town hitchhiking. So, dressed in full urban regalia of khaki tunic and shorts, plus the painful anti-dog savaging leggings, I phoned the central police station. I decided I would try and cop a free ride in a cop car. Amazingly they didn't tell me to bugger off and half an hour later I was sitting in the back of a Peugeot 404 B-car. At the single policemen's mess I was shown a free room and was delighted to meet up with Addie again, who had put on even more weight. He was stationed at Salisbury Central (Car Theft Section) - the jammy bugger. I also bumped into another china from primary school and Allan Wilson High, Norman Child. He was with Support Unit and was recovering from a bullet wound to the shoulder. I soon organised a batman for the time I was there and life was looking up (my Gokwe batman, Thomas, had been given unpaid leave.)

Driving lessons were a hoot. Once the theory test was (easily) passed, I, together with two other learners, were taught by an instructor in a long-wheel base Landrover. These models were painted grey and were kept spick and span, unlike the half stripped junk we had in Gokwe. In this vehicle we would take it in turns learning the most unbelievable crap. For a start, it was all incredibly old fashioned. We were taught how to double declutch while changing gears. Clutch in, move stick to neutral, clutch out, clutch in, move stick into new gear (what for, all modern gear boxes are synchronised?), and all the appropriate hand signals. Stopping was embarrassing as I imagined the drivers behind us pissed themselves with our antics.

Imagine going down the busiest road in Salisbury - Second Street at rush hour – back as stiff as a ramrod; hands on the wheel in the 10 to 2 position, when the robots (traffic lights) at Rhodes Avenue change to amber, then red, signalling you to stop.

In preparation, the first manoeuvre is the 'long wave goodbye': out comes your right arm - as stiff as the Fuhrer's salute - through the half open window (a sliding glass panel). Second move: wave arm up and down slowly, as if fanning away a bad fart. This is to alert other drivers that you intend slowing down (you also tend to receive tentative waves back from curious pedestrians). Double declutch the gears, lightly touch the brakes, look in the rear view mirror, fan fart again, but, before withdrawing hand, hold it up bent at the elbow in classic police halt pose, bring your hand in, put the clutch in, engage neutral, apply handbrake and collapse in a cold sweat over the steering wheel just as the traffic lights turn green.

This brain draining and physically exhausting process was only surpassed by a left turn. Here you were required to use the indicators, look over your left shoulder and, instead of the halt sign, you would switch from the fart fanning move to stiff armed, large anti-clockwise circles in three full revolutions. As you actually start to turn left, you hope that after all this effort you spot a pedestrian crossing the road before the instructor hits the emergency brake, causing you to hit the windscreen with your peaked hat, and throwing your petrified fellow learners in the back hard against their seat belts.

That first week I spent quite a lot of time in the evening with Addie at the police clubhouse. It had a neat bar and a snooker table which we used for a while. Addie was a funny bugger and he still had the annoying habit of flicking burnt matches at me but more annoying was that he cheated at snooker. It took me ages before I spotted what he was up to. He would steal a red ball and pop it in his trouser pocket. When it was his turn to play a shot, a red would mysteriously appear directly over a pocket near to where my last shot had taken the white cue ball. I was bloody sure it hadn't been there before. Eventually I got suspicious and while ordering more beer via the hatch in the wall adjacent to the bar, I watched carefully via one of the ornate framed mirrors hanging on the wall and caught the crafty sod.

    Still, these fun and games had to be terminated after my little 'accident'. I had a long shot down the table to try and cut a red into the corner pocket. I lazily placed a full pint of Castle far from the intended target but, 'illegally' on the wide wooden frame of the extremely expensive snooker table. I should have used one of the many small tables littered around the room. I let rip with the cue on the white with a force necessary to catch the red with a thin kiss. Unfortunately I missed - the hurtling cue ball smashed against the top cushion, took off at least head height, hurtled back my way at an alarming rate, and ploughed with incredible accuracy straight into my full pint, blasting beer and glass all over the immaculate green felt before my horrified eyes. The next thing I did was just as stupid. Without thinking at all, my panic reaction was to try and wipe the lot into the nearest pocket using my bare hands; promptly slicing my palms open and leaving a trail of blood soaking with the beer into the cloth before the pain woke me up. We got the hell out of there. No one had seen us and the barman didn't know my name. Such was life as young responsible police officers That meant I needed something else to do and I desired the company of a female.

I met Josephine when I was aged 18 going on 19 and she was 17 going on 18. I would end up feeling as daft as the Austrian *Nazi* who yowled that song in the *Sound of Music*, even if our ages were slightly out of sync with the ditty. It was one-sided love at first sight. The invisible and unspoken age difference dating rule between the sexes in Rhodesia still guided me. Josephine was not from my former high school; she was an outsider and, believe it or not, a blind date. In fact, she was a blind date I made myself. I couldn't get a date from any of the old Mount Pleasant High School gang (I wonder why?), so I needed a plan to find a prospective new mate. I asked my step-mom to recommend a couple of girls from the A-level history class that she taught at Oriel Girls High School. This turned out to be a big mistake. The first name she suggested was her favourite in the class, though Katherine did admit that her intellectual standard was perhaps above mine. In addition she had a 28 year-old boyfriend who was a major in the Rhodesian Light Infantry. After reading a couple of her history essays, I concluded that even telling her my name would sound clumsy. Her brilliance was impressive, but I was just plain randy. Besides, I wanted no trouble from the major. So, thanks but no thanks. Who's next?

Katherine's second favourite was Josephine Woods. Apparently, she wrote letters to my brother Michael. That sounded a bit strange, but I thought I would give it a go. Step-mum said she had heard that the family were a bit 'odd'. Odd? What is odd? My family were odd. How much odder could she be? I phoned her. Her father answered and only after an extremely long winded explanation of who I was, did I persuade him to call her to the phone. She was very surprised to hear from me. I asked if I could take her out for dinner that weekend. She seemed interested, and after concurring with her father, we made the date for Saturday at 7.30pm, outside the Bamboo Inn - Salisbury's best Chinese restaurant.

I didn't have any nice clothes for such a smart place and I didn't want to appear uncouth in my pair of prized Levi's obtained at enormous cost, so, after a quick hitchhike to my best mate Tim Bell's house, I borrowed a pair of pants in luminous green satin. Saturday Night Fever-style - so to speak. I don't think Tim ever saw those pants again, and he certainly wouldn't want them back now.

My next problem was how I was going to get from the driving school barracks in Cranborne which was at least six clicks from the town centre. I needed to scavenge a lift. Two middle-aged police reservists were taking the course with me. They were here to brush up on their skills before going back to Bulawayo to run their own version of a police driving school in the hopes of easing Salisbury's load a little. They were still in uniform, having a quiet pint in the police pub (the walls displaying all the plaques of the operational areas and the various fighting units, just like most public or private bars in the land), when I wandered in and started relating my story of *amour*, and, as they were really decent guys, they drove me into town. This obviously impressed Josephine's father, who had accompanied his daughter to our arranged meeting place. I remember hoping that he didn't think he was having dinner with us - unless he was paying of course. On my best behaviour, I assured Josephine's dad that I would return her by 11pm. I actually wasn't sure how I would achieve that, and getting her to hitchhike in that rather daft dress she was wearing looked a dubious prospect. In fact this was all very dubious. But, she was gorgeous: a nice pair of breasts looked very inviting under the oddly coloured nun's habit she seemed to be wearing (minus the hat), lovely straight brown hair falling well over her shoulders, clear complexion, eyes of blue and a mouth I wanted to play vacuum cleaners with. In other words - she was a babe. I wanted her to be my honey.

I recall next to nothing of that first dinner date, conversation wise. I know I was completely love struck and, knowing me quite well, that must have been as attractive as a chattering baboon tripped out on LSD. I do recall her telling me that it was only that she had told her father what a well-respected woman Katherine was, and therefore that I must be a respectable police officer for my step-mother to suggest her name in the first place. I hope I didn't let on that her teacher wasn't my real mother and that I was a raving loon. Most likely I was too busy blabbing what a hero I was in Gokwe, while grinning stupidly at her perfect face. The cost of the meal must have made me feel ill to my wallet, and at 10.30pm the question of how to get her home cropped up.

Once outside the restaurant, she suggested I call a taxi. I miserably concurred. I saw this option as an incredible waste of money, but at least I was clever enough not to put forward the idea of hitching, which would probably have got me killed twice: once by her father and again by my step-mom. So, knowing that there would be some taxis outside the Club Tomorrow discotheque, we headed in that direction. Sure enough, there were a couple of taxis and, better still, three police cars attending yet another fight - nothing unusual in that place full of pissed up troopies on R&R, kicking war stories out of each other.

I told Josephine to wait and I went over to one of the patrol cars. Whatever incident they were attending was now over, and the police drivers had already started their engines. I flashed my ID card to a very astonished mixed sex pair of senior patrol officers and explained that I was a fellow brother from Gokwe (emphasising the word Gokwe frightens most policemen), that I was on a date, that the dinner cost much more than I thought, and I couldn't afford a taxi. I gestured over to where Josephine was standing to relay the fact that she was not dressed for hitching and asked, very nicely, for help. They moaned a bit, but as I wasn't a staggering drunk and Josephine looked like Julie Andrews in a long haired wig, they reluctantly agreed. Even my date was impressed. They drove us all the way home up the Enterprise Road, where her old man owned a huge nursery (the trees and plants type), with me preening cleverly on the back seat next to her. I think she was so gobsmacked that she let me hold her hand. After I had been granted a quick kiss on the cheek and gained permission to phone her again, I sat well pleased in the police car until I was booted out in the middle of central Salisbury. The officers explained to me, in no uncertain terms, that I had a bit of a cheek and that, no, they were not going to drive me back to the barracks. Bastards! So it was back to plan B: hitchhiking and hoping that whoever picked me up wasn't way over the limit. I wouldn't have arrested him - I just wanted to be still in one piece when I got back.

Now with a possible new girlfriend to chase, I needed a driving licence *asap* and threw all my usual effort into this task. This meant of course doing the absolute minimum, while trying to have as much fun as possible in all available free time without lashing out too much money.

After two weeks of intensive lessons, it was time to take my test. The examiner, Section Officer Johnson, was in his early 30s and was a rather curious individual. He had only been in Rhodesia a short time, having left the Metropolitan Police Force in London before coming to Salisbury with his wife.

He failed me while trying to cross Second Street, claiming that I had not seen an oncoming car from the right, forcing him to use the emergency brake. For once I didn't argue, as I was a nervous wreck. I was told back at Cranborne that I would be given another week and one more test. This time I had to pass, so I specifically asked for SO Johnson to test me again, thinking logically that as I now knew him a little, I wouldn't be so nervous. It was also obvious to me that he rather liked my chirpy style and would not fail me again on such a minor thing as ploughing into a bus full of school kids or whatever. My hunch paid off; I received 60 per cent on my test, the minimum pass mark. Cool. I now had a licence to kill.

My next move was to see if I could extend my stay in order to get to know Miss Woods a bit better. I requested permission to take my motorbike licence, cleverly adding another two weeks to my stay. After a quick radio message to my boss in Gokwe, I received the answer I wanted to hear: permission granted.

Addie hired me his 1958 Volkswagen for a week for $10 so I could take Josephine out for a couple more dates, culminating (hopefully) in a few French kisses and love-struck pleasure. She remained rather aloof, however, rather as if I was just light entertainment and a cash cow providing her with fancy meals.

Motorbike school was a breeze, and I took to the bike like a natural. My teacher was SO Johnson, and, after the first week of lessons, he would tell me he had a few things to do and I could drive about unsupervised, so long as I was back for 4.30 pm. This was great fun, zipping around all day seeing family and friends on a nice shiny Yamaha 350cc bike; plus plenty of free petrol. A couple of times I visited Josephine after she finished school and she would ride pillion while I drove around her family's incredibly huge garden. I loved every moment of it: her long hair streaming back, holding me tight around the waist, laughing as I swerved and weaved between the masses of bushes and rock gardens.

Then, a couple of days before I was to take the test, SO Johnson didn't turn up for work. After a few fruitless calls were made, another instructor and I were dispatched to his house. I had visited once before and had been struck then by the obvious poverty of the couple, so much in contrast to the immaculately turned out professional who, at work, smoked a pipe with a Sherlock Holmes type of dignity.

They couldn't afford servants, so there were none there when we turned up. The back door was unlocked with the key still on the inside. We called out as we went into the kitchen, but there was no reply. We commented on the dirty dishes in the sink and walked further into the house. The few bits of second hand furniture were still in place and nothing seemed out of the ordinary. Still calling out SO Johnson's name, and with growing alarm, we went into the master bedroom.

The bed was unmade, but what stuck out like a sore thumb was the open bedroom cupboard, totally bare except for a few coat hangers with his uniforms on them. The house wasn't big, and a quick search turned up no suitcases. It was obvious now what SO Johnson had been up to during the last week while I was driving Miss Woods about. He was getting ready to do a runner. It didn't take long to find out what had happened. The pair had booked themselves on the South African Airways night flight to London and by the time we turned up at the house they would have already landed. But why? That puzzled me a bit. Johnson had appeared to be settling down and seemed to take his job seriously. I could only hazard the guess that they felt isolated, and I reckoned he would have been earning only $100 per month more than me. It could also have been that he had been told that he would be required to do some stints in the bush and perhaps he didn't fancy that. Either way, he was gone.

I easily passed my motorbike test with a score of 80% and managed to persuade my boss to grant me five days holiday at home. I pointed out that stuck in Cranbourne Barracks for the last six weeks could not really be seen as R&R. How is that for chutzpah! So I managed to bum a ride down to Mount Pleasant and arsed around the weekend with mates, hitching here and there as Katherine wouldn't let me use her car (this meant no date with Josephine). But on Sunday afternoon when I wandered in from wherever, my stepmother informed me that there had been a call from Gokwe police station to say I was to return immediately. I tried to ring back, but the line was constantly busy. I was puzzled, so I phoned Que Que Charge Office to see if I could get any information. After a while I managed to get through and heard the following garbled story from a very excitable patrol officer.

It seemed that yesterday, millions, billions, zillions of heavily armed gooks had attacked and torched Gokwe village and that the entire armed forces of Rhodesia had been mobilised and that included me. All leave was cancelled, and I was to get my ass back *asap*. It turns out that Gokwe had a problem trying to find out where I actually was. I quickly phoned Josephine and love-wailed a stricken good-bye, not that she seemed overly concerned with my imminent doom. Within 20 minutes I had packed my blue sausage bag and was ready to go, rifle and all. I wore jeans and T-shirt rather than uniform; it was acceptable to hitchhike in camo but not in police uniform. Katherine drove me down to the Bulawayo Road; I didn't have time to hitch out of the suburbs. A quick kiss good-bye, and I was on the road back to Gokwe, in love, with a licence to kill and the reality hitting me that the war had finally caught up with me big time. As I headed back one seriously worrying sentence kept going through my head that the PO in Que Que had told me over the phone: "I believe they shot up the police station pretty bad and the singles mess was destroyed".

My Precious wasn't insured. Could I sue Robert Mugabe?

Memoir mutterings

Of the central characters mentioned no longer in this memoir: -
9751 DSO Tim 'Addie' Addison. Pension and other benefits. June 1980.

I sometimes wonder why I was friends with Addie. I just remembered that the bastard use to put salt in my tea at Morris Depot. After about the fourth time he did this at breakfast, I snapped and threw the lot over him!

Email from Addie -

I was only in Cranborne Barracks (which were condemned in the 1950s but good enough for cops) for about 8 months of which every second month was spent in the bush; before being sent to the bush on a more permanent basis.

Keep up the good work and don't make me sound like such a shit!

Glossary

Babe. Attractive member of the opposite sex.

Honey. A babe that belongs to you.

Last of the Rhodesians
Chronicles of an African anarchist

The Gokwe Kid
Dick of the Bushveld

PART TWO

CHAPTER 19:

The Great Battle of Gokwe

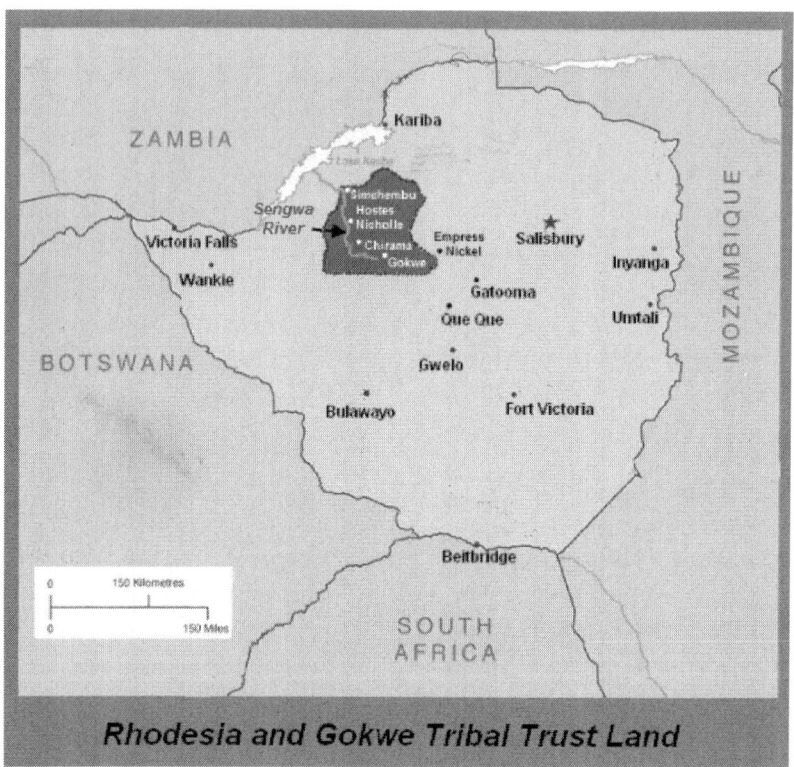

Rhodesia and Gokwe Tribal Trust Land

By the time I reached Que Que it was late, so I bedded down in their singles mess. The next day I managed to get a ride on one of the many military vehicles that seemed to be going backwards and forwards to Gokwe at an alarming rate. Details seemed patchy and everyone was in a high state of excitement with all sorts of rumours circling around – the worst one was that the single's mess had been torched and my beloved Precious had been cremated. Well, one thing was for sure, the kip that was the Gokwe gulag was now finally on the map.

When I pitched up at the charge office the place was in turmoil. It seemed that every Reservist available had been called up from Que Que. Loads of them were hanging around in small groups, all in camouflage and loaded down with kit bags. I went to see the boss to tell him I was back. It turns out the boss wasn't there and was actually on holiday in South Africa. Inspector Andy Gray was in charge and using Mike Harvey's office. The room was full with men being told by Gray where they would be sent to. He appeared absolutely exhausted and acknowledged my presence with a nod of his head. This wasn't the time for a chat, so I exited. After taking my stuff into my room (thank the Lord, my Precious was fine), and with knocking off time imminent, I didn't bother changing into uniform. But I needed to know what the hell was going on. I went to the office I shared with the others and I let Peter fill me in on what had happened. He looked a complete and utter nervous wreck! Whilst the direct attack on the village was now two days old, the whole circus was still very much active…

HALT - in the name of the lore! Time out –

The attack on Gokwe village, hey. Eish, the first and only time in the history of the Rhodesian Bush War that gooks organised an assault on an entire village. And I missed it. (Thanks to guardian angel for that!) As Mike Harvey later told me, it was the only reason that the *Rhodesia Sunday Mail* had bothered to send a reporter to the piss-pot hole. A bit of propaganda for la la land. And I quote from his Email –

You must remember that I wasn't at Gokwe at the time of the attack, but enjoying a holiday in SA, so what information I was briefed on when I returned has, regrettably, been lost in the mists of time. I don't recall the intricacies of what happened. The brief account that appears in the Rhodesia Sunday Mail was probably the nuts and bolts of my briefing on return from holiday of the whole episode. It must be remembered that the feature in the paper was because of the attack on Gokwe and its sudden rise to fame in the annals of the story of the bush war.

Ah, fame at last! Now, when I first wrote about this incident, I relied on memory. It was a bit patchy but almost bang-on. But now for this chapter, I have managed to get input from people that were also involved. Plus, I also have the bit mentioned rather casually from the above aforementioned governmental mouth piece. Some of the details I have gathered contradict a bit, but this is how I put it all together. A few people that could have perhaps provided more details are either dead or simply never bothered to reply to my Emails.

I really struggled to work a plan to describe the events that now unfold. To be honest, I arrived late and the whole shebam sort of ran in the background of my mind as it unfolded. So, I take a step back, and construct the incident as a spectator. I am not involved at all - hence a totally different writing approach; but it is very important because it was a turning point for us Gokwe BSAP – the war had arrived on our doorstep. So, take a deep breath, and here we go...

push starting a helicopter outside Gokwe police station

Pic - Max

Whilst I was brumming around on a police motorbike in Salisbury with my brain thinking only of one thing – Miss Josephine Woods; trouble had been building up in Gokwe TTL. Something nasty was afoot. It would appear that things had been a'gookin for Gokwe village for quite some time. But no one was sure what. My boss, Mike Harvey, thinks that the whole idea to attack Gokwe came from our own Scarlett Pimpernel – a gook by the name of Philemon. Nigel recounts -

He was a nuisance factor, not very active but he set the base for further infiltrations and created his own security structure.

Now I had of course heard of this individual who seemed to pop up all over the place now and again. I recall that he was supposed to have shot an elephant with his AK-47. What for? It is beyond me; must be a gook thing because they still seem to be at it thirty odd years later. Anyway, the guerrilla led our Special Branch a right merry dance for a long time. But exactly where he fits in is still a bit of a mystery. Mike Harvey explains –

I think the gook "Philemon", whom we were chasing around the district at the time, was ZANLA and had infiltrated with a group from Mozambique making their way to Gokwe. I was of the opinion that the attack on Gokwe was by Philemon's group.

The boss is very wrong. But it appears that Philemon, who can best be described as being a black man, who touted an AK-47, was about to have his charmed life terminated - but quite sometime before the attack. Nigel recalls –

Philemon the gook was a long story. Jim Ruddick and another CID lad from Gwelo, came out clandestine without even pulling into the cop shop on information they had. Philemon was culled as he tried to escape...they brought him to the cop shop afterwards. I saw his body on the area by the charge office outside...he had been well and truly put to sleep and even a shot went through his foot from underneath whilst he was balekering away from the boys. His AK-47 was next to him with the butt broken off and a back yard repair job done attaching the wooden butt to the rifle. He had previously been discovered by an off duty cop from the area and arrested, whilst the cop was taking him to the police station he somehow clubbed the cop on the head with the butt and broke it. I think he shot the cop after that.

But to be honest, whilst Philemon undoubtedly knew the area well, and even perhaps Gokwe village, it is difficult to actually think he was in any way involved in the planning of an attack on the village. Why would Mugabe's gooks come all that way from Mozambique? Makes no sense when Nkomo's terrs are not that far away and operating out of Zambia – no one is really sure. But Nigel thinks they were Nkomo's ZIPRA gooks as he makes a very good observation –

I think their mission was pre-empted from Zambia whose info was on Government establishments in the area. A successful attack would have resulted in a long reaction from the closest town which was Que Que. I suppose...this would have allowed an easy exit for them back to Zambia or where ever they came from and given them time to disappear, bombshell and re group. They clearly never had the local's full support because they were picked up on info as they entered Gokwe area and info was incoming right throughout their walk to the village. I would estimate they travelled over 160 kms from the Sengwa River in the north to the village....and I can't remember any info coming in that they took any vehicular transport.

The part where he writes that they were snitched on seems to confirm they were Ndebele gooks and thus not exactly very popular amongst the Shona's territory that they were a'gooken through.

So with all the information; the BSAP's top wanker of a Section Officer in Special Branch, Phil Drewitt, and his merry band of scallywags, are hot on the gook's tails. The problem is that Drewitt is a half-wit. (I describe this individual later and I do not mince my words.) Nigel didn't have much time for him either –

Phil Drewitt, that arrogant conceited prick from Que Que CID, was also out there because info had come about that there were 30 gooks travelling down from the Sengwa Base area progressing straight towards the village. They were following a river that ran south from there. They were heavily armed with serious back packs with arms and ammo - so something was amiss. He was assessing their daily progress and they were doing some serious mileage even with the heavily laden back packs...not sure if they used porters, but they had rockets, landmines, heavy machine guns and their AK's etc... When these 30 buggers got close to Gokwe they mysteriously disappeared off the radar and info screen for a few days and Drewitt was beside himself from frustration. It was clear that

Gokwe was a target but where and when they were going to hit was unknown.

Oh so clever-clever Drewitt is now hanging around with thumb up bum and mind in neutral. Meanwhile the gooks have sent out their sniffer dogs and even Nigel failed to spot something very queer –

When the gooks disappeared off the radar screen close to Gokwe itself and everyone was trying to get info on their whereabouts, it was assumed they had dispersed to avoid being picked up as a large group close to the village....but I recall that there were two or three youngsters in their 20's that sat for a few days on the bench area at the entrance to the cop shop and every time I went past them asking if I could assist, they said they were waiting for information to join the Selous Scouts. Now that was really an uncommon occurrence as the Scouts were usually turn arounds. They had been talking to the black cops about it as I saw them in chats with quite a few of them...I suppose with the commotion of an imminent attack or unknown intentions of the group of 30, everyone was running around trying to get logistics in place and it may have well been that the Scouts recruits were actually mujibas watching the lay of the land and to assess the potential readiness for the attack. In fact, I am very sure that was the intention and us being ass-holes never picked it up or did anything about it...suppose we were just so laid back and never thought beyond the direct contact with the gooks.

Oh yeah, laid back is very true. O.i.C, Andy Gray, is nervous though. Something doesn't add up. On the afternoon of Friday, May the 13th 1977, Nigel drives to Chirama to do some general enquiries that were due and more crucial –

I recall them wanting to secure radio contact at the base as the attack was anticipated and the fact that they came down from the North close to the water tank line north of Chirama was an issue.

Nigel is too late. He would have driven straight past at least one bunch of the gooks within minutes of leaving Gokwe village. They left him alone as they were getting ready. But the gooks had a flaw in their three pronged attack. It is a village after all - not an enclosed security base. It was shaped like a giant spider's web, three clicks in parameter, the threads are little dirt roads, except the umbilical chord to Que Que. The primitively built administration offices and accommodation blocks would have been scattered like dew drops on the thin silk in the morning sun. But what was the point taking this place on? Logically, they would be easily outgunned? Nigel thinks –

I suppose as it was a rural government occupied village where administration for the whole area was run. If you take it every occupant that worked in the village was a government employee...black and white, the three pronged assault attacked the three pillars of government which were the police station, the DC's offices and the DC's staff. The DC compound was separate to the offices - unlike the cops who were all housed in one compound.

And now comes the bleedin' obvious. The clue is Friday night. Yup, almost the entire white administration officers, ranking from top to bottom, are all gathered together – where? The only place to go - the unprotected 'sports club'. No fence, no guards, no nothing but piss-heads out their boxes by 10.30pm, rifles stashed in the tiny foyer. Nice! The gooks were daft not to spot that one. Think about it. A couple of rocket grenades straight through the thin walls and then machine gun any screamers that stagger out. Job done. Chain of command destroyed; panic stations all around and now plenty of time for murder, a bit of loot and pillage - perhaps a quick rape or two or three, and then bugger off before someone sends a message for help. And help was far away…

But the approximately thirty odd gooks cocked-up. They split into three groups almost equally. One bunch was to attack the District Commissioner's offices, (which doesn't make sense as no one would be going to work at that time in the morning), and also next to no one would turn up anyway as it was a Saturday. The second lot go for the DC compound, where their black staff sleeps. The final gang decide to snick up on the police station, via the black policemen's compound, just as the morning Saturday sun peeked a wary eye out.

All the white coppers are snoring their beer off, except maybe Peter, who was more than likely duty PO. I know Alan is not there. Nigel is at Chirama. I hazard a guess Leon and Ian are in bed inebriated. So at about fiveish, an observant sergeant on night guard (Andy Gray had decided to double up the guard – it was a smart move), spots a WILL-O'-THE-WISP which seems to be carrying a reaper's AK-47 and does the good old,

"Halt, who goes there in the name of the law?" Well,

something like that, but the reply is hardly encouraging – a blast on automatic and the bloke collects three rounds in leg and abdomen. He goes down.

The surprise attack is now well and truly blown because, bless our brilliant black coppers in the shop, they were well on the ball and as soon as they heard the gunfire – they hit the fog horn. Believe me; it kicks up a right noise, enough to awake the dead...drunks. As Nigel was told later –

> *I recall hearing that one person in the SQ [Single Quarters] running into an open cupboard door square on thinking it was the door to the room....the one lad from Internal Affairs had his gun stripped in his bedroom and couldn't fire back.....a real comedy after a Friday night piss up. The gooks actually came past the police SQ because they found a dropped RPG 7 [Rocket Powered Grenade] that had been thrown on the ground outside my window....*

With the entire hullabaloo, no one has a clue what the hell is going on and still semi-pissed and now loaded out of their heads on adrenalin, they gather at the Charge Office. The gooks are spooked and have disappeared after firing off some mortars, that flew off to who knows where. The other gook groups are popping away at some targets which can be heard in the distance. Chaos reigns supreme! No one is moving, Andy Gray is there and just then...BOOM! A massive explosion. The gooks had placed a cake tin in the road below the cop shop. As usual, a complete innocent ran over it. In this case a Gatooma farmer's seven ton truck. It had wandered in looking for casual labour that was always organised at this time of year; as it was now the cotton picking season. The truck is turned to scrap but no one is seriously hurt. The explosion adds to the confusion with thoughts of another attack. It is soon ascertained that it is a landmine - but now everyone is bricking themselves in case there are more.

The gooks are still around at first light but with their plans gone to pot, they decide to scarper before our lot can sort of think of some kind of counter attack – which was impossible. Whilst the villagers might have had a fire force of maybe a couple of hundred small arms, it wasn't in any way a fighting unit. As the gooks disappear they pass the water treatment plant and shoot up a couple of black employees. This information Andy Gray receives from another employee who had escaped and legged it quick to the cop shop. He in turn is very reluctant to send his lads down to check out the scene in case the gooks had set up an ambush. It is maybe after a couple of hours, when everything seems to have quietened down, the BSAP lads go down for a look see. Like the sergeant, the water boys are a bit shot up, but rapidly patched up and the three shifted asap down to Que Que hospital.

Now, exactly at this point in time *The Rhodesia Sunday Mail* has the story covered so

> On May 14 this year the terror war came to the heart of Gokwe village but only for half an hour.
>
> "A large group of terrorists had a planned three-pronged attack on the Police camp," said Chief Inspector Harvey.
>
> "As one group of terrs came in, one of our sergeants disturbed their plans."
>
> The Sergeant - now recovered - was shot three times before the terrs fired several mortars at the camp and then fled. In the follow-up operation one terrorist was killed. Two Water Development employees, who had been camping in a tent near the main camp when the attack on Gokwe was launched, were also shot, but not killed. Sergeant Bernard Watadzaushe has been based at Gokwe for nine months. Married with two children, he 'enjoys the bush' and hates the terrorists.
>
> "I love working in the kraals because the old men teach me about African history," said Sergeant Watadzaushe, who admits that most of his time is now spent on police administration. He also admits to his feelings about the terrorists.
>
> "They killed my aunt and uncle. They shot them," he said. "My aunt had been forced to make some terrs a meal. Then, two days later, more terrs came back to her and said they had been poisoned by the

food. Then they just shot them both. The sad thing is the tribe people here do not understand what is happening."

Sergeant Watadzaushe's father was a member of the BSAP for 12 years before retiring recently.

(Amazingly, that was all the paper reported about this 'incident'. Except exactly one more line which appears a bit later in this narrative.)

Of course, in the early morning of the attack the Charge Office phone would have been trilling itself stupid as the panicked whites tried to get information. Andy Gray gets through on the radio to Joint Operation Command (JOC). Well they are caught with pants down as well but manage to hastily muster up some troops attending the School of Infantry in Gwelo. Whilst this lot are on the way, JOC gets hold of an elite unit of the Rhodesian African Rifles (RAR), and sends them all tooled up and in the know. These guys were from an all black regiment and led by white officers. I hazard a guess they also numbered thirty odd in all. The fact that they arrived by late afternoon in batches by helicopter, operating out of Thornhill, in Gwelo (on standby for just such an occasion), is a testament to efficiency. These guys were superb soldiers; fit, keen and crucially – they had trackers. They quickly replaced the School of Inf blokes and hit the road…

Andy Gray accurately guessed that the terrs would head back to where they came from and the RAR were driven south of the village and were on the gooks asses chop-chop. It doesn't take long to spot that the terrs were still together and following the Sengwa River, which runs west to east behind the Chirama hills. This makes sense because it is May, and the Gokwe TTL is bone dry and water is crucial. The wide river bed was mostly dry, but there was still a trickle. Another point is that the gooks needed cover and the best was down by the river. Following the river was a bit of a detour, but safer. Starting near Gokwe village, it runs off the escarpment due west for approximately 100 kilometres before doing a perfect 90 degrees north for another 200 kilometres before gushing its guts into Lake Kariba.

But the gooks have a serious head start, maybe eight hours or more, and know perfectly well that they will be hunted. Our lads are moving fast, but soon darkness puts an end to any further advances, but presumably the gooks, still loaded down, are also exhausted and are taking a nap.

Sunday morning starts like any other with the sun roasting both hunters and the hunted by 10.00am - the chase continues hour after hour. More troops are constantly been choppered in and are getting closer and closer. Crucially, the gooks are tired and highly unlikely to have much in the way of provisions. Remember, they had marched a long way to get to Gokwe village and now certainly had no chance of stopping into some nearby kraal to 'persuade' some unfriendly peasants to rustle up some grub for a quick take away of 'sadza and nyama'. The RAR have shifted into another gear and the trackers have clocked from the increasing freshness of the spoor that they are closing in.

By Monday evening both sides are at exhaustion point and have already reached the turning point in the river, and would soon now be heading due north - something is going to kick-up very, very soon. Neither side would have slept that well. Adrenalin makes sure you don't get many *rem*s. In another 30-40 kilometres of slogging; both sides are going to have to contend with another big problem – the wildness of Chirisa Game Reserve, packed with just about most of Africa's dangerous predators.

Tuesday has the pilot, Roger Watt and his engineer/gunner, Rob Nelson, in their brand new *Alouette III* helicopter (no idea where the Rhodesians managed to borrow that one from), ferrying troops in the hope that they can hop them nearer to the gooks. As it is late, they leave the chopper outside the police station's front door and bed down in the PO's mess lounge. (A personal note – I seem to recall this and may have spoken to them.)

Wednesday has JOC decide, from the constant radio info from the RAR, to place the chopper at Hostes Nicholle Wildlife Research Station. Watt (early thirties) and Nelson (mid twenties), load up all their gear and fly to Hostes Nicholle. Ten minutes before they are due to arrive, Watt receives over the radio that the RAR had finally caught up with the gooks and the shooting had started. Two RAR lads had been injured and needed to be cassavaced out. Nothing too serious, although one bloke did have a rather large hole in his ear lobe. But, more importantly, the gooks had hot tailed it and the RAR's trackers were knackered. They were to dump everything at Hostes Nicholle, refuel, strip the chopper of back and front passenger doors, and pick up four National Parks trackers (three white, one black), that had just been informed of their latest promotion from following elephants to following gooks.

So, with the chase now in its fifth day - hunted and hunters are facing each other over a chessboard covered in bush. Now that the gooks have been located, it was time to bring in the eagle, especially one armed with twin .303, belt fed, Browning machine guns of pure Spitfire spattering death, capable of firing rounds at twenty a second, per gun! Bye bye gooks. Not only that, but the pilot, Air Lieutenant Roger Watt, is holder of the *Silver Cross of Rhodesia*. (That is one step below a British *Victoria Cross*.) This guy was a natural born sky dolphin. His unique instinct was to use the machine to trap gooks, just like the dolphins do when hunting their favourite fish. Tighter and tighter he could force them together, whilst dodging their poisoned darts of defence. Then the gunner would take them out. Now refuelled and loaded up with the four trackers, Roger and Rob set off back to the battle zone.

Meanwhile - Nigel, stuck up on the end of the plateau at Chirama base, alone with four black constables, is following the action on the radio. Working out that all the action was only fifty clicks away, he thought he could take his landy for a look-see by heading south to the edge of the plateau. This was pure bundu bashing – no road and Nigel has perched a constable on the bonnet to keep an eye out for rocks, holes and stumps hidden by the tall yellow grass. Needless to say, the constable decides that this is a bad idea playing at being a fairground gook target and yowls his head off, forcing Nigel to return to Chirama.

The gooks aren't garden boys no more but are a full platoon structured on conventional army set up of Platoon Commander, Sergeant, Sect. Commanders etc. The Commie trained bastards had been taught what choice to take when the eagle comes down from the sky - split or hit – flight or fight? They knew it was only time before their biggest fear would arrive above them. They are cornered, but know the ground hunters under the command of

Major Butch Zeederberg, are now also backed up by a platoon under Pat Lawless, and are moving in for the kill...

Leaving Hostes Nicholle, Roger is going like a bat out of hell as fast as the heavily loaded machine can go. Within fifty five minutes he is there. The Gooks have heard the chopper and even seen it and - they have made a decision. Now Roger's plans go askew because two of the rangers tell him, that as he was coming into land, they spotted the gooks. Roger is also informed by the RAR that the two members that have been hit in the firefight have decided the injuries were not that bad and decided to continue the chase. Two of the Nat Park trackers disembark to join the RAR sticks and Roger takes off again, with Rob getting ready with the machine guns and the two rangers acting as spotters. Roger climbs and starts to curve the *Alouette* anti-clockwise for Rob to swing the guns into action. But – they are too close to where the gooks are holed up...

The eagle has landed - but it is coming back...for them - so...together the gooks, all thirty plus of them, took the chopper on as one. They totally ignore the ground hunters. They just want to get that bird of prey out the sky - and now they opened up with everything they had from the covering shelter of the bush, and pumped round after round into the chopper, turning it into a sieve in seconds. Roger knows immediately that the *Alouette* is mortally wounded and was leaking badly – oil and fuel spewing all over the place and the gook's green phosphorus tracers would ignite the lot at any second.

That none of them in the chopper have collected terminating lead at this point is a miracle. Desperately, Roger banks away, climbing as fast as the stricken engine can claw its way out of the hornet's nest and try to get it in a position for Rob to open up to stem the gook's fireforce. The RAR lads can only watch in horror and pump some lead in the direction from where the gooks are shooting from; but the gooks are all well hunkered down and keep firing at the chopper.

Roger powers up and the stricken *Alouette* reaches 1200 feet (360metres), but still in range of the gooks' small arms, when finally white smoke filled the chopper, which rapidly turned black as aviation fuel and oil mixed, bursting into a roaring clockwise tornado as the rotor wash fed the flames. In seconds the rear wall of the chopper is burnt through and the cabin is engulfed. The control rods to the main rotor are now being attacked by the fire and Roger knows he has only seconds to make a plan and then…

Seconds seem like hours as experience and training become super heightened by adrenalin. His mind balances the few options open available in the terrible predicament they are all in.

He shuts down both fuel controls, instantly cutting any remaining power to the rotor blades. Immediately, the freewheeling unit automatically disengaged the engine, allowing the main rotor to rotate freely, and Roger, lowering collective pitch with his left hand, starts to glide the chopper down. The flames are reaching him now, burning his neck and the left arm that is desperately holding onto the collective lever. Somehow he gains a few more milliseconds from the flames by disconnecting his seatbelt and squeezing up tighter to the controls. His eyes desperately scan the fast approaching ground for a possible place to 'land'. There is the dry river bed, but logically this is too near to the gooks, or a ploughed field by a deserted village. He opts for the latter.

Above the roaring flames and the clatter of tortured metal - another sound enters his head – screams of pain. It is coming out of his own mouth, but incredibly his mind continues to take over his body's natural defence mechanisms and forces his left hand to stay on the collective lever - even as it starts to barbecue. Fleetingly, he realises that with the only door attached to the chopper, mainly his, could stop him getting out if, and a big if, they manage to get down still in one piece, perhaps trapping him in the burning wreckage, and he decides to jettison it. As he reaches for the lever, incredulously he sees that the two terrified trackers had climbed out of the flaming wreck and were now standing on the tiny boarding step, clutching desperately to anything that gave them some grip - outside of his door, and using it as a shield! With that decision decided not to eject the door, and with the chopper a plunging pyre - Roger's last instincts is to get the dying machine down because any time it could explode.

And then - the space time continuum finally ends and Roger drops the machine almost perfectly with a forty degree nose down, before it rocks back on its wheels. The rapid momentum downwards pushes still more fuel over him that promptly ignites. The two trackers are thrown clear and Roger, now a human torch, bursts through the door and rolls and rolls and rolls on the ground, extinguishing the flames.

Staggering up, he tries to gather his senses, and comprehends the sight of the two Nat Park trackers, relatively unharmed, but where is Rob? Almost incomprehensibly, he is told that at almost 30 meters (100 feet), Rob, trapped, and about to be engulfed in flames...had jumped. At that height and loaded down with body armour, he plunged head first and was mercifully killed instantly. Ironically, Pat Lawless, who recovered the body, noticed Rob only had a tiny burn on the back of one calf.

Roger, whilst trying to absorb this input and with the pain now becoming acute, has more problems as the chopper's ammunition starts to explode. The three stagger upwards to higher ground. The place is crawling with gooks and somehow one of the trackers had been able to keep hold of his FN. Dragging each other, they make it to the deserted kraal, but with only twenty rounds between them, the situation is close to hopeless. The adrenalin is wearing off and shock is starting to replace it, and Roger's burnt skin finally starts to hit him hard. Totally out of it, the three try to get their heads together; when they spot people approaching the burning wreck – and they could be gooks – not a white face amongst them.

Curiously, he didn't need to be worried because the gooks didn't hang around celebrating the downing of the chopper. They knew that they had had a lucky escape but they are now low on ammo. The Rhodies forces will not take this lightly, and with the possibility that there could be more eagles, and worse, *Hawker Hunter* jet aircraft, armed with incendiary missiles; they hit the river road again big-time. The RAR lads are stalled for the moment. The gooks turn the corner of the river, and are now heading north into deeper and deeper scrub; as they plough on in desperation to escape.

The three try to prepare for a showdown, but it turns out it is a stick from the RAR. They have no morphine. The stick supply them with water from the river, not only to pour over Roger's burns, but also one of the tracker's arm is also badly barbecued. As they do this, Pat Lawless arrives with Rob's body and brings it to the kraal.

Meanwhile the RAR lads are going berserk. The chess game they are playing just went tits-up - the white queen is down... Radio comms are blasting through the airwaves. We need emergency *casavac* now! We need more choppers - we need and need and need more eagles and the hawks...NOW! But respect - these gooks might have made a complete balls-up with the attack on Gokwe village, but they were more than willing to fight their way out...

Pat leaves four of his lads with the wounded three and returns to the battle. Thornhill, the Rhodesian Air Force base in Gwelo, gets the message and scramble pronto. Still, it takes over 45 minutes before two Hawks scream across the skies over Roger. He quickly, using the RAR's corporal's radio, explains the situation to the flight commander, Rob MacGregor. The jets are too fast, have no confirmed target and frustratingly circle about, giving cover, just in case.

JOC are desperate to get their lads out but Rhodesia's few choppers are scattered all over the country and it is an agonising five hours before finally, another eagle arrives having been sent from Wankie, almost 200 kilometres as the crow flies. Roger needs medical attention fast and the chopper's range cannot get them much further. However, 30 kilometres south of the westward part of the Sengwa is another river, the Lutope, running parallel before also doing a 90 degree to join the Sengwa just before the game reserve. On this river is a well maintained Internal Affairs base which was almost due south of the contact and had an excellent runway. Roger and the trackers are quickly flown there to be met by a twin engine Brittin Norman Islander with a doctor on board and they were flown to Salisbury. Roger would survive but would refuse any skin grafts. However, one of the Nat Parks trackers did need one for his arm burns. Roger was awarded the Military Forces Commendation, which entitled him to have a tiny gold pick on his Rhodesian General Service Medal, ribbon.

(Personal note – As far as I can work out, Rob's body was most probably picked up by Special Branch and brought to Gokwe before being transported down to Que Que. I distinctly recall seeing Rob's helmet on the boss's desk.)

Meanwhile...

The gooks had bought some time, but now the RAR lads have fresh trackers and are seeking revenge. Nigel is still up at Chirama, huddled in the tin shack listening to the tiny radio hissing and spitting, but he can hear the various sticks chatting softly between themselves as slowly, but inexorably, as the afternoon creeps into sunset, they are near...so near –

The tracker who had a nick name, which I cannot remember, but it was something like Chunky, was in front tracking with his support either side just behind him, he was saying he was very close to them and that a contact was imminent...they walked into the gooks.

I recall clearly the gooks were buggered, resting on the ground in a thick bushy area and got a fright when the shooting started...

Check - but not mate.

The gooks are knackered and after a short firefight, dump everything except their sidearms and leggit *asap*. The RAR recover substantial equipment, and along with at least twenty two backpacks, a mortar night aiming lamp. (The first one seen in Rhodesia). Plus one terminated gook. Daylight reveals heavy blood spoors of at least two more wounded. Our lads are all okay. Butch Zeederberg, guessing that the terrs may still want to keep together and be heading back to where they came from, now makes his plan as they continue after the group. With no maps, the gooks would be forced to keep following the river.

(Special Branch some days later were alerted to an individual seeking medical attention at clinic in Ume TTL. He was picked up and identified as having been wounded in the above contact. Another wounded gook was picked up by Ground Coverage two days later. It can be presumed that after being nicely patched up, the pair were sentenced and dropped down a hatch with a rope around their necks.)

Now with the follow up becoming the longest running battle in the history of Rhodesia, not only in days, but in hundreds of kilometres covered, Butch calls in vehicles and choppers at any opportune moment to leapfrog the enemy and set up an ambush. Now deep in the game reserve, they sit and wait...

Nigel is still following this on the radio and as night falls into the seventh day of the battle of Gokwe –

I recall listening to the radio in the tin hut at Chirama (the only white with 4 blacks) with the RAR buggers interacting on their radios....all whispering and short chats....the one lad said

" Hau! There is a leopard...there is a leopard next to me, can I shoot it?" The fear in his voice was pretty apparent. The White RAR officer came back and told him to keep still and not fire a shot - which he did...he was quiet for a long time....!!!

But, the RAR hit the gooks again as they walk into the trap. At least another two are terminated. The rest, at the end of their tether run off again. Butch waits for daylight and again they are shuttled out. The action is hot and the lads need cooling down. As Pat Lawless described to me –

I recall it being somewhat of a classic with Butch doing all the clever thinking in leapfrogging (using both vehicles and helicopters), my platoon with Jim Hardy's platoon (81mm Mor Pl, c/s 71) based on our spoor reports (straight out of the manual - NDAT - Number, Direction, Age, Type).and cross-graining. I recall it being described as one of the longest follow ups (150-200kms?) ever with us running on spoor most of the way. I recall Colin Krieger (Coy 2IC) meeting my platoon as we crossed a dirt track at some point in the follow up with a vehicle with Coca Cola and ice cream for the troops - I learned much about the value of good admin in sustaining morale from that!

Butch has it down to a 'T'. T for terrorist termination, and a day later, hit them again. More are taken out (not known exactly but at least one or two), but that was to be the end of it. The gooks split up and scattered. Checkmate. However, Butch, Pat and the lads are still hoping and continue all the way down the river till finally at Kariba, they find the small boats the gooks had used to come over from Zambia. Although it was obvious the game was over, the RAR are told to hang around for a couple of days in the vain hope some of the enemy may still try to make this their dash to freedom – it never happened. As Butch told me –

It was clear to us (not to Comops!), that they had exited. Can't remember total accounted for but think only four. Three days later we were in Mozambique!

The End

Not quite. Remember I said there was one more line from the Rhodesia Sunday Mail

In the follow-up operation one terrorist was killed.

And, that is that! Incredulous! The article, already half quoted in previous chapters and the rest somewhere in the next chapters, smothers just like - *tra-la-la* - the attack on Gokwe village, because the whole article is just complete, utter bull-shit propaganda. Oh yes, things went very nasty. No mention of Rob dying, no mention of the chopper down, no mention of perhaps one of the most amazing chases of the war. - ***Eish*** we don't want to panic whitey with bad stories in the newspapers, hey!

I did find one vaguely related press article. A tiny bit. It seems that Rob Nelson's older brother had also been killed a short time before in the war. The parents were devastated – they lost both their children. Mrs Nelson never recovered from the loss…

Well, it took three decades and a lot of research to find out eventually what most of us had no clue of what really happened. – and my memoir goes on…

So it was all very exciting with loads of people running around and wanting to be fed and bed and generally being a nuisance. I just tried to get on with the 'General Enquiries' -which had amazingly tailed off a bit since half the village had been shot to bits and people were reluctant to wander in moaning about some crime or the other. I wandered down to see the nice big hole the landmine had made. The truck had been removed. I found myself a bit of twisted scrap which I kept as a souvenir. Sadly, I never kept it. (Think EBay.)

Things would never be the same again. After a few days life returned to 'almost' normal. But from now on, all base camps would have a constant presence of at least twenty plus men to react to any new terrorist threat. Sand bags were placed in front of our doors and windows, and a mortar pit was dug just outside our bedrooms. It didn't look very safe and a short time later the roof caved in. One good side of all this was that Gokwe was classified by JOC as a fully fledged war zone and we no longer had to pay rent for our rooms.

That's another $9 in my pocket. Another bonus was all mail we sent inland was free. You just put the official police rubber stamp on the envelope. I had one of the shortest addresses in the land - PO Greenberg, Box 10, Gokwe.

Was I bothered with all this fame portrayed in the *Sunday Mail* – officially we are now Rhodesia's new white drunken hotshots loaded with tots? (Think about that one.) Yeah, so that was the attack on Gokwe. And did it make one iota difference to me that I was in a fully fledged war zone? Hah-hah, no chance...let the games go on. Bring it on man - I am tough enough and at last could give weeping willow Peter a run for his money when it came to wailing woefully of loves' bleeding hearts of separation...God help me if Josephine has kept any of my letters (Conceited hope?) I will never live them down, not because of the awful bleating drivel, but the appalling spelling, grammar and punctuation!

Still, my Precious was fine and I had something new to look forward to – The Muppets. Real ones from the UK - not the humanoids from Gokwe.

Memoir mutterings

6819 Gray, Andrew Jeremy. Chief Inspector. Pension and other benefits. September 1980. He would go on to found Gray Security Services in South Africa and make loads of dosh, but sadly would kick it from lack of breath at a rather early middle -ish age.
Rhodesia African Rifles - The Rhodesian African Rifles, or RAR, was the oldest regiment in the Rhodesian Army, dating from the formation of the 1st Rhodesian Native Regiment in 1916 during the First World War. Until the late 1970s, the RAR had exclusively black recruits and NCOs and exclusively white officers. The unit was not deployed outside Rhodesia during the war, but it established a considerable tally on internal operations. (Source – *Wikipedia*) Well, according to Butch – that last bit about not being sent outside Rhodesia is tosh. I salute you RAR – that was one hell of a bush battle you performed in Gokwe.

Glossary

Balekering. Running away.
Biscuit Tin. Land mine

CHAPTER 20:

People are dying but at least the Muppets are on TV

With everything now calming down, a nice bit of entertainment was greatly appreciated. Nigel and Alan had been going on about getting a television for ages, but besides a flag pole they had 'found' and some rather tatty bits of what should be an aerial, much hadn't happened. But, they had gotten their act together and there in our living room was a nice sized black and white television. Alan explained that the licence and $8 dollars a month rental fee would be split like the other household bills among us all. For once I didn't argue. I loved telly, especially when we had a problem with the generator or a heavy storm.

Now and then the police generator would kick up, maybe dirty fuel or whatever, and the next thing you know, the electric shaver is jammed on your face, with my Precious now warbling Boney M's 'Daddy Cool' like the Walker Brothers, and the overhead light flickered like a disco strobe. This phenomenon did wonders on the TV. Alan had laughingly pointed out that when they filled in the lease, he had lied and told the rental shop that we were on mains. They don't rent if you have a generator. It was hard not to see why. As the power decreased, we would all move our chairs forward and strain out of our seats to see the ever decreasing screen till it would be a little square barely bigger than a paperback, then suddenly the rooms lights became brilliant stars and the television would explode back to full size, sending us all back with fright. Great fun, but I wasn't that sure it was too good for the telly's innards.

The other problem was storms and even outside the rainy season we got the occasional serious ones. Stuck up on the plateau, plus the flagpole, meant we had quite a good reception since the next transmitter was in Que Que. Once the heavens opened, the picture quality crashed by 30 per cent, and even worse was when ferocious winds spun the aerial around. The flag pole had been attached to the lounge's back wall with hoops and was not concreted into the ground, so it spun on its axis in high winds. In fact, you could see it if you stuck your head out the window next to the television, which, it turns out, was very convenient.

Wilson, the cook, organised the various batmen for evening shift. There was always to be one on beck and call for tea or sandwiches. Anyway, one night, we are all gathered in the lounge watching our favourite show, *The Muppets*. Just as the old men up in the gallery gave out the classic line –'What do think of the show so far?', the wind spins the aerial and we have no reception. Nigel goes mental and hollers out for the duty batman. I am not sure who he belonged to, but I recall he couldn't have been more than 16. Nigel sent the frightened youth outside into the storm. It was seriously raging out there. The poor bugger was shaking with cold and fear, and Nigel, with one eye on the television, starts shouting instructions at the batman through the partially opened window. Every few seconds, a bolt of lightening would light up the soaked batman blinking over bulging eyeballs, making him look like a dark brown Kermit about to croak it, shivering like a tuning fork and attempting to twist the pole in the direction Nigel is blaring out. Anyway, he got it tuned in smartish, and I still thought it was good idea, the TV I mean - not sending out batman to be fried by lightening.

As usual whenever there was some action about that meant I could die a terrible death, I tended not to be around. It wasn't as if I was avoiding trouble but more vice versa. Strange world indeed. Having just missed out on the Gokwe attack (I know deep in my heart, that had I been there, I would have gallantly fought to the death rather than let the thieving bastard gooks steal my Precious), yet again people seemed to get inexplicably expired. Where am I? No idea. Sent here, sent there, but never around when it kicks off. So one night there is more trouble at Gokwe as Nigel relates:

Memoir mutterings

Email from Nigel Triggs -
A lone gook, who was drinking in the Gwelo beer halls and bragging about the fact that he had a stashed AK47, was accosted by some people from Gokwe and threatened with death and arrest if he didn't go and kill a retired ex-cop who lived in his kraal which was not far down the hill from the cop shop. So the lone gook was transported in a government white landy from Gwelo

through the night. He went into the retired policeman's hut and ordered him out. The ex-cop's son was watching the abduction and hid in the kraal. Anyway, the gook took the old cop down the road from his kraal, about 150 metres, and planted him in the head and took off.

The son then ran in the dark to the cop shop and reported that he had heard a shot and his dad never came back: he wasn't sure if he was dead but he was seriously shitting himself. Anyway, eish, middle of the night Mike Harvey vukas Triggs and instructs me to get the lads together. So we woke the single cops up and a few of the blacks. Harvey I think came along but was walking veeeeery far at the back: we actually walked from the station it was that close. Having the retired cop's son with me, he guided us to the road near the kraal .Then Harvey tells me to go in and see what happening. Geez, boet, the grass was about 7ft high and the path to the kraal was about landy width....just a sand road. So I leave everyone behind because I am kaking myself for an ambush and leopard crawl in the grass next to the path. There I see a dark thing lying in the path. Eish. I skirted the body that was the dark thing lying there, and went with the son to the kraal. All the time the others were well tucked away hiding maybe 100 metres away with no comms available - so it was a bugger up.

I cleared the kraal with the son and we went back to the body. If there was an ambush we would have been in the dwang. Anyway, after confirming it was the body, I called the other chaps, and we did the usual. Then the son told me that he was worried about his father's brother who lived about half a click away - he may have taken him as well. So Triggs in the lead, pushed there by Harvey (because he thought I was dispensable), and I get to the kraal fence where there was the concertina barbed wire gate which I started opening to let everyone through. Then the son said 'go this way' so I put the loop on the top of the pole back and went through the narrow upright trees they had for pedestrians. It was coming sunrise at that stage and we found the dead chap's brother to be fine. I asked that we stay there till light before we went back to check the deceased out.

Then Andy Gray arrives - top cop with a camera for photos. Anyway, while we were waiting for proper sunrise, the son came shouting "Check this, check this" so we went there and there was a stick grenade tied to the main upright pole at waist height with the string and key ring attached to the gate. So I nearly copped it there. Had the concertina gate been opened there would have been a good bang!

Anyway, the sequel to that story was that one of the constables had seen the white landy driving around the stores and taken its number down....this was traced to a Gwelo government department and the driver arrested. All the gook's details came out.

The gook and his AK then went on a robbing spree throughout the Gatooma area where he robbed and shot up the beer halls in mining areas and townships, taking money and enjoying life. There was a photo of him in the Que Que Charge Office. A young cop who was stationed in Gwelo was transferred to Enkeldoorn (I remember the chap but can't remember his name,) and many months later he raided a bunch of vagrants in Enkeldoorn town and arrested the lot. He took them to the cop shop and while booking them in he recognised the one from the wanted photo in Que Que. So that oke was transferred to Que Que, where I was with Special Branch at the time and worked with Alan Golden, who was doing some CID work. The boss gave me and a NSPO Derek Johnston the task of taking the very same gook on indications through all the beer halls he had robbed and shot the shite out of.

In the old Renault 18, I think it was, we spoke to the gook lots and he told us his story from entry into the country. He never fought, he just crossed, stashed his gat and went looking for work. Interesting story he had. We asked him what he thought would happen to him and he answered "I'll probably get the rope." We took the magazine off an Uzi and told him to strip it on the back seat.....he knew what he was doing. Anyway, he went to court and was hanged shortly afterwards for his murder charge.

That TV was a brown one and belonged to Triggs, stolen from his parents! There was an Intaf chappie, Ernie Happelt, who got hold of RBC and asked whether we could ever get reception in Gokwe: they said no but if he wanted to try he should build an aerial of certain dimensions and he did so in the Intaf workshop. The RBC said Gatooma had the strongest signal, so point it in that direction – and it worked – so I went with Happelt to his workshop and built one for the cops' single quarters. I got my folks to send out their old black and white TV and we set it up. It also worked.

But, amazingly, a year after I had left the cops and was called up to run SB Gokwe during the 1980 elections because the previous oke had wanted to klap the Member in Charge, the TV I had left for the lads after leaving was still there and working. We huddled around static-fizzing TV to listen to the election bombshell that Mugabe had won. Then, struz nuts, the bloody thing blew up in a puff of smoke. No bull ...it happened!

This is all very interesting, but my serious question - why was I paying $1.50 a month to watch the TV? Who owes me this money?

I note an interesting phenomenon in Nigel's narrative, which I still do. We adapted to metric in the early '70s. It seems distance and weight was not a problem and quickly through sports and later driving, we all adjusted very quickly. But, in heights, we still thought in feet and inches! Every one knows what a six foot tall man looks like, but not someone who is one metre eighty two point eight.

Glossary

Boet. Comes from the Afrikaans for brother, but used here in the same context as china.
Croak (it). Die.
Dwang. Same as being in the shit.
Kaking. Passing faeces.
Oke. Same as a bloke.
Struz nuts. It is the truth.
Vukas. Motivate into action.
Whacked. Hit (in this case by a bullet).

CHAPTER 21:

Sex, suicide and silly cows

Now that I was allowed to drive I whizzed around Gokwe almost every day. Obviously, for the first week after the attack I kept a very wary lookout for any signs that those nasty gooks had dug a hole in the dirt road and planted another explosive biscuit tin. This was a waste of time and eyesight because with my total lack of driving experience I was likely to be wiped out driving into a tree while steering around anything that looked freshly dug up. With so many dirt roads weaving in and out of the village, and all the traffic using them, after a while it was considered 'safe' from any landmines. Er, in other words, since no one else had been blown up yet, in theory, the roads were clear.

Still, there was never time to get bored. With Gokwe TTL having such a large population there was always something going on. Some of the incidents were tragic, some of them hilarious and some - just downright daft. With six months' experience under my belt I was quite well equipped to handle most crimes, incidents and accidents...

Responding to a report of the suspected suicide of an African Female Adult (AFA) in the cotton growing area due east of the village by the Umniati River, just about an hours drive away, I arrived with a constable at a small kraal. We were met by the headman. The rest of the kraal's humanity were silently sitting or standing around the entrance to a hut. I went in. An African female in her early 20s lay on the floor. She was clothed and in a foetal position. Her nostrils and mouth were covered in strange, whitish foam. There were signs of vomiting on the deceased's clothing and her grass sleeping mat. Next to her was an enamel cup.

The headman, after questioning, explained. The husband, who must have been in his 50s (the young girl was wife number three), had returned from a beer drink and accused his wife of being unfaithful and lazy. The deceased had gone into her hut and had made a drink using Rogor, an extremely toxic cotton plant insecticide. Witnesses claim her death throes took up to five hours and consisted of convulsions and constant vomiting.

I radioed Gokwe and received clearance that the body could be buried. On receiving our permission, the silent female observers proceeded to ululate and throw themselves about the dirt clearing.

We returned to Gokwe village.

When old man Kambasha phoned Gokwe Police Station at 10.00 pm, duty night officer (me) was just about to go to bed. The extension phone from the charge office rang and I was told I was needed. Collecting my rifle, dodging around the dark swimming pool, blinking at the bright lights, I smiled at half dazed, listless constables in the office and tried to ignore the howling hissing green box in the radio room as I listened to the phone.

"PO Greenberg here. What's up?"

"Ah, PO Greenberg, how are you? Unfortunately Number 1 son has chiya'd three mombes on the Chirama road with my truck, maybe half an hour from here."

Translated: His eldest son had driven a company 45 tonner into three suicidal cows, effectively extinguishing their lives approximately six clicks out. That wasn't too far, so I took off with two of the constables. It was dark, but when we arrived at the scene I could see by my Landy's headlights two mombes well and truly mangled in the truck's front bull bars. They would moo no more. I asked the driver where the third beast was.

"Ah, he is stuck on the exhaust pipe," was the reply.

Roast beef! I laughed and commiserated with him about the damage to the truck. I owed his old man for the free ride on his bus to Que Que and cashing my dodgy cheques. I told No1 son that he was a fine upstanding and responsible person for reporting this incident, and not to worry.

The next day a stroppy old man comes to the charge office, wailing and lamenting the death of his three cattle. Even without a translator it was pretty easy to guess what was coming next. He demanded I collect $300 from Kambasha for killing his cows. I pulled out the copy of instant fines for people trying to be a clever-clever. The tirade of rubbish got the cheeky man a ticket for 75 dollars for having unattended cattle wandering around on a public road. Shut him up very quickly. It didn't take long for the 'ticket' story to go around and my popularity amongst my black comrades increased.

It was a nice cool day in late June when a polite constable walked into our office.

"Ah, 'scuse me, PO Greenberg and PO Brockbank, but this man has come to report that someone in his kraal has killed himself." He indicated a very tired looking old man.

I looked at Peter. Peter looked at me. He who opens mouth first gets case. Weeping willow is an idiot and says he doesn't have time.

"Ah, Chief Inspector Harvey say PO Brockbank must investigate."

I sniggered. Peter was a bit pissed off, but asked the usual questions: When, where and how?

It transpired that a villager had hung himself from a tree three days earlier (it took that long to walk to make the report). That made it about a two hour drive through the bush. I decide to tag along as I couldn't be arsed sitting in the office all day typing up reports on my 19th birthday. A couple of hours later, after directions from the headman who had reported the case, we arrived at the kraal. There was a slight problem, though. The corpse was gone from the tree.

Luckily for Peter and I, being stuck in Gokwe (and Rhodesia), we hadn't been influenced by post counter-culture '60's spiritual revolutions and Zombie films and weren't worried that some goblin type apparitions that plague Gokwe to this day, screaming 'Death to Whitey', would materialise and sink its fangs in our necks. Still, with no corpse swinging in the wind, it was a little eerie.

The headman scuttled off into the deserted kraal before returning with the brother of the suicide victim. We hadn't bothered to take a constable as a translator, as the headman's grasp of English was rather good, so through him Peter asked,

"Where is your brother?"

It appeared that after hanging around for three days, the stench from the deceased had become unbearable so the brother had buried brother which was a bother. Well hung meat by the sound of it.

"Where is the man buried?" Peter asked, as I cast an eye for any signs of a fresh grave.

The brother seemed to be working himself into a rather upset state. He must have really loved the deceased.

"He says you have parked your vehicle on top of the grave."

I looked under the Landy and, sure enough, there were signs of newly-disturbed soil. Well that was rather handy, but the brother was to become even more upset when we told him to dig his brother up. It would take the poor bloke a while though. His brother was well down in that soft grey earth.

After moving the Landy, Peter and I chatted and drank a Coke each. I told him that the couple of letters I had received from my beloved Josephine didn't exactly contain any enthusiastic overtures of love considering she had cost me a fortune in dinners. In fact, they were boring. I shouldn't have mentioned love because that kicked him straight off yowling over his silly bint in Que Que again.

Before I had to listen to more of weeping willow's snivelling, the brother reached the corpse. With the earth removed and the blanket folded back I observed my first deceased by hanging. The face was grotesquely swollen, the swollen tongue, now black, protruded from the mouth, the bloated neck a massive circle of blisters. The sweet/sour, foetid stench of decay; almost made me hurl.

The leather thong belt he had used to hang himself lay next to the deceased. Peter and I both knew the drill: a complete examination of the body was essential to ascertain if there any other factors that may have contributed to the death.

Peter told me to get into the pit to check. I told him to piss-off. Forget it. It was his case so he could get in there and poke about. The poor, heavily sweating brother showed a release form for the deceased from Ingutshena, dated four days ago. The tortured soul had hung himself as soon as he had been released from the well-known Bulawayo mental hospital. A couple of eight year old nieces were eye witnesses to the hanging. They were called and they explained how their uncle had danced from the end of his belt.

All we had to do was radio Gokwe. Peter told the boss that, after exhaustive physical examination of the body; the questioning of eight year-old eye witnesses and the presence of the release form, it was an obvious case of suicide. The DC subsequently gave permission for burial and the brother shovelled the earth back into the grave.

We returned to base with the awful stench seemingly stuck to our clothes.

Early one morning, just after Wilson had served our tea, I heard this being shouted rather loudly -

"You dirty, filthy little bugger!"

Now that is not exactly what I heard from my office because it was spoken in Shona, but that was the gist of it judging from the noise perpetrating from the Charge Office, so I wandered out to see what all the fuss was about.

"What's going on here?" I enquired as a couple of constables, grinning widely, slapped a cowering youth of about 16 around the head.

"PO Greenberg, this person, he has raped his great-grandmother," one constable said, while pointing to the complainant.

I stared in disbelief. The crone was so old she most probably could recall seeing the Pioneer Column. By sticking my nose in I had also automatically set myself up to handle the case. I singled out a favourite constable I had used in my last rape case from three days ago as translator.

"Hey, stop slapping him around," I ordered.

"Let's go," I said, and signalled the constable to follow me and drag in the evil smelling hag dressed in rags to my office where they plonked onto chairs on the other side of my desk…

Rape. Another case. I sighed - they are never simple and we had no female policewomen to help us out. The last one I handled, just a week before, had turned into a fiasco when the complainant and translating constable broke out in hysterical giggles. 'Rape' seemed rather common in Gokwe, but it seemed more like Cry Wolf. In that particular case, the complainant, about 20 or so, looked remarkably healthy and quite chirpy once she was away from her husband (50+), who had brought his allegedly raped wife to the charge office the morning after the so-called incident.

After stuffing the ancient typewriter with a thick wad of paper and carbon, a quick flexing of my arms and cracking of fingers, I listened diligently via the translating constable to the 'facts',

With some dexterity, I belted out the complainant's statement, remembering to keep it brief and to the point.

There was a trick to all of this. To save a lot messing about you needed to quickly bundle key elements together. It was called leading the witness - Gokwe style. (In this case the complainant was obviously a witness to her own rape.)

I was tending to my fields. An African Male Adult about my age dressed in a trouser and shirt (I do not remember what colour they were) approached me. He told me he was a terrorist and I was afraid. He had no weapon but looked strong. He told me to follow him and I did. He asked me if I have children. I said that the dear Lord had not blessed me even after one year of marriage. After a while he said he requested a rest and because he was a freedom fighter he would help me become with child. He told me to wrap my arms around a tree and bend over.

Now, we all know where this is going. But first, I knew that acts of proclivity by the gooks were becoming quite common as the war progressed. Naughty crimes in the name of liberation were well on the up in Gokwe.

I was also interested in the dirty details - on a professional level of course, because luckily - social upbringing made most whites impervious to the dark side of the forces of lust (who was I kidding?).

There followed a lot of friendly chit-chat between the two. I soon figured out that the complainant was cleverly and coyly making my constable's crankshaft turn his brain to mush. I had to knock this on the head very quickly.

"So, then what happened?"

"Ah, PO Greenberg, it is difficult to explain," the constable replied while grinning at the giggling girl. There followed a veritable masterpiece of understatement:

The suspect then inseminated me with his seed.

Well, I guessed that was coming, but such eloquence! I must say that our black brothers in the BSAP were polite in the extreme – old school for sure. For example, when travelling in a Landy with Nigel driving, I would say, "Hey Nige, pull over, I need a piss."

But not our black colleagues. When I was driving, a bang on the roof would signal me to stick my head out the window to receive some information from a constable in the back. "PO Greenberg, is it possible to stop, please? Some of us wish to pass urine." That's just what they're like.

Back to the interview. Now that we had ascertained sexual intercourse had occurred, what happened next?

The suspect then made me walk in front of him for some time. The sun was starting to come down. He then said he was tired and he needed to rest and I must bend over and hug another tree.

Very impressive. And then?

The suspect then inseminated me for a second time with his seed and went off into the bush and I returned home and I was very late. My husband wanted to know why I was late and I cried and said I was raped by a terrorist. This morning we came to report. I do not think I could identify the suspect as he spent most of the time behind me. That is all I know.

All this was dutifully witnessed by my constable, who was by now in desperate need of a cold shower. I got the husband in, while thinking hard on what to say.
Obviously, she was a flighty one and in the modern age would have been Tweeting and texting the constable within seconds of swapping cell phone numbers. Now I have to do a damage limitation act. Also know in the trade as bullshit.

As young and inexperienced as I was, I instinctively knew that Nigel had, without even realising it, taught me a valuable skill - I had to save the husband's face because when it came to bullshit backed by a uniform - I was brilliant.

First, the facts: We have no suspect. The complainant isn't complaining a lot (well, if she was, it wasn't from the rape, but maybe the long walk). Meanwhile, the husband is a bit miffed that his muff has been messed with. Fair enough. Thanks to the Rhodesian Government, I have a fall back plan. It went like this -

"Constable, please explain that this is very serious, especially as a terrorist is involved." This I got my calmed down constable to translate.

"Luckily for you," I told the man, "we, as the police, will follow-up this complaint right up to the hilt for we treat rape very severely indeed - especially if it was done by a terrorist. However, at this point of time, due to the fact there seem to be loads of real ones causing some right hullabaloo all over Gokwe, this may take some time. BUT – here is a number. This is the number of the crime. Should you have any more details just return and use this number and we will make further enquiries. The Rhodesian Government hates terrorists and we will pay you $5000 if we catch this terrorist that raped your wife because you reported it."

With the paper work pretty well wrapped up, I took the docket to Mike Rowley's office, handed it all in, and said, "No suspect, very suspect, and sauce for the mongoose."

Anyway… back to the case of the great-grandmother, I am now investigating. It wasn't very pleasant. Not one little bit.

I asked how old she was. She didn't know. I asked what happened. The reply came via the constable who also seemed rather disgusted with the unfolding evidence.

"The accused came to her hut late at night and knocked on the door and said he was a freedom fighter and needed some food. However, she knew it was her great grandson and let him in. Then, after she made him some sadza, he lay down beside her and then he had sex with her."

I felt ill, especially as the toothless smelling bag was smiling broadly and cackling like the horrendous witch from the Wizard of Oz. Her face had more wrinkles than the dried prunes my step-mom used to force me to eat with my Pro-Nutro cereal to liven it up. Two yellow stumps looked out at me from a cavern of blackness when she smiled. Considering she hadn't exactly flown in here on a broomstick, but walked three days with the headman and accused in tow, she was seriously fit for her age.

"OK, ask her did she resist, call out, was it painful and please don't bother with any graphic details, as I have just had lunch."

"She says that she is too old to resist and it was painful. In the morning he went but the headman saw him and he was caught. She told the headman she had been raped and they have walked three days to get here."

What a pain this was. Unlike the previous 'rape', I had a suspect. So along with a constable and a bus pass, she was sent to Que Que hospital for a physical examination. I call in the accused.

"Tell him I can't be arsed listening to any cock and bull story. (Triggs had taught me well.) Tell him to just admit he is just a dirty little toe-rag and sign his mark."

I mean, what the hell was he thinking? Yuck. How could anyone fancy poking a pongy, soon-to-be corpse? It would be a long time before I understood the word 'fetish' in relation to sexual activity. But, I mean, doing it with a hag old enough to be your great grandmother – and IS your great grandmother?

With a confession wrapped up pronto, I threw great-granny banger into one of the holding cells. A few days later I received the doctor's report. I felt sorry for that doctor. What a horrible job, man. On the form it listed penetration of the examiner's fingers into the vagina as one, two or three fingers, kept stiff on top of each other. The doc had written four! It must have been a record. The doc had also noted that the penetration was 'easy' - thus disclaiming that the rape had been painful. Unless the kid was hung like an elephant, it was hardly likely that there had been much friction. He also had to swab the raped victim for any traces of the suspect's semen. Swabbed with a deck mop, more like it, but, hardly surprisingly, the little future terrorists had long dissipated into what bush remained.

I handed the docket to SO Rowley and the kid was duly packed off to Gwelo Court and prison. I didn't need no blue stone in my tea for a while, the incident definitely put me off sex for at least a week.

More suicidal cows! You can wipe out three mombes with one bus, but not with a '57 Ford bakkie. The vehicle, having no brakes, and going flat out, had in broad daylight ploughed into the cows crossing the road in single file at a sedate pace. This time, it was not a clean kill.

The first cow had kissed itself goodbye with the engine block and second cow was neatly executed with a tail board to the head. Third cow landed up lying grotesquely against the crushed body work and still very much alive. I got there at the same time as a representative from the Veterinary Department. Amazingly, the driver and passenger of the smashed-up ancient Ford were fine. The accident scene was complete carnage. The Ford must have bounced off the beasts like a steel flipper ball, spun around a bit, before, still upright, coming to a halt, sideways across the dirt road.

The driver started moaning about his bakkie and compensation.

My reply shut him up. "I'm sure you are well insured, but the lack of any braking marks, along with the bald tyres I noticed…"

He shut up very quick. Let sleeping mombes lie, huh! The vet bloke pulled the live mombe's tail, dragging its arse away from the wreck. The cow just looked at me with big, brown, sad eyes.

"This cow has a broken spine," the vet said. "You can shoot it." At that, he jumped into his Landy and drove off. Great! I've gotta shoot a stupid cow.

As usual, from out of nowhere, a small crowd of locals had gathered. With little entertainment available, incidents like these were as much fun as Roman gladiators in an amphitheatre. Then a man comes up to me claiming ownership of the two and half dead cows and pleads with me not to shoot the crippled one. I started to feel a little sorry for him, but explained that the beast was in obvious pain, and had to be put down with a severe dose of lead poisoning administered via my rifle muzzle. The cow's owner, still pleading pitifully, told me that if I shot it here, by the time it got to the butcher, the meat would be useless. Therefore, can I drag it behind my Landrover to Kambasha's Butchery, 10 clicks up the dirt road, alive, with a broken back, to be slaughtered? I told him I'd shoot him too, if he opened his mouth once more, and I shot the cow in the head. I then wrote the 'animal rights activist' a ticket for $75 for letting unattended cattle stray on a public road.

Nigel had taught me good, real good. There was a difference between us, though. He was a hawk, I was a dove, but we both got our own way. While he used a ruler to bring a suspect to book as an accused and all was fine - I simply used the copper's rule book of fines against any suspect accuser. It worked every time (think about that sentence for a while).

Memoir mutterings

This is what Gokwe did to you. You learnt to think on your feet – fast. In theory, had I gone by the book, the whole disaster would have cost a pretty penny in bureaucratic nonsense.

I should have opened a Road Traffic Accident Form. The little 'plan' of the accident area would have been a complete joke. All there was around the scene was bush. With no distance markings, I would have been forced to drive to Gokwe village and read the kilometres off the Landy's dashboard speedometer. Then, even if the driver had a driving license and insurance, they wouldn't pay out because the vehicle wasn't roadworthy. The owner of the cows DID have an obligation to keep his cows under control.

So, instead of all the paperwork, you simply do a crime v punishment assessment on the spot. In an instant I was the judge and jury. Everyone is guilty but at high speed the mind crunches mega bytes of mitigating circumstances. The driver now has no bakkie for whatever little business he had going. That alone is very serious. The cow owner, for all his wailing of paying a $75 fine, would have done an impromptu discount meat sale and slaughtered the beasts on the spot and maybe recouped over half of the mombe's value.

Job done. Cost to the Rhodesian Government – a bit of petrol, two hours of time and two rounds of ammunition – all nicely covered by the $75. However, had anyone been hurt or killed, that would have been another kettle of fish. Since no one had been damaged or terminated, we learnt quickly - just keep it simple.

Gokwe Goblins. In 2012, Gokwe became even more famous, firstly when they had problems with evil mermaids, and then in July, a goblin was captured and burnt alive after it was accused of stealing women's underwear whilst they slept. Just Google Gokwe Goblin - it is all there.

CHAPTER 22:

Lords of the Binge: The Fellowship continues

leopard, landy and Alan
Pic - Alan Golden

The Rhodesia Sunday Mail article continued...

DRINKING TOP PASTIME

Gokwe's big day is coming. Any day now, the village - which has a radio call number of 608 - is to get its first visit from 007. For a village which admits its favourite sport to be drinking, a celluloid visit from Mr Bond - travelling to Gokwe On Her Majesty's Secret Service will make light relief. 'The Godfather' came to town last week, but as he'd been there, the previous week as well, the Mafia was-a-not-a too a-popular. The villagers were shaken - but not stirred. The film shows are staged by the village's sole entertainment emporium, The Gokwe Club.

Each showing gets a full house of about 20 people, and then it's back to the bar.

Gokwe's main sport is drinking' said a resident, 'and the village record for downing three pints is 14 seconds.'

The Club also provides members - the entire village - with a swimming pool, a tennis court and an open-air squash court. Mrs Pat Sanderson, who organises the film shows, explained:

'We never really know which film we are going to end up with, and we have to have 20 people to watch it so we break even on costs. But everyone enjoys the films. We are hoping to get How to Save your Marriage and ruin something or other, soon.'

The 12 families and the bachelors of Gokwe were drinking a special toast whenthe Sunday Mail visited the village last week. The new Miss Bulawayo - Miss Debbie Erasmus - is a Gokwe girl.

As Mrs Sanderson said,

'Don't you dare forget to mention that in your story.'

Now that I think about it, I could have made a bloody fortune in Gokwe. As the article points out, the club needed 20-odd viewers (most of them were very odd), to break even on a film. There must have been easily 500+ blacks in the village. I should have rented the projector and sound system; got the local tailor to sew together four white sheets and down at the black's beer hall make an open air Kino. Charge them all 25cents and I would have been rolling in it. The place would have been well patronised with Suzie Matwetwes and I could have agreed to turn a legal blind eye for a share of the coming and goings. Ah, hindsight. Actually, showing a giant James Bond messing with voluptuous, semi-clad white females to the masses might possibly have not sat very well with the white Gokwians. Still...

One weekend I was the designated power man. That meant at 1pm on Friday I would come down to the sports club and fire up the diesel generator to power the lights, and most crucially, the beer fridge. This fiendishly large thing was in a back house shed and the day before I had been given short instructions by the outgoing power man. Presenting me with the key for the shack (to stop attempts to steal the diesel, which was rather ironic as I am sure the stuff was pinched at various levels from all the Government depots), I was shown how to work the thing.

"You see this small lever?" Gary asked, after he had opened the small room's door and we had trooped in to inspect the immaculately-kept machine. I nodded fearfully.

"This is the stop cock for the diesel. You must turn it on like this," which Gary duly demonstrated. It seems easy enough. Next statement churned my bowels a bit though.

"Then you take this iron bar and place it so." He waved a very thick piece of green painted steel and slipped it on a rod poking from the machine's guts.

"Notice how the grooves slide over the pins."

He stood back and I observed that this was like a vintage car's crank handle; in fact the same principal. OK, I could fathom that.

"You then turn this around and around till she starts."

Okaaay, that seems rather straight forward, but what happens to the handle then? Somehow I couldn't imagine the thing whirling around was a good idea. As if reading my mind, Gary said,

"It is very important that as soon as you hear the motor catch, quickly reverse the handle to unlock it from the pins, pull it off, otherwise it will break your arms and legs. Then when it spins off, it could kill you!"

Holy shit, Batman! Is nothing simple in this place? Maybe I should teach my batman to do this job. Being brought up a 'townie' one never presumed when turning on a light that someone, somewhere, is committed to perhaps die so that I could see. How enlightening was this!

So, on Friday lunchtime, it was with some apprehension that after pushing the lever to 'open', I slipped the lever on and cranked. First thing I noticed was the pain as I nearly tore the muscle in my right shoulder, and the heavy steel lever went flying backwards and fell off onto my foot. I sussed out that this thing had some serious compression and I really had to put my back into it. After four turns, nearly splitting my spleen, the bastard thing kicked in. I switched into reverse and pulled the handle off with such ferocity, I went staggering back, but I was alive with no crushed limbs. I went out, locked the door, generator brumming away nicely, and came back at 8pm - to be greeted by a lynch mob standing in the dark.

I was accused of forgetting to turn the generator on. I of course loudly denied this, and hoped to hell there was a very good reason for the lack of noise from the generator house. With luck some bad men had stolen it – call out the BSAP (Oh, I forgot - I am the BSAP!) With a couple of others carrying torches, we went to the shed to be greeted with a large pool of glistening diesel coming out from under the door. This doesn't bode well. Tiptoeing through this, I got the door open and we went in.

"You idiot, you detached the fuel hose when you pulled the lever off," some pleasant individual informed me, the expectant bitterness of warm beer apparent in his tone. Needless to say I was extremely unpopular that night…

Friday nights were always the same. It was darts night for a chicken. Even the women would play, but they didn't have to finish on a double, resulting in me having a few embarrassing defeats. Saturday nights were always the same too, just darts night without the darts and a free chicken.

Sometimes we had a movie. Mrs Sanderson would rent it somehow and we had a projector and an entrance fee. This would be set up in the largest room, the lounge. It was adjacent to the bar and was only used as a kids play area. Quite a few of the whites had young children and they would be brought along with their Nanny where they would mess about, fed with Willards crisps and Coca-Cola to keep them placated, and eventually fell asleep while waiting for their boozing parents.

I recall two films. One was a B class Kung Fu kind (Bruce Lee type movies being very in), *The Man from Hong Kong*. The best bit is the end when the good guy, who has slanting eyes, tapes a hand grenade inside the bad man's mouth, who now has very wide round eyes, locks him in his own armoury on the 23rd floor and abseils down the side of the skyscraper in less time it took the grenade to detonate. This removed the bad guy's fillings along with a large part of the apartment block's innocent occupiers' abodes. This bothered none of us and later a huge debate broke out at the bar that there was no way he could have fitted the grenade in the bad man's mouth. A grenade was duly presented and even I, with the commonly agreed consensus that I had a big gob, couldn't get it in. Someone came up with the fact the good guy had karate style chop-suied the bad guy unconscious, and as the jaw muscles had now relaxed, the good guy dislocated the jaw, popped it in and then taped him up. Sounded reasonable, and such intellectual conversation. The end music was cool too. *Blown it all Skyhigh* by some one-hit wonders called Jigsaw (I have an illegal download MP3 of that now).

Another film I remember well was the *Spy Who Loved Me*. In it, Roger Moore as 007 has a real neat Seiko digital liquid display watch which I knew cost £300. Besides the single men ogling at Barbara Bach's body, the film was (incorrectly titled) mentioned in the press, as Gokwe got its 15 minutes of fame after the place had been attacked. Just my typical rotten luck I was again away and missed out on hogging the limelight.

There was no real drinking up time. The bar would close when everyone had drunk enough. This oddly enough was legal. The DC had the right to extend the time as long as he liked. Once, he made this power quite clear when someone with a drink too many, decided to criticise him over something petty. Mr Wyatt didn't mess about. He called his wife and told the amazed barman to lock the fridges. This was at about 9.30pm. For good measure, he told the stunned patronage that the bar would remain closed on Saturday as well, and walked out. You didn't mess with this man.

And talking about messing - the article doesn't mention what happened when the daughters that had been at boarding school arrived back for school holidays. Mrs Sanderson, despite what was for me her advanced age, had a 14 year-old daughter. Well, the flirty nipper took a shine to Ian, who looked about 16, so it was rather funny watching this stiff, grey haired secretary clucking like an old hen whenever the two were at the club at the same time.

Another potential target was the DC's daughter. I will talk about this delectable lass later - and then there were the Erasmus girls - one of whom was the wonderful Miss Bulawayo. Well, she was a right prissy pain in the arse. She was the eldest daughter of the lady with the big bum that worked part time at the police station. Her 17 year-old, second daughter was cute and I had a little kiss and cuddle with her once, but the other one, Debbie…*Eish*! she had bunny boiler written all over her. Even the big cool cats of Gokwe didn't bother with that one. I, of course found out the hard way…

As Gokwe was now a bushwar hot-spot, loads of reservists were coming through on shift change en route to the outlaying base camps. What was now common throughout Rhodesia was the 'Troopies Canteen'. It gave away free food and tea to any troopie on the way in or out of the bush. So, here I was at the Gokwe canteen getting served by Miss 'Too perfect for Gokwe', and I asked how she was. She started moaning about the heat and she had better things to do than work as a servant for free. I, of course, had no problem telling her that I sympathised with poor little beauty queen getting her lovely lacquered nails knackered.

Ten minutes later, a bakkie driven at high speed turns up, and that massive bloke, Jaws, from the James Bond films, gets out. OK, he didn't have steel teeth, but his grip was of steel as he grabbed me by the throat and lifted me a clear off the ground. This was Debbie's dad. He had been a rather nice bloke till now.

"You talk like that to my daughter again, I will break your neck," he said dropping me and going back to his bakkie and drove off before the astonished eyes of the reservists.

Memoir mutterings

Reminder - I am definitely not going to make Debbie Erasmus my friend on Facebook.

Glossary

Suzie Matwetwe's. Women of the night peddling playful procreation.

CHAPTER 23:

Petrified peasants - lend me your ears for I need some wheels

Private transport was a problem. Besides the pain in the butt trying to bum a lift out of Gokwe and no one in his right mind would catch a dodgy Kambasha bus; when I did get to Salisbury, I was again stuck. Katherine was highly reluctant to allow me to use her Rhodesian assembled Renault 4. She thought I might dwang it and thus leave her without any form of transport. Which wasn't strictly true. She was now teaching at Mount Pleasant High School, just a fifteen minute ride away on a bicycle, and she could have used mine. I noticed that her daughter didn't come into the 'Can I borrow the car equation?', but there had always been a bit of favouritism in that direction. I was still more of the prodigal son type of family member when it came to borrowing the car.

So there was great incentive to have my own wheels. Even more so after one pear shaped weekend at home. I had arrived late Friday afternoon, phoned Josephine and she reluctantly allowed me to pop around. I was getting as bad as weeping willow Peter, as I begged to use the Renault. After much moaning from Katherine, I got it, and in the early dark drove up to Josephine's old man's place. I drove sensibly, indicated nicely (with the electric ones, none of the silly waving out the window stuff anymore - that had gone out the window as soon as I had passed my test), and as I entered the drive I had to cross over a cycle path that ran parallel with the road. There was an almighty bang and a very dark object, shaped like a human, went flying over the bonnet, along with a black bicycle.

I was in such a rage at the possible damage to the car, I ran over the comatose body several times, and threw the corpse into the middle of the road, along with the bicycle, and drove on. Not really, but the idea did enter my head for a second. I stopped, and in a genuine rage showed the black cyclist, who was hopping around wailing about a sore leg and damaged bicycle, my police identity card and threatened him with a ticket for having no light on his bike and possible negligent damage to the car.

Luckily, as the actual contact speed would have been at walking pace, I let him off lightly, seeing that there appeared to be no damage besides a couple of small scratches. My Step-mum never cottoned on, but Josephine had allowed me to take her out on another expensive dinner the following night but I was refused the use of the car and I wasn't willing to fork out for taxis. So, I had to get my own car…period.

Due to sanctions, cars, even second hand ones, had a horrendous price tag and required a minimum of 33% deposit before you could apply for finance. I still hadn't finished paying Katherine back for the airfare from Manchester, so as usual I was always short of bucks. No wonder that BSAP also stood for Broke Soon After Pay. Then an interesting radio message arrived from Que Que. They were looking for 'volunteers' for some new fangled idea that would help to win the war…

The police had several units for fighting Gooks.

1. **PATU**: As previously mentioned, meant that every now and then, you were bundled together with people you hardly knew, and spent four weeks of wandering around the bush, semi-trained, poorly equipped, looking for gooks and hoping desperately you didn't bump into any.

2. **Support Unit**: Also known as *Blackboots* because presumably they wore…oh forget it. This was a full time job slotting gooks on the same shift cycle as the army. Six weeks in and then ten days off for getting drunk, committing suicide, beating up the wife, or salt curing your souvenirs of ears and ball-bags - the former to hang from the rear view mirror, the latter to make a neat gearshift knob cover to show off to your like minded psychotic friends. I am not dissing the *Blackboots*, but unfortunately it seems every war throws up some real loons. I do not make this up. Some of the 'war stories' I heard verged on the criminally insane!

3. **Special Branch (SB)**: Part or full time job to 'persuade' the local frightened shitless peasant populace trapped in between, to 'confess' to the whereabouts of any terrs hiding out. Sadly, this unit did attract some people whose gospel was according to 'The little intelligence required *Gestapo* Guide to spilling beans *schnell*'.

4. **Interface Unit**: This was the new idea. It was based on the British success against communist insurgents in the Malayan emergency of 1948-60. Unlike the above, here the counterinsurgency plan was to try and win the hearts and minds of the local populace, rather than beat the black crap out of the blacks till they were black and blue – such as in job number three. The whole mumbo-white-jumbo was to last three months, with six days off in-between per 28 day cycle - so pushing it to almost another month.

5. **Police officer**: This job carried all the risks of all of the above without the immediate back up and was the least paid. When you were not forced to do any of the first four, you went about solving crimes and generally being nice to everyone. You didn't spend any time thinking much about gooks, otherwise you went mad.

By now, Chief Inspector Harvey was really pushed for white staff. His Section Officer Mike Rowley was out of action after having the crap shot out of him in an ambush and was recuperating in hospital. He would live, but never return to Gokwe. The boss still didn't have a replacement for him. Triggs's minimum of a year was up and he was gone and Alan was already on SB patrol. That left four of us. Well, actually three. Sending weeping willow Peter out with a unit was definitely a death sentence. He would be executed by his own side after twenty four hours of listening to his wailing declaration of undying love.

So, as it was me that intercepted the radio message, I mulled over it for a few minutes. I did some lust filled psychological equations. I knew about Einstein, and using that great formula I didn't have a clue about, I worked out - Josephine = no love – car + go into bush = extra money = car + love = Josephine + love making. Simpils! With that problem solved, I drew a deep breath. It meant no Precious for four months if I went for it. Still, I was besotted and I would/could make the sacrifice. I handed the radio message to the boss. He read it in silence whilst I refused to be dismissed. At the end he looked up at me –

"And?"

"Sir, I presume that you would have the authority to say where each group of us will be distributed around Gokwe. As you well know I have spent most of my time here around the Chirama base camp and as I have become known by the locals (as the local white loon), it would be best if I was stationed there. If you say you can arrange that- then I volunteer."

He looked relieved. I guessed he didn't like ordering any of us against our will. I hoped he had as much luck making up the demanded allocation of black policemen.

"Good Karl, I will radio Que Que that I am sending you." It was Karl now. It had been for a few weeks as we got to know each other better. I still had to call him 'Sir', but I had no problems with that. I had tremendous respect for the man.

Little did I know then, but over three decades later – this was the moment when I started to go insane and become the infamous Gokwe Kid. At this point in time I should have had my head examined, but no, they sent me out to 'talk' to the people. Rhodesia was doomed...

Cool Beans! As I left the office my wallet started working overtime - some quick mental maths. That's an extra $112,50 tax free a month, no rent, no mess fees, no batman (sorry Thomas, you're on 3 months unpaid leave, but I will let you come back to wash all my dirty camo whilst I go off on R&R), and as I can live off a dollar a day - it means along with the two hundred bucks I intended to get from the last of the money I inherited, plus step-mom would be paid off soon meant...at the end of the last patrol I had the deposit for my own wheels = Josephine = love = baby making with my honey using perhaps the tree hugging technique. Of course, this might have all been a bit of the well known Rhodie babe's favourite saying - 'In your dreams'.

What I and many of us didn't know, was exactly how badly the war was going. News at Eight, either on television or on the radio, always started the same way. 'Security forces regret to announce the death in action...' and then the names would be read out, usually followed with... 'and in the same period a total of XX confirmed Terrorists were killed.' Usually it was always more of them than us. Officially the kill ratio was one of us to ten of them. I had been in Chirama base camp eating dinner when the name of my former gymnastic partner from school was read out. That hit me hard. Two years we had been a team. Same first name as me. Karl had been a tall gangly kid of the same age. We hadn't hung out together but we had struck up a solid and reliable relationship. Some of the more complicated stunts we did relied on perfect understanding between us, for if something went wrong - a broken neck could be the result.

Now he was dead, killed in an ambush whilst fetching fodder for his unit's horses. He had joined the Grey Scouts, the mounted military wing of the armed forces.

So, when I freely volunteered to run around the Gokwe bush preaching propaganda - did it ever occur to me that I might also one day be in the newspaper column -'Killed on active service' - after the - 'Miscellaneous for sale'; with one standard entry from the BSAP? And then, even worse, just one entry in the condolences from my step-mom and Josephine wouldn't have even heard of my parting of mortal body and unloved soul. (Okay…let us not be toooo drama queen here.)

The answer - Nope. Not once ever. I believed that as I never went out of my way to deliberately hurt anyone, why should they want to do the same to me? Plus, whilst I still hadn't clocked it, trouble stayed away from me for the simple reason I dragged another self made version behind me. (Here comes trouble, and that's Karl in the lead.) But did I care about those snide remarks behind my back and in my face? No - because I was born for Interface. It was the Rhodesian version of the X-factor – fame at last awaited….

Interface school was interesting. No printed notes. We had to write everything down in our little books. (I still have this little book.) Right from the very start things went pear shaped. However - this is how it was to work in principle. A unit of five men made up between Internal Affairs and the Police would walk from A to B for three days and three nights. At each large kraal we came across we would gather the local folk together and have a nice cosy chat. It was supposed to go like this…

The introduction
Hi there, I am PO (whoever I am) from the police and my friend here is from Intaf. This you can see by the hats we wear and the grey shirts.
That bit with the hats and shirt we left out. Firstly there was no way I, or any of

us, would walk through the gook infested bush wearing peak hats and easily visible shirts. So scratch that one for a start.

Reason for visit.
To annoy the hell out of a load of severely frightened peasants caught up in a war whilst just trying to make ends meet and live in peace. Well not quite, I am here to save up for a car.
We actually just happen to be wandering through on normal patrol. *(Hah hah, normal patrol – my arse it was.)* The police bit is to see if there are any naughty criminals skulking about and the Intaf to hear if you have any problems regarding the administration of the land. Why are we carrying rifles? To ensure that the job is continued.
Whatever that is supposed to mean, but that's what it says in my little note book.

Warning about Terrorists.
Firstly these people are misguided and have been tricked into going over the border.
Then arrive in Tanzania, Zambia or Mozambique where they meet Chinese and Russian people.
At this point you could have said Kermit and Miss Piggy, for all the experience the locals have with these last two nationalities. I doubt if any of Gokwe blacks had been to one of the only two Chinese restaurants in Salisbury and the only Russians around was locally brewed Vodka. This you clarify with the next sentence.
They are Europeans and teach these boys to become killers of children and old people. (*Huh! Since when were the Chinese Europeans?*) Why do the Chinese and Russians help? They use these boys as puppets and tools to take over the whole of Africa.
It doesn't say in my book what the nasty Russkies and Chinkies want to do with Africa once they get it, but let's presume things will be worse than now.

What does a Terrorist look like?
He wears civvies or blue denim or camo, has a pack and carries an A.K /R.P.D./R.P.G. in his hand.
Might as well throw in: could be wearing a three piece suit, mirror sunglasses, chews gum and shoots people with a Tokarev pistol hidden in a crocodile skin brief case; but the thing that gives them away is that they are all black men.

Communism: How it works.
There are incidents in the area. Show them a little booklet called 'Anatomy of Terror' and describe what happened.

Unfortunately we don't have any copies at the moment but believe me, it's full of grotesque images of hacked up and tortured people of all races. (Google it.)

They stop the busses and the clinics and schools are being closed. The missionaries are unarmed and helpless. They plant landmines. The roads, schools, cattle dips, councils etc, no more new ones. No money. It is needed for weapons.

And a deposit for a car! No reference to Karl Marx or Engels, keep things simple.

Split of so called Majorities.
Nkomo / Sithole / Magabe / Mezarewa . How come these people say they are the true leader. Nkomo wants to kill Muzerewa.

As a white I wasn't too clued up on the spelling of some of these guys and had no idea who they were, besides being bad ass gooks.

Terrorist groups clashing.

This is true, what I didn't know was that Gokwe was a boiling point for this clash of might.

Smith and the security forces are all one.

That's pushing it a bit if you have seen a hondo in Club Tomorrow or Le Coq D'Or, but I suppose I believed it myself then.

If one faction take over there will be civil war. Freedom is democracy. The right to say what one likes and to be able to change government.

Amazing stuff this! The next bit in my note book makes little sense to me although one line says 'Land for everyone, Europeans have to pay'.

Message to Terrorists:
Security forces stronger, better equipped. We have radio, medical packs, food.

Terrorist fighting methods are of cowards. Hit and run.

They say come to fight yet they run away.

Security forces have casavacs (casualty evacuations).

If Terrorists give them selves up and help us they will be rewarded.

If villagers reports Terrorist they will be protected and rewarded, if don't report, face the consequences.

Any Problems?
   To be filled in later.
Question time.
   To be filled in later.

Got that? Good, now off you go and convert the masses. We are two white policemen, one black police sergeant, one black constable and one black member from Internal Affairs. My stick leader was called Andre Leo. He was a couple of years older than me, and had married young. A bit taller than myself, he had a gymnasts natural build and was quite good looking, with a head of curly black hair warming a very dull brain. He was alright even when drunk, so the next three and half months in his company, whilst not very intellectually enlightening, was never the less easily tolerable.

True to his word the Boss stationed us at Chirama. The routine was always the same. We would be driven out to an area that I planned or places that had been radioed to us from Gokwe police. Then we would walk in arrow formation about 30 clicks through the bush, stopping at kraals on the way and hold our Interface meetings. After the three nights sleeping under the open sky we would be picked up and spend two nights in camp.

So in the middle of October 1977 we started. For the first month I was really fired up by the whole thing. Whether I actually believed in the stuff we were putting over to the locals is debatable, but I became quite quickly a local local's L class celebrity.

Firstly, we would approach a kraal. This could be just a few huts with a couple of small grain storage constructions on stilts to keep wild animals at bay, and then ask who ever might be hanging still around, (because they couldn't leg it quick enough), where the headman was. This meant we would be directed a short distance away to a larger gathering of huts, some scrawny chickens scratching about in the sandy soil, along with the usual yapping, mangy kaffir dog covered in ticks, ribs sticking out and its tail stuck between its legs.

The maps we carried only showed the dirt roads and permanent constructions such as missions, schools, cattle dips, stores, Internal Affairs camps etc. No kraals. Certain kraals could only be found by asking the locals. The headman was then instructed to gather all his people for the meeting. This could take a couple of hours as they tended to be out in the fields looking after their crops. In that case we simply positioned ourselves around and waited in any shady spot. Morning and lunch time sessions tended to bring in slightly less than early evening meetings. Makes sense, but - but by 8.00 pm, it was prime time TV, less the TV. In the beginning, I would make the brightest black amongst us announce in a booming voice –

"Tonight, this is it! Tonight from Gokwe - live on the bush telegraph for the first and only time – PO Greenberg!"

Oh - how the crowds roared. I wandered into the dull light of a cooking fire, immaculately dressed in soiled creased camouflage, a pathetic stubble on my face, smelling as bad as my audience - and then I really gave it to them – the Gospel according to Great White Bwana Smithy. In my little book I note that alone at one such concert, 120 people turned up voluntarily. Why not, the tickets were free and I was unquestionably the craziest thing to hit the locals since their forced relocation en-mass to Gokwe TTL in the mid-sixties. My translator was useless. The stupid man was laughing so much he could hardly keep up with the garbage I was spouting. Who cared, I was the best entertainment the locals had freely ever been forced to witness. The last good laugh the peasants had had was when whiteman's clever bridge collapsed into the Sengwa River.

Perhaps it was then I would unknowingly get my Chimurenga name – the *Penga* one.

Sadly, after no Simon Cowell type signed me up for fame and glory, and suffering from premature ADHD syndrome - I got bored. My translator also had enough translating the same garbage three times a day. So on the second stint, we decided on a new strategy.

It was agreed to let the black members of our stick take turns to mumble the jumbo to a very bored crowd, and I would answer the questions. Andre's only job was to give a demonstration of our so called weapon power. This had caused a few embarrassing moments in the beginning. Pointing to a tree, I had signalled Andre to fire into it after explaining that the projectile would go straight through. It didn't. Damn, er, try a smaller tree. 'Bang', still no exit wound. After that we only picked trees with an approximate circumference of a man's thigh to be on the safe side. And talking about safe side - were we mad or what? Besides the fact that 100%

there were either gooks listening in or their mujibas; advertising our presence by shooting off FNs indiscriminately would certainly announce the whereabouts of the 'Rhodesia Has No Talent (and still lucky to be alive) Bush Tour'. I must have been totally off my rocker...I was.

All that transpired during the meetings would be written down in our little police note books and radioed through once a day. Andre did the first month and a half, I did the rest. What I pick up now, going through my note book, is the breakdown of people attending. We wrote down three categories, Male, Female and Juvenile. I noticed that the male presence was always far lower than the female counterpart and consisted mainly of men over forty. This anomaly, upon being queried, was put down to the fact that the able bodied men had gone to the cities and towns for employment. (Or were now gooks?)

    Question time was when I came into my element as an expert, not a clown, and as the weeks went by I had almost every angle covered. Some were harder to answer and with no guide lines I had to use imagination and intuition. I started to think personally that the whole Interface thing was a good idea and some of my explanations made for lively debate. One that popped up time and time again was the theme 'cattle'. These people adored their cattle and it was a sign of wealth and prestige. However, the tsetse belt went through Gokwe and I always had the same argument from the villagers on the 'wrong' side.

    We often had the tsetse blokes staying at Chirama and whilst chatting with them I understood the way they were fighting this very fast fly with the vicious bite, carrying the deadly disease *trypanosome* or, as it was commonly known, 'Sleeping Sickness', in humans. Another three kinds were fatal to cattle, horses, sheep, goats and dogs. The tsetse fly feeds solely on mammalian, reptile or avian blood, or in basic terms - me, my snake and my chick. Slowly but surely the fight was being won but there was still over a land mass half the size of Wales to be cleansed of this curse. The idea was to literally wipe out all animals with cloven hooves in a 16 km wide belt, as this had been calculated by the scientists as being the furthest roaming of the fly. This area would then sit dormant for ten years till there were no flies left. Then it could be inhabited but no cows yet, but donkeys were allowed. At the same time another same sized corridor would be wiped out. Only with a 32km fly free zone could the cattle be introduced, but even then they had to be regularly dipped.

So, how do you handle this argument?

"Sah, I am not worried about the sickness killing a few of my cattle."

To this you explain that his herd would all be sickly and be worth nothing.

"That is my problem Sah."

I try another tactic and explain maybe his next door neighbour, a half a day's walk away down the road, is not exactly impressed that his cattle are now infected because of his disease ridden herd.

"That's his problem, Sah, not mine."

Ah-ha, at this point - all are veeery extremely interested in my answer.

"Then I suggest you go and have a small chat with that neighbour and hope you don't get a knobkerrie over your head. In that case I will be back to fill in an aggravated deadly assault docket and you could be soon listening to your family," here I point around at all and sundry, "wailing above your head as you lie deep down here," now pointing to the ground.

This would be brilliantly translated by the black constable who was thoroughly enjoying doing the 'Black and White Ministerial Show' with me. Everyone would roar with laughter and we could skip to the next question.

Some were very basic in requests. We are short of water, we need a borehole. This could be fobbed off with the answer we short of money because of buying guns (and saving up for a car), but we will inform the District Commissioner. Or, we have a borehole but tired of hand pumping the water out, can we have a tap? Questions like these irritated me. Always want, want, want - but never can we get together, pool our resources, donate our labour, make a plan for brotherly betterment. Dig a well…do something for Christ's sake. Even my black companions would tell me that they despaired sometimes with this stubborn mind set of accepted position of perpetual poverty. Another example was in one remote kraal, where to my amazement, they said they hadn't been visited by any government presence for three years and the borehole is broken.

Why has no one bothered to report this? No answer- *Aikona hasa*.

I remember once, whilst on a patrol, coming across a Garden of Eden. I have not even seen white farmers create in such a small area what one solitary Blackman had created. A delightful fellow, dressed in blue overalls and black Wellingtons, he guided us through his garden. This was micro farming of mind boggling proportions. I think his 'patch' couldn't have been more than a couple of football fields, tops. It was packed stupid with every vegetable I could imagine. The maize was massive with huge cobs. He had planted the entire lot himself and we bought onions, tomatoes and meilies from him. Amazingly the neighbours' plots only had some scraggly and poor quality maize.

I was extremely interested in how he did all this. The man went on to explain that he had done a course at an agricultural college and with the qualification had been given a loan from the bank. That money had been invested in a borehole, irrigation pipes, some basic tools and fertilizer. He explained how the soil had to be carefully prepared and how the drainage worked. I asked how come the neighbours weren't doing the same thing. He just laughed and shrugged. (With hindsight – he was a dead man walking. Success under the whites = Sellout.)

We always asked the villagers if they had been approached by terrorists. To this they always replied no. At question time I would get some sticky ones regarding the subject of gooks versus us and with them stuck in between. From my notebook -

"If a terrorist comes to my home and he is in my hut with my wife and children and I inform you, what will you do?"

"If I lose my Registration Card or it is destroyed in the wash and I am on the way to Gokwe village to report this and you stop me. What will you do?"

"If security forces have been told that we have been harbouring terrorists but this is only a rumour, what you will do to us?"

"If I report terrorists and when you come they are gone will you shupa me?"

"If I am carrying a bag of grain to mill on my head and you stop me, must I put the bag down or leave it on my head?"

"If I am walking alone on a path and meet security forces must I put my hands on my head?"

Questions like these were from genuinely frightened people and as we wandered day after day through this wilderness, things were starting to get out of hand. We would receive constant updates of any terrorist activity in Gokwe TTL and in the space of two weeks alone in October, I filled my book with examples of how things were spiralling downwards -
6/10 : West Boundary store robbed.
10/10: Terrs at Gumuruya area.
14/10: Bus robbery. 4 C/Ts (could be pseudo terrs). Cattle Dip destroyed at Lower Latope. Number 4 and 7 Dip at Lutope also destroyed.
16/10: Dip attendant robbed of $50 (Terrs?) Latope man burnt.
18/10: Chief Jiri assaulted by Terrorists.

So it went on for three months...

Memoir Mutterings

Chimurenga and having a 'name'. This is rather interesting. Chimurenga is, according to Wikipedia –

Chimurenga is a Shona word for 'revolutionary struggle'. The word's modern interpretation has been extended to describe a struggle for human rights, political dignity and social justice, specifically used for the African insurrections against British colonial rule 1896–1897 (First Chimurenga) and the guerrilla war against the white minority regime of Rhodesia 1966–1980 (Second Chimurenga).
The concept is also occasionally used in reference to the land reform programme undertaken by the Government of Zimbabwe since 2000 (so-called Third Chimurenga, or Chidudu - The Fear).

Okay, but, and I mean it, I had never in my time wandering around Rhodesia recall this word. Now, strangely, as decades go by and thanks to the internet and the creation of cyber Rhodesia, I hear of fellow combatants having a 'Chimurenga' name given to them by the gooks. These are of course in Shona and could be variously translated in the same fashion of the Hollywood style of - 'He who dances with wolves'. As such, mine, if it ever did exist, is very appropriate.

Glossary

Aikona hasa. I do not know.
Dwang. Crash.
Hondo. Fight.
Penga. Insane.
Shupa. Cause trouble.

CHAPTER 24:

Pleasure and Pain

me and my new wheels
Pic - Gokwe Kid

After the first stint of Inya'face lecturing to the peasants that 'RHODESIA IS SUPER', I had garnered enough dough for a deposit for my dream machine, and on my six days off in Salisbury, I finally got my own set of wheels. I had no clue about automobiles. Someone, somewhere, once said a man only needs two kinds of friends to get through life – a dentist and a car mechanic. I now have the former but when I purchased my first car I lacked the latter, so as usual in the history of the world when it comes to second hand car dealers - I was ripped off. I had my heart set on a Toyota Corolla 1200 for the simple reason that the divine Cindi Tait, from Mount Pleasant High days, had been picked up after school by some dude in one, so I concluded it was the real mean machine for making babes desire babies.

The problem was time. I had little of it, so I nailed the first Corolla I found at Second Street car dealers next to the Reps Theatre. It was canary yellow with red plastic seats. It had been in a crash, repaired and re-sprayed. I didn't know about that bit and I was certainly not told of these minor details. A 1972 model with 86.000 miles on the clock, no heating, no radio, and retreads on the tyres, it was a steal for the sellers at $2200. (I didn't even try to negotiate! What an idiot.)

I spent all my days off zipping around faster than a tsetse fly to secure the purchase. I had to organise getting finance (the bastard thieving banks forced my step-mom to be the guarantor. Well they didn't force her - I did - along with a bribe of fifty litres worth of petrol coupons I had cadged from the Boss), road tax (What the hell?), fully comprehensive insurance that the bank insisted on (What the hell?) and after filling the car up with petrol (What the hell?), I was almost flat broke again.

I had just the last day to see my beloved Josephine. After phoning her (she seemed rather aloof and non-committal about a date in my new wheels), I went around to her place. I had cracked the mighty equation – Wheels = Josaphine + dinner = baby making. When I coolly rocked up, she was sitting on the drain culvert at the beginning of the drive with a clipboard doing some survey. Yes, it was a nice car. No, I don't want to go out with you tonight and you are terminated. I was dumped. Just like that! All that money spent on fancy restaurants - for what? A grand total of exactly seven, yes, exactly seven French kisses (I had counted every one), that had left me with severe lover's nuts. I hadn't even got a tittie grope! I was gutted. I will never look up the heartless cow on Facebook. When I am a rich and a famous author, she can bloody well come begging for my attention and I will refuse, unless she pays for twelve fancy meals at top restaurants. What else? Er…she can get down on her knees and profusely apologise for not leading me to the nearest tree on her garden's path. Erm – I hope she went on to grow up all obese and has horrible children like mine that do nothing but play computer games, and with luck her husband beats her every night. (End of drama queen rantings.)

I went to *Barney's* disco that night – alone - and whilst listening to ABBA yowling 'Dancing Queen' - I got completely shit-faced and swore never to fall for a woman again; the bunny boilers – all of them! (Actually…that isn't quite correct. So she was a…a heart boiler! Well something like that, because it really hurt. [Sob! Please play the world's smallest violin for me].)

Oh, and another thing, whilst I am venting my spleen - I spent TWO days wages buying an outrageously priced silver dog tag sized disc with neck chain. I had it engraved in large intricate italics; a *J* and *K* (the idiots managed to balls it up, so there was a strange scribbled tail at the end of the *K*, but that didn't stop the swines charging the massive amount. We had no consumer rights in those days), which I now realise you never wore unless I took you out for another f……. (splutter), expensive dinner whilst you still wore that daft Julie Andrews dress, because you were embarrassed wearing pendant and I bet you threw it away. If not, I want it back and I will sell it along with a signed copy of my book on EBay – to YOU for at least a hundred dollars because you have to save face…hah, hah, revenge is mine!

Then it was back to Gokwe, but at least I have some wheels, even if they did fall flat as pulling power.

Memoir Mutterings

I can already see the comments on Amazon.com
From the men –
"What a loser. He is as bad as weeping willow Peter."
And from the ladies –
"Aah bless. You never heard of 'treat 'em mean and keep 'em keen?"

CHAPTER 25:

Dumdums, death, dumping and a cat called Cat

Chirama base camp and longdrop
Pic - Nigel Triggs

After the attack on Gokwe, the base camps had been expanded to accommodate an increased presence of security personnel - mainly consisting of reservists from the towns such as Que Que and Gatooma, and some even from Gwelo. There was also the occasional presence of Intaf and Tsetse control. At Chirama, the government, for some strange reason, decided to build a brand new, and very expensive, camp further back from the edge of the escarpment, and it had just started. The construction engineer was a middle aged balding functioning alcoholic called Bill. He would stay the longest and never seemed interested taking any time off to return to 'civilisation' for a break.

To accommodate the large influx of whites, the recreational area needed to be extended. The octagonal tin radio shack had a massive green canvas tarpaulin attached to it, and this was stretched between several trees. The result was a large shady area for the grub and games table, plus shelter from the blazing summer sun on the paraffin powered fridge and deep freeze. Most of the police reservists were old enough to be my father, but with their vast years of experience they rapidly became well organised. They created a really smart camp with tents installed over dug outs, waist high deep pits, against possible mortar attacks. A ramshackle lot, these reservists, were a picture of all walks of white life. Bankers, shop owners, pen pushers, farmers, you name any white supremacy job – they came from all over the Midlands; sent to prop up the overloaded security forces. They came and went on various lengths of weekly periods. They actually liked the job! They just stayed put in camp whilst having a break from the wife and screaming kids or stroppy teenagers. On top of that they had free food, fully paid income by their employers, plus a government bush allowance.

A few I remember -

Paul was mid-thirties and the camp's designated cook. He showed me how to keep the fire inside the cast-iron oven stove ticking along nicely and how to make the most perfect meals of meat and vegetables. They were all well spiced and with lots of gravy. We got on fine - till he hobbled into the radio room one evening clutching his calf. I was in the middle of playing cards, when he announced my pet snake had just bitten him, and as I was also the resident First Aider, hopefully I had some anti- serum.

My new pet was an arm's length long and a forearm thick sized adult puff adder. For some strange reason, anything out of the ordinary was allocated to me and after it was discovered in one of the tents, I had gleefully caught 'Puff', popped him in a large cardboard box with some sand, stones, water dish; made him a nice cool warm home under the kitchen table. Paul was quite fine about this, and even gave me bits of steak to pop through the lid for him. But Puff didn't seem that hungry as he still had some fat bumps in him and spent the whole time sleeping his dinner off. It was also the reason why he had been easy to catch. Being naturally very sluggish, they only move fast when striking. I had simply wrapped some clothes around my arm and grabbed the thing by the back of neck.

But how the hell had it escaped? Also, NO, I don't have any anti serum, but yes, I can slash his calf along the muscle grain with my sheaf knife as soon as I have sanitised it in the fire which was in the kitchen...er... where the escaped snake might still be in. This was to bleed the poison out, or worse comes to worst; I could remove the leg at the knee with a shot gun blast. That will stop all progress of the venom. Paul looked at my white face, took his hand away and stood up.

"I'm not bitten, but the bloody snake is loose in the kitchen. There is a hole in the box."

A hole in the box? How did that happen? The radio operator chirped up then,

"I think that snakes aren't into prepared food and prefer it live."

Okay, and?

"Well, my guess is that the live rat we caught and popped in there this morning decided he wasn't too keen to be bitten and eaten and chewed its way out the cardboard box *asap*."

I can't believe this! I go away for five minutes on patrol and grown adults act like bored children, risking people's lives and my reputation! Poor sleepy Puff is easily caught skulking in a corner. I like snakes, so I was as gentle as I could be and released him free in the radio man's sleeping bag to teach him a lesson. Okay, I am kidding again. I took it a few hundred paces down the road and let it go.

And then there was Keith.

He was our heavy vehicle driver. They were in huge demand. We had a bullet proof Isuzu truck that was used to deploy us and ferry the reservists back and forwards to Gokwe village. He had just picked us up the day before and was a newbie. A tall boisterous man who sported a medium sized 'Rhodesian Front' beer belly. He had thinning reddish hair and a light skin that easily turned red in the sun. I would know him for just one night...

I was rudely awoken the next morning on my day off in camp, to be told, by a panic stricken radio operator, that they had found Keith lying on the shower floor.

Grabbing the nearest clothing, my dirt encrusted camo trousers; I rolled out the camp bed, burst through the tent doors and ran as fast as my brain started waking up. There lay the naked form of our truck driver, slumped against the back wall, his legs sticking out towards the entrance, the water still cascading over his bluish mottled form.

"How long has he been here?" I demanded from the circle of alarmed faces looking through the door, as I turned the water off and slid his naked form on to the flat of his back on the soaking floor.

Judging by the skin tone, I hazarded a guess he had been dead for at least quarter of an hour or more, but from my training I knew I had to try. The answer came as I balled my fist and smashed it as hard as I could over the prone man's heart five times.

"I was next in line for the shower and after maybe half an hour I came over and found him like this, and then we called you," was the reply from someone outside.

Too long, whatever struck him down had been fast. His eyes and mouth were wide open in an expression of surprise, the body relaxed and still warm from the shower.

I snatched a towel from the rail, bundled it up, and in my adrenalin rush managed to lift his heavy body up enough to get it under his shoulders. His head went back and pinching his nose, pulling his tongue down, I blew into his lungs twice.

I have read about death rattles, but it is eerie hearing your own breath rattle out of someone else, as I crossed my hands and started pumping over the heart. Seven times, then two breaths, seven pumps, two more breaths, each time I pumped, I heard my breath being forced out his lungs in that awful sound. How long I kept this up, I do not remember. I checked for his pulse, but there was nothing, and now the body started cooling and his normally very white skin was now a darker shade of pale blue…

I rocked back on aching knees and wiped the sweat with cramped tired hands from my burning eyes, along with the accumulated saliva of the living and the dead onto my hastily dressed and still unbuttoned, combat trousers…there was nothing more I could do.

Later, after his corpse was popped into his sleeping bag and bounced around in the open rear of the only Landrover at our disposal back to Gokwe village, I heard he had died of a massive stroke that had dropped him instantly. It was a small condolence for me, knowing that I could never have saved him - especially as I had guiltily concluded that his death meant an extra day or two in camp until a replacement driver for the truck was found. I thought about writing to his widow and two teenage daughters saying I had tried and that I was sorry. But never did.

We also had a cat, named after a short discussion, CAT.

We had picked it up from some kraal village on one of our patrols. She was a small black kitten, wriggling and mewling away in a sack. We all loved her, and took the mickey out of the poor critter something rotten. But she was spunky as anything, and loved the radio room. There the miniature black panther would cleverly use all available cover, till it was ready with claws and teeth, and then pounce on the exposed ankles of the unsuspecting operator. We would all laugh as, screaming in pain, he tried to shake Cat off. The room had a well cracked polished concrete surface and once we stuck a cheap Rhodie version of Sellotape to Cat's paws. We nearly pissed ourselves with laughter as Cat scrambled confusingly around the slippery floor, legs splaying everywhere, constantly shaking its paws. No matter how we tortured the poor thing, it came back for more. Tossing it in a blanket with four of us holding a corner proved that cats amazingly always land paws down, but I gathered from the spitting and raised hair, Cat wasn't too impressed with this stunt.

Andre liked to sneak up behind Cat when she was having a dump. Cat would dig a small hole in the soft soil of the camp area and start her toilet. Andre, beer in hand as usual, would tip toe up, and before the small black worm would land, he would leap into the air and, as his splayed feet crashed behind the poor bastard's straining arse; scream his head off. Much to Andre's delight the deposit went into reverse and the terrified thing would bolt off. I wonder if it ever managed to have a dump in peace after that upbringing.

Whilst on the subject of having a dump, as previously mentioned, we had in the middle of the camp, the toilet, better known as the 'Long Drop'.

The long drop had a proper toilet seat, but that is where the similarity to a Crapper ended. Once you opened the door, the stench really hit you, along with the swarm of very fat flies. This place was to be avoided like the plague, and if you had to drop a long one, then try and save it till late at night, when the heat had dissipated and the flies were in their beds. Sometimes, you got to go when you have to, and there was always a fear that a fly would zip up the rear passage faster than you could close it. There was a large bucket of lime taking up the space not allocated for your feet. This, with the use of a small gardener's spade, was used to sprinkle the powder over your recycled dinner. Once, very stupidly, I wanted to see how long a drop it was...

I had nightmares with the idea of running into the place, desperate, touching cloth, suffering the turtles head, slam the door shut, and before you could get your eyes to adjust to the little cracks of sunlight penetrating around the wooden door, your buttocks were submerged in some other person's defecated last supper. I had to know!

So once, I took a peek. As usual, it didn't occur to me to simply wait till night time and shine a torch in it. No, sadly, not me. Much cleverer to set fire to a long roll of toilet paper and pop it down. As the strip, spinning eerily, descended, the flames started to reach an alarming height. In the next few milliseconds, my brain realized that perhaps this wasn't such a good idea!

With eyeballs bulging at the awful sight of a huge pyramid of defecation in every tone and constipation/diarrhoea of brown imaginable, rearing skywards at least half way up the three metre deep shaft, complete with its own patrolling squadron of giant flies, I suddenly remembered that farts are flammable and Arabs use camel dung to make fires with! I shut the lid and burst through the door. I was about to shit myself.

I was wondering how to explain to everyone in camp and my Boss how and why - did I send the 30 year old Jacksie into orbit? The answer that I was interested to see how much poo there was in it, some how, would make a big brown mark on my report card.

Of course, we had a large contingent of black forces. All regulars and volunteers - the government didn't conscript the black population. Some were Police, some Internal Affairs, some just labourers working on the new base. They were allocated an area of the camp and did their own thing. I went over often to their 'side' and they taught me the game Mancala, but I was always soundly defeated, much to the delight of the onlookers. An ancient game that was extremely popular with the local populace, the version I played consisted of four rows of holes dug into the sandy soil and the outer rows filled with either bottle tops or stones as tokens. These would be moved around in turn till one player captured all the tokens. What appears as relatively simple for the on-lookers, it was fiendishly complicated and played at incredible speed. Games rarely lasted longer than fifteen minutes. Mine lasted a lot less. There was also a strange version of draughts and I was just as useless.

    I remember once tuning my mini-Precious into the enemy's signal being beamed from Maputo, Mozambique, where Robert Mugabe was retroacting the future, live on air. I would demand translations from the small black crowd, who had gathered around as they listened with growing amusement. It appeared that he was promising free farms and Mercedes cars to those that help free Zimbabwe etc, etc. Our lot weren't having any of it. I liked them all immensely and always queried if they were okay and had enough supplies etc.

We also did normal things whilst on our day off. Besides drinking, we had books and board games and masturbating in the shower (or if really bored - on night watch). But to alleviate the repetition we would occasionally go out with the Landy, gather a group of peasants together and after the usual spiel demonstrate a new (by me invented), demonstration of Rhodesian superior fire power.

    When I nipped, using pliers, the tip off a bullet to expose the lead, I made what is called a 'dumdum'. These were really cool to demonstrate the 'Exploding Tin' job. For this stunt I needed a used five litre tin of Sunflower oil, which was then filled with water and the top screwed back on. Perching it on a tree stump and letting fly, resulted in a great display. The water would explode in a massive cloud and the tin would actually spring forward from the force of the water exiting out the back. Then, to the amazement of the gathered spectators, I would show them the completely destroyed tin, now actually just a flat piece of metal, and the streaks ingrained into the inside surface as the water had actually scoured lines in its haste to get out. Best though was my 'Towering Inferno' stunt. Here I used a canister of camping Gaz, the miniature disposable tins that we used to cook with whilst on patrol. After a little trial and error, I had it perfect. First you perched it on some flattish surface, preferably about shoulder height, and sitting on a few layers of newspaper. Andre would set fire to the paper, run back to a safe distance and I would fire the dumdum through it. What a spectacular result! The compressed gas now 'air injected', would erupt in a huge ball of flame for an instant. The tin would disappear somewhere into the bush. I was forced to stop this bit of fun due to a shortage of available canisters.

Memoir mutterings

For all these fun and games, both on and off the battle pitch, my stick didn't break any rules. Gone were the days of lounging around and sending lies about our position each morning. There was no more night's off guard duty, unless it absolutely lashed it down, which it did on many occasion. The poncho's never got tied up as 'tents'. All that shite we were taught in COIN - forget it! After the last meeting, we would head out in the dark and after a couple of clicks, pozzie down and just wrap ourselves in the thing and hope it didn't rain too much. When it did, we were soaked, chilled to the bone and exhausted from lack of sleep. As the morning sun gathered heat, we wandered through the bush like steaming spectres till we finally dried out by 10am, only to be soaked in sweat by lunchtime.

Mini-Precious stayed in camp. I also raided the Gokwe armoury as it had been stocked up a bit after the attack on the village. I now had seven magazines for the FN. I needed more and on one of my extended weekends off to Salisbury, before I started with Interface, I put down my own cash at Faraday's and Sons to get enough magazines for the FN to suit my own requirements. They were Rhodesian made and a bit flimsy in comparison to the South African counterparts. There had been some moaning from other lads that the spring wasn't up to much cop. The trick was to oil the inside slightly, along with the cartridges; then they flew into the chamber like magic. I also purchased chest webbing for five magazines, and along with the pouches on my belt, and the magazine on the rifle, I had the firepower of two hundred rounds. Plus one. That was the one you kept in your breast pocket in case things went rather badly. This was the bullet you would place through your own brain. It was well known that gooks didn't exactly follow the principles of the Geneva Convention. The shop also had telescopic sites that could be mounted on a spare dust cover, but they were horrifically expensive.

I also had a plan to sort out my rucksack. Whilst the police had given me a Rhodie made 'A' frame in combat green, the thing was hopeless. I had to carry some serious weight. Along with food, Gaz stove etc, (we didn't bother taking any other clothes other than fresh socks), I had the first aid kit, complete with a saline drip (which made a nice pillow), two water bottles, and sleeping bag. We also took turns carrying the incredibly heavy TR28 radio. I must admit, many times we split it from the battery and divided it between two of us. Not the cleverest of ideas – but when you're knackered from walking in formation through sodden bush for at least ten clicks a day...

Anyway, whilst my UK imported rucksack was quite comfortable, the bright red was not so good, and wrapping the thing in my poncho wasn't really practical, so I thought up an idea to sort that problem out as cheap as possible. I had hitched down to Paramount Garments in Salisbury, where my old man had been the General Manager before he changed profession to pushing up daisies in the Jewish part of Warren Hills cemetery.

I recall that funeral well; I was 16 at the time. There was a lot of nastiness in the background, a story I will relate in a prequel – suffice to say it left poor Katherine in bits and financially in deep shit. Only one member of the staff had ever bothered to occasionally phone my step-mom afterwards. *C'est la vie* hey. So when I walked through the door and announced my name and desire to see the new manager (who I knew), well blow me down with a feather – the guy shot like a rocket into the reception. He was more than helpful to let me help myself to three combat shirts and matching trousers. No charge of course. If I had had to pay, I reckon I would have bounced a cheque on the firm. Hard to believe, but the owners had paid up my father's pension and last wage down to the last half-cent. They didn't even round it off a bit higher after a decade of faithful service. They certainly had plenty. Still, in a bit of *shadenfreude*, they lost the huge army contract a short time later due to... mismanagement. Hah hah – poetic justice.

I didn't want to wear the stuff. Paramount Garments used extremely heavy cotton, almost denim in thickness, from David Whitehead's cotton cloth factory in Gatooma. They were uncomfortable and stinking hot in summer. The trousers were okay, but only for winter. The plan was to find a tailor and get him to cut the shirts up and sew them all over the rucksack. I had come across a very busy tailor at an African store on the dirt road between Gokwe village and Chirama, which I visited regularly for some well needed supplies - beer and Cokes. I was well known and delivered the rucksack and shirts to the dubious in-house tailor and didn't haggle out a price. I reckoned he would wrap it up in a day and charge me two dollars.

I popped down a couple of days later and couldn't believe my eyes. He had taken the nylon pack completely apart and was systematically cutting the camouflage cloth into a clone shape and sewing it onto the nylon. He was doing this with an antique pedal driven Singer sewing machine. Then he was painstakingly putting it all back together. Amazing - but I grumbled about the ten dollar price tag a week later. Tight bastard I am! It was a bloody work of art and the envy of everyone. The fact it still had its original nylon carcass meant it was semi-waterproof, and with its well padded shoulder straps and the brilliant use of pockets, it was a dream. Granted, it weighed a little more (especially when the camo got wet), but it was rugged, comfortable, and could carry shit loads. I could run in it by simply pulling the quick release straps tighter, or use them in reverse to drop the pack if it there was a real high speed follow-up. The poor tailor took a serious risk doing the job, which he did totally in the open on the forecourt of the store. If gooks had come across him doing my rucksack, they would have planted him a bullet for sure...or waited for its owner to turn up, and plant us both. My guardian angel had definitely been at work again.

Glossary

Pozzie. Place to sleep.

CHAPTER 26:

Merry Christmas, I need a stiff drink!

me perched at my beloved Chirama
Pic - Gokwe Kid

On the 24th December (exactly one year since I first started here in Gokwe as a regular member of the British South Africa Police) - I am feeling pretty good with myself. I am slowly recovering from lost love, and I now own on tick, a car. I am the nearest thing to a pop-star amongst the local indigenous population - which is perhaps why I haven't been popped off yet. I can solve all sorts of crimes and even type them up well enough for them to be deciphered as English. Thanks to Christmas; we had an extra couple of days off, and I made a mental note to thank baby Jesus should I ever be converted from not believing in God. We had plenty to eat and… drink. But there was one small problem… Our biggest hassle at that moment in time- a terrorist assault perhaps? Nope; it was the paraffin powered fridge and freezer. It couldn't chill fast enough, and shoving the masses of beers (I was starting to get a bit of a taste for the stuff), into the deep freeze meant the meat never really froze and bloody water streamed out the poorly sealed door, attracting flies in swarms. And then - as if in answer to questionable prayers…

My boss turns up with the District Commissioner at Chirama camp. They had driven from Gokwe village to attend a funeral of a shot combatant, whose home, a couple of huts in a kraal village, was a mere half hour drive through the bush from our base. After a brief perusal of the camp, they carried on down to the escarpment floor where there was a small landing strip for light aircraft. Behind my boss's personal Landrover, followed the bases only Landy. Open at the back, it would accommodate the coffin being sent via 'Air Mail'.

I wasn't part of the entourage for the funeral. I was preoccupied preparing for the festivities ahead, including a little tree with some home made decorations. Moments before the sunset splashed us in hues of orange, the two Landrovers returned. The boss, extremely agitated, requisitioned the radio. I had noticed with some interest, that our Landy had acquired a rather long zinc alloy box, shaped like a coffin, busily steaming wispy coils of frozen air out the seams.

From the conversation Mike Harvey had over the radio, and his personal summary to us, the following happened and was about to happen. There is a mother of all ball- ups!

Everything had been going perfectly; the relatives had been informed well in advance, and the grave was dug. The paid local wailers were there (Bob M was banned in Rhodesia both Marley and Mugabe). The dead man's huts, personal possessions and wives had been, according to the local custom, divided up amongst his brothers. It was to be a grand funeral for a gallant black warrior, who had fought on the side of the white minority government. Respects were to be paid by the highest ranking white men in the Tribal Trust Land of Gokwe.

At that point, the 'coffin', was opened and it was the time to move the well frozen body, covered in dry ice, onto the blanket where he would be wrapped and buried. Words in Shona and English, spoken in respect for the departed, then wailing would start and that's that.

Before the body is out the tin and into the mud (rainy season going strong), a brother chirps up,

"Who is this man?"

Stunned silence (I imagine).

"The tag on his foot might say my brother's name, but he not my brother, and this is starting to look very heavy."

Oops! We have a problem.

No matter who the boss radioed, nothing was going to get sorted out till after Boxing Day. No planes, no boats or trains…helicopters, ox drawn Scotch carts, one body to beam up Scotty. Nope - It's staying here for a while. The metal 'coffin' was placed at the back end of our tarpaulin shaded area. The dry ice would keep it pretty cool, plus the evaporating carbon dioxide swirled chillingly around our Christmas tree making it really – Christmassy! The boss and DC zipped off to be at home with respective families and we have got a super cooled stiff!

Christmas day dawned like all those before. I saw nothing as I was still in my camp bed. You only get up when the heat from the sun makes it unbearable in the tent (or someone dies or there is a snake about). The cook had started the turkey in the oven and I went around the outskirts of the camp wishing 'Merry Christmas' to all and sundry, black and white. Both races had an adequate supply of alcohol. The blacks stuck to their traditional millet brew of Chibuku in normal summer temperatures of 30c plus, and us whites moaned at the bottled beers at 20c.

I think that it was during a game of Master Mind with brain dead Andre, that I had the very clever-clever idea. Whilst he struggled on row nine, (total idiot, I cracked most codes in an average of four, unless Andre was scoring), my bored eyes wandered around and settled on warm crates of Castle and Cokes… and then, lifting them up slightly, onto the swirling mist from the 'coffin'. The other members played cards or read and moaned over warm beer…

Three spring clips held the lid down and I swung it up on its hinges, swearing a bit as I lost a bit of skin on the sub-freezing catches. And, there he was, in all his shot up glory - our new fridge. Talk about heaven sent. The dry ice took up at least a third of the coffin. There was loads of it, steaming away. Dead brother was well chilled out, and I am sure he wasn't bothered as I shoved bottle after bottle in any gap I could find. There were no obvious gaping wounds apparent on his camouflage uniform, just some dark blood around a few small holes. His legs were slightly apart; perfect to balance the Castle beers as I slipped them in squeaking at a high pitch as they hit the dry ice. From the looks of the others, I knew they had been waiting for someone to finally make the move. Let's go and chill out with the dead this Christmas...

After a shift change of reservist personnel we had a new cook called John, who taught some of us to play Bridge. It is still for me the most elegant of card games. The teacher was one of the most amazing men I would ever meet. John was in his late forties, from the UK, divorced, alone with his own demons, and working as an engineer at one of the mines in Radcliffe. You don't have to wait long in 1977 for your call up papers once you become a resident of Rhodesia. Six months! Due to his age, John did cushy numbers. He didn't mind. No family, get paid one way or another, and for a brilliant six weeks, I had my own free university lecturer and he seemed to know about everything! He had explained to me that trying to top up my car engine with as much oil as possible was counter productive, and the 'max' mark on the oil dip stick was there for a reason. He took over the kitchen after Paul had left. He showed me how to place rolled bacon fat slices, garlic and onions, into deep slashes stabbed into the large roasts needed to feed us whites. I was also shown how to make a mix of oil and spices and baste the joint regularly in the wood fuelled oven.

He did us all proud with the turkey roast with all the trimmings, but kept the last surprise till darkness fell. He then brought out a large plate with what looked like miniature prunes swimming in a red sea.

"These," he announced to a rather inebriated group of on lookers, "are Snap Dragons."

He went onto clarify. The dark, small, round misshaped balls were raisins that had been soaking in almost undrinkable local wine for a couple of days. That's what they were also swimming in. Normally it was supposed to be brandy but we didn't have any in camp. It was also explained under normal brandy conditions the plate would be preheated and then set on fire. The idea was to plunge your hand into the flames, 'Snap' a 'Dragon' and pop it, still on fire, into your mouth, where upon biting the hot warm brandy mixed with the fruit, it would make a great party delicacy.

Instead, after all the car battery powered lights were turned off, using Rhodesian intuition, a large dollop of purple methaylated spirits was vigorously poured onto the plate and ignited. To everyone's delight, each attempt at a 'Snap' resulted in the flaming stuff igniting various parts of the drunken fool's body, table, floor and tasted appalling - but who cared, it was Christmas! Just as well Cat bolted as soon as the volcano erupted.

By the time we bothered to switch on the radio again the next day - after using the good excuse,

"Lightning storm, must close down," rather than the truth, "We on the piss and to hell with the world," our dead man fridge was starting to smell a bit - worse than the freezer.

When it was switched on again, I was called by the radio operator. Alan, in Gokwe village - had something to tell me...

Piet, Gokwe's government employed mechanic, as much as I knew him, was a nice guy. He must have been in his mid twenties. I didn't see him that much. Still, there had been weekends when we coincided at the Gokwe Sports Club. He seemed totally dissatisfied with life which he told me about when pissed. I couldn't figure it out. He had a South African Passport and was a top notch mechanic. What the hell was he doing in Gokwe? I never got a clear answer. But he seemed to be seriously depressed. He had been of huge assistance to me. That Gokwe main dirt road down to Que Que had knocked the hell out my Toyota Corolla's old exhaust. (I hadn't known about that either when I bought it.) I wasn't coughing up two weeks wages for a new one. Pete welded the scraps together. He told me it was just a temporary patch job. I bought him a beer at the club as thanks.

This is more or less what happened as told to me by Alan in an email –

There wasn't too much snow in Gokwe that year. With temperatures in the 30's Father Christmas would have needed an air-conditioned sleigh with 4x4 capabilities.

Christmas Day in war torn Gokwe! Now there's an experience to be shared. A long boring lunch with the DC - trying to quaff down as much free beer as possible. The prime of Rhodesia's young fighting men ogling anything in a skirt older than 12. The lads couldn't wait to get to the retreat of the Gokwe Club and continue the ritual - three easy steps; drink, fall down, sleep. The lesser mortals had already fallen by the wayside, CMED mechanics, asthmatic cattle counters from the District Commissioner office, and even a few of our hardened 'top of the food chain' Patrol Officers.

As we sat wondering how many more beers we could squeeze in before the generator switched off, the clatter of distant fireworks drifted through the alcohol induced blur that we called consciousness.

Fireworks...? A slow surfacing of reason....
Fireworks...? The wave builds through the haze of Lion Lager bottles...
Fireworks...? Holy shit - that's gun fire!

He didn't say a word, but in one look from the OiC (Officer in Charge, Mike Harvey), conveyed a complete set of instructions to me - Move your ass, find out what's going on, meet me at the station. Grabbing Chris, the young inebriated Intaf officer, by the scruff of the neck, I roared off into the darkness in my Landy, armed to the teeth. Driving without lights through the sombre dirt tracks that doubled as roads in un-electrified Gokwe, we reached the houses on the edge of the compound.

"It came from over there," yelled an unidentified resident, indicating the direction with a brief flash of a torch, before scurrying back behind their sandbag defended veranda. 'Over there' was Pieter's house, the Afrikaans CMED mechanic who was built like an ox. We approached cautiously; bullet ridden walls and windows faced us.

"Pieter!" No response, "Pieter, we're coming in!" Still no response.

Our cautious entry did not mimic the SWAT house clearing techniques we see on TV today. With blood pounding in my ears, I stepped over empty 7.62 expended cartridges and empty magazines. With growing concern, the images of the day began replaying in my head. Debbie, the young attractive daughter of a Gokwe stalwart family - flirting with the socially inept Piet. Teasing him with pouting lips and rebuking his advances when he took a step closer. A sad and lonely Pieter, that we ignored and left crying in the corner – Wanker - real men don't cry.

Piet had slipped the safety catch on his FN rifle onto automatic and sprayed the house with magazine after magazine until he ran out of ammunition. He then took his last round, slid it into the chamber of the rifle, and placing the red hot muzzle of the gun into his mouth - pulled the trigger. That's how I found him. His skull and flesh blasted onto the rear wall of the bedroom at a muzzle velocity of 1,200m per second. Merry Christmas everyone.

Yeah, Merry Christmas – Rhodesia really is Super! It was Boxing Day; I still had the day off. I cracked another beer bottle that ponged a bit from our freezer of rapidly rotting human meat. I was really starting to *really* like this stuff...

Well 'our' Christmas cheer was flown out lunch time on the 27th to be buried in the right place. We didn't get a replacement. Instead, someone had to go back to the village...and explain...there has been a mix up and actually ...he has not been terminated, and, er...the ex-dead has been granted compassionate leave and will be here in a few days.

Great! Brilliant, super, and as senior Gokwe based police officer it is my task to go down there and tell the village inhabitants this wonderful post Christmas news and survive. I took the most senior black policeman with me as translator. I did not understand that much of the indigenous customs and rituals, (not part of the white school curriculum), but in my European mind set -

How the hell do you clear up this mess? The so called deceased man's brothers are shagging his wives and taken all his stuff and...and...and...

I couldn't even ask my black accomplice, some 15 years my senior, for advice. I simply told him to explain to the headman of the village the mix up and get us out of there. His taut face was the real answer, one I could only vaguely understand, but he complied.

CHAPTER 27:

Pulled over whilst pulling on the piss

As another month of lecturing to the peasants that 'RHODESIA IS SUPER', (whether you like it or not), slips painstakingly by, I had reluctantly forgiven the female race and decided I missed them quite a lot after all. Besides, I was getting bored with pudding pulling in the shower.

Back at home in Salisbury on my next six days of R& R, I soon got sick of the Rest bit, and wondered how I could kick-start the Recreation bit, (I was not stupid enough to ask Katherine for another top class recommendation), when who should happen to wander in through the door? Alison Howard. Actually, she wasn't there to see me, I wasn't that desired yet, but to visit my sister. I was more than interested to see her again. A couple of years before, whilst at school, I had wangled a lunch date at her parent's house. What a performance that had been...

The father was there. Sort of. The man was immaculately dressed in a serious looking banker's type suit and I had been informed that he was some top notch business man. He seemed so old; I thought he may have arrived here on Cecil Rhodes newly built imperialistic railway service. Unbelievable! The mother was a lot younger, but was in my eyes a right dirty cow if she had let the old goat on her 15 years ago to make Alison. I mean, what were they thinking? We all know that old people shouldn't desire sex after they have reached the age of thirty eight. *Ag sis man*!

Mrs Howard shouted all through lunch, explaining that her husband was slightly deaf. I think he was more than that; I thought he was slightly dead! Several times I thought he would keel over into his lunch. The sound made by his knife and fork on the plate, as he tried to cut a piece of lettuce, reminded me of a drum roll at the circus. I was grateful when the comic show ended, as I was about to break out in nervous giggles. Back in Alison's bedroom, I had managed to attain an interesting position of attempted *amour*, when the next disaster struck. I am not sure how I managed this, perhaps being a gymnast had something to do with it, but Alison was standing in the middle of her room, with her legs gradually moving apart, as I, kneeling, with my upper torso under her mid length dress, slowly moved my kissing lips up the very strong and trembling inner thighs, heading towards...when suddenly - my head got clamped.

For about three seconds my hearing was cut off as her thighs squeezed my head so hard I couldn't put my tongue back. Then just as suddenly, the grip relaxed and the skirt was pulled away from my head. That was the end of the passion run - totally ruined by Alison's mother popping in and wanting to know if we were alright...

Now she looked even better. She was seventeen going on eighteen with long blonde hair, a tiny mouth with red lipstick, almost as tall as me, not my usual buxom bosom type, but she had a nice sized arse as compensation. I started my peacock show and before Bridget lost patience with me, for hogging her visitor, I got Alison to agree to a date on Saturday night, providing her mother hadn't remembered the attempted toad-in-the-hole incident. The next day a phone call confirmed that her mother had approved her daughter going out with my step-sister's respectable police officer brother. Yeah...like shit I was.

 Poor Alison. Maybe I was still on a 'hate women' kick after Josephine had taken an assegai, torn my heart out, and tossed it nonchalantly onto the Enterprise Road – to be run over by any passing car; because by the time we left the Meikles Hotel restaurant I was semi-wasted. Trouble had started when it came to pay the bill. At $20, I had chokingly written a cheque, only to be informed by the head waiter they don't accept cheques! I wasn't carrying much cash because as usual I didn't have much to my name. Still, I explained that on the reverse of the cheque was the rubber stamp from Gokwe police station, here is my BSAP card, and if that is not enough, what you gonna do? Call the cops? Hah-hah - bloody no chance.

 From there I dragged the alarmed girl to the Monomatapa Hotel where we sat in the foyer lounge till I was well oiled, whilst gibbering some gibberish about me being Rhodesia's answer to Garry Glitter preaching propaganda to the peasants rather than paedophilia (read that sentence out loud when you're drunk!); and we were kicked out at 11pm when the bar shut. Home time, and don't spare the stallions planning a drunken delusionary good stomping humping. Still, it appeared that the couple of glasses of Rhodie made Cinzano that Alison had drunk could assist me in my bedroom for further adventures of discovering what was under her clothes, and with that in mind, I headed my Toyota Corolla onto Second Street.

I think it was at the junction with Rhodes Avenue that I decided to demonstrate the prowess of being a hot shot from Gokwe, when, on the completely empty four lane road, a Citroen frog looking type car, pulled along side at the red traffic light.

"Watch me drag these fuckers off," I pronounced to a very white faced Alison, and as the lights turned amber, I was revving the shit out the poor little 1200cc engine, and to much screaming retreads, bolted down Second Street like a bat out of hell.

Sadly, just before I reached the Second Street Service station a couple of clicks down the drag, the French pile of junk had matched my top speed of 92 clicks an hour (the mile version), and had pulled up along side. What I had thought had been a really good race, had turned into a no fun reality game without the virtual PC, when the frog's interior light were switched on, exposing two uniformed police officers signalling me to pull over. Oh Shit! This was bad news, man, and to assist my anxiety, Alison burst into tears - accusing me of being an awful person! I would normally have agreed, but I was seriously intoxicated with my own invincibility. At least I still had a few sober brain cells left to pull over. I couldn't outrun the bastards; I guessed they had my number, and now my ass.

The passenger was a male at least twenty years older than myself. He instructed the female police officer, who had been driving, to go to the petrol station and phone for a 'B' car - the flying squad. Eish - I was in serious trouble - and as I managed to stand up, after falling out the open car door, I leaned against my police pulled passion wagon, and considered my fate. The boss would not be impressed for a start. With no driving license I would land up on patrol for at least another year. The car would be sold at a loss and I would still be paying the rest off and, 100%, I was looking at two weeks in the box with no pay. Neither would Katherine be very impressed. Sod the wailing Alison's grave yard candidate parent's opinion of me. I might as well jump head first into the Chirama longdrop, until - I suddenly spotted a loop-come-possible bolt hole.

The police officer had started to explain that they had just finished duty and would make sure I was 'well copped', when I happened to notice a small gold coloured 'R' in his uniform lapels. He wasn't a real policeman - only a Reservist! What do you do when ambushed? Go on the attack. I whipped out my police card (for a start I outranked him even whilst pissed out of my head), and started a tirade against the man, that whilst I, stationed in GOKWE, risked life and limb, whilst useless lazy bums like him had a pushy waster job pulling poor bastards like me for having a few drinks before they get sent out to DIE again and again…etc, etc. (I am a serious drama queen when it comes to getting out of trouble.) Now, the stunned bloke is desperately trying to defend himself, claiming that he had done a stint here and there, but I brushed this aside, shouting louder now to override the howling coming from Alison ('Alison? Who the fuck is Alison?'), about how she can't phone her mother to pick her up; because she hasn't a mobile phone as they haven't been invented yet, and I have been arrested, howl, yowl…

Bloody hell, she sounds worse than weeping willow Peter, but I am now in full righteous swing. The man didn't know of course that I had just spent the last two months having my own Rhodie law show to the accolade of hundreds of captive –vated, non paying fans - and really let him have it…

"GOKWE, man, Gokwe…you know where it is? Yeah, that made you quake – it's the end of the fucking world man - only insane people are posted there! I don't give a monkey's toss where you have been man, because I come from GOKWE where there are GOOKS, man - millions of the fuckers - all over the place. I'm with INYA'FACE man, that's more fucking hard core than you have had nightmares about."

I hadn't personally actually bumped into any gooks yet (not that I was going to tell him that), remember, I had a guardian angel, and I sure as hell needed it here right now. I was in serious kak. All this I told the man quite politely. I hadn't used the C word and besides, all white members of the BSAP were used to the foul language of drunken idiots. Whilst I drew breath and my Dutch courage brain pondered the next line, the police women returned and signalling her partner, informed him the petrol station was closed and no phone was available. Ah. Now what? It was half past eleven by now. If he stayed with me, and sent the female officer back to Salisbury Central Police Station and she got a response… in that time I would have talked myself sober and my so called arresting officer would have either shot himself or me by that time. He wasn't armed, but I was. I had that cute little pistol I always fancied from the armoury in the glove compartment. I could always lend it to him. (I had correctly signed out for it. Oh, if you're wondering where my FN was, it was under my bed at my step-moms place – frightened the hell out of Julia, the maid, when she vacuumed cleaned under it.)

"Get in your car and fuck off," was the next instruction from a completely outclassed reservist police officer and I thought this was a good idea. Alison didn't seem that relieved and insisted I take her home.

Then it was time up and back to Chirama…and pulling my wire yet again…*Eish*!

Memoir mutterings

I never saw her again. She refused another date. I did see a picture of her on Facebook a while back. Her hair is shorter now. I asked to be a friend and she never replied. Eish, Alison, I know it's a bit late, but I'm sorry hey! When I am rich and famous and if your husband lets me, I will take you out for a really nice dinner and order two taxis.

CHAPTER 28:

When the lion feeds, I hit the jackpot

Pic - Gokwe Kid

Now that the peasants have been so brilliantly converted to the gospel according to Ian Smith, by non other than myself, and I have not managed to get my ass shot off, it was back to the 'normality' of the police station. Even though I was almost top dog with Nigel and Alan gone, much to my alarm we had someone new in Nigel's ex mini house. I had been hoping it would be mine one day. Instead of me, we had an overweight middle-aged bachelor that didn't seem to do much all day in Nigel's ex office (which also should have been mine), besides making nice charts. He was a Section Officer with over seventeen years in the BSAP by the name of Jan van Staaden.

Oh, almost forgot. I was also alone in my room. Weeping willow Peter had managed to get himself shipped out two weeks after my return. He had been sent to Que Que to pick up wages, supplies and papers, fuel coupons, etc., for the boss. He had ignored warnings and had spent an afternoon trying to revive his school girl's desires for him. As a result, the fool drove back in darkness and just outside Que Que, went at full whack into a herd of cows. (Which ironically, might have saved his life because he could have landed up being ambushed.) He later wailed that an oncoming car had temporarily blinded him, but I think his head was still stuffed up his arse trying to work out his love life. If it wasn't for the triple seat belts, and the armour plating, he would have been dead. As he now automatically lost his licence to drive police vehicles until an internal enquiry had been completed, the boss sent him back to Que Que. Best thing to do with him, Peter wasn't the type for the bush.

One day, the boss sends me out on general enquiries again, not to my beloved Chirama, but up to Chireya, the badlands. This time I had a licence to kill with me. For an extortionate $5, I had wangled a permit to exterminate a kudu antelope. This amazing achievement made me the envy of all the white community. The District Commissioner was the only authority with the power to issue shooting permits and kept them to himself and his cronies. I just fumbled with his eldest daughter in my passion wagon one night to qualify for mine. She was a nice kid, but as she was only sixteen, I kept my animal lusting to some serious snogging and tittie grope. After all, I was an officer and a gentleman, but I did have some strange carnal feelings for her mother who thought, along with her husband, that I was a nice person. If he could have read my mind, he would have shot me – with or without a permit.

 I spent more time chasing kudus than doing police work. Kudus are clever and knew the hunting season exactly, and were also smart enough to know which side of the National Park fence to stand on. Once, I was hot on the heels of a lovely well horned individual in the Landy, bouncing around as it ploughed through potholes and huge troughs in the dirt road running along the park fence. This was really *Daktari* stuff! Then the bugger simply, with one fluid bound at full tilt, sailed over the twice my height fence into safety. As it stood there, watching me spill out the Landy in a cloud of dust, it chewed some grass and sort of winked. Now, if I wasn't such an honourable gent, I could have dropped the cheeky sod with my FN and dragged 270 kilos of potential biltong through the large gaps in the fence. Then I would have some smart curly horns to mount on my bedroom wall, as well as a nice new rug for the floor.

The day the permit ran out, so the bush suddenly became full of visible kudus. In compensation I managed to bag a huge adult black mane lion without firing a shot. Whilst out on investigations from base camp, a couple of locals flagged me down. Translating through my constable, I was informed that a couple of lions had been nibbling at their goats. So what! I wasn't going after a couple of shumbas to arrest them for chewing on a few mangy goats. Not quite. Next thing I learn is that the pissed-off goat's owner had laced the half eaten carcases with Roga cotton insecticide - with very effective results. They had found the male that very day, not far from where we were. This sounded very interesting, so the incident was well worth a look. Manoeuvring the Landy around rocks and stumps, I managed to get as near as possible without snapping the chassis.

Eyes, very wide open, and loaded rifle in hand, I got out and walked over to the beast. What a sight! A massive, fully grown male, without a mark on it. The cause of death was apparent. Roga, as I knew from that suicide I had attended, was very poisonous. This poor cat had died an agonising death and the foam was still apparent around its open mouth. No sign of the female, but I was still a bit nervous.

I was wracking my brains. This was some prize and protocol directed that this must be reported back to the DC. I knew the man would promptly claim it for himself, whether I am playing with his daughter or not. I needed to make a plan. I informed the complainants that poisoning giant pussy cats was against the law, but being a kind policeman, I would give them $2 to skin it for me. They happily agreed to this and told me to return in three days.

Back in camp, I was in trouble. I had been away from Gokwe police station for nearly two weeks when I was only supposed to be away for five days. One of the reasons is that I had come down almost straight away, upon arrival, with flu or similar symptoms. Where I was now, it wasn't like you phone the local MD, nor as legends of Africa decree, do you bang a drum and the local witch doctor turns up, complete with a bone through a broad nose and a magic bag of get well cures.

In fact, you are normally returned 'home', but the thought of every day's tax free $2.50 away allowance kept me strong. Plus, even dying, I could still tune into Springbok radio and hear the new Number One, 'Magic Fly'. I was ordered, after the third day of the shivers, to go to the local mission clinic. This clinic was run by a bunch of Catholic do-gooders from Portugal who loathed the security forces. I was informed of this fact by newly promoted Inspector Jan van Staaden himself, who was presently the highest ranking man at Chireya camp. This was the same man that made nice charts back at the police station. So off I go and I present myself to a rather good-looking chick in a silly hat, called Sister Goldenhair - which was rather odd because it was as black as the leg hairs weaving intricately underneath her semi transparent stockings.

I received very little sympathy. Number one smile was obviously weakened from my illness, and rather than get a date for a little exorcist hanky-panky by moonlight, I got six aspirin and was told in Portugese to *vá-se foder*. I am not sure what that meant, but it didn't sound very nice. I was told in camp the gooks were often sheltered there and our 'lads' had done a few 'search and seek' missions on them - hence, her reluctance for a candlelight dinner. A short time after I left, I think most of the Portuguese were murdered and the place burnt down to the ground. Holy retribution. Never feed the hand that shoots you.

Now I am in a pickle, and all sorts of lame excuse doesn't hide the fact I was to return to Gokwe village. Gawd! What about my ill gotten fortune, all beautifully pegged out and well covered in salt crystals. I had paid up front! $2 could buy two crates of Cokes. I would turn for help to the only people I had learnt to trust. My fellow black policemen. I had noticed that a proportion of white Rhodesians, as the war dragged on, were getting some rather nasty habits. Doing some one over was getting common. But not my 'Boys'. They all rather liked me. Dunno why, but I think in their culture, mad people are treated with special deference. A quick explanation and I was assured that all would be arranged. They really were stars…

Until five days later, when some rather silly constable shouted out at the top of his voice, as his hand pushed a huge black plastic telephone receiver against his ear,

"PO Greenberg, SAH, your **Lion Skin** is at Kambasha's store, to be picked up."

I nearly died! Again the guardian angel was around, as no white officers were in ear shot, and as soon as knock-off time came,

I took the Corolla for a quick spin up to the shops. I went in and was welcomed with a huge hand shake from the proprietor, Kambasha himself. I liked this guy, plus I respected the fact he was a very astute businessman. After all, he did sell me half a rotten cow at seven bucks a kilo. My lion skin was sitting in a corner in a huge sack. I couldn't believe the size of the rolled up stinking and crackling object as I hurriedly stuffed it into the boot, filling its empty space in entirety. Kambasha explained there was no charge for the transport, as he owes me one for the mombes and his son driving into them incident. I thank him profusely, shake hands and I am out of there very quick before some curious eyes kick-start wicked wagging tongues.

So now I have an undetected very bad smell in my car boot, AND - I was about to go on holiday. It was my very first real, working man's proper holiday. I got days off, of course, but after one year of duty, you could apply for HOLIDAYS. I duly filled in the form and had 19 days approved. One problem; as usual, I was broke. With so much money coming in from running around converting the blacks to think white, I had given my Precious an addition of a foreign imported record player. The second hand thing I had purchased from the robbing buggers at Radio City for $130. It wasn't like we had EBay at the time and the Rhodesia Herald's Miscellaneous section wasn't actually full of many foreign made turntables. From the same thieves I had purchased a set of Phillips speakers, larger than my Sony ones. They in turn had been dismantled and installed into the interior door sides of my Toyota Corolla, which now had a Rhodesian made WRS cassette player supplied by the same swines for over a hundred bucks. These guys ate an entire month's bonus and salary – but I had cool tunes in my wheels. You can't pull babes with no vibes in the car.

 Now completely skint - I had to shift the lion. I also needed petrol. Shit loads of it. I have got a mate's thirsty speed boat to supply and, I am only invited to the two week session with ex-school pals at Lake Kariba, if I can come up with the petrol coupons.

 To obtain as many petrol coupons as possible, you can revert to two methods. Buy them on the black market, which of course, as an honest tight copper I would never do, OR - lots and lots of bullshit. Which, of course, is absolutely free, and I have bucket loads of it. Officially, because my car was registered at Gokwe, I was allocated exactly five litres a month. That won't get me far. So it was time to initiate some X-factor.

First stop is easy. The boss. Switching to my drama queen mode, there is much wailing about my poor step-mom, who only has a few pitiable coupons and she can't get enough to go to Inyanga, in the insurgent riddled Eastern Highlands, to check if the gooks hadn't razed my dead father's retirement cottage to the ground and must pay poor old Enoch with his seventeen kids, who looks after the place...etc, etc.

I was rewarded for my Oscar winning performance with thirty units equalling 150 litres. I am doing well. Next stop, in uniform, using the police Landy and being paid to go pilfering, I was down to our local Governmental Department dealing in such stuff. As usual there is the delightful greeting from some middle-aged bored house wife known from the Sports Club, and after presenting my 'Holiday Approved' certificate, managed to wangle another fifteen units of five litre coupons. She was only worth No 2 smile.

Now it was time for the kill. I still needed more. Speed boats eat a lot of gas.

The District Commissioner's daughter was nice. That my little lessons in love had made the poor girl gabble to her parents how wonderful I was; meant I could systematically abuse my sexually aroused privileged position into the Gokwe hierarchy. Besides the free dinners, a kiss and cuddle in the car, a licence to blow clever kudus apart, I needed juice coupons. I didn't have to fall into my well rehearsed swan song, as I sauntered into the DC's office with No1 best nice smile. Without a batter of an eyelid, he swung the safe door open, to expose enough coupons for me to fly out to the UK.

I wasn't too greedy and thought two entire sheets of fifty by five litres would tide me over quite well and hope you and the missus and ...er ...what's her name, are fine. Actually, I am being cruel in this case. She was sweet. And pretty. Her folks were very nice and oddly enough, landed up moving into a house just down the road from my step-mom's place. It's...just... I am a bit odd.

Anyway, off we go on holiday - giant stinking pussy and me. Arriving at home in Salisbury, the evil beast was fired into the back of the garage, along with promises to Katherine that before the

Department of Wildlife execute her after strenuous torture, I would dispose of the rancid thing as soon as I had a plan. More yowling from step-mom as I insisted on using the phone - only placated with $5 and 25 petrol coupons.

A call to the tannery confirmed my suspicions. With no official hunting licence or a letter from a farmer stating the lion had been wasted on his property, no tanning. It might have occurred to me to forge a letter. Easy enough, but that wasn't as deep as I wanted to dig. Bad enough skirting the skins and things laws, but down right forgery baulked against my moral conscience. I have to find someone with a farm. A few phone calls and a meeting later, pussy is unloaded for $70. I am off to Kariba and the Rhodesian way of life at last - sun, lake, speedboats, booze, babes and…the Casino.

Casinos and I are bad news. Just like my gamble for love with Josephine, it was all one sided. I loved handing over my money and the Casino loved keeping it for little reward. This self destructive addiction (I have many of these), first started at one of those fundraising fetes that usually a school or church organised to try and raise money for a good cause. I was a kid of 14, wandering between stands of home made cakes, various games, raffles, whilst being bombarded with loud, semi-incomprehensible noise as music pounded out off ancient PA systems. One stand was very busy. It was totally surrounded by big, loud, beer drinking men in standard uniform of various coloured crumpled Safari suits, stained and battered veldskoens and long blue socks with a comb pushed into the top. There were very few women and just a handful of kids. I wandered over. Working my way through an outer ring of watchers, I cast my eyes on what was to become my first true love. It was a Crown and Anchor table - GAMBLING!

Like those hypnotic snake eyes of Ka in Walt Disney's *Jungle Book*, I watched entranced - the spinning dice stops and piles of 20 and 25 cent coins being taken or doubled or even trebled up. Within minutes I left the circle feeling ill, as I realised I had dropped my entire pocket money for a week in 30 seconds. Confused and dispirited I cycled home. BUT, I was bitten, badly! It had awoken that Jewish side in me. A side, my father had occasionally mentioned, as ruining some of his relatives. Who cared? I saw myself getting rich quick.

My next pocket money was wisely invested in Faradays Sports and Guns shop in town on a set of Crown and Anchor dice. Weeks passed as poor Bridget was subjected to games of Crown and Anchor using matches. No matter what combinations I used, who ever was the bank, won. This was proved at every visited fete for the next 2 years. I needed a new drug - a superior quick fix.

The annual Salisbury Manufacturers and Agricultural show provided it. There, it was amongst the Luna Park machines at 10 cents a go for the Danglers and 25 cents for the Octopussy, (That particular 'ride' had a dubious reputation ever since one of the spinning cabins flew off and landed on two passer bys, killing them.), I came across ROLLER BALL! Here you simply placed money on blue or red at evens and white at 3 to 1. You pushed a billiard ball slowly down a runway and watched it plop into a painted shallow indentation. If it landed on your colour you won. It never did. I managed to get shafted at a couple of Salisbury shows. I once bumped into Bruce Grobbelar there. I hadn't seen him for a bit since he dropped out of school to go to a private college. Now he was betting 10 dollar notes, because he had a job playing as a football goal keeper. We all knew football was a blackman's sport after you turned twelve and it had no future. I felt ill again and went.

Checking out other forms of gambling led me to poker and pontoon or 21 we called it. Kid's stuff of course, matchsticks became dollars when I joined the police. Many a night was spent matching wits with the others POs in Gokwe. Here I could win. Not always, but always a little ahead. I was 19, a real gambling man now. It was time to hit the biggest drug of all- THE CASINO!

Katherine still possessed the holiday cottage on Valley Road, surrounded by whooshing pine trees; it nestled in a huge valley ... directly below the Montclair Casino Hotel. On a clear day, I swear I could hear the fruit machines.

me at the pad in Inyanga
Pic - Gokwe Kid

Now, on a couple of long week ends off, and once more doing my Good Samaritan bollocks, this time it was different. I had taken my car and had loads of petrol. Instead of just moping around during the day, I drove up to the National Park and spent many pleasant hours trout fishing. Murdering trout at Mare Dam in the day was lovely fun but the screaming din from a million frogs in the little dam below our cottage at night was a killer. So presenting step-mum with my rifle one night, (I still had the pistol), I told her I was off to check out the scene in the Montclair Hotel. Should anything happen, I am sure to hear the fire-fight and call for help. I gave her an extra two magazines and explained that the single bullet on the mantelpiece was to shoot herself in the head should I not turn up with reinforcements on time. She nodded and carried on knitting and reading.

The first barrier was the sign at the door. Minimum age 21. A true poker player simply ignored that and so did the staff. I was in. There were women everywhere doing nothing. Croupiers to a ghost casino. Welcome to the Hotel California! I was home at last. This was magic; a glittering world all to myself. The government had granted the hotel a casino license in the hope of boosting tourism to the area. It hadn't worked much. Now and then some other punters wandered in, but for the next few trips she was mine. My expensive whore, she bled me dry. I could choose any dealer I wanted. Open the roulette table ... "No problem Sir," ... open a Blackjack table ... "No problem Sir." The people who worked there were so nice to me. Once, Paddy, the very Christian manager, took some effort to help me out. After knowingly bouncing a cheque on him, in the vain hope of buying it back with my winnings, I confessed my sin to him. He wisely and kindly took me to one side and asked when pay day was. I miserably told him, and he promised to hold the cheque back till then. So kind of him. I struggled to survive the next month.

The Montclair was nice even after a terrorist RPG (rocket propelled grenade) hit its roof. The girls told me about all the adventures the next night after they were attacked. Great fun! One customer refused to hit the floor as he had hit the jackpot on a fruit machine. And -

"You should have seen the assistant manager with an FN, hopping and rolling around like James Bond, using the gaming tables as cover. Hilarious stuff!"

I think it was that night at the roulette table, when I threw the keys to the Toyota Corolla on red. It was all I had left. Again Paddy helped me by throwing me out...

Now I was going to Kariba for the first time in my life. Rhodesia's Las Vegas...Sin City here I come. My mates were camping and after some performance managed to get a place on the packed out grounds of Caribbea Bay Casino resort. I was buggered if I was going to pay to sleep on the ground. I am a policeman from GOKWE - that must pull some weight even here, so I zipped up to the policemen's singles mess and wangled a cost free room, complete with balcony and a view from the Heights overlooking the stunning shimmering lake. Breakfast was served for a mere 50 cents as well. What a life! THIS; is living.

After breakfast, I would take my passion wagon down the steep winding road to the resort. I didn't bother paying the outrageous $2 entry fee by simply telling the man at the entrance gate that I was only going to the harbour. Then I park up by reception and lounge at one of the pools, drink beer in my mates speedboat, water-ski, look at the women and eat well. I tried to keep my distance from the usual large crowd of camouflage dressed troopies that seemed to be attracted to the bar by the first pool like flies to dung. A few times several would land up fully dressed and play some hooligan game of trying to drink bottles of beer underwater.

But it was the night I wanted…those tables were full. There were loads of people wanting the same thrill as me. The place wasn't as stuffy and correct like the Montclair Hotel. Open shirts allowed but no jeans or trainers. The fever on us all, women gathered around and chatted me up when my chip piles are high. Flushed with success, I am the glibbest, coolest mouth in town.

I was well pleased with my holiday. Then I hit the 400 dollar jackpot on the fruit machines. Three triple black bars. I had shoulder cramps for a week from pulling that bastard handle. But the thrill as the machine rang those bells of victory and all the other punters gazed in envious fascination at the ultimate win flashing at me, plus my very broad smile. It was during one of these sessions that I met a waif of a girl with soft, short blonde red hair, Victoria.

She was only 17, but I took her into my brothel of hedonism - the world of roulette and Black Jack. That late evening we kissed on the pier that jutted out into the lake. She was there for a short holiday with her sister and when she flew out three days later, we were 'hitched'. No hanky-panky, mind you. Before leaving we went up the Heights to look at the Dam wall. This two lane wide concave construction held back the might of the Zambezi, powered two nations and created a water paradise that was the second largest man made lake in the world. This place was the stuff of fantastic legends. When they built the main road down to the valley in the fifties, the Minister of Transport scoffed at the plans and costing of the finest British surveyors; claiming he could do it twice as fast and at half the cost. And he did. Didn't need any plan. Just follow several thousands of generations of elephant routes they used to get down the escarpment. They were not stupid and knew the easiest way. As a result you tend to see a lot of elephants wandering around on the tar road.

Meanwhile, with a couple of days to go, I was informed that the speedboat was consuming some serious petrol. I didn't have to contribute to the cost of the stuff, my mates had rich parents, but now I had to find more coupons. The lads had plenty of babes queuing up to go on the only speedboat that never seemed to run out of fuel. So I took a quick spin up to the local cop shop. I couldn't help but notice the government's poster on the wall 'Don't Drive Rhodesia Dry', but it was for a speedboat, I needed them, so no problems with my conscience. This time my bullshit to the Officer Commanding of Kariba town police station didn't hit a sympathy nerve much, even after explaining I was from Gokwe. Till now the Rhodesian version of, 'Open Sesame', had done wonders. The tight sod only gave me 50 litres of units. I handed these over, (the ones I needed to get back I had wisely kept separate), and told my disappointed mates it was definitely their lot. Eish man, they must have gone through almost 1000 litres posing away!

Still, I was well impressed with my holiday. All costs covered, including the petrol home, a new girlfriend, and the lion's $70 still in my pocket. All good things have to come to an end and I dutifully turned up for work…and later found out my lion skin was sold for £1200. I felt very ill for years!

Memoir mutterings

The attack on the Montclair Hotel is a bizarre one. The owners of the place had taken in an orphaned black kid from an early age. They paid for him to have a top notch education and treated him as their own son. In his early twenties he was being trained as the future manager until – he was caught thieving. I gathered it was quite serious account fraud. The couple were devastated, but they didn't call the police in, just chucked the bloke out on his ear. He promptly rewarded them by going over to the gooks and getting them to do the hit.

The hotel was a soft target. The nearest police were in Inyanga village, over half an hour away. Weirdly, besides the rocket blowing off a bit of the roof, nothing was that serious. It was claimed they lined up the couple of clients and staff from the hotel (not the casino) and fleeced them of cash, jewellery and watches and then went off back into the night. I vaguely recall that security forces caught up with the group a short time later and slotted a couple before the rest managed to get over the border.

Glossary

Veldskoens. Also known as vellies. A light shoe, or lowcut boot. Made with soft rawhide uppers and sewn onto a rubber sole.

CHAPTER 29:

How the chain of command works when there is radio silence

Once upon a time - on a bog standard insignificant day of rapes, murders, stolen bicycles and a couple of chickens, along with the average bestiality (not necessarily with the stolen chickens) - the boss calls me into his office. He hands me a file.

"I would like you to read this now. Here in my office. It arrived with the police post from Que Que."

Ooh - sounds all cloak and dagger stuff - very exciting! I take the file eagerly and look at the cover. It had my name on it (wow, that is so cool), but disappointingly had no 'Top Secret' stamped anywhere. There were a few sheets of paper inside and I started to read them in chronological order. Within seconds it became very clear and I nearly passed out with fright. This was the worst case scenario – ever. The first two I already knew -

Rhodesian Broadcasting Corporation
License Department
Salisbury
Autumn 1977

Karl Greenberg
BSAP
Box 10
Gokwe

Failure to renew your radio license.

Dear Mr Greenberg,

According to our records, your radio license has expired. As of this date we have no record of you renewing it. I wish to point out that if should you not do so within the next thirty days we have the power under the Radio and Television Broadcasting License Act of 19 hundred and voetsak, to really give you a serious hard time. Evasion is a criminal offence - it will be prison for you, and a fine that will break you financially for life.

Yours threateningly,
Rupert Mudcock
Director

P.S. If you write a nice letter to say you don't *really* have a radio anymore, we will hold fire, BUT, mark my words, we could spring a surprise visit, and woe is you hey if you have a radio – *china*.

British South Africa Police
P.O. Box 10
Gokwe
Day after your threat

Director Rupert Mudcock
Rhodesian Broadcasting Corporation
License Department
Salisbury

Re: Get your licence or get liquidated

Dear Mr. Rupert Mudcock,

I take deep personal affront to your offensive tone. I can only postulate that you suffer from megalomania brought on by polymorphous light eruption. As you may notice I am a police officer, and a highly respected one, based in a place you would struggle to find on a two-dimensional, geometrically accurate, static representation of three-dimensional space - commonly known as a map.

Your ignorance of the law empowered under your jurisdiction is staggering in its incompetency. I am surprised that you have attained the position that you now seem to relish with the pathological psycho of a power obsessed maniac. I find it disturbing that you should accuse me of being a common criminal with no proof of any crime committed. Contrary to your misguided belief, it is not a crime to own a radio without paying a levy for it. It is, however, a criminal offence if I turn it on and listen to the propagated propaganda garbage churned out by your broadcasting company. Should I simply have it tuned into Radio Maputo to listen to Comrade Robert Mugabe without a license, that is his problem, not yours! Nor am I legally required to formulate, transcribe and communicate to anyone, when and if, I engage my receiver of electronic media into the appropriate mode for deciphering and henceforth regurgitated out via an electro-acoustic transducer into comprehensible harkening

However, in fairness to the predicament I have now put you in – to wit, your demand is a load of bollocks – I will take time to explain and offer some advice that you are in desperate need of. I would have continued paying the extortionate sum to listen to *Forces Requests*, simply because my present honey sends me messages because, as unlike you, I have a war to fight; but sadly my beloved mini-Precious (such was the name of my recently departed radio - for use of a better word), passed away – violently.

It was whilst I was gook hunting deep in the bush at Chirama base camp. I was tired and well sauced from a few toots, when I was required to drive off and fetch some beers from the nearest store about an hours drive away. Upon my return, after and enduring a few more for the road, I forgot where I had placed my mini-Precious and drove over it. Its dying scream will haunt me forever. The squawk the loudspeaker made as it was flattened into a Frisbee, still makes my bones chatter chillingly. I have neither had the time, nor the inclination; to purchase a replacement. That would dishonour the ghost and soul of my mini-Precious. Some of its happier ditties - *Schweppes Orange, Lyons Ready Maid, Five Roses Tea*, and *Rixi Tixi Taxis* to sadly mention a few - still fill my head when I dream.

I buried mini-Precious at the edge of the escarpment where the reception had been the best. I placed its terribly mutilated, crushed face pointing in the direction of Springbok Radio, a channel we both had loved. Its little twisted aerial I left poking out the small, shallow grave. I placed the inverted fired FN cartridge from the gun salute onto it in deference for a lost comrade taken so cruelly by the hell that is war.

Now let me give you some facts of life and some advice re: reality. The population of Gokwe TTL is almost quarter of a million. Through my travels throughout this massive land mass, I have become aware of a huge proliferation of radios used by the local populace. The noise they emit I find, quite frankly, irritating to my Western tuned ear, but this is beside the point. I roughly calculate that if 10% of this population possess a radio, you should, in mathematical terms, be receiving on the average - 2000 renewals a month. I have been informed by Gokwe's Postmaster General that he has no recollection of this ever happening, and would struggle to find the forms in the tip he calls an office. (Saying that, I err on the cautious side. He could have been pocketing the lot because he tried to shaft me over some digital watches, but this is just an unproved theory.) I also notice that in all my time I have been in Gokwe, I have never seen you or any of your goon squad rock up here and spend a few weeks driving through bush and mud, checking out the peasants' licences.

Your racial inequalities match the Department for Dog License fees. I have yet to see a collar with obligatory dog tax dogtag hanging around a Kaffir Dog's neck. The only things that are hanging there are ticks and fleas, but this is not so of the white dog owning Gokwians who comply with the law. Must they also write a letter for tax exemption if their beloved pet gets inadvertently run over by a drunk? I beg to differ.

Sincerely Up Yours,

Patrol Officer Karl Greenberg
Gokwe Police Station

Oh-oh! This doesn't look very clever-clever anymore. I had written the letter on police time, with police paper, using a police typewriter, with the fancy Gokwe police rubber stamp under my signature and posted my reply in a police stamped envelope (free post). I have typed out rape statements faster than that letter. I had worn a dictionary out putting the masterpiece together and had shed buckets of tears of hilarity over my sparkling wit – now I wasn't so sure. I didn't look up at the boss, and went on to the next sheets. They were all letters...

Rhodesian Broadcasting Corporation
License Department
Salisbury
Day after Greenberg's letter

Assistant Commissioner of Police
Patrick McCulloch
Midlands Province
British South Africa Police
Gwelo Headquarters

Greetings Pat, dear old friend,

I hope you and your wonderful wife are fine. We must get together down on the farm for a bit of chin wag in the near future. Chat about the good old days over some gin and tonics. Those wonderful times when we were hard, disciplined police troopers, what-what, arf- arf.
    Listen old boy, sorry to bother you, but it seems you have some unruly element under your command. I have enclosed the necessary documentation and I believe you will be shocked by this young whippersnapper's response to my perfectly written, standard request. Quite shocking, old boy, quite shocking! I told my beloved of course, and she almost swooned, and now threatens to bring it up amongst her fellow Bridge players.
    This cannot continue. We have to uphold the regiment dear chap. We cannot allow this rubbish to bring down the noble name of the BSAP! Next thing you know -the disease will spread and every Tom, Dick and Harry will scribble illiterate memoirs of their pathetic contributions. All rabble Sir! Unlike us Sir, unlike us. No, old boy, this evil must be stamped out before it spreads. Good God man, if the enemy got hold of this scandal; we will be the laughing stock, old boy. Laughing stock, I tell you!
    I will leave this in your capable hands, dear chap. I am sure you will act with all the powers at your disposal.

Yours faithfully,
Your friend Rupert

I let out a small, silent fart. Bloody hell! This bloke has had a serious sense of humour failure. The way he was going on, this Rupert Mudcock twat would splash this as a scandal all over the News of the World. I bet the slimy bastard was even hacking into the police phone trying to find out if I really had a dead radio. Still, this was looking bad. The boss was still watching me silently, as with shaking hands; I read the next letter –

Assistant Commissioner of Police
Patrick McCulloch
Midlands Province
British South Africa Police
Gwelo Headquarters

Chief Superintendent Toady Scheisskopf
Officer in Charge
British South Africa Police
Que Que Province
Que Que Headquarters

Good God, Toady, what the hell is going on down there? I give you command of some run of the mill joint and I am having to handle nonsense like this? What in God's name are you doing man? Have you lost your marbles? Too much playing golf, I gather, rather than controlling the men under your command. Totally irresponsible. An absolute disgrace. I want action from you Toady, action I tell you; otherwise you can kiss any more promotion good-bye. I will not tolerate this.

Make it so.

> Chief Superintendent Toady Scheisskopf
> Officer in Charge
> British South Africa Police
> Que Que Province
> Que Que Headquarters

Chief Inspector Mike Harvey
Officer in Charge
British South Africa Police
Gokwe

Harvey, have you gone mad? Are the lunatics running the asylum? I know that Greenberg. A very cheeky sod. Last time I was up there he was hanging around like some X-factor candidate, scruffy and with long hair. When I asked him to get a haircut, you know what he said to me?

"In case you haven't noticed - we lack white people's barbers or hairdressers. But if you wish, I could go to the local's one and get myself an afro just like Black Belt Jones or perhaps some reggae locks like Bob Marley."

I want his guts for garters, Harvey. I want him flogged, drawn and quartered, Harvey, you hear me. A disgrace. Some lip on that boy. Listen up Harvey, if you don't want to rot in that hellhole till your bones are bleached to alabaster marble, pull finger and sort that cocky bastard out once and for all. A bloody disgrace allowing such a fool to run amok under your command. Bloody hell Harvey, sort yourself out man and bring that imbecile down a smart peg or two.

I demand immediate action.

Chief Supr. Toady Scheissekopf

I closed the file and handed it back to the boss. We faced each other in semi-cemetery silence. Even the cicadas and cooing doves that you normally heard through the open windows seemed to have shut up. They were waiting quietly for my firing squad to gather.

Maybe five seconds we stood there emotionless - but it seemed forever. For one of those rare occasions in my life…I had absolutely nothing to say. At last, Mike Harvey spoke, but there was something wrong with his facial muscles. They were twitching strangely around the corners of his mouth and his eyes seemed watery.

"Karl. May I give you some good advice? Next time you want to pull another stunt like this - please refrain from signing it in an official capacity and using our rubberstamp."

Then, before my astonished eyes, he took the folder and dropped into his wastepaper basket.

"Dismissed."

As I sneaked Gollum-like out of his office I suddenly realised that with all the stuff that went across Mike Harvey's desk – this bit of 'bad news'; had just made his day.

Memoir mutterings

I got lucky, as usual. I recall from private correspondence with Mike Harvey that Toady wasn't exactly his best china either. I recall an incident when Toady comes up for one of his inspections. (Ah, bless, he must have had a golf game cancelled.) So, it turns out that we single POs 'have' to invite him to have lunch with us. Wilson puts up a right feast for a rare full house of at least 5 POs. I am as usual chattering utter garbage during the meal. Then Toady, with a look of pure venom, says,

"You! Shut-up! I wish to eat my meal in peace and not be forced to listen to utter rubbish."

Now, I seethe. For a start, it happens to be OUR singles quarters, thus sacred hallow ground. Secondly, my dear Chief Superintendent Scheisskopf, we had to allow you to come and eat with us. We need that pleasure as much as I need a frontal lobotomy. AND, thirdly, my dear Shithead (which is English for Scheisskopf); I am also forced to pay for part of your bloody meal!!! Which, I have just now concluded, is the chicken leg and I am going to shove it up your nose.

I didn't, because if I had - this would have been the final chapter. Still, with that wonderful thing of hindsight and the attitude problem I have – I should have tipped his meal into his lap and legged it *asap* to Mike Harvey and begged him to hide me.

I wish I had that file now. It would be gold worth on EBay. Still, the boss was right to get rid of it.

Glossary

Voetsak. Normally means bugger-off or get lost. In this case - 19 hundred and voetsak - the word is used as 'no idea'.

CHAPTER 30:

The rise and fall of the Gokwe Kid

Part 1 - Super sleuth struts his stuff

It wasn't a dark and stormy night - but the dark clouds would soon be gathering when finally, my antics would send shockwaves through the community and I would become the infamous Gokwe Kid – *Dick of the Bushveld*. At this point in time I was officially the longest serving Patrol Officer in Gokwe. As previously mentioned - besides going mad, bush, suicidal, killed by gooks, or crashing Landys - the only legitimate way out of Gokwe was through a transfer request after exactly twelve months service at the station. I hadn't bothered, for I rather liked my status. Parts of Gokwe I knew really well, I had excellent relations with the black staff, and was barely tolerated by the white 'Gokwian' community. The Boss relied on me more and more, and vice versa because I needed him to help me to do the mess accounts. (I had inherited my old job back.) The DC's daughter's tantalising tickling during her school holidays meant I went home swimming in petrol coupons every time I had leave for a few days each month. I had a girlfriend and the cash flow was just above poverty level – so all in all, mine was a happy lot. It was all too soon to go seriously tits-up…

It all started on an autumn morning - the sun blazing away gently outside the window with a few clouds breaking the monotony of perpetual light blue. I neatly filed my last bit of paperwork and bantered with Leon and Ian, the last of the gang that I had sort of started out with. The two dim-wits puffed furiously on their fags whilst swearing at the ancient typewriters and threatened me with the usual disembowelment if I didn't shut it. I didn't mind, they were both ignorant twats, but it was nice to have some company for a change. My desk was clear and I was wondering if I might pop out for a little cruise around town under the pretence of maintaining an active presence of smiling, happy caring cops. (Just keep an eye out for the missing landmine.)

I snickered loudly as Leon ripped a thick bunch of papers and carbon from the guts of the protesting machine, whilst screaming obscenities about the stupidity of carbon paper that prints mirrored on the back of the page instead of the next one. I ducked the screwed up paper ball aimed viciously at my head just as the boss walked in with a huge pile of papers stacked under his arm.

A quick scan of my two partners, whose sudden eruption of typing and frenzied paper pushing showed immense skill in trying to avoid what was coming next; my stupid smiling face and cheerful "Good morning Sir" settled my fate.

Dumping this mountain on my desk, my greeting was repaid with an added line,

"Sort this out, it's a bloody mess, and soon."

He walked out and the gleeful cawing from the peasants at the other desks really rattled my cage as I gazed at the evil mound of mixed recycled brownish paper, along with a pile of white crime report forms, enough to open up my own police station. This didn't look too good. This was a mess, no doubt about it and it took four long studious days, and a second desk, to get some kind of picture in my head of what was going on.

What I had here, spread neatly over two desks, was, technically, theft and fraud. What looked just like a simple case of stolen cheques fraudulently cashed, didn't show that many entire families existence was threatened by starvation. The picture doesn't always tell the whole story. At last I had something to really get my teeth into. So far, all cases were wrapped up in hours or a few days, weeks, months... It was all so simple. We got an accused - job done. We have none - job not done – pass the paper work up the ladder. There was nothing complicated to test my detective skills acquired from years of reading *The Hardy Boys* detective novels and *The Three Investigators*. I now had my wish, because in this game - there are snakes that counter the ladders and the serpents had all landed on my desk. Time to roll the dice and this time - I dice with death...

Over a period of the last four months, from a far south west corner of Gokwe TTL, adult Africans of both sexes and various ages had been haphazardly arriving at the police station with a similar story. Each complainant had been interviewed by a different constable who had reported the sad facts, and passed it on up the chain of command for comments. All the complainants had the same thing in common. All were small scale cotton growers neighbouring the belt of commercial white farmers in the Gatooma area. All had had their small cotton bales picked up by the Cotton Marketing Board's (CMB) trucks and all had waited for their cheques in vain. Most of them had written to the CMB, and along with the crime report there was an attached letter with a photocopy of a cashed cheque from the CMB explaining that they had been paid.

I was stunned. Someone was systematically stealing all that these people were supposed to live off till next harvest time. Some of the amounts were small, $30, the biggest well over $2000. There were at least 30 cases; the entire sum exceeded $8000. This was a huge amount of money. $8000 was more than two years pay to me; to these people it was everything! I also had a small idea how back breaking this work growing and harvesting cotton was. Before I became a rogue Boy Scout, I had been on a camping trip and we visited a cotton farm. There I spent an hour till my finger tips hurt, filling a large heavy hessian sack with the freshly blossomed buds. With the massive sack hardly disturbed by my efforts, I had been informed by the laughing farmer, who weighed it for my curiosity, that it was about 10 cents worth of effort…

Amplifying the problem was the fact that none of the reports had been followed up. Some were as old as 14 weeks. That did make sense. As each case had been handled individually as a no hoper, (no clues, no suspects), it got tossed 'upstairs' to the Section Officer, where it could have sat for… gawd knows how long, to be eventually placed among tons of other paper on the boss's desk. However, viewed as a whole, a pattern started to emerge.

All the complainants used a single posting address - a Postal Box number in Que Que, used by a bush store. Amongst some of the complainants' statements appeared repeatedly the name of the same bush store. Here, just like Kambashas in Gokwe village, the enterprising owner owned the bus that linked the store with Que Que. The store supplied the area with provisions and acted also as Post Office, bus stop and clearing bank. Local trades sprung up around it, tailors, millers, bicycle mechanics, you name it. It was a hub of activity. Music blared all the time, great place to meet and drink cold beer and have a game of table football.

So the next logical step was - who fetched the post? Oddly enough our police station wasn't the nearest to the store. Whilst it was in our jurisdiction, an all black staffed police station under Gatooma rural police, based at the Empress Nickel mine, was much nearer.

So I sent a radio message to them requesting that they please interview the store owner and ascertain who collected the post or the person that had done that job for the last four months. Sounds easy hey! Just wander into the radio room, look up the frequency and gab away. No way. No, we typed out radio request sheets, sent them to Que Que to some impatient bastard who loved shouting at us youngsters for being so slow and not saying enough OVERS and forgetting to take your finger off the send button. I noticed he never shouted at Mrs Erasmus when she did the radio shift. Maybe that was because he had seen the size of her bum - or the size of her husband. (That is the same bloke that nearly throttled me.)

With the radio message sent, knowing it would take a few days before I received some comeback, I wrote a request for the CMB to send me all original cheques made out and cashed and photocopies of all the complainants' letters and their replies. This was duly done and when the huge parcel arrived I sorted it all out. Quaint, but not unsurprising, many of the complainants' letters to the CMB had the same handwriting. This was due to another enterprising person based at the store – the letter writer. For a few cents, he would compose any genre (including love) for the illiterate peasants. The English was rough, but fully understandable. But it was the cheques I was really interested in. I needed to be very careful - I needed tweezers - by Jove! No careless fingerprints from me. Okay, so we had no tweezers (or gloves) and I wasn't going to ask Mrs Erasmus for the use of her pair, and I reckoned Mrs Sanderson didn't use things like that any way, so I held the cheques 'gingerly' at the tips. It was the back of them I needed to look at. There was the signature of the so called cheque bearer, usually followed by the store owner who had cashed it, who himself had signed the back when depositing it in his bank account. A few had Que Que clearing banks with different store owners' signatures on the back. 80% were from the city of Gwelo, 80 odd clicks further south, all countersigned by the same shop owner. That's interesting, either the man was blind or he was bent, because even an amateur like me could see that all the different signatories were of a similar scrawl, more printed, and how the hell do you confuse Grace Marufu with Gideon Gono - for crying out loud! A letter to the bank and a week later I had the address of my

African merchant's store in Gwelo. Those were definitely the days. You try getting that sort of detail out of a bank today; you need serious court applications or *Wikileaks*.

This meant another painful radio transmission to moaner in Que Que to relay to Gwelo Police for one of them to interview this 'blind' shop owner and why he had never asked for the casher's *Stupa* (the obligatory identification papers for Africans), before handing the dosh out? Actually, the answer was bloody obvious; he was taking a massive cut and insisting a lot of the payout be in goods from his store; he didn't give a shit. That should put the wind up the bastard a bit, he was a white actually and a known 'fence', but I didn't know that at the time.

Days go by and whilst I wait for more input, I sorted all the cases, with crosschecking numbers and dates creating a chronological list. I had taken the crime to heart. I was going to get my man. I carefully mounted all 30 odd cheques on a huge piece of stiff cardboard, protected with transparent film, ready to send to forensics for fingerprinting and handwriting analysis.

Then a message from Empress Nickel police station arrived. The store owner stated that a certain Raymond R., a self-employed Scotch cart maker at the store had been volunteering to go with the bus to Que Que once a week, fetch the post, and return on the next available one. It seems he had been doing this saintly task for almost five months but had disappeared a few weeks ago, leaving several irate cart owners with paid deposits for repairs not done. I had a name and also, a stroke of luck, his address. Well, for us bush cops - a district, a chief, and a headman's name; was more than enough. This system worked a treat and could pin a man's home down to a radius of a click or so. One problem though, he came from Sinoia, a small farming community west of Salisbury. It was famous for its incredible limestone caves with the cobalt blue 'Sleeping Pool'. My man and chief suspect, Raymond R, liked to move around.

So it was back to the radio. This time, again via berkhead, to Sinoia Police. Confirm that Raymond R is a registered resident and should he be there, he was to be detained. The next bit sounds unfair, but that's how we flushed the baddies out of the bundu. If he wasn't there, they were to detain any wife/wives and children for as long as possible. Also let the kraal head know why.

No, they were not detained in cells. They were well fed and accommodated and had free use of the police compound. They were like on house arrest, except they weren't at home. I wasn't sure how long Sinoia police would hold them for but I gambled on at least a week. After that, I would be running out of options…

It worked. Three days after my radio confirmation from Sinoia police that one wife and two children were being detained, Raymond R. was shown into my office. A tall, middle-aged balding man, quite eloquent and with excellent English, enquired why I was looking for him and why had I detained his family. I was gob smacked. He didn't look like no nasty cheque thief to me. He was dressed in the usual mixture of semi-clean, crumpled cheap western clothes of trousers, an open shirt and dark jacket. I asked had he worked at the store as a cart builder. He happily concurred saying he was on his way back after a short holiday. This wasn't balancing up. I asked for a sample of his hand writing. He produced graceful flowing words with swirls and loops, nothing like the crude printing strokes on the back of my cheques. Almost crying with frustration now, I sent him away to be fingerprinted. After a quick radio note to get his family released, I returned to my desk and pondered the next move. I didn't like it. The thought that he may be pulling a bluff didn't seem possible to me. I gloomily started to conclude that I had the wrong person.

Still, I had to go down to the area where the crimes had been committed. At least two of the initial complaints were from a friend or other family member of the victim. I needed the victims' statements, plus an interview with the store owner and hopefully meet with some outraged clients of Raymond that might be interesting. One drawback…my boss. As soon as it's official that some poor sap of a Patrol Officer was going deep into an area, he got ALL the cases needing attention. Some of them were weeks old. Pick up suspect 'A', interview witness 'B' etc, loads of clicks apart in the bush, some addresses just a vague dirt track. It was no use, I landed up with a senior sergeant by the name of Mandashona and a raw green constable to accompany me. With an open backed Landrover, we went off, with Raymond and the constable sitting happily in the unprotected back, a two week tour ahead of us. Plus a pile of dockets!

Things were slightly improved by the fact we would be staying at the Empress Nickel mine. I had passed this huge set-up that employed almost 1500 people several times as it sat on its own tar road some 50 clicks south-east of Gatooma. I would use the road as a shortcut when I was going up to Salisbury. Providing it didn't rain too much. When that happened, the low slung concrete bridge over the Umniati river would become awash and had taken a couple of bus drivers and their passengers for a bad surprise, resulting in several drownings, as the raging waters lifted the huge, fully loaded commuter bus and spat it out onto a sandbank several hundred paces downstream. My associates would stay at the all black police station, and I at the single quarters of the mine employees. It was mind bogglingly boring there.

A hint of what lay ahead occurred on our second day. I hadn't worked with Mandashona before. He spoke English fluently and had over 17 years experience in the police. However, I noticed his temper after I hit a covered tree stump, and, as he wasn't wearing his seat belt, he cracked his head a bit hard on the windscreen. His rifle actually chipped the bullet-proof glass! He threatened to inform Chief Inspector Harvey about my driving. There was nothing wrong with my driving. I still refused to walk and it wasn't my fault there was no road. A few minutes later we arrived at a kraal and were guided to the suspect's hut. He was not one of my cases - I was just there to pick him up. Luck had it he was there asleep on his grass mat upon the hard earth.

Before I could compose a nice politically correct wakey-wakey speech, like,

"Hi we are the police and I'm here to arrest you," Mandashona snatched up a large stave leaning against the hut wall, and proceeded to bring it down with some force on the prostrate body. That woke him up! I watched for several more seconds in absolute astonishment. Mandashona laid into the screaming man with profound abandon whilst shouting that the man was a thief and we have come to take him away, and he must confess on the spot. The suspect's howling appeals to me for this to stop finally entered my mind and I ordered the sergeant to cease. SHIT, this was bad news. I asked an excited Mandashona what the hell was that all about. His reply relating that this was the best way to get them to confess, I found a little disturbing. He made Triggs's methods saintly in comparison. We took the poor bloke in handcuffs, along with his wife. The suspect gave some long winded story and after

Mandashona had looked her over, told me she had to come along to cook for her husband whilst he was being detained. All this was in Shona, so I just gave up and said, like, "whatever - lets go." This was to turn out to be a massive mistake.

Back at the mine's police compound, Raymond was still happily wandering around the place, free to do what he wanted and waiting for his promised lift back to the store. For me it was back to the boring singles' quarter's room and plan the next day. Then just read a bit and early bed. I really missed my mini-Precious.

I spent a couple of mundane days chasing up some old crime reports, which all led to naught and did the paper work at the mine police station. To relieve some of the boredom I had blabbed myself cheekily into being shown through the nickel mine. My own private tour. Abuse of position, definitely, but who cares; going down a mine is an adventure. I had even wangled an invite for Mandashona. So one mid-afternoon, after being kitted up, we went underground. My sergeant gave up after a short 20 minutes, claiming the constant descent on the ladders was too much for him. I think he was afraid as we went deeper. He returned to the surface and got a lift back to police camp. I went with my host, deeper and deeper. It was exhilarating. Deep underground he showed me a huge hole, so large that our torch beams could neither reach top, bottom or the opposite side. I had a ball and unlike school, I didn't have to write up a project about the trip.

Then it was time to follow-up on my intricate case which would lead to plenty of excitement. We had an early start with just Raymond in the back with the constable. The suspect and wife were being held in the police cell and compound respectively. Of course, travelling in the back was all very forbidden due to the fact that if we hit a mine, the two in the back were mincemeat - but shit happens. Also, what else are we supposed to do? Drive around in a fully armoured Landrover conversion called a Kudu? We had one of those back at Gokwe by now, but they were only used to transport security personnel.

So, off we go to get some statements from two victims of the cheque fraud. At one village where we stopped to ask directions, I was approached by two locals who seemed very irate to see our, 'stopped grinning all of a sudden' Raymond. Well what do you know! These two had a written contract with 'innocent Ray' for a cart repair he hadn't done but knocked them for a fifty dollar deposit! Best of all, it had been written by him, complete with poorly printed text and fancy flowing signature. BINGO. I didn't need to be a graphological cryptologist to realise I had my man - I was now a proper detective after all - Dick of the bushveld! He knew it that same second I twigged. Gotchya! Handcuffs were quickly applied before he had any thoughts of doing a runner, and just for safe measure I told my armed constable in the back with him to keep a wary eye. Meeting these two new complainants meant more paper work as I had to now take a statement from them both. Still, I was in a great mood as we drove deeper into the bush. I already had visions of being awarded the Commissioner's Commendation for excellent detective work above and beyond the normal abilities of the average Patrol Officer. I could even see him pinning to my tunic the little silver baton on a green ribbon bar next to my General Service Medal that was still in the post. I would be on the front pages of Illustrated Life of Rhodesia, The TV and Radio Times and, in the not to distant future, have a dedicated Facebook page – I was a super star at last.

Still dreaming away, and after negotiating the Landy for at least two hours along the dirt track I had been following, it brought me along side a large clearing. The size of a football pitch actually. I know that as there were two make shift goal posts and about 14 young men kicking a battered ball about. This was a surprise. I had never come across a piece of cleared land in Gokwe that wasn't for the sole purpose of farming. For recreational purposes (outside perhaps one of the bush schools), this was unheard of. It never occurred to me that it could be being used for something else besides sports. The track seemed to end here. The very fit looking young men, mostly my age, wandered over, with very blank expressions - if not a little hostile. They were dressed in various ragtag clothes, and soaked through from their game. Raymond was in the back, manacled and looking miserable. Us three policemen were in sweaty and dust stained uniforms.

I asked through Mandashona, who was acting as my translator, if they knew the way to the villages of the two victims I needed to take statements from. By this time we were surrounded, and there were demands as to why there was a man in handcuffs in the back.

Now, I was in an excellent mind set of triumphant detective ability, Mandashona, unfortunately was not, (he was still pissed off with me). Now I, loving an audience and being the reigning X-factor winner from Chirama – announced, with quite some drama as I exited out the vehicle, FN in hand, and waved it at Raymond.

"This man here is a very bad man. He is the notorious thief and forger that I, PO Greenberg, the Gokwe Kid, Dick of the Bushveld, *aka* my *Chimurenga* name, 'The *Penga* One' - has hunted down and caught. For this bad man stole 8000 dollars from the poor people that grow cotton here."

Mandashona was translating very excitably and was having a problem keeping up. Also, I wasn't so sure he was doing it quite word perfect, but so what? The young lads all seemed to know some English. I explained I needed statements from his victims and then the bad man was going to jail for a long time. There were a few barked commands and four of them scattered, to find these women either at home or in the fields, one of the kind youngsters explained. I was well impressed. I asked if I could maybe drive there, but he smiling explained it was not necessary as they will be here soon. A barrage of questions about friend Raymond here, led me to describe the whole crime.

By now, something happened that is unique to Africa - If anything of the vaguest interest occurs, drop everything you're doing and rush over to see what's going on and stand around with a dumb-ass expression of aloofness; whilst clocking everything that may be worth telling your mates, family or anyone else down at the beer hall. So, of course, miraculously, I had several dozen locals pitch up and stand around. What an opportunity for me this was! I was a star and the peasants needed to find out why! They don't exactly get the local tabloids out here. A true stand-up comic needs a stage, and I jumped into the back of the Landrover and gave a performance... as if my life depended on it.

Of course, by this time I have my head so far stuck up my arse I had long gone past seeing the shit I was in. I told them down to the last detail, and after winding them all well up about my paper chase; then just like Tommy Cooper, I fumbled around and then presented them with the discriminating Ox-cart contract. This delighted the peasants and they jeered at the cowering Raymond something rotten, who by this time looked as if he was swallowing molten steel. But I had wound the locals up a tad too much for they thought this would be a great opportunity to give Raymond a clap or two. I thought I better intervene as I had yet again, inadvertently, organised a lynch mob.

"Hey, that will do. He will get plenty of that when he goes to Chikarubi."

"How long he get?"

I had no idea, but wanted to impress them,

"Fifteen years at least! And he will spend most of the time trimming the municipality's lawns!"

That did the trick and they left him alone. The young constable at the back seemed very nervous from all the attention. I knew that he was almost straight out of Tomlimson Depot, so I guessed he was a little overwhelmed with this all. It is not often you get to work with a famous celebrity. Actually, he looked like he needed to pass a very urgent stool - and not the three legged type.

Flushed with my audience approval, I asked the fit young men why they didn't have any jobs. This cooled the bantering some what, but to the frosty question of "doing what" my answer "Fit young men should join the BSAP" - had them in fits! Mandashona, sweating curiously in buckets, constantly mopping his face with a handkerchief, was almost hysterical with laughter - me too - such nice blokes. I couldn't understand why Mandashona was suddenly my new best friend and thought I was the greatest orator since Mark Antony. Although, I must profess, that after three months of Inya'face, performing before hundreds of enthusiastic bush theatre goers - it had given me speech skills worthy of any Shakespearian play. The sergeant, catching me curiously looking at him, commented,

"It is very hot today, PO Greenberg," as I briefly studied his rather off whiter shade of pale black face.

The constable fingered his rifle nervously and grinned idiotically. Raymond look petrified, like he was about to be executed. Stupid bugger, we had laws and he would go to court. Mandashona then says to me,

"Sir, they are asking what they get if they would join the BSAP?"

Good question. Flushed with success I told them -

"You will qualify for a brand new shiny bicycle painted in your favourite colour – BLACK! Because who has ever seen a white bicycle? AND you also get a really nice watch with a matching black leather strap. Not for free mind you, but in interest free instalments from your excellent wages that come complete with a pension plan."

I grabbed Mandashona's left arm and showed them the watch he was wearing. I was dead jealous of that watch, we never got one when we joined. Us stupid whites were expected to have one. I often thought about throwing my crappy digital watch away and seeing if I could get a neat police arm piece as well. They all gathered around Mandashona's watch and agreed it was a really cool time keeper. It had large numbers that were luminous at night, and was water resistant between droughts.

This was brilliant! All I need is a few crates of beer and we got a great party. Still, I had a job to do and before I got to the Inya'Face bit about the gooks being a bad lot etc, Mandoshana announces, in a rather exhausted and summative voice, that the complainants have arrived. I had to excuse myself from my new friends as duty called.

They retreated a respectful distance whilst, through Mandashona, I took the statements. I added of course that No 1 suspect was in the back of the Landrover and I was more than happy to let them give him a tongue lashing. Bloody right, these two old girls of about 50 plus had been robbed of six months income. My new friends gleefully encouraged the tirade. Excusing myself once again I explained I had to be off, and thanks for the delightful chatting. Oh, and please could they take a serious thought about joining the police. I pointed out that they had been witness to what we do - help those that had been wronged and also bring the culprit to reckoning. Their leader, I guess that as he had been asking all the questions, smiled and assured me they would give deep thought to it. I was wished a pleasant journey and as we didn't have to keep stopping for directions, I returned to the mine police station before dark and dropped everyone off and went back to the single quarters for another boring evening. The constable and Mandashona looked well shattered. Feeling exhilarated with my successful day, I showered, heated up another tin of cheap whatever on my mini camping Gaz stove and, dressed in civvies of boxer shorts and T-shirt went to the bar.

I was sitting, attempting to chat with some miner twice my

age, nursing my second beer, when the phone rang behind the bar. The barman picked it up and spoke briefly into the hand set. Just as I was explaining Raymond's plight and my claim to instant fame to a semi-bored miner - the barman called out.

"Excuse me Sah. But are you PO Greenbag?"

Amazed, I said I was.

"It is for you Sah!"

Totally confused I took the handset the man proffered and said hello. The reply came from a very excitable constable. My constable.

"Sah, Raymond - he has absconded!"

CHAPTER 31:

The rise and fall of the Gokwe Kid

Part 2 - 'Stupid is as stupid does'

(Forest Gump)

"What the fuck you mean Raymond is gone?" I screamed into the mouth piece.

I never swore at the black staff. The other white POs got it back from me as fast as they gave, but the black police officers never swore in the English language and it would be considered extremely impolite to use whitey profanities in any discussion with them. But I said a bad word then as my world promptly imploded. I thought about having a heart attack on the spot, but guessed the pain would kill me. This was a juddering blow. My mind simply couldn't comprehend the situation. I just knew this was bad news. I raced to my Landrover, and drove at breakneck pace down to the police station in under two minutes. A frightened constable explained. As the Empress Nickel's police had negligently not been informed that Raymond was now under arrest and Mandashona was on the piss at the local beer hall, it was hardly surprising that whilst he, loyal constable went to urinate, Raymond, who had been released from his manacles once inside the police compound, had simply walked out the open front gate and disappeared amongst the hundred of black miners heading to the beerhall and shops.

Check Mate. Great detective and sleuth shot down in flames. *Dickhead of the Bushveld* sprung to mind. Shit, what am I going to tell my boss? I had had enough of Mandashona. Fuck him! That still didn't help. I knew I would get the rightful rap for this train crash. I told the constable we leave at 7.00 am the next day for Gokwe - mission uncompleted and an unmitigated disaster. I went back to that impassionate bedsit. I was gutted. All that work in vain. Even worse was imagining Mike Harvey's face when I told him. I had failed miserably. Thinking of all those promises I had made to my fans only a few hours ago – all gone. My confidence was shattered and I felt like throwing up. I crawled into bed and tried to sleep. For the first time in years I missed my teddy bear.

As soon as I finished a quick breakfast, I returned to pick up Mandashona and the constable; plus the earlier arrested suspect and his wife. Mandashona, whilst neatly presented, was stinking of beer. He sheepishly acknowledged he also forgot to tell the Empress Nickel's police about Raymond being an accused. Ah... who gave a shit at this stage? Let's go. He very enthusiastically agreed. The Landrover was packed, my rifle stuck neatly between door frame and seat. Just as we were about to pull away the Sub-Inspector from the police station asks me for a private word. African Sub-Inspectors as far as I was concerned were as equal as their white counterparts in experience. You don't get to run a police station controlling hundreds of black miners by being an idiot. He want to speak to me, I listen. Mandashona swore in Shona under his fetid breath.

I followed the Sub-Inspector into the radio room. There I was introduced to a short, middle aged man in blue overalls and bush hat. This person, explained the Sub-Inspector, is the night guard. So what? It's not his fault Raymond walked out. He didn't know. That was beside the point. In careful polite tones I was told what Sgt. Mandashona had been up to last night. Besides getting appallingly drunk and having sex with five prostitutes at the beer hall, he had returned to police camp and made trouble.

"What kind of trouble?"

"Your sergeant was caught by my night watchman having sex with the wife of your suspect against her obvious vocal overheard consent. When he asked what he was doing, your sergeant shouted abuse and threatened the night guard if he were to inform anyone."

What the hell was going on? None of this made sense. What was Mandashona doing shagging this guy's wife? I needed this bull-shit like a hole in my head.

Okay... calm down. Make some kind of plan. I am the senior officer present because I am white. Under my brown leather belt with the magnificent polished brass clasp, I have already personally dealt successfully with two rape cases and experienced Triggs wrapping up a rape case in his own imitable style, but - none involving police officers though. The Sub-Inspector made it clear that he wasn't impressed with my sergeant's conduct and exactly what was I going to do about it? A first class question! I was up to my neck in a giant pool of poo and thought for good measure I might as well submerge my head in the stuff as well. At least the expression 'Having shit for brains', would neatly sum up the insanity of what I did next.

I wasn't thinking straight anymore. With my head swirling with a cyclone of contradicting thoughts, drowning any logical lifeline (the obvious – radio Mike Harvey immediately – you're out of your depth), insanely, I organised an impromptu kangaroo court. I arranged for the Sub-Inspector to use his office and with the night guard and two other senior policemen from the station, I called in the woman. Through the Sub- Inspector I asked her if she had had sex with Sgt. Mandashona last night and if it was against her will? Her denial tipped the scales and turned this whole facade into a circus fiasco. The protests from the night guard and the loud angry bursts in Shona to her from the others in the room didn't need translating. Not only did they know that she was lying, but they were all well pissed off with this Gokwe pisshead Mandashona stuffing up their well ordered police station.

I hit the woman. I totally lost it. In sheer desperation I did what I thought I was incapable of; hitting an innocent person and a woman at that. I slapped the back of her head hard enough to make her duck and bend with shock but not pain, and repeated the swipes another three times, most of the half hearted blows glancing off her hunched shoulders. All I got was a weeping woman pleading on her knees to me. The others looked at me with puzzled questioning expressions. Christ, what they want from me? Do a Mandashona and beat her with a stave around the room till she was half dead?

The Sub-Inspector realised my total failure and saved my face with an alternative.

"Call in her husband and ask him to interrogate her, Sir."

Clutching at that straw, I agreed. I looked away as the husband beat the truth out of his wife. The others were well pleased. I felt like hell. Yes, she had had sex with him. Mandashona had said he could arrange that the white officer would release her husband if she slept with him. He had also threatened to arrange that the white officer would send her husband to jail if she told anyone. Only the interruption of the night guard caused the whole sexual adventure of my sergeant's deceit being brought to light.

Super – a world class confession! I managed to make the worst of it and called Mandashona into my kangaroo court and attempted to read him a Warned and Cautioned statement as he was under arrest on the charge of rape. He went totally berserk! Sweating profusely in the now baking tin hut, shouting, switching from Shona to English, glaring at us all; I gathered we all needed our heads examined and he was having none of this. With that he stormed out and sat down on the small step in the open doorway of the police armoury, about twenty paces away from my parked Landover. In his arms was a fully loaded FN rifle. There wasn't a weapon amongst us. Mine was in the Landrover, so was my constable's, who had joined us a few seconds before Mandoshona did his blown mind trip and sat on the step. The sergeant's body language didn't bode well and the way he was cradling the rifle, along with the glazed expression, gave me goose pimples. Maybe he contemplated a ruined career because of a nosy young white and would go down fighting. It was only a couple of days ago he had told me he was due to get his medal for 17 years of outstanding long service. I was urinating big time on his parade and if he really went off the rails there was enough in the miniature armoury to start a small massacre.

The radio room could be accessed out of his line of fire. I got there with the others and radioed the Empress Nickel mine's security section. I requested armed reinforcements, saying we had a possible amok policeman. Within minutes they were met at the gate and led to the radio room. As these white middle-aged congenial men looked through the window at, gazing with glassed eyes at the sky Mandashona clutching his rifle, one asked what the plan was.

Plan? They were the sodding plan! So plan something! As a heated debate broke out, my constable walked in with Mandashona's rifle.

"How you get that?" we shouted.

"He went to urinate and left it there," was the calm reply.

I thanked the miners profusely and went to the Landrover and armed up. Feeling better, and with no Mandashona in sight, I ducked back into the radio room and did what I should have done at 7.10 am that morning - call my boss.

Now when I miserably asked for him (that alone is an awful thing to do. No PO called the boss unless it was something very important), I knew I was now in big trouble and it was all self made!

I told him the whole story. He spoke then to the Sub-Inspector. After a brief conversation, I was then told to call Mandashona. He was around kicking his heels. I just shouted out the door,

"Sergeant Mandashona, Chief Inspector Harvey wishes to speak to you on the radio."

He came of course. The boss told him he was to go with me to Gatooma. The whole mess was in their jurisdiction. He would radio ahead and arrange that this car crash would be processed there. I was requested again. Chief Inspector Mike Harvey was extremely pissed-off. I was to drive to Gatooma police station. The tone of his voice was enough to hurt, but when I told him Raymond was gone -

"Looks like you blew it big time Greenberg. Over and Out." No more Karl. Takes time and respect to earn the boss calling you by your first name.

With a silent Mandashona in the front seat, the constable, the woman and her suspect husband in the back, we left. It's tarred all the way from the mine to Gatooma. Within an hour we were there. After being questioned by a very serious senior officer, I went and chatted a bit with the other young POs. Whilst they seemed sympathetic, they didn't exactly offer much hope or advice. One of them, 'Goofy', who I knew from Morris Depot days, offered me a cigarette and I took it. It tasted like soot and made me light headed. After the third - I decided to buy a pack of Kingsgate 20's. I was told I wouldn't be returning to Gokwe that night. The whole sorry affair would take a while. I was to sleep on the couch at the singles quarters.

At 5.00pm I pondered my fate. I was stuck in a strange place for a night on a serious big downer. I wanted only one thing - my girlfriend Victoria. After a quick change into the only 'civvies' I had with me, boxer shorts and a T-shirt, I hit the main road with nothing but a rifle, an ID card and a thumb. Estimated time of arrival at home in Salisbury: 8.00pm. It took almost two hours longer by the time a kind farmer dropped me off at the top of the Lomungundi Road and I ran the last two clicks home. I jumped the locked gate and hammered on the door. Babbling uncomprehendingly to my completely stupefied step-mother, awoken from deep sleep, I just grabbed the phone and dialled.

Victoria's Mom answered. Phoning this late in Rhodesia was associated with bad news. I was plenty of that! There was no way, even if Katherine lent me her car, that I would be allowed to see my honey but after much pleading, I was allowed five minutes on the phone. She had school tomorrow. That's that. Not even enough time to tell her what a mess I had made of everything, just time to tell her that I loved her. I put the phone down and some brain cells, that hadn't been totally obliterated, pushed a very important detail to mind. If I did not turn up in uniform in the OiC's office at 8.00 am the next day – I was absent without leave and no one had a clue where I had gone. I also realised that rocking up late and announcing arrogantly –

"I just popped up to Salisbury for the night, with no clue what time I will return, because I was feeling a tad stressed, and thought a grope with my honey would clear some of my anxieties around the predicament I now find myself in – which, funnily enough, I have just managed to increase ten fold – so perhaps just take me outside and shoot me because I believe it would please everyone including myself."

Now I had to tell step-mom. I went into the kitchen where she was making a cup of tea. There was no point at this late hour trying to explain about Raymond and Mandashona and rape and…so I just said if I wasn't in Gatooma Police Station by 8.00 am tomorrow, it would be my end. I begged that she take me to the Bulawayo Road at 6.00 am and wait, and if I didn't get a lift by 6.30am; to drive me all the way to Gatooma. It was a hell of a request. There was no way she could get back in time for school. She didn't hesitate.

"Go to bed son. I will wake you in the morning."

I didn't even have the chance to say hello to Bridget or Michael.

Leaving a note for the kids, we hit the Bulawayo Road at 100kmh after waiting futilely for a lift for half an hour. I was a bag of nerves. The Rhodie assembled Renault 4 was blasting flat out. Just after Norton, some thirty clicks out from Salisbury, we slowly approached another car. It was also a Renault 4 with three young women in it. I had a plan. If we could overtake them and get some distance, I could maybe flag them down. Hundreds of those painted white stripes in the middle of the road flashed by as Katherine fought it out. I had never seen her so determined. Normally she was a mouse at the steering wheel, her left hand used to always habitually touch the gear stick in a nervous gesture of confirmation. Then we had them. Uphill and a short straight - no on coming traffic, our few kilos lighter made the difference and we overtook. As soon as step-mom couldn't see them in the rear view mirror, she hit the brakes and I stood with my rifle in the middle of the road. The girls pulled up. I gabbled that if they were going as far as Gatooma and, if so, could they take me? They were more than pleased to have an armed accompanist, even if my usual chatty personality was somewhat dampened from the thoughts of what lay ahead. So I kissed Katherine and thanked her and turned up in time to change into police uniform and present myself.

No one noticed I had been missing and it was well after 2.00 pm when, after signing my statement at a second interview, I was told to go. So I headed back to Gokwe village with the constable. The other three were being kept behind for more questioning. I braced myself for the confrontation with Chief Inspector Harvey...

the boss - Mike Harvey, wife Heather and daughter Sally
Gokwe 1977

Pic - Mike Harvey

CHAPTER 32:

The rise and fall of the Gokwe Kid

Part 3 - Savaging the savages

By the time the boss had finished debriefing me, the early evening shadows were being cast by the magnificent huge masasa trees before the entrance of my police station. I didn't get a tongue lashing; his eyes said it all. I wandered to the opening and looked out onto its dirt forecourt. Various strange, armour-plated *Made in Rhodesia* mutants, all named after some of our wild life, were parked up amongst the last few working Landrovers – It looked so peaceful.

I suppose I was coming down from one hell of an adrenalin rush. It seemed all so mad! Like - was it really just 48 hours since I went from being the winner of Rhodesia *has Talent*, along with fame and glory... to self-destruction and the tears of a clown? I don't know how long I stood there silently. Word had spread fast and the black policemen left me totally alone in my thoughts. I dreaded to think what they were thinking about me! I didn't mix with them socially and vice-versa. For all I know Mandashona might have been a total twat amongst them and several may be secretly pleased with his demise or, maybe he was well popular and in that case?

As I listlessly pondered over all this, three Landrovers turned up and the green painted, unmarked vehicles pulled up sharply in a cloud of dust. Loads of filthy black and white men piled out. I recognised the leader of this motley crew immediately; Special Branch Section Officer Phil Drewitt. The man was as popular as a pork chop thrown into a Mosque/Synagogue/Vegetarian Take Away, Yup, SO Piggy (so nick-named by me for his physical similarity to Miss Piggy from the 'Muppets'), was the clown who cocked up the intelligence on the gooks that hit Gokwe village. The same one that Nigel doesn't exactly mince words about, but nor do I, for I disliked this guy a lot. He was a total knob end. I didn't have much affection for some members from Special Branch. They were the nasty elements in this war and SO Piggy was a primitive backward jerk with a cruel streak to match his large gut now exposed in bright pink between strained buttons of his camouflage shirt. I stood back as, completely ignoring me, he swaggers his obese form into the cop shop with grenades and ammunition swathing his sweaty body. Stopping in front of the charge desk and with fat legs splayed, he shouted out to all and sundry…

"I want to know which dickhead of a police officer tried to recruit six gooks I've been chasing for three weeks - into the fucking Police force?!"

Luckily, my brain decided at that point it had had enough of the circus and would like to mull over for a while the mundane tasks like eating, bathing, drinking and chain smoking. So, ignoring the loud mouthed twat, I wandered back to my room. Home. I greeted Wilson half heartedly and ran a big bath in our communal tub. I had just started to relax in the steaming waters, when the internal police phone on the wall in the corridor started to shrill its ear piece off. Since it wasn't quite knocking off time, there were no other POs around. Just great! Wilson answered and knocked politely on the bathroom door.

"Chief Inspector Harvey wants to talk to you."

What the hell does he want? Jeez, I need a break man! But you don't tell Wilson to tell the boss you're in the bath and I will phone back later, and besides, it's almost 4.30 pm, I'm knackered and want my peace. So I wrapped myself in a towel and said

"Hallo." I kept it short and sweet. I wasn't in a chatty mood.

"Who said you could have a bath? Get into my office now and fully kitted in camouflage." He slammed the phone down on me without even saying goodbye!

Semi-soaking, I got my ass into camo and was in the boss's office in five minutes. It was packed. There was at least six Special Bastards including their slimy black side kick, and some large, young bearded white bloke. They were dressed in a mixture of civilian and army camo T- shirts, along with dark green boxer shorts and calf high desert boots. Piggy liked to pose in a combat vest packed with FN magazines and grenades and shit - a real walking arsenal arsehole. They all looked at me and waited.

"Did you in the last couple of days talk to some male Africans at a make shift football pitch?" the boss asked.

I didn't like the drift this question was going and looking around at the Gestapo surrounding me, the penny dropped. I told him briefly what had happened. I left out the part where I thought I had been so very clever-clever with the X-factor stuff. Piggy looked at me,

"You're lucky you are not dead. We have been following them for almost three weeks. They are most probably the same bunch of Gooks who took out the Reverend and his wife a few months ago and YOU wanted them to join the BSAP!"

I didn't say anything. What for? I guessed Mandashona and the constable had realised something was odd. That's why they were shitting themselves! This was all Raymond's fault. I impregnated his image into my mind; I would cut and paste that any time for the rest of my life. I looked back at the boss.

"Draw ratpacks for three days. You have no time to get supplies. Get your sleeping bag and webbing. There are four constables waiting outside. You will go with NSPO Blackbeard back to the area you were in. You are to supply SB with protection and back up."

With that the boss dismissed us. As I went out, Piggy asked me a question.

"Didn't you find it odd coming across that football field in the middle of no where?" he sarcastically put it.

No, because I was doing my bloody job as a policeman solving crimes and I had been doing quite well out of it - so for once, the sodding war wasn't running through my head and had it been I would be dead by now - isn't that so? I just said,

"No."

I didn't have to call him Sir. He might be SB, but still only a Section Officer; which at his age meant he was too thick to pass the promotion exams.

So I got my sleeping bag and paraphernalia of gook extermination kit, and driving the fully loaded 'Leopard' armoured vehicle (made out of a VW Beetle), I followed Blackbeard and his loony tunes into the sunset. It was well dark by the time we swung up in front of a fenced Internal Affairs camp. This is where we will be based for a while, Blackbeard informed us. After much shouting at the compound, it brought out a guard who let us in. I found the kitchen, warmed up some junk from the ratpack, and snatching a stretcher, I went to bed on the veranda. The whole situation seemed surreal. This wasn't really happening.

At 5.00am we were woken up. Thank God I hadn't had to do night watch as well. My nerves were killing me and I was hitting the fags at twenty a day by now. An hour later, clever NSPO Blackbeard, as I now found out he was only a National Service Patrol Officer with 'A' Levels, doing his stint (called a Rhodesian gap year), before going to university, was running the show and explained his plan. A few clicks down the road was a bush store where he reckoned the gooks, if they were still around, would hang out. I and my lads were to surround the place and his boys go in and question anyone in there. The big surprise was that we weren't going to walk; his plan was to surprise them with a speeding assault with all vehicles. That suits me, but I now knew from experience this would be a mistake. Nigel had been right about this over a year ago.

Judging from the din our two vehicles were making and the dust clouds pouring after us, when we showed up through the trees about 200 paces from the store, the people gathered there started running. Hitting brakes hard, everyone hit the ground and from screaming NSPO Blackbeard's instructions, we ran after anyone. I heard some shots to my right. My target in a bright pink shirt was legging it at a high rate, so I let loose twice into the air whilst vainly shouting in English and dodgy Shona, he must stop. That must have been obvious enough since there were about twelve of us running frantically around shouting the same request in different versions.

Within 50 racing strides into the bush I stopped. No hope of catching him now, the chap had well scarpered, bare foot as well. Blackbeard was directly to my right and came running over.

"Why the fuck didn't you shoot?" he shouted, red face surrounded by masses of black hair and beard.

"I did and it didn't work," I flatly stated.

"Not in the fucking air, man, at him," he raved.

Ah… now this piss-ant, barely out of 'skive army national service by pretending you really want to be a policeman' training school, was maybe in charge of the operation, which sucked, but he wasn't in charge of me! I had been in Gokwe over a year now and was older than this cock-sucker, plus as a regular, I had a rank advantage. I had taken an instant dislike to this man poncing around MY Gokwe!

"I am not shooting anyone in the back!"

"But it could have been a terr," he babbled.

"I doubt that. The young man had no shoes on and I have never heard of gooks running around in bright pink shirts. Well, even if he was a mujiba, your wonderful arrival style might have triggered his flight along with everyone else's."

This point duly sunk into his over qualified brain, so he shut up and we went back to the store. Besides arresting maybe a few tins of imported South African pilchards as foreign invaders that were sitting on the shelves, there wasn't much point in sticking around. Clever Mr Blackbeard realised that too and ordered us back to base camp, but not before I spent almost six dollars on some beer, fags and pilchards. At least the brave owners had stuck around. They of course, when asked by our genius team leader, had never seen a terrorist around and knew nothing. Back at camp, Blackbeard's disappointment was replaced by his latest brain storm. He and his *shutzstaffel* would go out and round up some locals for questioning. My four constables and I were to do…nothing. I liked this plan. So I had a shower, the local Internal Affairs lads had started up the Rhodie boiler, so there was plenty of hot water. Feeling much better, I cheerily waved Nutter and his pets goodbye and had a lovely pilchard and onion sandwich lunch, washed down with a Castle or three and a Kingsgate fag or ten. A poke around the few rooms found me some books to read. Oh, I did have a small job. I was to organise a 24/7 guard roster. As there were enough black police and Internal Affairs able bodies, I left us two whites off the list.

I had just settled down with a Sidney Sheldon best seller when Special Branch National Service Police Officer Blackbeard and the nasty boys arrived back. They had been very busy. He had commandeered my Leopard as well, and had brought back a dozen African males for questioning. He had them march off smartly to a corrugated, asbestos roofed carport behind the main building. I didn't follow the manacled, frightened, shabbily dressed motley crew of youths and middle-aged men. Not my business. I asked what time Blackbeard wanted to eat dinner as I was making us a corn beef stew with rice.

"I'll get it later," he replied in a voice strained by excited adrenalin, as he trotted off.

I went to my camp stretcher and back to my book. *The Other Side of Midnight* was getting really good. I think it's that part where the betrayed Noelle uses a wire coat hanger to incite a miscarriage, when my concentration was disturbed. There were some bloody odd noises coming from behind the building. I rolled off the cot and walked slowly to an outside back corner and took a peep. I had heard in inebriated war story chats with other lads about torture being used. This was the first time I saw it first hand. Two men held a third bent over a chair by his arms. A fourth 'policeman' beat with enormous force the exposed buttocks with a large stave. Another with a loaded FN kept an eye on the others sitting on the concrete floor and being forced to watch their compatriot. Blackbeard sat relaxed on a wooden desk chair, rocking it on its back legs as he shouted questions.

As I said, this is not my business. I went back to Sidney Sheldon. Smoked some fags and had another beer. Beer had lost its bitter taste since I had started smoking. In fact I was getting to like the stuff quite a lot. Super hero came in late. He warmed his food up over the still smoking wood stove, and as I lay slouched in camo on my stretcher with the book spread open in the middle, rifle and beer within easy reach, he filled me in on his total lack of success. I said goodnight.

Next day I awoke at the crack of dawn. No choice since the place was surrounded by stinking cockerels and Kaffir dogs going mad. Magic man and the ghost hunters were getting frustrated. So off they went and dropped off the first well battered civilians and arrived a couple of hours later with the new human load of potential harbourer of terrorists.

As they were led away to be settled in, I told Blackbeard I was going back to the store.

"Get me a crate of beer, this is thirsty work," was his reply.

I took my time. I drove up slowly and no one ran away. We went in and drank a couple of beers. The two constables I brought along to protect me were delighted for the break and supped on cold beers too. I was paying. I wasn't in any hurry to get back. I was getting extra money for doing nothing besides churn over what I had witnessed in my head along with the weird fact it was all, somehow, my fault. At lunch time the head torturer came in to eat and sup on a bevvie. Quite exhausted he was. He then proceeded to tell me, that while he still didn't have much information, one of the suspects had defecated himself from the beatings. Wonderful, like as in, beat the shit out the poor bastard?

"Dirty fucker stunk disgustingly, so we had to hose him down, bet it's the first wash he had in ages anyway," he laughed as he shovelled food into his mouth.

I was now at the part in the book where they are plotting to murder Catherine; so I wished him a lightly guarded sarcastic good luck. Blackbeard, failing again in getting whatever he wanted, took his crew and battered victims off again and went looking for more volunteers. By the time he returned, it was too dark for fun and games. So the next manacled batch was given food and some light weight blankets.

Next day brought a breakthrough. I had just finished the book where the two anti-heroes get executed and the supposed dead, innocent Catherine winds up mad in a convent, when bearded super sleuth brought me exciting details. This new batch had 'struck' pay dirt. One unlucky peasant had finally succumbed to this artful form of questioning and admitted that he knew of a village where the terrorists had been staying. We must pack and get back to Gokwe police station now, and, he added in his unconcealed excitement,

"Dig this," he laughed, "the Munt told me we have to beat those villagers too before they will admit."

I was so pleased to get out of this place of pain and we were back in Gokwe police station by 2.00 pm. I stayed behind after the debriefing in the boss's office. I wanted the time off I deserved, and how I needed it. My head was in a serious mess. Knowing the *gen* by now, I added that there were two POs at the moment in the charge office, I haven't been home for four weeks and been on duty every weekend in that time. He pulled out the huge roster that recorded our whereabouts - past, present and future. It was Thursday afternoon.

"Be back by Monday 8.00 am," and pencilled it in.

Not bad! So whilst I'm still begging, and with one success, I sweetly asked for some petrol coupons. I wasn't exactly his hot-shot copper at this time but he knew I had been through the wringer. Chief Inspector Harvey looked very tired. Three years Gokwe had been his home. His transfer request had been approved and he was going soon. I had known him a year. He was a good man and a fair one. I got 17 units…Shit loads.

I ran to my room and packed fast. Victoria will be with me this weekend. Connecting up the battery leads to the Toyota in my own carport, formerly Nigel's, I was on the road in less than an hour. I drove as fast as I could on the dirt road. At 100 kmh, the back started to slide on the loosely graded stone road that constantly flicked up chunks onto the undercarriage, but generally, besides a dodgy repaired exhaust by the late, blasted his own brain's out, Piet, my yellow passion puller was fine. Tyres were a pain and the retreads were running thin. Sticking the FN's barrel out of the window as a serious heavy deterrent to ambushing gooks, opening a bottle of beer whilst guiding the jittery machine with my knees, I hit the Empress Nickel mine's tar road an hour later and opened her up to almost full whack. I looked about half hopefully for Raymond. Just over an hour later I was home.

Coming home was always brilliant. Katherine never knew when I would turn up. For once I would gladly sit at the table and I did all the talking; after I had phoned Victoria of course. I knew I couldn't see her that night, but I would be outside her school in my wheels waiting for her at lunch time.

Sitting looking cool in my Toyota Corolla with a pair of shades on and my WRS tape deck blasting out Rodriguez 'Cold Fact'; at last I was the smart arse picking up my own Cindi Tait.

Victoria waves at her pals and has her boater tilted back cheekily on her golden red hair, in what Stephanie calls the 'Tart' look. White blouse and straw hat -the badges of rank as she was a sixth former and a school prefect. She was excellent fun and I liked her family too. They owned kennels on the Old Mazoe Road. Well out from the suburbs. Tonight I was taking her to *The Cellar*. I had reserved a table. Jacket and Tie, and long dresses obligatory for Salisbury's best restaurant. Beer please waiter. Smoking was changing my taste buds and the Rhodesian wine still sat heavily in my stomach from my overindulgence three years before in the Boy Scouts. Evil stuff.

Sunday night was always spent till 9.00pm at her place. Victoria was cute and she sent me messages via Sally Donaldson's

Forces Request on national radio, (which always cost a round if others heard it, which you gave out groaning embarrassedly - but secretly pleased), and when she could, a goodies parcel of chocolate and stuff, along with love letters.

Then it was back to work - I hit the Bulawayo road at 5.30am on Monday when Julia the maid came on. No traffic on the road, so I get in for 7.30 in time to change into uniform and with rifle slung over my shoulder, greeted good morning to the duty black policeman at the front charge office, who dutifully noted my presence in the book, and I went to my desk...

CHAPTER 33:

The rise and fall of the Gokwe Kid

Part 4 - Hasta la vista, Gokwe

I felt seriously sick looking at all my Raymond stuff - all lying so neatly there on my desk. I had to wrap the sorry mess up. I carefully collected the cheques and, along with the Ox-cart agreement from Raymond I had obtained on my travels, which now seemed a million years ago, I posted it onto our forensics department. At least I had had him fingerprinted on the first day, so I sent that as well. I didn't bother sending another request to have his wife and kids rounded up again. I concluded that now Raymond knew the game was up, he wasn't exactly going to walk into my office - all full of smiles and apologies. Not a lot more I could do. I wrote out my report and carried on with other crimes. Mandashona was back on the scene. We didn't talk. No one mentioned the subject. I wasn't going to talk about it either. At night I would write letters, listen to music, or go watch the television.

Something was wrong in my head. Okay, most of it was usually obvious, but there was something else. I didn't feel like me anymore. I dunno, but the whole Raymond business and its aftermath had taken away something – innocence? Yeah, for sure I had not only been naive, but extremely lucky, but hells bells, I was still alive and kicking. But, plenty people were not and just when I thought the whole crazy episode, like a conclusion of Rhodesia's *Strictly come Soldiering*, the end should have been in sight – guess who turns up?

Piggy and his dogs of war were back. Now this time they had really gone overboard. Using two huge armoured Isuzu truck transporters, they had rounded up the entire village that the beaten bloke had told them about. Leon, Ian and I were told to get to work. Charge: aiding and abetting terrorists. Minimum punishment - five years imprisonment. This was a huge amount of work. All day we sat there, each of us with a constable translating. Always the same answer to the same question.

"Yes the Terrorists were at our village." *(No point denying it, since several of them had been worked over to get this fact out.)*

"Yes, we gave them food as they demanded it." *(Otherwise we get beaten, mutilated and shot.)*

"No I didn't report to security forces as I was frightened." *(Oh well, so much for Inya'face. Waste of time if you have the locusts following you.)*

African Male Adult or African Female Juvenile, it made no difference to what we had to do like autonomists. Name, age, kraal's name where you live. *(Which was rather ironic when you considered that the entire villages' inhabitants were now enclosed in a barbed wire fence thrown hurriedly around trees at the back of my bedroom.)* Situpa number. Sign here or as in most cases, a scribbled X would do, with the charged person's clumsy fingers being guided by the constable to make the two wobbly crossing lines. AND

"The next," shouted Leon as the scream from the typewriter confirmed another four times copied Charge formula being pulled out. Now we are having a race! At least we were allowed to keep proper hours. By 4.30 pm I was a typing wreck. My finger tips were almost raw from smashing ancient keys again and again to try and correct mistakes, whilst the soft recycled paper collapsed from the force. The carbon sheets all had holes in them from the 'O'.

Next day wasn't too good. When the others and I arrived at 8.00 am the black staff's faces were looking black. That's a bad sign when they stiffen their shoulders and talk very extra-extra politely. One of the apprehended had died in the night. Pneumonia! It was getting cold at night up here on the plateau as winter approached. Was I glad that it wasn't my responsibility? Let's get this behind us before they all die out there.

As fast as we could, we charged them, and just as fast, they were trucked down to Gwelo. We were getting good. All cracked fifteen each that day. Just faceless, smelly frightened humans huddled in rags on a stool, one after another. Next day we finished them off, which was just at the time as Piggy and the loony tunes turned up again from their latest adventure. They looked very flustered and were not their usual swaggering selves. Well, it didn't take long for the news to go around. With the information they had 'freely and co-operatively' received, they had followed the gooks to a village, taken up an observation point and called in an air strike. The small napalm bomb, *Made in Rhodesia* and called a *Frantam*, fired by the Air Force took the targeted hut out perfectly. One problem though. They found just three incinerated children in the smouldering wreck of a hut. There were no terrs in the village. I wrote in my police note book in a dastardly scrawl...Air strike, 3 local kiddies killed. Underneath I drew a wiggly line.

Forensics sent my stuff back a couple of weeks later. They confirmed all my suspicions. Raymond was our man, but he was gone. I packed the whole lot carefully into a cardboard box and presented it to Alistair Barr, the new Section Officer. He, accompanied by a wife and two small children, had moved into Mike Rowley's house. He was a nice bloke, but had serious hassles with his missus who was not very impressed with Gokwe and the social life. Ali looked at the pile in the box and just kept his comments to,
"What a shame he got away."
So all that work just received a short comment and ended up in the file room.
I had let everyone down on this one. Most of all I had let the complainants down. They would have never seen their money again, but should have had the satisfaction of knowing Raymond was going to jail; just as I had boasted. Well at least he wouldn't be operating his various scams around Gokwe anymore. I knew I would never get Raymond out my head for the rest of my life, as in a perverse twist of fate, he had saved it!

Things started to happen around me at a brisk pace. I was kept mostly at the station now. I took our new addition, a gentle, softly spoken kid who introduced me to the pop group Supertramp, out to my beloved Chirama. The new base camp was almost completed, but it wasn't on the escarpment edge. Somehow I knew it was the last time. How things had turned around since that day I first arrived and started my education under Nigel and Alan. Now I was the teacher. Then Chief Inspector Harvey was transferred, and our new boss was a Jock from Macheke Police station. What had he done to get promoted here? All hell was breaking out and his arrival speech to us POs that things would be changed, didn't bode well. I gave him two weeks before I put in my transfer request. Gokwe wasn't fun anymore. It was a war zone. Every week saw more police reservists being shuttled in and out to the three main bush camps.

Even the sports club wasn't even vaguely entertaining. The District Commissioner, along with his cute daughter, was also gone - along with my petrol coupons. You couldn't look out the windows of the sports club anymore due to the sandbags. The mortar bunker's roof outside my bedroom collapsed along with my enthusiasm for my new boss. It was time to go. My cleverly worded appeal to be transferred to Salisbury failed badly and I was posted to Gwelo Charge Office. After fifteen months in Gokwe, it was time to say farewell...

There was some weird tradition whereby, if you had been part of the white community for at least a year, you held a send off party at the sports club, and received a copper engraved mug from your adoring Gokwe chinas. Fifteen months gave me the time span but not the accolade. I had spent most of that time in the bush and my lack of social skills at the club, re: to swallowing large crates of beer, left the chances of getting a mug at nil. Also, with all the comings and goings, most of the crowd I had started out with were long gone. I wasn't spending good money on people I hardly knew and not get a mug either. However, I meant to thank some people that had most definitely been my companions and help in all that time.

So I remembered something my late father once did on his birthday. It was at Paramount Garments, where he worked as the general manager, tradition to buy cakes for the white staff. At dinner on that particular birthday, he had told us that he hated the habit. Why give cakes to people he hardly knew and had limited contact with even at the workplace? So instead he bought little sweet buns and a Coke for all 300 plus African workers. I had been well impressed with the gesture – shame he never showed that side to me, but I absorbed the lesson.

So I invited twenty plus black staff of all rank and file. Especially Sammy. I would miss this man. Also Wilson and the other single men's mess staff. I drove down to Gokwe village beer hall and bought a huge drum of Chibuku beer; never could get into the stuff, the smell of fermenting maize and millet always left me weak. Even Mandashona accepted his invite. We met behind my sleeping quarters and sat on the grass in civvies or uniform and prattled about our adventures together. Mandashona never spoke the whole time. I was pleased that I seemed to be liked and spent a great three hours with my ex-partners, me sitting on a side mounted crate of Castle. I was liking the stuff more and more and it was simple to slip a full one out and return the empty to its slot. That was that!

With my car packed to the roof, I drove out of Gokwe police station for the last time, rifle loaded besides me. I rocketed down that long dirt road. I passed the place where Peter almost died after hitting the cows, and a little further on, the ambush spot where the preacher and his wife had been murdered. The Que Que lads said his wife wasn't killed in the hail of bullets that took out her husband and crashed the Landy he drove. They said she was taken into the bush and raped before being shot. They left six children orphaned. I had even met the guy. All white visitors to Gokwe TTL had been required to come into the police station for a briefing update. I had done the man's briefing. Brand was his name - I have an entry of his name in my notebook. Even my boss couldn't stop the man going to preach to his flock. He wasn't armed, a real do-gooder. His prayers didn't do much good for him and his wife though.

And then the tyres touched tar. The Toyota would never touch a dirt road again under my ownership. A huge shiver shook me as I entered the suburbs of Que Que - something was gone out my life for ever...

Memoir mutterings

On October, 23, 1977, the Reverend Andries Louw Brand (40) and his wife Tabina Metje Brand (41) were killed in a terrorist ambush. They were murdered while returning to their home in Que Que, after celebrating communion in the Gokwe area. Mr. Brand belonged to the clergy of the Dutch Reformed Church.
They left six children.
http://www.rhodesia.nl/mission.htm

Email from Nigel
I do have a copper mug chum...somewhere in a box in the garage...still there the wife says... you can have it...!!!!

Of the central characters mentioned no longer in this memoir –
6121 Superintendent Mike Harvey. Pension and other benefits. February 1985.
8934 Patrol Officer Nigel Triggs. Own request. May 1979.
9312 Detective Section Officer Peter Brockbank. Pension and other benefits. March 1983.
9479 Detective Section Officer Alan Golden. Pension and other benefits. May 1980.
9612 Section Officer Ian MacKinnon. Pension and other benefits. May 1982.
9614 Patrol Officer Leon DeBeer. By purchase. October 1978.

Glossary

Bevvie. A beer.

CHAPTER 34:

'And...The winner of 1978 Rhodesia's X-factor is...PO Greenberg!' (Fame at last - triumphant, the Gokwe Kid arises from the ashes – only to get bored with it all.)

Well, exactly as my Gokwe adventure had started, no one knew of my arrival and I was made to sleep on the floor of the Gwelo's single policeman's mess lounge for the second time in my life. 8.00 am the next day, and wearing my city uniform for the first time since driving school, I presented myself to my new boss. I liked Chief Inspector Brian Hayes immediately and we chatted a bit about my life in Gokwe. He explained he would organise which shift I would be allocated to, but for today; just hang around with one of the charge office Patrol Officers and get the feel of city policing.

I had hardly been introduced to my 'guide', PO Tony Knobbs, when a call came through regarding a pick pocketing incident. But - it had been long enough to notice and flash my boyish number one wolfish smile at a very well endowed young lady working at a typewriter. The smile in return showed promise. Things were looking good here. With two constables in the back of the grey painted Landrover, my chaperone explained on the way to the public bus depot, that the buxom bunny at the typewriter was called Noaline, was bound for Morris Depot and in the mean time was a police recruit in waiting. And, no, as far as he knew she had no boyfriend. I licked away the excess saliva that had gathered on the end of my canines. Things were looking even better. Curiously, we were not armed. My FN was locked in the small armoury in the Charge Office. It felt weird not having that thing with me all the time.

At the bus depot we all disembarked, and sure enough along came the complainant. Tony talked to the excited victim whilst I looked about. There were maybe fifteen of these huge long distance buses piled high with personal belongings in multi coloured cardboard suitcases or wrapped in blankets. The thick, sickly sweet smell of rotten fruit permeated the air. The noise was amazing. Hundreds of Africans queuing before the buses, milling about or buying vegetables, razor blades, bars of soap, bottles of Coke and Fanta from the dozens of rickety stands. The whole place seemed to have a carpet of chewed and spat sugar cane pith and strips of its hard outer cover. The only difference between Kambasha's terminal in Gokwe and here was this bus depot was tarred. Most of the amassed blacks gave us a curious look over. Meanwhile, Tony had ascertained that the complainant, besides missing his wallet whilst standing in a queue for one of the buses, had no idea of what the suspect looked like, nor were there any witnesses. I had been handling grand theft, rape, bestiality and suicides for the last fifteen months. This was a load of cobblers. It was totally futile and a waste of time. Before I got back into the Landrover, I threw one last glance around the files of people and…stared - **straight into the eyes of Raymond!**

As our eyes locked, he let out a loud piercing wail of agony and tried to hide his tall frame behind the others in the queue. I was already running, cursing that I wasn't armed and screaming for the others to follow. My head was pounding, and even with those stupid, cumbersome anti-dog savaging leather leggings impeding my running, I was like a rocket. I saw nothing but him. I needn't have worried. Raymond had collapsed on the ground in shock, his worst nightmare had just come true. I handcuffed him and passed him over to the very confused constables.

"Watch him well," I excitedly said, "he has escaped me before."

Tony asked me what the hell was all this about. On the way back I explained briefly. I was elated - on fire, buzzing, bubbling like a popped bottle of champagne. This is brilliant. I stormed into the Charge Office dragging a still wailing Raymond. Every one, black and white looked in amazement as I grabbed the next free typewriter and charged him. The docket numbers, stolen amounts, time frame, everything… coming out my head with ease. Raymond made my day even better by gabbling away and confessing the lot. Still pumping with adrenalin I put a call through to SO Ali Barr up in Gokwe as soon as Raymond had put his flowery signature to the charge sheet. No pissing around with sending radio messages. A delighted Ali told me to send him up with the next truck of reservists and after putting down the phone, I booted Raymond up his arse into a cell. I was an instant star and Noeline appreciatively shared my bed that night in my new room on the first floor with a shared balcony. The Gokwe Kid (Cad?), had arrived and as I am neither an officer nor a gentleman – Victoria was history. The Show Must Go On!

I was allocated to the Number One shift in the Charge Office under SO 'Bones' Buchanon. There were a couple of other POs, both slightly senior to me, Keith and Paddy. By pure coincidence we all had a room on the first floor of the single's mess and shared a balcony. I rather liked the set up and had no problems with my new compatriots on the shift. Keith came over as a bit of a dandy but Paddy was a seriously clever dude who had dropped out of university in South Africa due to too much partying. We had many fine chats whilst on night shift together, but he was seriously depressed with his lot.

Shift work was new to me. There were three and it sort of went like this –

It started with five in the morning till one in the afternoon. This was a killer if you had been on the *Fellowship of the Binge* the night before. This shift would be awoken at the awful hour of 4.30am by the outgoing night shift that had started at 7.00pm the previous night. This night shift was so boring, with almost nothing going on unless it was the weekend, we struggled to stay awake. Things were made worse by our official 'lunch break', where in theory we had an hour off to munch on rancid sandwiches of Lobel's bread and rock hard roast beef supplied at enormous cost from our mess kitchen.

In turn, nightshift had been picked up by the afternoon shift that was an absolute dream. You could go on a bender and sleep in, and had six easy hours to recover before going on another one. Well, usually at the weekend.

The whole set up whilst looking fair on paper with days off after each shift, two for the day shifts ,and three after a week on nights; played havoc with socialising with your mates, such as my old Morris Depot china, Jeff. He was busy with a babe and was on a different shift; so catching each other wasn't that easy. I had actually seen Jeff just recently – it had been a visit that wasn't (yet again) one of my brightest ideas…

About a month before I left Gokwe, I was sent down to Que Que to pick up in cash the wages for the black staff. Along with the cash, there were the petrol coupons, radio messages and whatever. After weeping willow Peter had piled his Landy into the mombes, and the murder of the preacher and his wife, I had no desire to head back at sunset. With nothing else to do, I radioed Gwelo and found out that Jeff was on nightshift. I waited till seven and when I called (all this 'illegal' of course), he said to come on up. So I did. Dressed in T-shirt and shorts, off I went on the usual one hour drive by armoured Landy till I ran out of petrol. Mmm, this was a bugger, especially since the Landy radio didn't work. So, I am stuck on the side of the road, in a rather desolate area of bush on both sides, presumably full of gooks, and feeling rather stupid.

After what seemed an eternity of scratching at my palpitating petrified hole in the hope of activating my brain into a plan; the lights of an approaching car gave me the idea to stand in the middle of the road and flag it down. That nearly got me killed, and the extremely frightened white bloke and his female companion, were in a right state when they stopped the speeding car.

"Bloody hell man, I nearly wiped you out!"

Flashing my Police card,

"Would you be so kind as to go to Gwelo police station and inform PO Swindells that I am stuck here and to bring some petrol."

The kind man agreed and Jeff duly turned up – three hours later! I was in bits. What the F? I was gagging with thirst, half frightened to death, with an illegally procured piece of government transport, and he thought it was funny!

"Sorry about the delay, but we were called out on some misdemeanour."

"Great, did you bring some petrol?"

He had, and I followed him back to the charge office. After an hour's chat, I bedded down in his room for a couple of hours till he woke me at 4.30am. I had to get back before anyone missed me. I also need more juice, which wasn't a problem, as Jeff simply let me into the compound where they had their own pump, and filled up, noting down in the log my Landy number. I hoped that no one would work out that the number was of a vehicle from Gokwe that had no reason to be there.

Almost at the halfway point between Gwelo and Que Que, the Salisbury – Bulawayo train line crossed the road at a place called Hunters Road Crossing. There were no booms or other forms of safeguard; drivers were expected to slow down and have a good look before proceeding. I didn't have time for the nonsense, besides, there couldn't be that many trains going up and down at this time. To be on the safe side I switched my headlights off. This neat trick would make it possible to see any high powered beam emitting from the train engine. There was none, so with the Landy going flat out, I approached in safety.

Sadly for me I had neglected to take into account a row of trees that grew along the track that effectively blocked any light from the oncoming goods train that was about to meet me in the middle of the crossing. I hit the brakes, but there was no way over a ton and half of steel reinforced Landy was going to stop in time. Oh, it would stop alright, when I ploughed into the thing. In a fraction of a second I lifted my foot off the brake and shoved it flat onto the accelerator again and went for it. How close it was, I am not sure, I wasn't exactly looking out the side window for a good view of the grim reaper approaching. As the train rumbled past me, I pulled up, jumped out and threw-up all over the road. I was shaking almost uncontrollably. Eish, I was pushing my guardian angel a heck of a lot recently…In fact, that guardian angel was going to have to work some serious overtime in the next five months…

Gwelo police station, a large two story colonial style building, was a throbbing hub. Upstairs was the rural section, along with the offices of various top dogs. Downstairs was the charge office and another couple of offices for smaller top dogs, such as Brian. We had been on first names within a couple of weeks after bumping into him at the Fairmile Motel bar, and had a nice chat. Just as well, because within three weeks he had called me in with bad news.

"Karl, I have to send more of you POs out on PATU patrol. I need one more. You up to it?"

Like hell I was. I put on another Oscar winning performance, clutching at my heart, staggering around, bleating pitifully how I had spent fifteen months fighting gooks in Gokwe 24/7 and needed a bit of a rest – preferably on top of a nice sweet girl. Brian understood and he let me off. Look, it wasn't that I was frightened of being terminated by terrs; I just hated the walking around whilst carrying heavy packs, sleeping in thin sleeping bags on rocky ground, and all the bullshit involved. I was skint as usual, but to hell with the extra money this time. Eish, fifteen minutes later, Jeff comes into the Charge Office and pulls me aside.

"Karl, you know I just got back from a four week stint?"

I acknowledged this fact, but I had a bad feeling about what was coming next.

"Hayes wants to send me out again, man. Yususs, I got a honey and hardly seen her, man. Will you take my place?"

And now? He was my friend, but better him go and chase gooks instead of me, so I gave another bullshit speech about Gokwe etc, etc, and the poor miserable bugger went off. I did feel bad for a while, especially since he landed up in the police box for two weeks…

Jeff was no stranger to the box. He had spent a week in it for 'borrowing' petrol. Petrol was now a big problem. None of us had much. I was allocated exactly five units a month, just like the rest of us. You either got a lift back to the mess, or walked. Brian couldn't cough up any extra and occasionally we could get a 'going home' allowance, which was a pittance. We were effectively trapped in Gwelo! Jeff needed juice to see his chick and drive about. He foolishly would drive his bright blue Mini Estate car into the police compound whilst on night shift and fill up whilst booking it down to a police vehicle. After a couple of these trips, he was snitched on.

Now, he was back in the box again. Being rather hacked off with having to go out gook culling once again, he had been dropped off with his stick in the bush and promptly told his black members to go chill in some kraal, see you in a week, and with his side kick Sloane, returned back to Gwelo and sent false location reports via his radio from his girlfriend's bedroom, where he was holed up. Rather daft, but even dafter when he was spotted driving around in his unmistakable Mini. The BSAP hit him hard for that. His transfer request to Gwelo Rural was refused, promotion chances set back a year, and along with two weeks in the box, a very short haircut, two weeks pay lost and a fine.

Was it my fault? I dunno… Sloane wouldn't have gotten such a harsh treatment, for Jeff had been stick leader, but he landed up in more shit after his return. He threw his kit onto his bed and went for lunch and when he returned – his FN had been stolen! We single POs had a good idea that it must have been one of the dozens of reservists that always wandered in and out using our pad as some makeshift hotel. They were becoming a serious pain, always moaning about our parties, loud music and scantily clad girls.

After one particular weekend bash, about thirty of us were mustered into Inspector Strict's office after a particular complaint from a load of wasting reservists kicking up that they couldn't sleep on Saturday night. Amazingly, we were informed that as from henceforth, we were no longer allowed girls visiting us in OUR quarters. The lunatic was definitely deranged. We paid rent and loads of dosh for the privilege of eating our German matron's dodgy food, and he is telling us how we spend our time off in OUR pad!

"One reservist complained that 11 o'clock on Saturday night he had gone to the toilet for a wazz and the door was unlocked and a young girl was in it half naked; giving him a shock. All this must cease!"

"What he do, knock her off the toilet with his hard on?" Jeff shouted.

We were crammed like sardines into his office, and immediately a riot broke out with everyone shouting. Insp. Strict stood there flabbergasted as we went mental, and then one loud voice –

"I'm not putting up with this shit; you will have my resignation on your desk in fifteen minutes."

That started a chain reaction –

"And mine."

"And mine."

And so on till all of us threatened to resign. Okay, we knew it wasn't as easy as that, but it left Insp. Strict in a right pickle explaining to the top dogs upstairs that the entire single POs of Gwelo (we would have got the rest to join *no problemo*), had quit en masse. I was so excited with all this I wanted to shout '*Vive La Revolution*', but wasn't sure how to pronounce it.

Stuttering a bit, and also rather red faced,

"Okay, er, just try and keep your parties a little quieter after 10 pm. Dismissed."

And that was that, and we carried on as before...don't mess with the boys from the BSAP!

But I was getting rapidly bored. Charge Office did relatively little. Whilst Gwelo City had a population of about 50,000, they seemed rather well behaved. I am sure that Rural upstairs had plenty of Gokwe type crimes to work on, but in the Charge Office – boring, boring and boring. Most things were petty. You soon learnt not to write anything down till you heard the whole story, sorted it out and wrapped it up *asap* without plunging yourself into daft crime report forms.

I just don't get it. Why were we sent to places that we didn't know? Okay, places like Gokwe wouldn't exactly have any home grown whites, but the distribution didn't make sense. I knew no one in Gwelo. Gwelo boys should be here, not people from Salisbury or Bulawayo. I mean, think about it. You're brought up in an area, know the people and presumably, come any trouble, they wouldn't hesitate to talk to you rather than a complete stranger. It was worse for the farmers in the bush. Why were they sent as reservists to completely strange areas? It made no sense. Farmer's boys who joined the BSAP, should have been patrolling the districts that they knew backwards…I dunno, it just seemed a waste of potential.

By the end of two months I was extremely frustrated. Gwelo had a disco once a week on Saturday night at the Midlands Hotel, situated a short walk away from the cop shop, and there was a rather small mangy cinema on Main Street. The same street also had the usual assortment of shops and that was that! No one went out to local dams fishing or picnicking. Firstly, because we had no petrol and secondly, you could get shot up. There was a drive-in cinema on the outskirts but I only bothered once. I had got a blind date with the daughter of a reservist I had met in Gokwe. He wasn't impressed with the idea, but agreed after I explained Keith would be coming as well with his girlfriend and that we would be armed to the teeth. The whole evening was a joke. There was maybe only twenty other cars and all spent the first ten minutes of the movie juggling their vehicles into the 'middle'. The idea of that was if the place got revved, the outside cars would get blasted first. Since I couldn't drop the seats back, because of the two in the back, it was a very poor passion wagon indeed.

I knew I was stuck for a minimum of a year in the Charge Office before I could apply for another transfer. I half heartedly applied to the CID, but you usually needed two years behind you before even being considered. I am still not sure what triggered the thought of getting out of the BSAP was. Perhaps an accumulation of several factors or simply; I just couldn't be arsed anymore. So I decided to make a plan to get out after exactly two years…

CHAPTER 35:

The Beastie Boys say – (You gotta) Fight For Your Right (To Party)

By the middle of 1978, Rhodesia had its back against the wall. Where was the so called 'Rhodesian way of life' we were fighting for? It was certainly not in Gwelo, or anywhere else come to think of it. And - what the hell was the Rhodesian way of life? Drinking and dying had replaced drinking and, er, go fishing? I wasn't doing any more of that either. Not being able to get up to Salisbury very often and having no spare fuel coupons, going up to Inyanga with step-mom was impossible. The costs and the difficulty of maintaining the cottage became too much; and she reluctantly sold the place. Even that was a huge problem. Property prices, especially in so called 'hot zones' were depreciating rapidly. In the end she shifted it for a paltry $4000 – the buyer was the oil conglomerate

Shell - as a getaway cottage for management. Four grand for 1.6 hectares, and a fully kitted-out three bedroom cottage…*Eish*! Smart bastards, they got it for zit - knowing full well, that come the revolution, they would still be there.

It seemed that everyone was on some weird trip. The only thing that superficially appears to unite us Rhodesians was a hatred of gooks, but that wasn't enough basis for any solid friendships. You had to make do with the company you were thrown into, whether you liked it or not. But things were going seriously tits-up and the government continued pumping out messages of imminent solutions to a terminal sickness – the death of white ruled Rhodesia. It was the dying that was a bit of a bummer. Especially when slowly, but surely, like a leaky tap - drip, drip, drip - news of school colleagues going moggy or giving up the ghost, came through the grapevine.

One that had been with me in Mount Pleasant High had been blasted to smithereens whilst attempting to defuse a gook anti-personnel mine. It was said they just found ragged bits of him dangling from trees. Another mate from school had lost the plot after a heavy drinking session and shot-up his own police station. Luckily he only riddled the outside walls with holes, but that got him a couple of weeks in the box. Even more crazy, a former class mate from Alan Wilson High had been with a group of inebriated lads on R&R, and had fallen out the back of a car whilst horsing around on Second Street in Salisbury. He scattered his brains all over the tarmac.

Some could handle the trauma, others couldn't. One night I took out for dinner a pretty girl that was a Woman Patrol Officer in Gwelo. I knew the story of what happened to her previous boyfriend, but hearing the story from her own lips, in a sort of impassionate - almost abstractly detached reciting, was harrowing. He had been on a PATU patrol and been in a contact. Gooks died. He was observed standing over a victim and saying,

"I wonder how his mother must feel when she finds out."

This is not good. His stick leader reported the incident. But, it wasn't like we had an in-house head-shrink or psycho-crisis trauma unit. You either took it or lost it…and he took the latter choice. After his debriefing he went to this young girl's home, still fully tooled-up and in camo. Whilst in her bedroom, he had asked for her hand in marriage. Crazy, they had only been dating a short time, but, hell, life was fast hey! To try and buy time, she had said, something like,

"Oh, stop being silly, I will make you a cup of tea."

She then told me, between servings of fine food and dodgy wine, that as she walked down the corridor towards the kitchen, she heard the unmistakable sound of a FN being cocked. Guessing instinctively, she turned, ran back and as she entered the room, he pulled the trigger. The barrel end was in his mouth. He painted her bedroom ceiling and walls red and grey. Just like that. He was only nineteen.

One lad in our singles mess, Tony, a seriously amusing and popular lad, had started to go to pieces. Whilst on patrol, he had seen in the distance a person that looked like they were carrying a weapon. As his stick advanced, the fleeting figure took off, and after firing three warning rounds into the air and hollering 'STOP' he took a shot that downed the person. It turned out to be a peasant woman with a hoe. She was dead.

Of course, there is more. All of us knew someone that had died…or…taken the gap. Which, I had now decided, I would do. I calculated to leave after two years of service. Since that meant I had served six months longer than the obligatory national service, I was comfortable in my own skin about that. But I still had another year left of my contract, and judging from Scummy's attempt to get out all that long, long time ago, the excuse of -'I can't be arsed' - had no chance of being accepted. Also, I wasn't going to have **'DESERTED'** after my name in the BSAP nominal role. Not quite the best path if you want to sell a memoir! As I considered myself an expert on fraud after the chase and capture of Raymond, I reckon a little fraud would be ideal to get me on a one way ticket out of *Rhodesia Was Super*.

I fired off a letter to my mother in Manchester. I needed her to pop down to her local GP and do some drama queen antics of terrible depression and anxiety due to the fact her son was being brutally murdered on a daily basis by terrible gooks. I also needed a letter from her pleading with me to come home as she could no longer handle the stress of facing my imminent departure from this world. When they duly arrived I submitted my resignation, 'By Purchase', based on compassionate grounds, and submitted my bullshit. Timing was essential. Under two years it cost 250 bucks, but after two; it was a minor detail of fifty dollars.

The next phase could be a little tricky, but my Boy Scout experience came to play and I was well prepared when I was called in for an interview with the upstairs Superintendent. It was his job to persuade me to stay and continue the good fight. I had noticed that he wasn't exactly going out into the bush a lot slotting gooks. After listening to his blah-blah, I simply thought of my dead beloved pet alsatian and turned the taps on (discreetly mind you, didn't want to over do it) - and had my application approved...tee-hee. When Inspector Strict heard the news, he pulled me over for a quiet word.

"Greenberg, I reckon your application is a load of crap."

I just replied, "Prove It."

I still had almost three months of twiddling my thumbs till departure day. The plan was to liquidate my assets of a car and my beloved Precious, and pay off debts of...a car and a rather expensive watch I had bought on hire purchase whilst bored on a trip to Salisbury. Since I was due to get my entire pension back of almost two grand, I figured I should have enough readies when I took flight. For the time being; I just needed to keep my head low, nose clean, and try to stay alive. But first, I was to have a birthday party. Yup, I am turning 20 - so you must have party. Yeah, a party – the surreal Rhodesian way of life.

Now, its six months almost exactly, since I opened beer bottles from a dead man's spread legs for Christmas and exactly a year after I saw my first hanging for my last birthday. Hopefully this time it would be a pleasant experience...Rhodesia is, *still* after all, hey - Super...

It is the longest night of 1978, and I am having a party. I am on the way out of here, two and half months to go, so it was bit of an early farewell party. So, on Friday the day after my birthday, it was planned and all and sundry to be invited. That basically meant any acquaintance met in the last two and a half months - mostly the police single guys with or with out chicks. I organised half a dozen crates of beer to be chilling on the balcony. I didn't need a coffin this time. It was plenty cold enough at night at the height of a Midland's winter, sometimes down to 0 Celsius by three in the morning. That necessitated the uniform of heavy long trousers, the stifling wool jacket and tie, for night shift, but as I was on the afternoon shift, summer tunic was still warm enough. I would be knocking off at seven pm - so perfect timing.

Five minutes. That's all. Five minutes before I finished my shift and return to the mess to await my guests, when Inspector Strict storms in. He was another of those authority figures that didn't number on my Facebook friends, especially now he thought I was pulling a fast one. He demanded that all available man power was to be commandeered for a search and seek operation at one of the township's beer halls. That, above my loud protests, included me! I managed to make a quick call to the mess and told Jeff to kick start the party without me. I was bloody fuming.

The briefing went as follows: Special Branch possessed information regarding a possible meeting of known terrorists in a certain beer hall. The huge fenced complex, accommodating at least a thousand black, weekend start, freshly paid revellers, would be surrounded by a unit called in from the School of Infantry. They had strict orders to shoot only outwards, as we would be going into the complex and may only shoot ...inwards! Hah-hah; how is my sodding luck?

I took a 9mm pistol and an extra magazine out the gun safe. We had no bullet proof jackets and I knew I would be freezing in my summer khaki tunic and shorts. The sun was well gone and the winter chill moved in fast. My job was to flush out any one hiding in the out-buildings under the concrete tables or benches. Special Branch would gather the clientele in rows onto the beaten earth clearing used as a 'beer garden', and then one by one check their Stupas. Should an 'incident' occur, don't forget - do not to shoot in the direction of the perimeter fence. I was furious, how long this shit gonna take? Even if we machined gunned all in sight, I couldn't see us back before ten. What a pisser!

The drinkers and the whores reacted the same way, but it was still early, and there was no sign of a drink fuelled riot on our hands. Moaning a lot, they complied to leave their tables and drinks of Chibuku; and I started searching. Logic dictated that should there really be a bad man under a table, I might get more than the evenings planned alcohol poisoning, but more like a rather serious lead dosage, so as I peered under tables, seriously shit scared, I had the pistol cocked and ready.

No one was around, so I returned to the beer garden just as

the last irritated customers were being checked out. I observed that one man had been singled out and Special Branch were 'guiding' him towards the open back door of a riot proof Land rover.

I noticed how he broke from their grasp...

I noticed he ran back through the gates into the well lit beer garden, darting desperately around tables, still covered in half-drunk plastic containers of millet beer...

I noticed people shouting, as the fugitive headed towards the perimeter fence in the opposite direction of the entrance...

I noticed how the back lit figure climbed desperately over the mesh wire fence twice his height, and landed with a thump...

I noticed in the diffused light, twenty paces further, the shadowy figures of the School of Infantry boys, a mere twenty paces apart, in the tight enclave they had created...

I noticed more shouts as the target ran unhindered through the ring of men and suddenly - the sounds of two shots being fired in warning along with the millisecond flash of flame blasting upwards from a perpendicular held rifle, then...

I noticed the sounds following the horizontal flames seemed to lift the now very dark fleeing shadow, a little to one side, and then throw him violently down.

That was that. Next I can recall all the police involved, black and white are crammed in the Charge Office demanding explanations from Inspector Strict who was directly responsible for terminating someone's life. This was obvious by the blood soaked corpse lying in the back of a Landy - held together by his clothes.

I glanced at my appallingly expensive Swiss *RADO* watch that was over a month's salary, and already causing problems with repayments. I think it was half past ten, and Strict was attempting to debrief us with words of? No idea, why he ran or who he was etc. I just thought of my rapidly ending party, when a distraught African voice shouts above the babble,

"Sah! You have killed my brother; he is a member of the army, SAH!"

This is heavy, and this, IS, my brother! What has gone wrong now?

In the ensuing melee of shouts and counter shouts, I mentally switched off and walked as fast as I could back to the mess. A: To keep warm and B: I hoped the physical exertion would take away the horrors. Fuck this for a lark! I'm not made for this shit and I certainly didn't sign up for it.

I arrived totally breathless by eleven, to be greeted by about twenty odd teenagers and early twenties, in various forms of intoxication.

Loud greetings of 'Happy Birthday' and where have I been, and so on? I changed quickly into warm civvies, grabbed one of the meagre beers from the last crate, drank greedily of its bitter taste - just like life at that moment. I had no invited female there to attempt to copulate with, but what couples the balcony held were strewn over the hastily pulled mattresses from the three bedrooms opening onto the balcony, and the single men were fired up for trouble. In a way, I suppose the aggro that followed kept my brain occupied in the present, rather than what had transpired an hour ago. I didn't need to worry, because I had hardly knocked back the first bottle when -

"I have heard that someone here that is on Number One shift, recently arrested a young black girl, took her to the cells, forced her to expose her breasts and then had a wank. And that person is Irish!"

We had only two 'Irishmen' living in the single's mess. One of them was making the accusations, the one nicknamed 'Irish' (as we already had a 'Paddy') and who was a relatively new addition to the Gwelo BSAP. And in pure *pikey* class of intoxicated jealousy, announced this as loud as possible, whilst 'Paddy' snogged some chick on one of the mattresses.

I was surprised by Paddy's reaction. I didn't think he was a violent type but something snapped, plus, what the hell, I had seen plenty madness tonight - why not some more? In the ensuing shocked silence, as all eyes swivelled to Paddy, who had been quietly engrossed seducing a willing prospective mate - and he reacted as a mad man.

A bespectacled intellect, my senior in age, and education, he launched himself off the bed, and grabbing a bottle by the neck, went for 'Irish', who was grinning in self satisfaction that at last he could 'have it out' with a compatriot!

"You fucking Irish peasant," was about all Paddy could scream, before I dived on him.

There were bottles smashing everywhere, Thomas, our German mechanic, with a couple of others, held Irish back, as he lunged forward for the battle, also bottle in hand. Girls screamed - the party was exploding in mayhem, shouts from below, as reservists tried to sleep on the lounge floor before being shipped out to the bush.

The party was over, clean up tomorrow. Both wasted souls, still roaring death threats at each other, were escorted to bed, the chicks split as did all the rest...Happy Birthday me!

Memoir mutterings

Oh, I almost forgot. Turns out the poor man who was shot to shit on my birthday had a twist of 'Dagga' (hash) in his shoe. He had most probably panicked at the thought of being caught with the stuff and then be kicked out of the army...

Glossary

Pikey. Is a pejorative slang term used mainly in the United Kingdom to refer to Irish Travellers, gypsies or people of low social class. (Wikipedia)

CHAPTER 36:

A gook in a kia, backing a winner, and a mad German

Well, I suppose I didn't exactly sit on my professional arse all day or night awaiting imminent release from Rhodesian paradise – so, depending what shift you were on; occasionally things did wake me up from a comatose idiocy from the near perpetual crimeless society - with a touch of gook sauce. Sometimes my brain cells would be invigorated by nonsense...

Dring- dring, dring-dring -
"Gwelo Charge Office, PO Greenberg (yawn) speaking, how may I help."
"Oh, hi, good evening, I have just had a strange phone call and an African voice had told me to watch out because I have a gook right at this moment in my maid's kia."
This sounded a bit odd, but I took his address down and promised to be there in fifteen minutes. Grabbing the two largest constables falling asleep over some desks (I ignored the one with the insane dog that just wanted to rip us whiteys apart), I trundled off on what I predicted would be another boring lemon. Meeting the complainant, we surrounded the kia, and after I banged on the tin door,
"Here are the Police, open up immediately," I stood to the side just in case there really was a gook in there and he may let rip with an AK.
Instead, the suspect jumped out the back window straight into the arms of the complainant. As my constables bundled the semi-dressed, silent figure into the Landrover, the complainant said something very strange.
"Listen, something is queer here. As the bloke was speaking to me on the phone, I distinctly heard a radio crackle in the background, and someone say 'Yes, this is the guardhouse, over.' "
I assured the man I would get to the bottom of it and off we went back to the police station. After about five minutes, the

suspect suddenly chirped up,

"Ah, Sah, I am a Special Branch policeman stationed here in Gwelo. I have my ID and think I know who phoned."

I pulled up. "Start talking."

"Well Sah, ahh, you see, that lady is my girlfriend, but there was another one after her and he wants to cause trouble."

Well, this was nothing new. In Gokwe even the rabbits were considered sexually conservative compared to the locals. Eish, the way I see it; only a Sony Play station game of rabbiting would keep them so occupied as to stop them procreating for hand outs in the near future from the UN. After inspecting his ID, I asked whom he thought it was.

"Sah, I believe he is a soldier working at the School of Infantry. Please Sah, please do not report this, as I will be in big trouble."

He didn't need to worry. BSAP protect their own, especially from the dickheads of the School of Infantry and the Rhodesian Air Force stationed just down the drag in Thornhill. It didn't matter if we were white or black; there was no love between us because we all fought over the same respective treasure – women. In the war we expected and nearly always got each others support. Best of chinas, thanks lads, but come weekend free time and R&R it was war (again).

I dropped 'my new best friend' off outside his quarters, assured him he would not be reported, and decided to go after the shit-head who had tried to land one of us in trouble. Like - it could have gone really pear shaped and I could have landed up planting the bugger because of this love rivalry. As I drove the ten minutes to the entrance to the School of Infantry, I pondered my move. I had not a lot to go on, but, I would try a bluff.

I rocked up at the guard house and wandered in with my two constables. A black soldier in camo with fancy School of Inf badges attached to his shirt looked rather surprised at my entry, and went into the body language mode I could recognise so well by now – me know nothing. That made him guilty as hell.

After introducing myself, I asked,

"Did anyone in this guardhouse make a phone call to the outside about an hour ago?"

"No and why you want to know?"

Eish! How stupid was the bugger. The answer made him

number one suspect.

But, before I could reply, two black fellows behind him started to crow big time.

"He lying Sah, we heard him make the call." This came from what must have been the School of Infantry's version of the misdemeanour box. Well, it was more like a cage with some beds in it, but the occupants were more than delighted to make sure 'clever-clever' was going to get well dropped in the shit.

"I see, and please tell me what you heard?"

Stupidly, the oh so clever-clever in charge of the entrance to the Rhodesian School of Infantry, attempts to be now super clever-clever with me. Such a sad man. He then recklessly, with absolutely no idea that he is dealing with the famous Gokwe Kid, impertinently tries to *diss* me – the tosser.

"You have no right to talk to the prisoners, I demand you leave now. You have no rights here at the School of Infantry."

Yawn... no rights hey! Try this for rights – with just a snap of my fingers, the cheeky tosser was pounced on by my delighted constables, handcuffed, and chucked into the back of my Landrover. The charge - being a cheeky clever-clever. Up yours School of Inf - arrogant bunch of wasters; all of them. Still, I couldn't exactly bugger off and leave the entrance to Rhodesia's prestigious officer training school with no one at the gate. I could get into some bother for that. I chatted with the two 'prisoners'. Obviously the tosser in my Landrover wasn't exactly their best friend but I garnered through there delightful chirping that I had the right man. I looked around and spotted the white night duty officer roster and rang the number.

Some rather startled bloke arrived half dressed, apologising for the delay. I didn't have to call any one from the School of Inf or the Rhodesian Airforce, 'Sir', unless they were ranked Captain or above. This bloke was just a recruit and called me Sir! Still, I must admit, I was pretty cool in my abilities by now - although my hairstyle was still rather Justin Bieber. I explained the situation. What I needed was this bloke to take over because I couldn't be arsed with all the paperwork. He enthusiastically agreed. As I released tosser, I set the fear of hell into him,

"Listen, my friend, you phone once more, or give my lad any more problems, I will make sure you sit a long time in our cells."

The bloke was crapping himself now. I took the white recruit aside,

"Listen, just blast him out a bit, and let him back on his job. But tell him if I hear he gives the two prisoners any stick…I will be back."

So, that was another exciting night. (I phoned the complainant and had explained what happened and assured him it was all sorted.) My constables were roaring with laughter over the whole episode. They really thought I was the dog's bollocks. It wasn't just my reputation about the arrest of Raymond; it was something more important – horse racing. On another boring afternoon shift, I had watched all our black staff fill in the ten cents bet on accumulative winner's forms. The *Rhodesia Herald* always had some smiling blackman on the back page who had won thousands for just twenty or thirty cents. (Lucky swine.) I knew the odds were appalling, but it was that Saturday when the Schweppes Gold Cup was running in Borrowdale, Salisbury, that gave me a short lived reputation. I looked at the name of the horses and recognised one. I knew this nag. A tiny grey I had once backed on an afternoon out at the races with Victoria. I announced to all and sundry that I was going to the betting shop on Main Street and I was putting two dollars on the small grey mare. I got 8-1 and walked home half an hour later with sixteen bucks (less tax) - a half dozen Cokes and steak burgers for all. After that, I was inundated with requests for winners, but sadly that died along with my lack of success two weeks later…

Of all the weird, wonderful and wankers I met in the BSAP, the funniest, and downright craziest, was Thomas Lenzen. I don't think his name is for real and even using the BSAP nominal roll, I cannot trace him. Any combination of his surname, and the address he gave me that I noted in my little police notebook, is definitely dodgy. Facebook nor Google can find this crazy German. Main Strasse 2 or 8, Saarbrucken. Mmm…

Gwelo had attained city status in 1971, presumably after they installed a second set of traffic lights. Perched on the main communications link between Salisbury and Bulawayo, it was an important industrial centre but, if you didn't need petrol whilst on the way to anywhere else, you didn't bother to stop.

Ah, but you can't forget those Saturday nights in the disco. Situated almost bang in the centre of Gwelo, the Midlands Hotel disco was the scene to be seen. Come to think of it, it was the

ONLY joint in that tiny 'city' to hang out in. It was a melting pot for Rhodie macho aggression. We, the BSAP boys were always there if we weren't on duty, or in the bush. Then there were the recruit 'Blue Jobs' from Thornhill Aerodrome, training to be pilots. Finally, there was always some budding new army officer material from the Rhodesia School of Infantry. We all had one and the same goal for our free time - the local available women. We coppers had the home advantage and we abused it with glee.

The Charge Office was just around the corner from the hotel. If trouble started at the disco, we didn't need a cell phone to callout our pals on night shift for reinforcements. It took a mere 30 seconds of drunken meandering down the road to get them. The POs were all bored senseless anyway, and eagerly awaited the aggro call. Before you knew it, our 'Brothers in Arms' had the perpetrators locked up. The cheeky ones were given a hosing down in the back yard - to extinguish their flaming passions, you understand.

It was on one of these delightfully entertaining evenings, when I first saw our Thomas in action. Well, with the war depleting the viable stock of 'normal' youngsters to join the BSAP, they were recruiting all sorts by now. 'Irish' was also very dodgy about his background, but if he could pick up an FN and speak some English, that was good enough. Thomas never had to pick-up either a weapon nor much English for that matter. I have to explain a bit about Thomas. He was a totally unknown element who had sent a shock wave through the single men's mess in Gwelo. For a start, he was slim, darkish skinned, rock hard (er...I mean he was very strong), and at least a head taller than myself. At twenty eight he was almost the oldest member of our mess.

Surprisingly, for a fully qualified white policeman in Rhodesia, he hardly spoke any English. It seems our Thomas came from Düsseldorf, and was a highly qualified mechanic from Mercedes Benz. Even stranger was his sudden appearance here in Gwelo with the title Patrol Officer. He was never called up to play 'dodge the Commie bullets'. He never wore anything but greasy overalls. It was also strange that this occurred whilst our motor depot was on the verge of collapse because all home grown available police mechanics were out experimenting with lead poisoning tests on insurgents. In fact, by this time in 1978, if you had a rather strange past, enlisting with the Rhodesian forces was the next best thing to joining the French Foreign Legion. All were taken and no questions were asked so long as there wasn't an Interpol arrest warrant out on your head. Make your self at home. Rhodesia Is Super!

Anyway, on one particular night, the disco was heaving as usual. Flashing lights, girls flashing flesh, and lads flushed with pints. The Bee Gees are pounding away 'Staying Alive' from the banned film *Staying Alive*. (Hah-hah-hah, staying alive, hah-hah-hah. Yeah - great song, but staying alive was turning into a problem.) Thomas wandered in and sat down at our table. I don't deny that on that evening someone had previously been sitting in the chair but the occupant had not been part of our police group and, in any event, he had been long gone - at least the duration of a dance. Thomas sat in the vacated chair and signalled to one of the hard-pressed black waiters for a beer.

"Hey china, you're sitting in my chair." This drawled out comment came from a rather well built budding officer from the School of Infantry, who had now returned from wherever he had been.

"You hav name on chair? I see no name on chair for you," said Thomas, as he swivelled around and pretended to look at the back of the chair for a nameplate.

This looked really good to us. We eagerly awaited 'tuff nuts' reply. Poor bastard, he didn't know our Thomas.

"My chair! You get out of it, or there is going to be trouble," was the silly twat's next clever demand.

This was definitely getting better from our point of view. We drunkenly started arguing over who was to do the alcohol induced weave across the road to call for back up. Thomas pushed the chair back. He stood up and, almost matching the moaning officer recruit's height, said to that poor unsuspecting innocent,

"I giv you chair," and Thomas promptly snatched up the steel framed and wooden slatted chair, swung it over his head and, faster than a striking cobra, smashed it over the poor sap's skull, dropping him like a stone.

Bloody hell! This was pushing it a bit. Two of us got Thomas OUT very quick and one went off for back up. I comforted the poor sod on the floor, as he came around slowly. This was my very clever ploy so as not to get beaten to death by a load of mad drunk, very upset fellow nutters from the School of Infantry. You may find it useful to know that, in such a situation, when you shout authoritatively,

"I'm a qualified medic and this man needs space and air," it keeps you from having your head kicked in by the outraged well-pissed colleagues...

There was no doubt that Thomas was mega cool and was having a ball here. He would pull any stunt for a party ending in a shag. Let's face it, the Rhodie girls were short of men, And - this man was definitely exotic. We single coppers loved him. In fact, he and his newly found immigrant police 'pal' Irish, turned up to enhance our police force at almost the same time. Actually, Irish's real name was Paddy, but we already had one Paddy so, in our Rhodie way, we nicknamed him 'Irish'. Of course, there was nothing but aggro between Paddy, the intelligent intellectual, and the drunken uncouth Irish, especially after the event at my birthday party. Irish would happily raid the Gwelo single nurse's mess with Thomas every weekend, bouncing the accommodating bonnie lasses in the back of the police Landrover that Thomas always managed to acquire whenever he needed some wheels - like at every opportunity!

Thomas didn't give a shit about rank or protocol. He called no one 'Sir'. When asked his name from some authoritative figure, he shouted,

"I AM DA MAKANIC THOMAS!"

He could get away with it because he could fix a motor like a dream and was as sneaky as a Smeagel/Gollum. He had balls the size of coconuts, but even his chutzpah reached extraordinary heights one weekend...

One Friday afternoon, I went to the back compound behind the police station to see if Thomas had finally repaired our only going Yamaha 350cc motorbike that was coughing its guts up on one cylinder. It had recently made me die in embarrassment after I had to give up chasing a Renault 4 for jumping a red light, because the damn bike couldn't push more than a wind assisted 35 kmh down hill. Rolling out from under a Peugeot 404 that he was working on, Thomas laughed and asked,

"Wat you want?"

He confirmed what I expected to hear. Nothing had been done. There were no parts available. Then the police internal phone rang. Thomas's side of the conversation that followed consisted of a roar into the mouthpiece,

"THOMAS DA MEKANIC," followed by "WAT AH YOU? I FIX KARS, WHAT YOU WANT?"

Then there was a long pause

"NEIN, DA VIER NULL VIER, HE KAPUTT, GET PART NEXT WEEK. BYE BYE. AUF WIEDERSEHEN."

He hung up, looked at me with that mischievous grin, winked and showed me a motor part in his right hand and lowered his voice.

"I go Salisbury. I need car. I get de Big Boss 404. You kuming?"

I couldn't, I was on weekend shift.

It took someone with a lot of balls, or who was a total nerd, to report to his superior officer in the Salisbury Central Police Station next Monday morning, that it had been a relatively quiet weekend - except for a queer incident involving the car belonging to the Senior Assistant Commissioner of Gwelo, Pat McCulloch.

It appears our Thomas, seriously pissed-up, had caused another riot and had gotten himself into a mighty battle in the disco Club Tomorrow on Saturday night. Having no faithful backup, he did the smart thing. He did a runner. Salisbury's 'finest in khaki' came after him. It was Peugeot 404 against Peugeot 404. The police, whose drivers still doubled the clutch and put their arms out when turning, with flashing blue lights and yowling sirens, against Thomas, THE MAN, the West German Mercedes mechanic, who had been drunkenly driving cars, with or without their owner's permission, on no speed limit German Autobahns since he was six months old. Thomas, of course won easily in his 'borrowed car'. He got clean away but he left a trace - the car's registration number.

I was in the compound at about 11.00 a.m. on Monday, bitching once again to Thomas about the Yamaha motorbike, when the internal phone rang. Thomas's conversation with the Senior Assistant Commissioner of Police and the highest-ranking officer in the Midlands province went like this.

"THOMAS DA MEKANIC."

Pause.

"HUH?"

Pause.

"YOU KRAZY; AUTO KAPUTT; I TELL YOU ON FRIDAY I WAIT FOR PART; MAYBE WEDNESDAY ME

GET."

Long pause.

"NEIN, NOT POSSIBLE! AUTO KAPUTT, NO DRIVE. I NEED PART. AUF WIEDERSEHEN."

As he hung up, he winked at me, and pulled the car part out of his overalls.

CHAPTER 37:

The greatest Rhodesian wankers or the massacre of Allan Wilson and the Shangani Patrol revisited

Gwelo BSAP 15 - they were Men of Men (not)

Pic - Gokwe Kid

There are two kinds of wankers. Real wankers are the likes of Pockface and Beergut. Lesser wankers tend to be relatively nice people that do stupid things with sometimes disastrous results. I happily fit into the latter category. Some people are born wankers, some achieve wankness, and some have wankness thrust upon them. This was definitely the case with a certain Major Allan Wilson and the doomed Shangani Patrol. I quote Wikipedia –

The Shangani Patrol was a group of white Rhodesian pioneer police officers killed in battle on the Shangani River in Matabeleland in 1893. The incident achieved a lasting, prominent place in Rhodesian colonial history.

That's for bloody sure. It was crammed down our necks at Allan Wilson Technical High School. They even had some souvenirs, well scraps really, from this battle. These wankers had been chasing loads of gooks belonging to King Lobengula. As you can see, nothing has changed much – the gooks still moan about stolen land and such rubbish, but now they have AKs instead of spears to make their point.

Still, in 1893, these gooks caught Wilson and another 33 men and had a merry old time killing them. The story goes that they fought to the last bullet. That makes sense. The gooks said they kicked up a right ruckus and that they had died 'Men of Men'. It was claimed that as the last of them received an assegai or two, they burst into song and did a stirring rendition of 'God save the Queen.' However, since none of them survived and the gooks were not that clued up on 'Pioneer Hits of the Week', this can be regarded as foolish propaganda. History shows it was a bit of a Custer's Last Stand type scenario – in the wrong place at the wrong time, and "Fuck me, where DID all these very angry gooks suddenly come from?"

But, even now, all these years later the coolest dudes, the Rhodie machos, Men of Men, would occasionally let their guard down and woe betide those that achieved this title of incredible wankness, even for a short time. It is rare however, and here I misquote the great Winston Churchill,

'Never on the rugby field of human conflict was so much humiliation caused to so many by so few.'

Because what transpires in the following story had the entire BSAP force become the laughing stock of Gwelo…

The lads who occupied the singles mess in Gwelo were generally a great lot. All so different, and each with their own unique personality. They were like me - full of bullshit. One lunch time we had quite a full house in the dining room. Not only the urban and rural regular POs, but my recently added room mate, Peter Tannahill, turned up for a change. He was a National Service Patrol Officer, but being a very witty and smart individual he was accepted by the regulars. I had been to school with him at Mount Pleasant but as he was 'A' stream clever-clever and a 'Rugger bugger', I, as a gymnast lightie had been excluded from his 'Fellowship of the Ring Pieces'... Now we shared a room and amazingly we were like two dogs. After sniffing the qualifications, we were quite happy to wag tails. I rarely saw him as he had a really shite job. The poor bugger worked at the PATU training camp as Mad Mike Moore's sidekick.

So, Peter wanders in just as we all started eating. Whilst greeting all and sundry, he kept picking at the skin on his right palm.

"What's up with your hand?" one of the local wits, Tony, shouted out over the bantering babble.

Peter holds up a hand pitted with large holes from dried and burst blisters received from digging bunkers. Awed whistles all around,

"How the hell you get all of them?" asks Tony.

"Wanking too much," laughs Peter, along with the rest of the room.

Unfortunately, in a millisecond of thoughtlessness, Tony, having been the interrogator and had eyes still on him, lifted his own right hand instinctively to almost table height and glanced down at his open palm. Caught red handed, the roars of ridicule from the baying pack could be heard as far as the police station. Now that Tony had openly declared his qualifications to everyone's delight, conversation turned to the theme of the greatest debacle ever planned in the history of Rhodesian Rugby.

Mainly, these cowboys wanted to organise a Rugby 15 and take on the local area schools' first teams. There were enough ex-Rugger buggers to make up a full squad and plans were well underway.

The first school the leader of this loony lot contacted had spoken to the headmaster. He had flatly refused to let them play against the first team. Our lads had at least 18 months to 2 years average age advantage and he didn't need his top team mauled by a bunch of desperados. However, he had reluctantly agreed to let our lot of brave lions maul his 2nd team. Our *conquistadores* were definitely fitter and stronger than these kids. They could each sink a crate of Castle every night if need be, whilst puffing on thirty Madison a day. They were gook killers, brilliant military strategists and most of all, they were - Men of Men.

There had been moans and groans and shouts of cowardice that went around, but the first game was on for the weekend. I wasn't much of a rugby fan then but agreed to come along to try out the second-hand camera I had purchased off some Christian freak that had a happy-clapper bookshop on Gwelo Main Street.

The magnificent 15 had had a short training session in the

police pub and it was really just a matter of sorting out the small details, such as who brought the crate of beers for half time. Down at the quartermaster's store they had managed to get some blue police rugby shirts from bygone days of fame. Socks and shorts at each player's discretion. Rugby boots an optional extra.

On that fateful day, I had by now managed to load a film into the Russian made camera I had bought off the American loony in the bible bashing shop. The first attempt had cost a disastrous fortune when I was informed, when picking the pictures up, that, sorry it appears the film has not been exposed. You idiots developed an empty film?

My Zenith commie cam had come with some screw on telephoto lenses. Very impressive! What wasn't impressive was the very primitive light meter, along with the fact the exposure settings had rubbed off. As a result, in the end I shot one film and sold the camera to some poor sap for a loss, as usual, prior to leaving the police.

Now as the official photographer/reporter for the BSAP magnificent 15, it was intended that I write and send pictures to the police rag-mag, *The Outpost* along with suitable tales of glory and an educational hammering coming to the youth of Gwelo. Before I could select a suitable lens for the dramatic opening, the whistle blew and the sneaky young bastards had scored a try before our fly-half had put his fag out! The few bribed supporters we had dutifully sighed, and clasped their hands together. They were to keep them that way for an agonisingly long time.

If you have a dog or know some one well that has one, try to think of a huge Rhodesian Ridgeback, soaking wet and stinking before the fire. It starts to bite itself with that lip curl over the teeth that reminds you of the film Aliens. As it snuffles frantically up and down its steaming fur, you, with your 15th Castle lager of the day in your hand, and stupidly watching the dog's contortions with growing amazement for 40 minutes, think;

'If he is such a clever dog, as every idiot says to him, how come he can't catch the fleas?'

THAT is exactly what I thought of the BSAP 15.

It was awful to watch. Like hordes of Matabele gook warriors, the school kids totally overwhelmed our brave, gallant, wheezing, cramp riddled wankers. No chance of one on one mortal combat as the swift and expertly trained squad worked together like marauding Impis to hamper the efforts of the booze-cruise professionals. I have the rudimentary idea of rugby tactics, but I had never seen Shaka Zulu's *Buffalo Horns* military strategy used on a rugby field. God help the BSAP. At times it seemed that our trapped men were being illegally outnumbered. It was an optical illusion. They were only fifteen, but they were all standing, whilst half of our squad seemed to be gasping on the ground, gobbing out tar stained phlegm from heaving lungs.

Few of our team were interested in a beer at half time. By now the blue police rugby shirts stunk like a stale brewery and fags were passed around with shaking hands. Puffs were interspersed with doubled up dry retching, as the accumulated lactic acid in the tortured muscles wracked their bodies in spasms of pain. I have seen deep sea divers suffering from the bends look happier.

The second half just got silly. These kids took the piss now and danced around the magnanimous, but zombie look-alikes of the fighting police 15, as try after try went over. I felt ill. What a waste of money on the crate of beer. For the first time since joining I understood what the British South Africa Police insignia of a lion with an assegai shoved deep into its pulsating heart stood for.

None of our Men of Men had garters and as the socks slid down, the playing field became littered with their combs. I lifted my eyes up into the clear blue skies - not to look for any divine assistance - but to see if the vultures were gathering. In fact, they had landed long time ago, and taken up residence in the unused opponent's half of the rugby field. They patiently waited for the final whistle, when they would pick the corpses down to their stupid bones.

The score board was a primitive affair with just HOME and VISITORS written in large white letters above two hooks for the numbered cards. The entrepreneurial youngster in charge, noticing that for the first time in the history of the school, the score could go to triple digits, had cleverly removed one of the hooks from the unused VISITORS and placed it in preparation under the HOME part.

At last, the final whistle went, and the lightly sweating youngsters took the trembling claws of our fallen warriors and thanked them for a spirited fight. It could have been worse and with a score of 56 to nil, it was a fair result – even if the ref was of Irish descent and would go on to shaft the Welsh in the 2011 World Cup – the bastard.

The debriefing lasted all week with the team members selfishly blaming each other. Some complained they had never even touched the ball. Others pointed out that they were the ones standing around scratching at their own balls instead of trying to catch the cheeky monkeys that did have the ball. Now there were still two schools to go and this time, the headmasters were phoning us and offering the first team! A girl's high school had asked if we had any wankers who played hockey. It seemed they need to hammer some big lads as prior training before some of them go off to win the Olympic Gold in Moscow two years later. Some of our squad were cowards and immediately applied for patrol duty in the terrorist riddled death trap of the Honde Valley, or an immediate transfer to Gokwe - rather than go through this humiliation again.

With more balls than brains, the revamped squad took on the next lot. Allan Wilson and the Shangani Patrol were Men of Men, we are Men of Men. This time the spectators had increased, as parents came out in force to see their sons kick some copper's ass, and get away with it. I flatly refused to take any more pictures than the one I had wasted at the previous game. Although still nursing severe stiffness, the mighty BSAP 15 went forth with heads high and hope in their stitched together hearts. The hammering this time was of such intensity, that any reasonable referee would have stopped the game out of pure human compassion. The score went over the 60s to nil. A grateful headmaster thanked our butchered upholders of the peace for the fine entertainment. His only regret was that he should have charged a spectator entrance fee and raised enough cash for a new school rugby academy.

The final match? I didn't witness; as even I couldn't bear the pain. I believe the score went something into the 70's to nil. I resorted to walking to the Charge Office for my shift wearing a large coat covering my uniform.

CHAPTER 38:

The Leopard and the Donkeys plus - Gooks! Run for your lives

men of men - the Gokwe Kid on his last patrol

Pic - Gokwe Kid

Well, I suppose it had to happen. I had done enough dodging and diving but with only six weeks left before jumping the sinking ship; I got roped in for another bush tour with PATU. I wasn't exactly thrilled about this. I wouldn't be sent to Gokwe, but to another Tribal Trust Land, bang in the middle of Rhodesia, surrounded by land thieving white commercial farmers. In other words, whilst it was only a fraction of the size of Gokwe, it was a very nice place for gooks to hang out whilst doing their thing – such as shooting-up land thieving white farmers *et al*. According to the rumours, this place had more gooks than ticks on a dirty troopie's scrotum.

Being sent into the bush, and figuring out who did more time out there than some others, became like toxic pus eating at our respect for each other as individuals. Idle bitter talk that so and so had managed to get another note from the doctor for gout, so he didn't have to go, would start the paranoia off again. Maybe some of the guys really did have gout or other ailments. But this paranoia ran deep in the psychology of us all.

The end is nigh – six weeks early – what a pisser, but this time I was tooled up something rotten. Gone were the days of sixty rounds in a box and a bright red rucksack. Over time, and after each patrol, I had systematically built up a nice little arsenal. If I bump into any gooks, they gonna see some serious fireworks. At Gwelo armoury I also managed to get myself a Model 32 Zulu rifle powered flying grenade and the necessary blank cartridge needed to fire it off the end of my flashguard. It would have been a rather costly mistake to have a live round up the spout instead. They also supplied me with a dodgy Mills grenade.

By now, things were getting really well out of hand, with more and more elderly police reservists filling positions vacated by young regular officers. It was known as the 'Chameleon job'. One minute you were in your smart, perfectly ironed khaki tunic and shorts with a peak hat, the next in dirty, smelly camouflage - playing at soldiers. It was 'drop all police work and get out shooting'. I even had my bank manager on my shift once, and I think the bastard knew I was leaving as he refused to up my credit limit. The call ups played havoc with the judicial system. Cases are just not paperwork. You carry the crime in your head - till its conclusion. Now off you have to go on sudden death duty, so you try to clear your desk and pass over all you know to whoever takes your place. I didn't really have much on my desk. I didn't have one! I just had a small pigeon hole with nothing in it.

First of all I had to spend another couple of nights on a refresher course with Mike Moore again. Whilst I had enormous respect for him as a thoroughly top professional in what he did – killing people, I wasn't that pleased to see him for now the fourth time. Not because I disliked him as a person, on the contrary, we were quite chatty with each other; but I hated being made to crawl like a leopard and run around in the cold and damp of the nights and climbing gomos in the mid-day sun.

I was introduced to the rest of my stick. Luckily there was one white PO with longer service than myself, so Martin Oostehuizen was designated as leader. That suited me fine. I didn't want any responsibilities at all. Our stick was surprisingly seven in all. There was another white PO on his first patrol (poor sod), and the last four were black police officers of various ages and rank. I garnered that they all had had quite a bit of experience chasing gooks. I just hoped that none of them were in the mood to garner some more. The fact that we were seven didn't bode well. So, after a bit of the old -'Gooks! Run for your lives,' we are duly considered fit and popped off to our designated slaughter houses.

Our completely fenced in base camp at Ngezi TTL - bordered on the east by the Wanezi range and the Featherstone farming area - was run by Internal Affairs under the command of a white man aged about 21 or 22. It was hard to tell exactly how old he was, as the bloke was a skinny shell and completely off his trolley. It was well known that these Intaf lads had it hard, with some of their camps regularly attacked at night. This poor bloke was constantly on the bottle, and his unpredictable mood swings made us all edgy - never mind the nights he spent screaming his head off in his sleep. The camp was rather busy with not just Intaf blokes doing guard duty, but also another stick made up entirely of old toppies of reservists, all in their early forties. Depending on circumstances, we rarely bumped into each other at camp as usually our days off didn't coincide. But they all seemed a nice cheerful lot, all married with kids of various ages.

Anyway, there we were, kilometres away from home comforts like birds and warm, soft beds (beer we had aplenty in camp), deep in the heart of the Rhodesian bush. The first couple of weeks were uneventful and followed the usual procedure. We would be dropped off somewhere and wander around looking for gooks. I must admit that Martin took his job rather seriously, which I was grateful for because this was a really hot area. There was none of this dossing around stuff, and night watch was strictly adhered to. One good point was that he was a great fan of doing OPs (Observation Points) which consisted of the others looking for hours through binoculars at the movement of local villagers, whilst I read books.

One night, with no moon to see by, and still icy cold from the hint of the passing winter, I was pretending to be, and getting literally quite clever now as 'acting' second in command of our seven man stick when - we had an incident. We had been observing a village for two days from a nearby hill, but due to a lack of any enemy activity, we decided to move on. It was pitch dark when we packed up from our OP. We proceeded to move to the next tactically brilliantly chosen hill to look at more kraal occupants going about their daily routine. I was starting to panic by now as I had no more books to read, plus we had another two nights to go before our well deserved one night's rest at base camp to watch Charlie's Angels. This broadcast was on a black and white TV powered by a diesel generator that caused the picture size to change as the power fluctuated, but who cared - I was in love with the one with the short black hair.

Martin decided that we should leave our OP in single file. Perfect for the enemy; not so good should we walk into an ambush. But at night there was little choice. I didn't care. So, there we were, a stumbling and a silent mumbling, through the savannah bush, about 7.30 pm, when to our great surprise, we came across a huge piece of bush cleared for the purposes of farming. This was bad news. How the hell were we to cross such a large open area without being used for target practice by some observant gook on night shift?

The solution, straight from our first class training in 'go out and die' tactics, was... take the long way around, using all available cover, with a scout ahead and one man up the rear peeping at regular intervals behind him in the vain hope of spotting any sneaky gooks slicking up. Whispering, stick leader Martin addressed his part-time second in command (me) - who immediately passed the buck on.

"What you think, we go around or try to cross?"

As far as I was concerned this was his attempt to blame any stupid decision on a majority vote should things go wrong and people died. This was African democracy, north of the great Zambezi at its finest. One Man - One Vote - Once. There was a brief concurrence with the other super trained PATU members, and the decision was made.

And…we all decided on the lazy option, balls to playing hot shots, we were tired and wanted to go 'doo doos'. Bed a stupid word. Reality was a thin sleeping bag on hard earth with some one waking you up for guard duty just as you succumbed to the pain of rocks crushing your spine as you slept fully clothed.

With the decision made, Martin's next brilliant advice –

"Keep your eyes well open."

The man must have been stark raving mad; we couldn't see jack-shit, and there was no cover for 200 knee trembling paces. So with that input ringing in our highly tuned ears, we started to cross.

In single file. Like the proverbial sitting ducks. I silently sent up a prayer to my guardian angel, who had kept me alive so far…only another two weeks to go.

You have to use a bit of imagination to visualise what happened next. Have you ever accidentally stepped on a cat's tail? Or heard the yowling when it's gagging for a shag and there is another Tom fighting for pole position? It's a god-awful din that comes straight from Hell. Now multiply that by ten, remember it was a dark, quiet night, and you have a sure fire recipe for instant loose bowels syndrome. It's a serious spine shuddering racket.

Without hesitation, our stick leader reacted with superior training insight and opened up with all that he had. In just two seconds he had emptied a 20 round magazine… at nothing. Well, that started us all off. This was the absolute fire-power trip - seven men shooting at god knows what or where - in *single file*. I was in third place in this mad line of instant chattering death. That I didn't suffer immediately from lead poisoning is a wonder as some of our members were a bit challenged when it came to targeting and shooting. It was utter chaos. Every third round in the magazine held a tracer projectile, which was clearly visible as it disappeared over the hills in the far distance. I thought this seemed a little excessive, as whatever the problem was, it seemed to be almost at our feet. I sensibly raked the ground in front of me, nearly turning Martin and the bloke next to him into instant cripples. The tracers looked really cool as they spouted the last bits of lit magnesium from some small anthill I'd just taken out.

And the gun smoke! With seven of us each emptying three magazines into the sky or the ground, and till now amazingly not in each other, what little visibility we had was now gone in a cloud of bittersweet cordite. Martin's screams of "Stop firing" gradually came to us during magazine changes, and the night again became quiet. Saying that, there was a hell of a buzzing noise in my ears, and I was coughing from the fumes.

"What the fuck was that?" The demonic squealing had now stopped.

"I think it was a pig," was the reply from someone inside the cordite cloud.

"Well, whatever it was, any terrorists in the vicinity must be fucking amazed at the major battle going on without them," was my cynical reply. Besides, even a pig being slaughtered was more into squealing 'oink-oink' rather than yowling like a pussy on a skewer.

"Everybody reload and move forward," ordered Martin.

We must have gone about three paces when the nerve torturing screams began again.

"Leopard!" someone screamed and the 'shoot em up' was repeated, but now stick leader was getting really carried away in the pre-funeral festivities by shooting off pencil flares. Balls of red phosphorus light shot into the sky, turning the landscape salmon pink; every bush and stone became a moving pale shadow, which was promptly shot to bits in our fear.

The adrenalin rush…dah dah dah dah,,, "Get that ya bastards,"….dah dah dah… "Yeah…die ya mother fuckers!"…

Load of tripe. It was… I'm gonna shit myself… go away scary thing… help! Run for your lives.

An unusual calm descended at last, as all of us realised that we were down to the last half magazine of ammunition each, and that we wouldn't survive a terrorist attack with what we had left.

"Pull back!" shouted Martin. This was the best idea I had heard all night.

"What about lobbing a few grenades to end our firework display in a grand finale?" I asked innocently.

So there we were - 100+ rounds of ammunition between seven of us, our backs to a large tree, rifles pointing out, and seriously kakking ourselves. Everything was quiet. After a few minutes, stick leader had recovered himself sufficiently to think straight again.

"I'll radio for evacuation first thing in the morning," he

informed us.

This was great news! We just had to hope that we didn't get a little visit from a group of freedom fighters in the meantime. I couldn't quite see our last stand being so romantically depicted in oil and hung on PATU Headquarter's 'Hall of Famous Idiots', next to Allan Stewart's painting of *The last stand of Major Allan Wilson*.

Ours would be titled, *The Gokwe Kid, last man standing*, complete with a blood stained air ticket hanging out of a breast pocket. I am firing away the last rounds using two FN,s, surrounded by my brave fallen comrades. The gooks are closing in on me; I am singing my swansong 'Rise O Voices of Rhodesia', and my guardian angel, riddled with bullets lies crash landed before my Bata trainers shod feet...

All bad things come to an end sometime. Dawn broke, and with chattering teeth we radioed for help. With the arrival of back up and a proper trained tracker, we went back to our 'contact' place to see if we could make any sense of the night's amazing events.

It turned out there *had* been a leopard; the spoor and its kill, a half eaten donkey, were evidence enough. Our tracks and piles of expended cartridges, sparkling with the morning's heavy dew, put its warning screams and its dinner about twenty paces from our fireworks display. Even with all the lead we shot off, we didn't hit it; there was no blood spoor at all of any wounded leopard gapping it. However, at the end of the field there was another donkey, tethered to a small stake. This one resembled a hairy red sieve. Very sad - donkey very dead! It was difficult to ascertain how many projectiles had pounded it into mincemeat inside a very leaky skin bag, but I am sure it had made a very swift trip to its maker.

The owner of this fragmented animal turned up at base camp that afternoon and started yowling as much as the leopard had. There was a 'Victim of Terrorism Relief Fund', and I suggested to the Intaf mad man in charge, to use it to obtain the $50 the owner was ranting for in compensation because of 'loss of wealth due to inappropriate action taken by the protectors of the realm'. There was no way I was chipping in my own money just because we had acted like a load of dumb-ass donkeys.

Back in base camp, with our nerves rather frazzled, we crossed paths with the PATU reservists who had just come in from a patrol that had produced some interesting results. A dead gook! I had only seen people shot dead that were on our side, so it was nice to see one biting the bullet from the other end of the war spectrum.

What had happened was that the three old toppies, along with four black reservists, had been diligently patrolling through the bush just after midday when they spotted a small group of gooks heading towards them. Quickly and silently they set themselves up into an ambush position, which basically meant hiding in a row in the bush with perhaps a few trees as cover. They had literally only seconds before the enemy would bump into them. Normally the plan was to wait until the group were along side before opening up, but they were spotted. Before the gooks could even think of the dilemma they were in, our lads hit the triggers. The leading terr went down instantly. Another seemed to have been hit in the leg, but along with two more, he high-tailed it pronto. The stick sent them on their way with several more fired magazines of hot lead. With no tracker, they did the smart thing and radioed in for support.

The follow-up found no sign of gooks and the blood spoor had stopped, presumably the recipient had managed to staunch the wound. They then all returned to camp with the body.

Well, how do you describe looking at your first dead, certified terrorist - CT, for short?

He didn't look very terrifying lying on the hard ground of our compound with the flies buzzing in and out of his blown apart skull. The FN round had entered just above his right eye. It came out taking a third of his skull with it. A bit of brains sort of still hung bloodied from his split head. He had been brought to the compound in the back of a truck after the contact, complete with weapons. The body had been almost stripped, checking for any papers which might have intelligence of their intentions past and present. His dark blue, filthy trousers lay in a heap next to his feet. Whilst still wearing what appeared to be some form of combat jacket of dirty green, this was spread open about him and above his chest. The left hand had the thumb missing. A passing shot had amputated it. His genitals were not exposed or disturbed. They were still hidden by green underpants with white ribbing around the legs and waist. Strangely, who ever unloaded him had put his corpse onto a large hessian sack, so he didn't lie directly on the ground.

I examined the weapons the gook had been carrying when he was taken out. One was a ten round SKS, a Soviet semi-automatic carbine, which used the same ammo as the AK. This one was most probably a Yugoslavian copy that the Mozambique government had been given and passed onto Mugabe's gooks. It had a rather evil looking integral folding bayonet which hinged down from the end of the barrel. The other weapon was a really nasty piece of work – a rocket-propelled grenade (RPG), which is shoulder-fired from a launcher. It is similar to and does pretty much the same job as a Bazooka. Judging from the area where the contact had taken place, it was reckoned that this was more than likely the same bunch that had attacked a convoy on the Salisbury to Fort Victoria road a couple of days before. They had fired a RPG rocket but had missed.

One of the old boys involved in the contact, Tom, told me the details. Tom must have been in his late forties, married with a couple of kids. He was a devout Mormon and neither drank alcohol or smoked. Nor would he even drink tea or coffee, claiming it was against his religion, but enjoyed cups of *Rooibos*, the popular South African redbush herbal tea.

The next day the body was unceremoniously dumped at the nearest kraal. The occupants could bury the lad. Yup, a lad. He couldn't have been older than seventeen. At the same time, a bit further on, our stick got dumped for what would be the last patrol I would ever do.

Martin, as usual had a plan. I just hoped it wasn't going to be another donkey type one. He was trying to work out where the remaining gooks might be heading or hanging about, and as such decided we would spend our last three nights doing another OP. I liked this idea of sitting on my arse reading my replenished book supply. What I wasn't so hot on was the gomo he chose for us to perch on. It was a massive outcrop of granite. After scrambling for almost two hours, we arrived at the top, but had to keep low so as not to have our silhouettes spotted. The view was magnificent and Martin had managed to get us a good position to observe a kraal, just under a click away, nestled at the foot of a small donga flowing from where two heavily vegetated gomos met.

I did of course take part in lying down in two hour shifts using binoculars to observe the coming and goings of the peasants as they went about their daily tasks. Very boring stuff. All conversation was in whispers, and all cooking and sleeping was done well away from the edge. On the last day, just before mid-day, we hit pay dirt…

The peasants were of course caught in the middle of this war. They were damned if they helped the gooks and damned if they didn't. We observed two armed gooks make their way into the kraal and disappear inside one of the huts. Martin decided to call up an air strike. I thought this was a much better idea than simply wandering down the hill and having a showdown. Plotting the exact location was easy. I had a weird instinct to convert rapidly all the swoops and swirls of map contours into tangible landscape, and along with Martin, nailed down the kraal's co-ordinates perfectly.

Now, because we were so high up, comms using the small VHF radio worked well. What didn't work so well was the time it took to get the request through. We waited and waited as we kept watch and saw how a peasant woman had gone into the hut a couple of times with what we guessed was food and water. Our nerves were in a high state of excitement and even I was warming to the hunt. But still the promised air strike hadn't arrived. And then, just as the radio finally crackled with the news that an aircraft was on its way, the gooks left the hut and headed west – to rapidly disappear into the bush. Martin was almost shrieking with frustration. Twenty minutes later the small Lynx (a Rheims-Cessna 337), a weird looking contraption with twin-engines in a push-pull configuration, appeared. Its engines were mounted in the nose and rear of its pod-style fuselage and twin booms extend aft of the wings to the vertical stabilizers. A twin barrelled .303 machine gun could be seen sticking out the side of an open side door as it buzzed overhead.

Using a separate frequency, Martin could talk to the pilot. There wasn't much to say. They were too late. Just for some limited effect, the Lynx strafed parts of the gomo west of the kraal, but it really was pretty hopeless, and after ten minutes the plane buggered off. What an anti-climax. There was absolutely no point in hanging around as it was obvious that our position was compromised and it was hardly likely that the gooks would return. Martin told us to pack-up. We were due to be picked up at a set rendezvous later in the day anyway. And then...we spotted the gooks again!

Incredibly, the direction we wanted to take down the gomo was in the same line of sight of the rapidly walking gooks. However, they were at least a click away. I cursed. Whilst not being a trained sniper, I understood the workings of wind and gravity on a projectile and had rapidly calculated the walking pace of the gooks. I reckoned with a good telescopic lens, I could have had a bloody good go at them. I told Martin I could still have a fair chance if he played at spotter with binoculars. The gooks wouldn't even hear the report of the rifle. He disagreed. Looking at the map he said,

"If they continue in the same direction, and we go down the gomo, here, pointing to a point at the bottom of the huge hill, we could intercept them about here."

I disagreed.

"Martin, the terrain down is steep and well thick with bush. It will take us almost an hour. They are in light scrub moving fast and they know we are around."

By this time the gooks were no longer visible, but we went down the gomo in hot pursuit. That none of us twisted an ankle or worse, was more down to luck, and at the bottom we rapidly fanned out into formation and started the sweep in the direction Martin was guessing we might bump into them. Crazy shit this, but all the training was paying off and we all cruised through the bush with itchy triggers, highly tuned senses and, to my surprise, I had a hard-on. For what seemed an age, but maybe only an hour, we came across a kraal and Martin ordered us to attack.

I wasn't quite sure what the hell we were supposed to attack, but he started to open fire. This was followed by the others firing away at the silent huts. There wasn't even a Kaffir dog around. I guess Martin was hoping that the gooks might have taken shelter in them, but I wasn't too keen on this idea. The rounds would go straight through the flimsy mud covered pole walls, and make a mess of anyone inside. What happens if there were only civilians in them? I fired into the straw roof tops and kept a wary eye out for any gooks that could, in rather minimal theory, break out and run for cover.

Even Martin must have realised that this was all very futile and after emptying a magazine he screamed for us to stop. The surrounding bush was silent. Even the cicadas were in shock. There was a wailing coming from one hut, and a lot of crackling noises from two others. It turned out that I had set them on fire with my tracer rounds.

" Check out the huts," Martin ordered, and I headed to the one with the wailing noise and kicked the door in with ease - to be confronted by an absolutely petrified old woman clutching a small child to her bosom.

"Baas, baas, please no shoot," she pleaded, as my eyes rapidly adjusted to the dark interior.

Thank the stars; none of our bullets had hit the two, which was remarkable judging from the streams of light pouring into the dark hovel from the holes our rounds had made as they were passing through.

"Police, police," she said, and dug from an old cardboard suitcase a coloured photograph of a young black police officer standing next to a police vehicle.

"My son. He my son – policeman"

Brilliant! I took the picture and went over to Martin. The others had cleared the remaining huts and found nothing. My adrenalin rush was wearing off rapidly and I felt ill, and very, very angry.

"Listen Martin," as I thrust the picture in front of him, "we nearly had a major fuck-up here. Her son is a sergeant in the BSAP."

"Find out where the rest of the villagers are and if she has seen any gooks." he replied.

I called over one of the black constables. The child hung to her grandmother crying uncontrollably. As he asked the trembling bag of rags, I searched the suitcase, finding wage slips and more evidence of her son's involvement on our side. I was horrified. If gooks ever found this stuff, she would be butchered on the spot, along with the infant, as a 'sell-out'.

"She say no Sah. She not seen any terrorists. The others of the kraal are in the fields."

Two huts were now burning rapidly to the ground.

"Okay, tell her, we are sorry. It is a big mistake (that's for bloody sure), and tell her to hide all this," I held out the papers and picture, "because they could get her killed." Oh the irony of it all!

I went back to Martin.

"Let's get to the meeting point – now! "

He agreed and three hours later we were back in camp. Tomorrow we were going back to Gwelo and I happily got utterly shit-faced and stupidly sold my fabulous rucksack to the screaming Intaf loon for ten bucks. I could get maybe five hundred pound for it on EBay now…aargh…

Eish, that was close. Guardian angel had pulled out all the stops this time. Before being dropped off back at the mess we were first all dumped at Mike Moore's office. He congratulated the old toppies on their kill. As I waited for my lift, I had a couple of photos taken with the lads. I also had a quick word with Mike Moore. I told him about the unstable bloke in charge of the camp. He knew about it but as the nutter was Intaf, it was out of his jurisdiction. I then told him I was out of here. He didn't seem surprised.

"Tell me Mike, what are you going to do when this all goes tits-up?"

We were totally alone. He didn't even pretend that we were winning the war.

"I suppose I will go to Israel."

"Another war? You never get enough of this all?" I asked.

"I am a soldier Karl, always was, always will be."

We shook hands and wished each other well. I had six days off followed by three days in the Charge Office, and then I was free…

PATU - Gokwe Kid in the middle
Pic - Gokwe Kid

Memoir mutterings

Of the central characters mentioned no longer in this memoir –
9335 Inspector Mike Moore. Pension and other benefits. March 1981. I am surprised he stuck around so long. I never did find out what happened to him. He will be somewhere out there – running against the wind.

Glossary

Donga. A stream.

CHAPTER 39:

The Road to Perspicacity – Part One

It is all well and good chanting, 'Rhodesians never die', at every drunken opportunity, but by now I was thinking much like a member of the Hitler Jugend, who was finally seeing the fruitlessness of screaming 'Sieg Heil', over the din of Berlin being pounded into a large refuse tip.

Oddly enough, I very nearly changed my mind. One of the people I went around to say goodbye to, on my six days R&R after my last bush patrol, was an old school pal, Nigel Eames. He lived just down the drag from home in Mount Pleasant. We had been quite close, even getting over a slight disagreement when I once went behind his back and shaped with his girlfriend Shirley Groper, but I had been forgiven. It seemed he dumped her soon after; as I wasn't the only one playing up to the girl's surname.

Nigel wasn't there but I had a small chat with his parents. Nigel's father was also in the police. Actually, it had only recently come out that he was in fact a Senior Assistant Commissioner and head of the CID. (Criminal Investigation Department.) I had never clocked this fact! He was a really nice gent and had often told us kids, when we went around playing in the early 1970's, anecdotes from his life. He would sit in his rather English country style living room, and puffing a pipe, relate exciting times gone past. One story involved a small black faced clock, mounted in a piece of solid wood, which adorned the fireplace mantelpiece. He had removed it from a destroyed German tank after a battle during World War II in North Africa. Mr. Eames (as I still called him), surprisingly knew I was going and 'instructed' me to go down to CID Headquarters and see him the following morning.

So somewhat puzzled, I turned up and informed a nonplussed officer at the front desk, that no, I didn't have an appointment with the 'Big Boss', but I had been told to come and see him. Taking my name, he disappeared, to turn up a minute later, and looking well surprised, ushered me into Mr Eames's office. I didn't like lying to this man, and I also had an uneasy feeling that he saw right through the façade of my excuse for taking 'the gap'. What he had to say was almost like a dream come true. If I withdrew my resignation, I would be transferred to the CID, would wear civilian clothes, could grow my hair, and best of all; could opt to be posted anywhere in the country. I could stay in Salisbury or even have Kariba or the Victoria Falls tourist resort areas. For the second time in my life I was given an offer I would be stupid to refuse. (The first had been from my headmaster with the offer of becoming a Monitor if I stayed on at school. I didn't.) Mr Eames told me to think about it overnight and let him know the next day. So somewhat filled with conflicting emotions of self preservation as against duty, I went home to mull over the incredible opportunity. I didn't tell my step-mom what had transpired. But it was too late. I had burnt my boats. Airfare was paid, my car, my Precious and all other possessions had been sold off. I was literally left with a few piles of clothes and my tape and record collection in Gwelo. I phoned the following day and respectfully thanked the man for the offer, but - 'No thanks'.

Returning to Gwelo after my six days R&R, I was called up to the Superintendent's office. My discharge papers lay on his desk. I was asked if I wanted to change my mind. Perhaps if I just went on an extended holiday to see my mother in the UK, it would be enough to settle her anxiety problems? I switched into my best, 'woe is me', mode and thinking once again of my dead dog, I did the old 'Uriah Heep' of wringing my hands together, whilst squeezing a few crocodile tears, and that was that. All approved - I am out of here.

I had my foreign currency allowance to the max as I had cashed in my pension. This was the amazing amount of 2300 Deutsche Marks in *American Express* traveller's cheques. The Rhodesian Government heavily restricted foreign currency for the simple reason they needed it to pay for petrol and bullets. Married couples with kids were expected to emigrate with little more than double this sum! As a result, there were many reports of shifty shenanigans. One trick was to build an ocean going yacht in your backyard, and take it on holiday to South Africa, then hope it lasted longer than the Titanic's maiden voyage, and then sell it. The government tried to stop that scam by insisting you had to leave the house deeds as guarantee the yacht would come back. They never did, and since the homes were unsellable, many simply did a runner and - sod the house. The other way was to purchase anything that could be converted into hard Forex. Jewellery was an obvious one, but it was overpriced and typically received only a fraction when sold. Rhodesian First Day Covers was another popular misconception of value. Even today you can't shift them for more than a couple of pounds on EBay.

The bank had wanted to transfer my allocation into an account in England. I wasn't having that. I didn't trust the bastards. They had never trusted me (no overdraft and bounced my cheques now and then), so I explained I needed it in traveller's cheques because I was flying into Luxembourg and then touring. So I got my way.

I also collected a fancy letter from the CID saying I had never been convicted of any crime in Rhodesia, and a little blue certificate stating that I had been a member of the British South African Police for *one year and three hundred and sixty three days*. What the Fuck! It was supposed to be two years on the dot! This was an unfortunate error that cost me an extra two hundred dollars. In my calculated plan of deceit, I had stupidly not bothered to check the exact date of enlistment. That meant that in the space marked 'Reason for discharge', the typed answer, 'By purchase' neglected to add that, according to the small print, for service of under two years, the cost of freedom was two hundred and fifty dollars. I was gutted. How pathetic does that look? Had I stayed another two days I could have saved twenty day's pay - and received two day's pay more! In revenge - I stole my police belt.

The cheapest flight to Europe was with *Luxair* - flying from Johannesburg, South Africa, to Luxembourg - payable in Rhodesian dollars. After arriving in Europe I would hitch around for a while absorbing the culture and history of civilisations far more advanced than ours. Well - that was the plan.

Between handing in my uniform at Gwelo police quartermaster depot (minus one belt), and leaving African soil, I had a couple of weeks to kill. If I had to go to South Africa, I might as well visit my ex-next-door neighbour in Durban for a bit. Before that, it was up to Salisbury to sell off the last possessions, pack and say goodbye to the – soon to be raped and murdered (by the advancing communist infiltrators or whatever), Katherine, Bridget and little Michael. I intended that my departure from Gwelo be stylish and dignified. The train would leave at 2 a.m., and the night shift had kindly agreed to pick up my luggage and me from my room at the mess. I was going to miss that room and the fun and games that had gone on in there. I was still a bit miffed that two hours before the end of my final afternoon shift, Inspector Strict had forced me to have a hair cut - the bastard. When I had kicked up something rotten, he had politely informed me the only place I would be going was the box for a week for refusing a direct order. He also nicely pointed out that my BSAP certificate, with the typed bit next to 'Conduct' could also be changed from 'Good' into 'Very Bad'. I complied through gritted teeth.

That final evening was a Saturday. So I decided that a visit to the disco at the Midlands Hotel would while away the hours as I said goodbye to mates and those I had once mated with. After getting warmed up on some beers, I switched to my old favourite - vodka, lime and lemonade. And I drank shit loads of them.

I vaguely remember getting punched by my now ex-shift boss, Mike Yoko, after tipping his beer all over him, whilst staggering around with double vision. Some uniformed police, now my ex-mates; 'assisted' me from the disco to my room, where the same gentle officers came to pick me up a few hours later for the train. Actually, I had to pick myself up. Several well aimed kicks to my torso enabled me to recover well enough from my alcohol induced stupor to gather, rather incoherently, that I was covered in vomit and lying on the floor of the mess toilet.

"The train is leaving in fifteen minutes, we are waiting in the Landy downstairs," was my chauffeur's caring comment.

I was in an awful mess. Scraping as much Rhodie made Smirnoff, Mazoe lime concentrate and Sparletta lemonade as possible off my clothes, I bounced off the walls and staggered around, reeking of god knows what, till I had my stuff in the Landy. They drove me to the station, where I was booted out onto the train platform. I was so drunk, that it was impossible to understand in the darkness that the luggage trolley should be pulled and not pushed; so with four sails into the wind and tacking desperately, the outcome was an acute zig-zagging, resulting in a large loss of luggage, which was never to be seen again. I felt and smelt very ill when Katherine picked me up. History was repeating itself: I had made my exit from the boy scouts with a similar *coup de grace*.

By the next day I felt better (as you do at that age), and proposed the usual 'prodigal son' invitation to my step-mom for dinner. These sessions had become a regular feature of my rest and recreation stints during the last two years. Much to my surprise, I was turned down. She had a date! Bingo! At least ten bucks saved. Still, I was now seriously interested in this unnamed snake in the grass that had mysteriously been mentioned. I put some careful, considerate and loving questions to the woman who had unselfishly kept me on after my father died; when she could have more easily kicked me into legal touch.

"Okay...who is he, how serious is this and how long has this been going on?" was, for me, a reasonable start to the interrogation. After all, I was the famed Gokwe Kid - Dick of the Bushveld, capturer of the infamous fraudster Raymond, a legend in my own mind or simply a mindless leg end, semi-finalist in Strictly come Soldiering, winner of the Rhodesian X-Factor and holder of the title of Rhodesia has no Talent.

"John Withers. We want to get married. Over six months." Her high speed answers were enough to impress the quizmaster of Mastermind.

I was appalled. How had she managed to keep this relationship a secret from the greatest bush detective/ex boy scout for so long?

"That's nice. So why don't you?" was my time saving reply, whilst my befuddled brain wrestled with this latest input of multi-changes to my life. Too many alcohol binges in the last two years were obviously dangerous - I was losing it at twenty years of age!

Before I could even get to the phone book to look up the number for the Salvation Army (the Rhodesian alternative therapy for working class, fucked-up, brown bottle addicts; I know this as we had one stay in our house for a bit, but that's another story), step-mom is on the phone. Calling her date - an old midget with an appalling temper, and a tendency to drive huge cars (the last one I remember was a Studebaker, with tail wings to rival a Boeing 747 and I think it was two-tone). I know this also, because this guy, who wanted to marry my step-mum, was, or at least had been, the woodwork teacher at my last high school. He hadn't taught me, but I had seen him around and knew about his reputation for strictness from the other kids.

She chatted to him for a while, babbling like some fourteen years old that had just had a Bay City Roller sweaty jock-strap thrown her way. After she hung up, I was informed that a last minute civic reception would be arranged and that he would arrive at the house in twenty minutes to present himself to get my 'stamp of approval'. I felt more like stamping on his head - the dirty git! What would my mates say? She was far too old for these kinds of shenanigans. I knew this because I was doing it myself and found it very exhausting.

She went on to explain that they didn't want to take the risk of upsetting me; so would have waited to get hitched until after I had 'gapped it'. Wasn't that sweet? I desperately needed feedback from Bridget. What did she know of this plot? How long had this old dog been peeing on our driveway gates? Worst of all - he was obviously poor because he was a teacher at Mount Pleasant. I came to the informed conclusion that he was definitely a treasure seeker and... a filthy old man. I mean, he must have been at least in his early fifties. Disgusting!

In the few minutes before his arrival, I cornered back-stabbing co-conspirator Bridget. She had thought it might be a passing fad, but now expected the din of squeaky bed springs from the bedroom next door to hers in the foreseeable future. But it was agreed. We were all happy. Step-mum was happy and little Michael would have some male adult to emulate. At nine, we hoped Michael was young enough to make the adjustment. We would call this ageing buccaneer by his first name - John.

I met the randy bugger, as agreed, and thoroughly worked him over. At last a pupil was kicking a teacher's ass. He was very sweet and obviously in love, but I caught him with his hand a bit too far up Katherine's skirt; - this dude was out to have his cake and eat it too.

So, the day before I left, never to see step-mum again under a Rhodesian sky, they were married. I went out that night. In the morning the glowing bride made me tea and sandwiches and there were hugs all around, John drove me to the Fort Victoria road, the meeting place for the convoys. I noticed he looked tired, if you know what I mean, heh-heh-heh.

After a quick handshake, John left. I was alone. It was too early for the first convoy. By now the war was causing all sorts of problems. Nearly all major roads had these convoys. After a couple of minutes, a two-door 'Yank Tank' Camero turned up.

"Where you going?" asked the driver.

"South Africa."

Katherine and the Gokwe Kid

Pic - Gokwe Kid

"Hop in; you can ride shotgun. I can take you as far as Fort Vic and I am driving fast."

This was a reasonable offer. Single cars at high speed rarely got taken out by gooks waiting in ambush. The convoys, although protected front, back, and middle by armoured vehicles, were forced to go at the pace of the slowest vehicle. So off we went, with me pointing a shotgun out the window. Big deal – this was guaranteed to frighten hordes of Chinese trained guerrillas. A thought occurred to me. Instead of naming all our weird armoured vehicles after African animals, like Leopard and Rhino, the forces should have named them after Chinese animals. Like - Panda bears! In addition, they could all be painted black and white instead of the boring green and tan used now. Surely no well trained insurgent would dare to shoot at a panda bear.

To begin with, the drive was uneventful. We travelled flat out down a perfect road with well maintained verges and grass cut well back. It was just after we shot through the farming town, jokingly self-christened as the 'Republic of Enkeldoorn', that we first got a hint of trouble. I say a hint, but it was more of a shout. A very loud banging noise was coming from the area where my feet were, and the car was swerving dangerously all over the place. When we eventually stopped and had a look, we found that one of his brand new retreads had thrown and was shredding huge chunks. There was much ranting from the driver. I could have told him about retreads. I was so tight that I had mine on my Toyota Corolla retreaded twice. The useless things couldn't handle the Gokwe dirt roads though, and had peeled apart pronto. I had almost had a heart attack buying new tyres for the car before selling it for $1200 with over 100k miles on the clock.

This, however, wasn't quite the place to ponder on the quality of Rhodesian vulcanisation techniques. We were in the 'badlands'. I could smell it. I was a highly trained killer. It said so in the newspapers! In fact, I think I smelt the nervous bursts of gas emitting from my rear end. Luckily, Speedy Gonzales had a spare and without much more ado we hit Fort Vic.

For the next stage of my journey, to Beitbridge and the border, I hitched a lift with a family going on holiday in a Peugeot 404. What was it with Rhodesia and 404s? You were sort of considered a big deal if you owned one. But they looked like a sugar cube perched upon a wheeled matchbox. You had more chance of pulling a chick in a 1940's Volvo. I'm no artist, but I sketched identical designs of the 404 when I was four years old. I remember the amazing wire cars the black Rhodesians made. Just using fencing wire, they would create an almost perfect scale model of a car. You even had a steering wheel that moved the front wheels, as you happily pushed it down the road. The cheap models were based on 404s because they were the easiest to make.

The smartly dressed immigration officer didn't even want to look at all my correct and proper documentation. The anxiety I had felt at leaving Rhodesia for good culminated in a cursory glimpse and not even a stamp in my passport. Instead of a handshake and perhaps
"Good luck, china, thanks for trying to keep the braying hordes at bay, shame about your dead mates," or "please stay and save us from the communist onslaught, think of your soon to be raped and murdered step-mom and sister, if you desert us in this hour of need," etc. etc.

It was an anticlimax. All I had was a blue ballpoint scribble in the back of the passport: 'Emigration status approved' along with a stamp from Barclays Bank. No speeches from the immigration officer besides,

"Next."

I had successfully taken the gap - the chicken run - follow the yellow brick road.

Regrets? Who are you kidding? I was twenty, full of myself and (I reckoned), a star in the waiting. I was *The Gokwe Kid* – I had the X-Factor.

CHAPTER 40:

The Road to Perspicacity – Part Two

I was now in South Africa. It was about 2 pm. and hitching on the same stretch of road, was my new guardian angel - the bad kind. He was one of those men that got the shit kicked out of them at Club Tomorrow by troopies. He was dressed in a dirty, sloppy shirt, caftan type jacket, along with torn jeans, and had long, black, greasy hair. Definitely not SAS, and not even in my wildest fantasies could I place the yob as being an undercover Selous Scout.

We got chatting. Well, there was nothing else to do, and short of killing my unwashed new friend, there was little chance of getting rid of him. Like me, he was on his way to Durban where he told me he lived in a commune (presumably with other smelly hippies). To the question "What unit did you fight in?" he answered "None". It seems he had bunked National Service. This last piece of information, along with the hair and clothing, would guarantee him a good kicking in every night spot in Rhodesia, never mind Club Tomorrow, which was famed for attracting the sort of visitors that would happily take a few penalty kicks in the direction of such lowlife.

He seemed nice enough though. After a while, a car pulled up. Another 404 - but this time in light green. To my delight, the driver announced that he was pissed and needed to sleep it off. If either of us had a driving licence, we were in charge. For a change, I was the winner - my new mate was either too dozy or had no licence.

So off we went. It was the first time I had driven an automatic, and I had great fun at South African police roadblocks explaining that it was not my car, nor did I know where it was destined, but I hoped to find out soon from the gentlemen lying comatose next to me when he eventually came around. The owner eventually woke up, bought us a beer in some backwater Afrikaner village and chucked us out. By this time, Dopey was getting on my nerves bumming fags all the time.

The next lift was with a real gent driving yet another 404 (white). It was getting dark and he was only going as far as Jo'burg. It had never actually occurred to me that it would be nigh on impossible to hitch from Salisbury to Durban in a day. So when he asked us where we intended to sleep, I became panic stricken. I hadn't the foggiest notion. I wondered what might be the latest stats on murdered white bums hitching in apartheid South Africa in the middle of the night. My guess put the percentage at quite a high level. For the first time in two years I didn't have my FN rifle, and suddenly I really missed it.

I need not have worried. The driver was a real gent. He took us in. He even turfed his little daughters out of their beds to make way for us, and his wife cooked us a goulash. All this at about 11o'clock at night. In the morning, he went out of his way to take us to the road going to Durban. I regret not recording his name because if ever I get back down to that area, I hope he can put me up for free again.

So there we were, on the road to Durban, and Dopey is my new best mate. My original plan to go and stay with Susan, my ex-neighbour, and her mum went out the window. I was gonna stay with the hippies and learn to be a cool skate. We duly arrive at Dopey's pad; a small flat, two roads down from the beach near the promenade. This was brilliant! That I had to sleep on the floor with seven others was irrelevant. This was living. And to top it off - they were smoking illicit drugs. I was staying with Snow White's seven dwarfs and *all* of them were called Dopey! It was only a couple of months before that I had been involved in a drugs bust in Gwelo. That time, I was on the giving end. And now? Even if the South African police had kicked the Dopey's door down and shouted

"Ya freaking heepie freaks, man, a bit of sjambok hippo tails flaying ya back, that sort ya bloody morphs out."

I wouldn't worry. My background was impeccable. I would stand my ground and announce *AUTHORITATIVELY* that,

"I am a former member of the infamous BSAP, capturer of the fraudulent X-Factor and Gokwe's star dickhead. My name is Raymund Bushveld; and fuck-me, am I stoned or what?'

In the state I was in, they would have been welcome to call me Dopey 8.

I phoned Susan and explained my delay. It was agreed that we would have dinner together that night. I was also informed it had to be a 'quickie' as she was meeting her boyfriend Marc at 8.30. How stupid can I get? Instead of simply firing a hamburger down her unappreciative throat from the tacky fast food place down by the aquarium house, I invited her to the best restaurant in town, the famous India Room at the Malibu Hotel.

I hadn't seen Sue Grundy for a couple of years, and it had been an incredible stroke of luck that I bumped into her dad when he was sent to Gokwe as a reservist. He had supplied me with her latest address in Durban and I had written to her. The reply had comprised of rather weird and insane babblings of being a born-again Christian and her suggestion that I should - 'Go with Jesus' - bullshit. At this point of time I was really trying hard to see the light. I suppose Dopey and the guys were pretty much the dregs of the film and musical *Godspell*, and I was as close as I would ever get of seeing the Lord after several hits on the bong...

Like me, Sue had been a useless tosser at school. Although admittedly, she was academically better gifted than I was – just. She was skinny with an uncontrollable mop of short curly hair, and we got on great. We were two useless kids with loads in common, and we accepted we would never turn into much. This finding religion thing was a rather alarming development. Sue no longer sounded like my perfect female nemesis. I had lived next door to her for years, on both sides. I always thought number fourteen was best because the access to Sue's pool was quicker. Besides, when we had lived at number 10, before the old man gave up the ghost, we had our own.

"Could I have a swim in your pool?" I asked her mother one day. I was granted permission, which I took to mean unlimited access, and boy - did I take advantage. Sue grew, mostly up, and became a drum majorette. I seemed to be growing as well and became captain of the gymnastics team. The tossers were making good after all. By the time I was seventeen and she was sixteen (and had the use of her mum's car), I jawled with her on Saturday nights. This way I got to go to parties outside my usual boring circle. The taste in music to the parties we attended was a bit different as well - Bad Company and Led Zeppelin, rather than the George Baker Selection and Band on the Run.

I hadn't seen her since August of '76. I had popped around to visit her and her mum in a smart apartment they now lived in. I had just arrived from the UK, with my golden locks and fancy clothes and…a bottle of 73% proof Captain Morgan's dark rum. All that seemed a hell of a long time ago. Tinker, her mother, was a 'B' celebrity as she had at one time presented a cooking show on Rhodesian TV sponsored by Gloria Flour. In other words, she was a very good cook and I threw up the huge portion of leg of lamb she had so carefully worked on, all over her highly polished wooden floor. I was so drunk that Susan let me sleep in her bed…less her. Now here I was, two years later, hoping my behaviour at dinner this time would be slightly more agreeable than the drunken, vomiting orgy I created last time we sat down at a table together; till I fell off the chair and was dragged to bed.

Amongst the clothes I had brought (I was dragging around a very tatty suitcase), was a very smart black jacket with the awesome embroidered BSAP logo of a lion being stabbed to death with assegais, stitched onto the left breast pocket. I managed to wash some grime off this impressive garment in Dopey land, and I arrived punctually at the restaurant. Sue hadn't arrived. Maybe she had stopped off at a church on the way to burn some candles for my soul or more than likely had been delayed polishing her cross.

When she turned up she looked nothing at all like Julie Andrews after a howling session on a green hill far away, but more like Cleopatra in high heels, towering at least three inches over me. I was a bit nonplussed. Where were the sacks and ashes, the huge wooden crucifix, the crown of thorns and a stolen copy of a Gideon's bible in one hand and a tin with a 'Save the poor children of Africa' sticker in the other? Susan always greeted me in a friendly way. The one I received, "Stupid tosser!", was one of her favourites. I suppose it was better than "You filthy sinner, get on thy knees and repent thy sins." Considering we only had an hour left to order and eat, repenting my sins would probably mean I would miss my flight - never mind my dinner.

We were the only people in the India Room. That was just as well, as I would promptly manage to make a fool of myself as usual. First the wine card. Ah, I was still off wine ever since my self-imposed poisoning at the Boy Scout AGM. Regardless of the fact that I was on a tight foreign currency budget, I let her happily order some fancy plonk whilst I settled on a Castle. I had strangely gone off the vodka, lime and lemonades and the rum for a while. The wine waiter was a splendidly kitted out individual with a huge silver dinner plate hanging around his neck. Whilst he fussed about opening a bottle of wine that was going to cost me three days of bush patrol pay, I enquired what the dish was for. This, I was informed, was for the customer to spit into when tasting the wine. Really! I was very intrigued. He explained that you swill the wine around your mouth to savour it, and then spit it out into the proffered silver platter. Very posh! I was well impressed. Normally if I drink something, it zips down barely touching my taste buds. But this made sense. After all, after the wine has been gargled around a bit and picked up last night's dinner still stuck between your teeth, it's obvious you don't want to swallow the evil, stinking brew of old biltong and well foamed wine.

Since I was paying, I was presented with a small amount of wine to taste. For all I knew, it could have been aviation fuel, such was my etiquette in wine tasting, but I did fancy gobbing in this bloke's plate. With a skill reminiscent of a TCP advert for bad breath, I gave the stuff a full spin wash around my teeth, and then signalled to the waiter to stick out his bowl.

"Ah! No! No, it is only for show Sahib," the pseudo-Indian waiter informed me as I sat there, cheeks swelled out, eyeballs bulging and little dribbles of brown foam leaking out the corner of my mouth. I couldn't even mumble 'Bastard' as I gallantly swallowed the evil brew.

Chucking half a glass of Castle down my throat to make me feel better, I asked Susan what was with the Holy Grail - as that was no nun's habit she was wearing. If she had wandered into a church clothed in that regalia, the best compliment she could have hoped for was 'harlot'.

"Oh I gave that up, far too boring, I'm now into men whose eyebrows grow together," she explained with that amazing insane cackle she had. I plucked mine. I never could bear the thought of looking like a werewolf.

"My latest beau, Marc, is very hairy," she went on. "I love it!"

There were plenty of that kind around - usually we called them baboons. She had definitely cracked.

It was time to order. The menu looked good. The assorted sea-food starter from the cold buffet trolley sounded ace, and we started with that. The main course would be six lobster tails in flaming brandy sauce for me. I can't remember what Susan ordered, but I do remember being fascinated that her version of the menu had no prices on them. This was to be my first introduction to sexual discrimination. In macho Rhodesia there was only one menu; this was given to the man, and he told his partner what she was going to eat depending on the amount in his wallet or the odds of getting a shag. No chance = hamburger. Good chance = two hamburgers; and a T bone steak for me please. How do I like it cooked? Cut the horns off, wipe its arse and kill it; was the standard reply.

The trolley pulled up and I couldn't believe my eyes. There were seven huge revolving trays stacked with just about every creepy crawly that wandered the floor of Davy Jones's locker. Since this entire farce was costing a small fortune, I wanted my money's worth. I made the waiter put two heaped serving spoons of everything onto my plate. I reckon it amounted to over a kilo of the stuff. Whilst shovelling this lot down, I informed Susan that I would spend my last two nights at her place. No sweat. I would have to sleep on a couch and she wouldn't be there much. I gathered that monkey man took up a lot of her spare time. Who cared, I needed a clean bath and a pad where the fleas weren't the size of rats and the rats the size of cats.

My main course arrived and I was very impressed, if a tad full. Our waiter made a great show of setting the lobster tails on fire. I hadn't seen anything like that since I went on a Boy Scout jamboree at Ruwa Park and took part in a first aid competition. I had witnessed a group of black Scouts cover a white victim's 'wound' (in reality kneaded dough and ketchup), with methylated spirits and set it alight. The idea was to cauterise the 'hole' in his leg. I had never seen a whitey do so much 'shakin de ass'!

Finally the lobsters were presented to me, looking lovely and pink and, as the brandy burnt off, I grabbed my weapons and went to work. I wasn't a total peasant and had been taught that you use the middle set of knife and forks for fish. They were definitely wrongly designed for this job. Cutting a piece off a lobster's tail was a nightmare. It was like trying to slash your wrists with a blunt razor blade. Thank God no one was around to see me fight with these creatures of the deep. Eventually I separated a piece and, looking as cool as possible; I popped it into my mouth and started to chew. It was disgusting. It tasted awful. And the noise - I am sure eating glass would have been easier and quieter. For a while, Susan watched me intently as I tried to force the muck down my convulsing gullet, assisted by huge swigs of Castle. When she could watch no more, she leaned over, and in a loud voice asked

"Exactly what are you doing, you dumb fuck?"

"This is rubbish," I said, prodding the mauled carcass.

"You are eating its shell, you moron. You are supposed to take it off."

I looked at her in amazement. I tried to imagine ordering Nandos style Piri-Piri chicken in a basket at the Mazoe Hotel back home. Then only to find it served up covered in singed feathers. What a load of idiots. First they lie about gobbing in the wine tray, and now the overcharging *faux* Indians are serving me food still dressed in armour plating. Susan kindly showed me what to do, and it was delightful. Slinging the last glass of wine down, Susan cheerily breezed off to rendezvous at the Planet of the Apes while I miserably signed one of my hard earned traveller's cheques.

Next day I said goodbye to the seven Dopeys, who didn't really notice, and went off to the Grundy's pad. Tinker, Sue's mom, was delighted to see me and brushed off my apologies for not finishing her leg of lamb. I was totally forgiven, she said, but could I try to not vomit in this new flat. I spent a relaxing couple of days with the Grundy's and then on the last night Susan asked if we could meet up at the Father's Moustache bar so she could introduce me to her latest orang-utan. It seemed like a good chance to pull some naïve South African chicks. We Rhodies were world famous lovers. The papers told us so. Or I am mixing that up with 'greatest anti-insurgency force'? Not sure, but I did fancy some insertion, not forcefully of course - for I am a BSAP gentleman.

Again in my very smart jacket, I turned up at the popular bar on the promenade road and was duly laughed at by the South African chicks. Between getting the knock back and Susan and Hairy pitching up, I took the time to experiment on a new drink. I ordered a double brandy, which arrived in a large goblet. Recalling my flaming brandy sauce with the lobsters, I tried to set the brandy alight. I am sure I had read in a Wilbur Smith book that this was like a hot toddy or something. Then I remembered that the brandy sauce had been preheated. So with my Lion brand matches, I proceeded to warm the goblet. The next match applied into the now sooty glass had the required effect and, lo, I had a small fire. The first attempt to blow it out resulted in my eyebrows being singed. Panicking, I tried to cut off the oxygen by putting my hand over the glass. By now I was receiving some curious looks. My first thought was that I had created a vacuum; it seemed as if the glass was trying to eat my hand. The next feeling was of intense pain as the red-hot rim burned into my palm. Nearly screaming in agony, I shook it off and it bounced onto the carpet floor, spilling the rest of the boiling brandy. After switching tables and waiters, I ordered another. Two brandies, and a bit of trial and error, and I had developed the perfect technique.

Eventually, Susan and a guy resembling Chewbacca the Wookie, strolled in. No, really, that's what he looked like; same size, but wearing some clothes. I shook his hairy paw, and after a chat and a couple of beers, I introduced him to my newly acquired stunt. Carefully keeping the glass a good distance from the match, I revolved it expertly, swilling the brandy lightly around the rim. Puffing the match as elegantly as James Bond blows away the cordite from his PPK, I slid a beer mat across the top, extinguishing the flames, and delicately swallowed the perfectly warmed brandy in one shot.

"That's for morphs," grunted Chewbacca. "You got to drink it while it's on fire."

I ordered another and offered him my matches.

"Please, be my guest."

Of course, what happened next was bloody obvious, but I nearly wet myself in anticipaaaaation (from the Rocky Horror Picture Show).

As soon as Chewbacca's lips touched the flaming glass, his head was set on fire. This was an inferno waiting to happen. This guy had so much flammable fur he made an Inyanga bush fire seem harmless. I never did see which way the glass went; I was too occupied with trying not to fall off my bar stool. By this time, I was pissed on the warm brandies I had practised with, and the entertaining sight of watching this Great Ape slapping his own head to put out the flames was too good to miss.

I wisely took a train back to Johannesburg. Susan saw me off. Her lasts words to me

"Get on the fucking train, you next-door neighbour from hell. If I don't see you in the next thirty years - it will be too soon."

And then I flew away. I wouldn't set foot onto African soil again for five more years, and it would be in a place called Zimbabwe. But, that, as they say... is another story.

Memoir mutterings

There will be a prequel as yet unnamed and hopefully a sequel about my time in Germany. Wait and see.

Glossary

Jawled. Go out and hang around partying.
Sjambok. A heavy leather whip.
Skate. A milder version of a yob

Acknowledgements

It is hard to believe that it is almost a decade since I had the divine inspiration to become a writer. Only the public will decide if I should stay at my day job of being a penniless drunk.

Along the way, scattered by mountains of empty beer bottles and cans, many people attempted to point me in the right direction. Rather a waste of time but I have to thank them all for the support and encouragement. Hopefully I haven't forgotten anyone. So, in no particular order or priority of how they contributed to my masterpiece –

Audrey Horne, Stephanie Brooks, Ryk and Susanne Basson, Katherine May, Andrew Field and his BSAP web site and Facebook page – (there many ex members helped me with missing details), Mike Harvey (The Boss), Susan Grundy, George Hall, Breda Gajsek, Nigel Triggs, Alan Golden, Willie Mackenzie, Nicky Berry, 'Kudu Eye', Tim Addison, 'Netsai', Roger Watt, Butch Zeederberg, Pat Lawless, Mike Paterson, Ian Neill, Carlsberg Lager, Beri Hayter, Alistair Fall, Liam and Sue Sheahan, Mitch Stirling, Mike Shute, Ruth Kerr, Captain Morgan, John Polenski, Miriam Causon, Andrew Edmondson, 'Cool Beans' Brown, Roy Bushell, Ken Tilbury, Mitch Stirling.

And last but not least – **The Open University**

Printed in Great Britain
by Amazon.co.uk, Ltd.,
Marston Gate.